T0305404

Reuters Institute Global Journalism Series

*Series Editors: Rasmus Kleis Nielsen and
the Reuters Institute for the Study of Journalism*

Matthew Powers, *NGOs as Newsmakers: The Changing Landscape
of International News*

WORLDS OF JOURNALISM

Journalistic Cultures Around the Globe

Edited by

Thomas Hanitzsch, Folker Hanusch,
Jyotika Ramaprasad, and Arnold S. de Beer

Columbia University Press

New York

Columbia University Press
Publishers Since 1893
New York   Chichester, West Sussex
cup.columbia.edu
Copyright © 2019 Columbia University Press

Library of Congress Cataloging-in-Publication Data
Names: Hanitzsch, Thomas, 1969– editor. | Hanusch, Folker, 1975– editor. |
Ramaprasad, Jyotika, 1949– editor. | de Beer, A. S. (Arrie), 1942– editor.
Title: Worlds of journalism : journalistic cultures around the globe /
edited by Thomas Hanitzsch, Folker Hanusch, Jyotika Ramaprasad,
and Arnold S. de Beer.
Description: New York : Columbia University Press, [2019] |
Series: Reuters Institute global journalism series | Includes bibliographical
references and index.
Identifiers: LCCN 2018048847 (print) | LCCN 2018061249 (ebook) |
ISBN 9780231546638 (electronic) | ISBN 9780231186421 |
ISBN 9780231186421 (cloth : alk. paper) | ISBN 9780231186438 (paperback) |
ISBN 9780231546638 (electronic)
Subjects: LCSH: Journalism. | Reporters and reporting. |
Journalists—Attitudes.
Classification: LCC PN4781 (ebook) | LCC PN4781 .W74 2019 (print) |
DDC 070—dc23
LC record available at https://lccn.loc.gov/2018048847

Cover design: Lisa Hamm

CONTENTS

ACKNOWLEDGMENTS

This book is founded on a project that has come a long way since its inception. The seed for what would later become the Worlds of Journalism Study (WJS) was planted in October 2006, when a group of scholars started a small pilot study with the aim to compare journalistic cultures in seven nations. Ten years later, in early 2017, when data collection was completed for the second wave of surveys with journalists, the project had developed into an intercontinental endeavor of researchers from sixty-seven nations, whose contributions sustained the project through its various stages, and which has now culminated in this book.

This book stands on the shoulders of giants and owes much to our many good friends and supportive colleagues across institutions around the world. David Weaver, whose seminal collection *The Global Journalist* appeared in 1998, was a major inspiration for us. Weaver's *Global Journalist*, as well as the scholarship of Wolfgang Donsbach, notably his work with Thomas Patterson, set the stage for large-scale, cross-national investigations into journalists' professional values and aspirations. With these models in place, it seemed the next step was to begin large collaborative projects in journalism studies, and the WJS and this book are our attempt to do so.

The unique nature of the WJS, an international research endeavor driven by a collective of scholars from all around the world, necessitated a distinctive approach to collaborative publication. Readers will quickly realize that the book does not fit squarely into established classifications of scholarly publications. Reflecting the collaborative work ethos of the project, each chapter was written by a team of up to twelve authors. In addition to contributing as authors to various chapters, the four of us served as editors, overseeing and facilitating this sometimes complicated process of collective knowledge production. Perhaps, if there is any single term that can reasonably describe the nature of this book, it is "edited research monograph"—a genre that has gained popularity at a time when collaboration has increasingly become central to research and science. Altogether more than forty scholars have contributed to this book, bringing their rich knowledge and cultural experience to bear on the analysis of a data set that contains interviews with more than 27,500 journalists, as well as on interpretation and explanation of findings.

Now, as the task of writing is done, it is time to extend our deepest gratitude to those who helped make this book possible. We begin with the recognition of the hard work of the research teams in all sixty-seven countries, many of whom also contributed to this book; their dedication stood us in good stead through this undertaking. Our project website provides a full list of the principal investigators in these countries (http://www .worldsofjournalism.org/research/2012-2016-study/principal-investigators/). We next thank our colleagues who have served with us on the current and previous WJS Executive Committees—in alphabetical order, Ashraf Galal Hassan Bayoumy, Basyouni Hamada, Epp Lauk, Claudia Mellado, and Martin Oller Alonso. We also owe our gratitude to the nine eminent researchers—Lee Becker, Joseph Man Chan, Joaquim Fidalgo, Beate Josephi, Henrik Örnebring, Paschal Preston, Zvi Reich, Elena Vartanova, and David Weaver—who advised us as members of our Scientific Advisory Committee.

Many friends and colleagues have helped us bring this project forward by engaging with us in numerous informal and insightful conversations. We are grateful to all of them. In particular, we would like to mention Jay Blumler, Frank Esser, Bob Franklin, Martin Löffelholz, Herman Wasserman, and Lars Willnat. We are also deeply grateful to Philip Leventhal at Columbia University Press and Rasmus Kleis Nielsen, editor of the Reuters Institute Global Journalism Series, for making this book project happen. We have benefited from the general professionalism of Columbia University Press editorial staff, specifically from the rigorous and patient editing of Anita O'Brien, and from the creativity of Lisa Stamm, who designed the cover for this book. We are also indebted to the two anonymous reviewers for their intellectual rigor and generosity.

A large-scale, multinational project such as the WJS would not have been possible without the support of the universities we work for and those who provided funding to us to carry out this project. First and foremost, we thank LMU Munich, which not only has hosted the WJS Center but also has contributed significant funds to at least partly cover field research in more than twenty countries. In addition, the German Research Foundation, South African National Research Foundation, University of the Sunshine Coast, University of Miami, University of Pennsylvania, and Stellenbosch University have all provided substantive funding for field research in the countries we studied. Our national investigators, too, received funding from more than thirty organizations—too many to list here. A full list of funding institutions is available in the appendix.

On a personal note, Thomas thanks his awesome wife Minnie and his beloved children Lisa and Tim for their eternal patience with a husband and a dad who always carries a laptop and who keeps promising that things will change once this project is over. Folker thanks his parents for their support in enabling him to embark on a university education in a far-off country—it was worth it in the end! He also thanks Stephi, the best partner one could wish for, and their two boys Finn and Felix. He is grateful for their support, encouragement to reach for lofty goals, and endless patience living a migrant life that has taken them to the end of the world and back again. Jyotika thanks her parents, who encouraged girl child education and aspirations in India at a time when this was not the norm, and her husband, Ram, and daughters, Charulata and Jui, who have allowed her the time and space to pursue her work. Arnold remembers his wife, Nicolette, who passed away in 2017. Over a period of more than half a century, she made it possible for him, in more ways than one, to pursue his journalistic and academic ideals and goals, as with this book.

Above all, we are grateful to the more than 27,500 journalists who responded to the study. They all gave up significant chunks of their already busy schedules; the insights they allowed us into their profession have been invaluable for the success of this project. For all of us, to see this study grow and make an impact on the field was, and continues to be, an exciting experience in its own right. We look forward to the next phase.

Thomas Hanitzsch, Folker Hanusch, Jyotika Ramaprasad, and Arnold S. de Beer

WORLDS OF JOURNALISM

1

EXPLORING THE WORLDS OF JOURNALISM

An Introduction

Thomas Hanitzsch, Folker Hanusch,
Jyotika Ramaprasad, and Arnold S. de Beer

Challenging assumptions of a universal understanding of journalism, *Worlds of Journalism: Comparing Journalistic Cultures Across the Globe* charts a "world of journalism" populated by a rich diversity of journalistic cultures that operate in varied societal contexts—in the midst of transformation themselves—marked by their own characteristics and traversing their own paths. The book details how journalists in countries around the globe experience their profession in different ways, even as they retain a shared commitment to some basic, common, professional norms and practices.

The overall aim is to contribute to a more current and globally appropriate mapping of the various worldviews and orientations of journalists regarding their editorial autonomy, as well as the influences they experience in their journalistic work, their roles, their ethical conventions, and their institutional trust. The book also deals with the changes that are currently shaking up long-held, firmly planted, macrolevel ideas about journalism, founded in both ideology and experience. Essentially, what this book (and the Worlds of Journalism Study on which it is based) attempts to do is to present an understanding of the multipolarity of the journalistic world, setting it apart from the Cold War bipolarity represented in such seminal books as *Four Theories of the Press* (Siebert, Peterson, and Schramm 1956). Firmly grounded in the conviction that there is more than one form of journalism, the study brings international and cultural diversity into focus. To this end, we deliberately opted for a pluralist perspective on the institution of journalism, with the aim of demonstrating the diversity of journalistic cultures rather than criticizing them from a normative point of view. Such normative approaches, we argue, generally privilege Western journalistic norms, which were in turn exported to various parts of the world through training and textbooks, as well as through Western media capital and ownership, and which have been accelerated in recent years by globalization and economic liberalization in many countries of the Global South.

While this exportation is often understood to be hegemonic in nature, we also acknowledge agency of the recipient countries to accept, adapt, or reject these norms. We position this transfer in more complex terms: as a dialectic, rather than simply as the dualism of an eager "imperialistic" sender and a passive, reluctant receiver. Journalists in the Global South, we believe, react to these norms in the context of local contextual conditions, such as authoritarianism and development needs, which govern their receptiveness to, support for, and active application of these norms in practice. This approach exemplifies the book's framework of (and empirical approach to) the importance of contextual factors.

In the following chapters we draw on a survey of more than 27,500 journalists in sixty-seven countries from around the world. Together these societies cover almost three-quarters of the world's population. The data were gathered through the Worlds of Journalism Study (WJS), a collaborative framework for comparative journalism research open to scholars from around the world. As such, the project not only is the largest comparative endeavor in the field of communication research to date but also comprises a sustainable community of comparative journalism studies researchers. The participating scholars are united in their goal to regularly assess the state of journalism globally. The main mission of the project "is to help journalism researchers, practitioners, media managers and policymakers better understand the worldviews and changes that are taking place in the professional orientations of journalists, the conditions and limitations under which journalists operate, and the social functions of journalism in a changing world."[1]

In this introduction we explain why we believe a project such as the WJS is needed and useful. We outline the genesis and development of the study and introduce its methodological framework and structures of planning and coordination. As part of this discussion, we also highlight some of the important challenges we faced in the research process. Finally, we lay out the key narrative and organization of the book.

Western Bias and the Value of Comparative Journalism Research

In journalism and communication research, much has been written about the importance and value of comparative research (e.g., Esser and Hanitzsch 2012; Gurevitch and Blumler 1990; Hanitzsch 2009). An increasing number of publications catalog and critically examine the expanding wealth and breadth of comparative research in journalism studies (e.g., Hanitzsch 2013; Hanitzsch and Donsbach 2012; Örnebring 2012). Comparative research is indispensable for establishing the generality of findings and interpretations, and it can keep us from overgeneralizing from our own, often idiosyncratic, experience (Kohn 1989). Without comparison, national specifics may become "naturalized," possibly even to the point that they remain invisible to the domestically bound researcher (Blumler, McLeod, and Rosengren 1992). Engaging in comparative work also helps to foster global scholarship and sustain networks of researchers across continents. It facilitates the international exchange of knowledge between scholars and institutions, including those operating in regions still inadequately represented in our field (Esser and Hanitzsch 2012).

Since the early 1990s the increasing recognition of the benefits of comparative research by communication scholars has led to an enormous increase in cross-national inquiries. Additional facilitators are the changes in the political and technological environment that have made the world more accessible to researchers. The end of the Cold War and the onward march of globalization have made it much easier to exchange ideas and interact with colleagues from afar. Further, new communication technologies are immensely useful in establishing, maintaining, and managing large international networks of researchers (Hanitzsch 2009).

By the turn of the century comparative work had almost become a fashionable way to do research in areas such as journalism, political communication, and media policy (Gurevitch and Blumler 2004). These studies, as well as the growing number of publications from non-Western scholars, gave greater visibility to journalism practice different from that common in the Western world (Wasserman and De Beer 2009). Consequently, we recognize that in comparative research the conceptual underpinnings of a study, such as the Western liberal pluralist idea of the institution of journalism, may also drive its results, findings, and conclusions (Josephi 2005). We were aware of this fallacy as we undertook our study.

In the Western world, shared understandings of journalism tend to build on the idea of the separation of powers, accomplished through a system of checks and balances. In such a context, the news media act as a Fourth Estate alongside the traditional three branches of power: the executive, legislative, and judicial. Grounded in a liberal pluralist view, such a perspective sees journalism as essential to the creation and maintenance of participatory democracy (Gans 1998). This model assumes that the news media are independent of the state and that journalists are mostly autonomous agents who represent the people. This autonomy is granted to journalists by the news organizations in which they work, as well as by the societal expectations of the role of the media in a democracy (Nerone 2013). This approach privileges liberal democracy and individuality, which are different from norms that exist elsewhere, as exemplified by the ongoing debate over the value of development journalism (De Beer et al. 2016; Romano 2005). For countries newly emergent from colonialism, development journalism—based on a collectivistic precept—was one way to overcome the destitution left behind by colonialists, but for the West it constituted a stifling of the press by the government.

As we show in the following chapters, Western democracies, and the United States in particular, may arguably not represent the dominant model of journalism in terms of numbers, both of media and of population. From a global point of view, the number of people exposed to Chinese journalism, for instance, is significantly larger than the combined populations of those consuming news in all Western countries. For this reason, we have tried, as much as possible, to avoid any normative biases in our study. Our view, then, counteracts the default assumption about one's own country or language group (e.g., the Anglo-Saxon research and publishing world) representing what is "normal" in journalism. That assumption went surprisingly unquestioned in the discipline for a long time (Livingstone 2012). Instead, the purpose of this book is to show, through a variety of journalistic understandings, that journalism is a complex and multifaceted concept when explored against a global background. Our aim is not to suggest that one is better than the other but rather to explore the contextual settings, which may be related to the existence of different journalistic cultures around the world.

Still, progress notwithstanding, the genesis of journalism theory, research, and practice as it has been promoted in the English-speaking world lies in Western, if not mostly U.S., tenets. Many areas pertinent to a global understanding of journalism and journalistic culture remain uncharted owing largely to the field's continued strong reliance on studies originating from the West. For instance, an analysis of comparative journalism research published between 2000 and 2015 in journals listed by ISI Journal Citation Reports found that eight of ten articles were exclusively authored by scholars based at institutions in the United States and Europe (Hanusch and Vos 2019). Further, more than half of all studies included the United States in their comparisons of journalism, demonstrating the country's centrality as a reference point in comparative research.

This large Western presence in knowledge production and country focus is complemented by the fact that the English language has become the lingua franca of the international academic community (Josephi 2005), allowing for a larger circulation of Western ideas than of knowledge produced in other languages. As a result of these interacting influences, scholars from the Global North have an automatic advantage in furthering theoretical and empirical work that is "designed in the North [and then] applied in the South" (De Beer 2010a; Josephi 2005; Wasserman and De Beer 2009), creating a cycle that reinforces Western dominance. Together these lead to a culturally asymmetrical recognition of academic research and intellectual authority in global knowledge production. Western researchers often take it for granted that their work is relevant to readers around the world and rarely face criticism when they make little reference to scholarly work from outside the Anglo-Saxon world. Researchers from non-Western contexts, however, are often criticized if they rely heavily on literature from their own regions (De Beer 2010a).

The paucity of recognition of non-Western scholarship is reflected in the way journalism scholars recognize and distribute scholarly prestige. The dominance of U.S. scholarship is particularly noteworthy. For example, more than 52 percent of the members of the International Communication Association's Journalism Studies Division work in institutions outside the United States.[2] Yet the field's symbolic capital—indexed through major awards honoring scholarly achievement—tends to be allocated to researchers based or educated in the United States. Between 2011 and 2018 ICA's

Journalism Studies Division has given all its book, dissertation, and out-standing article awards to scholars from universities located in the West. Of the twenty major awards, thirteen went to U.S. researchers.[3] Further, conversations among journalism researchers on social media channels heavily used by academics appear to coalesce primarily around issues related to media and journalism in the United States and Western Europe.

We argue that the Western dominance and researchers' uneven cover-age of world regions have had notable consequences for our understanding of journalism. Western journalism, particularly the news media in the United States, has become the prism through which researchers have con-structed normality for our general understanding of journalism. The West-ern experience has almost become the standard against which to gauge journalism in other regions of the world. Consequently, journalistic cultures in some, mostly developing and transitional, countries are sometimes por-trayed as needing to "catch up" with the norms and practices celebrated by the West (Golding 1977, 292; De Beer 2010b). Such a transfer of ideology can be problematic as cultural contexts and communicative needs in many of these societies differ considerably from those in the West and may thus call for a different understanding of what constitutes journalism and what jour-nalism ought to be.

Nowhere is the problem of generalizing and exporting the Western view to other parts of the world more evident than in academic and professional discourses that assert a global crisis of journalism (Franklin 2012; Mancini 2013; McChesney and Nichols 2010; Peters and Broersma 2013). In response to a widely diagnosed "collapse of journalism" (McChesney and Pickard 2011), scholars have recently issued calls for "rebuilding," "reconsidering," "remaking," "reconstructing," "rethinking," and "reinventing" journalism (Anderson 2013; Alexander, Breese, and Luengo 2016; Boczkowski and Anderson 2017; Downie and Schudson 2009; Peters and Broersma 2013; Waisbord 2013b), and even for "rethinking again" (Peters and Broersma 2017). Notably, these calls are very much informed by professional devel-opments and journalism research in Western countries, and most of them have originated in the United States.

The alarmist tone of this debate may be appropriate in the context of journalism in the United States, but the situation in most other countries may not call for such a response. The political and economic conditions of journalism in the United States, as well as its historical tradition and cul-tural mythology, make the American media system very different, if not exceptional, when compared with media systems in other Western nations (Curran 2011; Hallin and Mancini 2004; Hardy 2008). A high polarization of the American public and shrinking trust in political and media institutions make the country a breeding ground for public disaffection from "mainstream" news media, effectively pulling U.S. journalism in directions farther away from journalism in most European societies (Hanitzsch, van Dalen, and Steindl 2018). Evidence presented in this book further corroborates this assertion, notably about journalists' perceptions of their roles (see chapter 7).

While traditional journalism may be contracting through economic pressures brought on by technological change in the Global North, as chapter 10 argues, it is still expanding in many rapidly developing nations, such as China and India. Further, in some regions, journalists are coping with realities and problems quite different from those experienced by their colleagues in developed democracies (De Beer 2009). These include issues pertaining to journalism as an institution, such as journalists' safety and issues of impunity, heavy censorship, and media bans, as well as power rent-seeking, clientelism, and an instrumental use of the media mainly by politicians. Other issues are more broadly related to the societal conditions of journalism, such as pervasive corruption, low human development, and strong socioeconomic inequalities. After all, the proclaimed crisis of journalism may be, at least in part, a crisis of the professional paradigm celebrated by journalists in the West, and—by extension—the expression of an intellectual blind spot in journalism scholarship.

Furthermore, the lopsided coverage of world regions in international research can become a serious impediment to our understanding of journalism derived from comparative research. In the context of comparative politics, Barbara Geddes (2003) and Linda Hantrais (1999) have demonstrated how case selection affects answers to research questions. Arguably, similarities and differences revealed through international comparison can result, to a substantive extent, from our choice of countries (see chapter 3). Thus, increasing the number of countries in a comparative study to cover a significant proportion of the world's population can effectively reduce selection bias and lead to conclusions that are more accurate.

An example illustrates this point well. In a now classic study, Thomas Patterson and Wolfgang Donsbach (1996) noted striking differences in journalists' professional orientations in Germany, Italy, Sweden, the United Kingdom, and the United States. The study found that German journalists were significantly more partisan in their reporting than their American colleagues. In the previous WJS, however, which covered twenty-one Western and non-Western countries, the differences between German and U.S. journalists shrunk to relative similarities within the context of a macrolevel comparative perspective (Hanitzsch et al. 2011). Hence differences at a regional level of analysis may become similarities in the broader context of global diversity.

With the inclusion of sixty-seven countries in the present study, we have greater power to evaluate the robustness of findings and lay claim to the cross-cultural validity of our conclusions. While this number of countries provides a fair representation of world regions, we also recognize that quantity alone does not necessarily make for a groundbreaking study. It is not always true that we learn more as we study more countries. Hence incorporating larger numbers of societies in a comparative study without adequate representation of countries with different journalism ideologies can only partly resolve selection bias and insufficiently eliminate Western dominance. Moreover, despite intentions to represent more researchers from the Global South (as is the case with the WJS), researchers from the industrialized North are still more likely to lead or join comparative projects than are their colleagues from the Global South owing to global inequalities in terms of scholarly capital and financial resources.

In sum, we believe that "international" journalism research still too often problematizes journalism from within the Western experience and a Western analytical framework. This dominance has led to the normalization of the Western journalism paradigm, to which journalistic cultures outside the Western core are fitted in normative, conceptual, and empirical terms. These are all strong indications of a continued hegemony of Western scholarship over journalism studies as an academic field, a hegemony that the WJS has attempted to counter. While only one of the editors of this book is from the Global South (and he too was socialized into a Western academic culture), the WJS project as a whole has attempted to counter Western hegemony by taking deliberate measures during the research process to involve researchers from the Global South. Non-Western researchers were included in the methodological decisions, in particular in the formulation of the questionnaire, and as authors of this book, enabling the representation of their interpretations of the findings. Further, the WJS includes a wide range of countries from the Global South, allowing us to examine journalistic cultures that are very different from those of the West but also show remarkable similarities.

Challenges Along the Way

The researchers involved in the WJS have devoted considerable effort to the development of concepts that deliberately serve a comparative purpose that applies to both Western and non-Western contexts. Some of the difficulties of this exercise are discussed in chapter 2, which outlines the study's conceptual framework. We found it particularly challenging to strike a healthy balance between two, sometimes incompatible, demands of theoretical universality and cultural specificity. On the one hand, we tried to develop concepts in a way that enabled us to adequately capture journalism's major facets in often very different cultural settings to avoid comparing apples and oranges. On the other hand, we wanted to make these concepts sensitive to the contextual conditions in the countries included in the study. To resolve this dilemma, we had to compromise on a few conceptual issues.

The definition of who is considered a "journalist" in our study is a case in point. Finding a workable definition is central to our research, given that the study is about journalism and journalistic cultures based on interviews with journalists. There is no universally accepted jurisdiction over journalism's boundaries and, more specifically, over who should have the authority to speak on behalf of "journalism." This renders the very definition of being a "journalist" highly contested, within and across national boundaries. In academic and professional discourse, "journalist" can mean anything from the professional hard-news-producing reporter at a news organization (Patterson and Donsbach 1996) to the "redactional" citizen (Hartley 2000, 45), or simply everyone who employs and reproduces journalism's discursive techniques, for instance, on social media platforms.

The spectrum of definitions suggested by members of the WJS broadly ranged from hard-news journalists alone to producers of user-generated content, such as nonprofessional bloggers and columnists who only occasionally contribute to news outlets. We opted against limiting the study to "classic" hard-news journalists because this would have excluded a significant proportion, if not the majority, of journalism focusing on "softer" beats, such as sports, lifestyle, and celebrities. At the same time we chose to exclude nonprofessional contributors because including them would have rendered it impossible to arrive at a definition that we could operationalize consistently across the study. Ultimately we adopted a somewhat conventional definition: journalists are individuals who contribute journalistic content to news outlets as either employees or freelancers and who earn at least half their income from their work for news organizations (see chapter 3).

On the practical level, this definition helped us to generate samples of journalists that are broadly comparable across the participating countries. Our definition, however, created new problems on the conceptual level. Journalists working for community media, for instance, may not always fulfill the criteria mentioned above, as in many cases their work is not traditionally remunerated. Community media of different kinds are widespread in parts of Africa, Asia, and Latin America, and they have gained ground in many Western countries (Berrigan 1979; Deuze 2006a). University-owned media, for example, have a long tradition in the United States and in parts of Latin America. Following intense deliberation with the principal researchers in the relevant countries, we decided to include community media in societies where they play an essential role in the country's news ecosystem, such as in sub-Saharan Africa.

Thus the second wave of the WJS (2012–2016) followed conventional pathways by understanding journalism as professional work and as an institutional practice. We accept that this decision is subject to valid and legitimate criticism. However, when we designed the study in early 2010, many developments in the technological environment, such as social media and computational journalism, were still in their infancy or nonexistent in many parts of the world. In fact, even independent online journalism did not exist at the time to any significant extent in many parts of the world, including even in an economically and technologically emergent country such as India or a media-rich country such as South Africa. Hence the relatively long planning stage required for a large-scale comparative study such as the one presented in this book would inevitably lead to a situation where ruptures in journalism and its environment that emerged later could not be captured in the study's operational stage.

Another case in point with regard to resolving conceptual issues is the use of the nation as the unit of comparison. The diversity of journalistic cultures is addressed at the level of cross-national comparison, making the country the primary reference point. Such a focus on national territories as units of comparison may seem anachronistic in a time of increased globalization of business, politics, culture, and almost all aspects of human life (Cohen 2013). We argue, however, that the forces of globalization notwithstanding, journalistic culture is still articulated and enacted within national spaces. News production is strongly geared toward news agendas that prioritize domestic news; media coverage primarily features national actors and interests; and journalists speak to national or local audiences (Tunstall 2008). The relevance of the nation for journalism's conditions of existence still holds true, despite the fact that national borders do not necessarily reflect cultural, ethnolinguistic divisions or correspond to a common sense of identity (Hantrais 1999).

Hence journalists still cover the world in national frames and operate within a space marked by national boundaries (De Beer 2009), although this has become more problematic with increasingly deterritorialized news spaces spanning national borders and continents. At the same time, despite the rise of global consciousness, the significance of the nation as a frame of reference is still underscored by substantive, and in part even growing, distinctions between countries, for instance in terms of public values (Inglehart and Welzel 2005). Researchers have made similar arguments in communication and media studies. In a comparative assessment of foreign television news, Akiba Cohen (2013, 328) argues that even with the onward march of globalization, mostly in the realm of business and commercialization, "a 'global village' has not been created, and is not likely to happen." This is not to say that we advocate a view suggesting that national borders "contain" journalistic cultures. Borders are porous, and journalistic cultures have always traveled across geographic boundaries. We do not think that boundaries other than national borders are irrelevant to the study of journalism. To the contrary, the country level is only one of many ways of distinguishing between journalistic cultures—a way that we found particularly productive in this effort to study forms of journalism around the world. There is much to say, for instance, about organizational journalism cultures or other cultural distinctions within the institution of journalism, but this would merit another book.

The Worlds of Journalism Study

The Worlds of Journalism Study has made a notable conceptual and empirical contribution to our understanding of journalism in its diverse forms and has broken new ground in terms of its comparative design and the way in which the study was organized, coordinated, and orchestrated. The magnitude of the WJS in terms of geographical coverage and the number of respondents and researchers involved is unprecedented in the history of journalism and media studies research. It has become the largest and geographically most inclusive collaborative effort of its kind in the field of journalism and media research. Facilitated by communication technology and annual in-person meetings at WJS conventions, it has also created a sustained community of researchers across the globe who are interested in the comparative assessment of journalism. The experience of exchanging ideas and garnering cultural understandings about journalism has advanced our goal of integrating viewpoints and strengthened our interpretations as we traversed the path of this international, comparative, decentering endeavor.

The WJS is participating in the trend to include larger sets of countries and regions that other disciplines, such as political science, sociology, and psychology, have been following since the 1980s (e.g., Hofstede 1980; Inglehart and Welzel 2005; Schwartz and Bardi 2001). Standing on the shoulders of giants, the project reported in this book has continued some of the important work other comparative journalism researchers have undertaken in the past twenty-five years. David Weaver's (1998a) collection of journalist surveys from twenty-one countries and regions—the *Global Journalist*—was an important starting point for the WJS. Still, despite the fact that the *Global Journalist* gained enormous traction in the field, it also had its limitations. A key point of criticism was related to the absence of a strict comparative design. The book compared different populations of journalists at different points in time. Interview methods, questionnaires, and sample sizes varied widely among countries. Weaver (1998b, 455) himself conceded that making comparisons based on such methodological variability would be "a game of guesswork at best." In the follow-up volume, edited by Weaver and Lars Willnat (2012) and expanded to cover thirty-one countries, the editors still noted an urgent need for comparative studies to employ standardized survey questionnaires and representative samples.

The WJS has its origins in a pilot project created in 2006 in response to the deficiencies in comparative studies noted above. Inspired by Patterson and Donsbach's (1996) systematic comparison of journalists in five Western countries, and with initial support from the German Research Foundation (DFG), we carried out a comparative survey of journalists in Brazil, China, Germany, Indonesia, Russia, Uganda, and the United

States. Over the following four years the project developed into a collaborative effort that ultimately included twenty-one countries, covering all inhabited continents and a wide array of political, economic, and sociocultural contexts (Hanitzsch et al. 2012). A grant from the Swiss National Science Foundation in 2007 made possible the inclusion of this larger number of countries. Major findings were published in the field's leading journals, giving the study broad international visibility.

In early 2011, when it became clear that the project would continue into its second phase with an even larger number of countries, the participating researchers officially founded the Worlds of Journalism Study as a semi-institutional framework with a mission statement, its own statutes, and a governing body, the WJS Executive Committee. To a considerable extent the inception of the WJS was inspired by, and the study itself modeled after, the World Values Survey, a worldwide network of social scientists who, since 1981, have been examining people's changing values and their impact on social and political life in almost one hundred countries.[4]

As the participating WJS researchers prepared for the second wave of the study (conducted between 2012 and 2016), the network rapidly grew into a large collaborative effort that eventually covered sixty-seven countries and territories around the world. The group's approach to academic collaboration is neatly summarized by the credo "Give a little, get a lot," famously coined by Robert Stevenson more than twenty years ago with regard to the news flow study by UNESCO/International Association for Mass Communication Research.[5] In other words, collaborators were entitled to receive the full comparative dataset in return for contributing data on their own countries.[6] The expectation was that participating researchers would creatively analyze the data and test hypotheses in ways that would not have been possible with data from a single country or even a few countries. In response to some of the shortcomings of earlier studies, the researchers participating in the WJS collaboratively designed and adopted a common methodological framework, including a standardized questionnaire, to ensure cross-national comparability (see chapter 3). In the Northern Hemisphere's summer of 2012, the new study was ready to go into the field as the second phase of the WJS.

As the geographical scope of the study and the number of researchers involved in it grew, the network implemented a more structured managerial framework that would enable it to coordinate a study of this magnitude. Here too, we believe, the WJS has broken new ground in the field of communication and media research. A WJS Executive Committee was created to provide leadership and strategic planning for the project, recruit new members, organize meetings and workshops, promote publications and dissemination of results, and raise central funding as well as assist members in their fund-raising efforts. At present the Executive Committee is assisted by a Scientific Advisory Committee consisting of leading scholars in the area of comparative journalism and a Statistical Advisory Committee, which since 2015 has been providing help and support to members of the network in matters related to data analysis and statistical procedures.[7]

What makes the WJS distinctive among comparative studies in the field is that the researchers participating in the project elect the Executive Committee members. Each country is entitled to cast one vote.[8] The network has adopted this democratic process for a number of reasons. For one, the voting process gives Executive Committee members a considerable degree of democratic legitimacy to steer the study and present it to external stakeholders. In addition, the leaders of the study want to ensure that everyone involved has a say in all decisions—from the design and planning of research to the publication of results. From its beginnings, the project has taken steps to avoid being governed by the strategy that James Halloran (1998, 45) famously identified as "research imperialism." The emphasis on inclusiveness over exclusiveness allows participating researchers to see theoretical, methodological, and cultural diversity as an advantage rather than a threat. Consequently the WJS has developed into a democratic tribe of scholars rather than an academic empire (Hanusch and Hanitzsch 2017).

As positive as our efforts and their results may sound so far, the WJS was not free of problems: the complex collaborative structure created research problems on many fronts (see chapter 3). The successes we garnered and the problems we encountered have, however, provided us with insights for the next phase. The researchers collaborating on the project come from different theoretical, methodological, and cultural backgrounds, and they have distinctive understandings of teamwork, the division of labor, work structures, academic hierarchy, information exchange, and, perhaps most important, communication habits. Researchers participate in the project on a voluntary basis, and their level of commitment to the study varied by researcher and over time. For most collaborators, the WJS was one among many academic endeavors, including teaching and managerial and other academic duties at their home institutions.

To ensure that the final data set met the highest standards in terms of data quality and integrity, data management was centralized at the WJS Center based at LMU Munich. As a service to the entire research network, the WJS Center carefully reviewed all country data sets for potential problems, clarified issues with local teams, and turned all data files into a standardized format for dissemination to the whole group. Owing to the sheer number of countries and the complexity of the data, this project eventually turned into full-time work for Corinna Lauerer, a Ph.D. candidate at LMU Munich at the time, who devoted about two years of her academic career to data management for the WJS.

The Central Narrative of the Book

Amid the calls for de-Westernizing and decentering journalism theory, research, practice, and education (Grüne and Ulrich 2012; Waisbord and Mellado 2014), the WJS provides a concrete example of how this can be executed, at least as part of comparative journalism studies. The study's theoretical narrative privileges de-essentializing, which in turn seeds its methodological decisions and analytical framework, and together the two inform the interpretation of results and the derivation of conclusions. As a result, this book presents a diversity of beliefs and perceptions of journalists rooted in a collaborative effort that did not begin with any notion of a particular journalism that is more normative or desirable than another. Comparative research that is mindful of this issue can foster and calibrate our understanding of what journalism is, or ought to be, through cross-national contextualization. In this book we argue, based on comparative empirical evidence, that the universe of news making is populated with different life forms of journalism that produce a fascinating multiplicity of journalistic cultures articulated in many different ways across national borders, geographic regions, political systems, levels of socioeconomic development, and cultural value systems.

It is important to point out that despite our attempt to erase ethnocentrism in our work by decentering it, we have not fully explored or implemented the decentering project. We have, however, moved it forward.

Among the myriad dimensions that constitute decentering, our main effort has been directed toward de-essentializing journalism. At the theoretical level, we articulate journalism as a discursive social institution that spawns a kaleidoscope of journalistic cultures, which are manifested as products of local societal and professional contexts. At the empirical level, we acknowledge cultural influencers as well as indigenous ideas about journalism. We understand that we still have work to do—include more scholars from less-represented regions, include variables and measures in our questionnaire and analyses that capture other realities, and explore more indigenous writings and modes of thought for our explanations—as we traverse this path toward decentering our research. At the same time we believe that this book will set benchmarks for future journalism studies research that will allow for a more democratic understanding of the field.

As we demonstrate throughout the book, journalism and the way it is articulated in professional, academic, and public conversations are substantially influenced by a variety of contextual factors. By emphasizing the discursive properties of journalism and journalistic culture, we challenge an essentialist understanding of these concepts and show how notions of journalism are varied, traversing different pathways in different contexts. We note that ideas of what constitutes journalism are deeply embedded in various cultural histories, which have led to differential developments across the world. The comparative evidence presented demonstrates how deeply journalism is grounded in its historical contexts and the political, economic, social, and cultural conditions within which it exists. It follows that journalism's normative compass needs to account for culturally disparate realities on the ground. Hence the various characteristics and manifestations of the dimensions of journalism—roles, ethics, and so on—as articulated by journalists in different countries within their societal contexts, past and current, are simply that, not to be judged by their relative proximity to or distance from some Western or other culturally specific norm.

It is important to recognize that we consider our work as exemplifying decentering, a recognition that there is no single central operational paradigm of journalism as an institution or of journalism as practice. This approach does not remove or discard Western narratives or, for that matter, narratives of various origin, nor is it reductive in its approach; it simply allows these narratives their due space, proportionate to their similarities and variabilities. Even so, in the end, the book demonstrates that news making in Western democracies still has a number of features that set it apart from journalism in many other parts of the world.

The authors of the WJS are also cognizant of the fact that, despite some key similarities among forms of journalism in developed democracies, such as a strong emphasis on journalism as a "Fourth Estate," journalistic cultures differ considerably among many Western countries too. As the evidence presented in this book demonstrates, the United States, most notably, is far from being a truly "typical" case even within the group of Western democracies. Journalism in the United States constitutes a unique, sometimes even extreme, case against the backdrop of global comparison. In a similar vein, no single model of journalism can be applied to what is commonly considered the Global South. Journalistic cultures in countries in the non-Western world differ greatly in many ways, as the following chapters demonstrate.

Hence our approach to the WJS project, its very underpinnings, and its reasoning have immense currency today given the demise—with the fall of the Berlin Wall in 1989—of a world in which there was a bipolar distribution of power and ideology. Today power is more evenly distributed, allowing ideologies of a different tenor to surface and find a voice. The book provides a theoretical orientation and a methodological roadmap for journalism studies researchers to engender inclusivity, to allow for an epistemology that includes various voices within a framework of multiple normalities that are contextually determined, rather than some universal norm that is considered to be an ideal. While we do not live in a balanced epistemic world (and it might be utopian to expect this), today scholars, aided by global travel, economic strength, and digital technologies, can be liberated from intellectual imperialism while they resolve and satisfy their intellectual curiosities. The WJS has allowed our community of scholars to have such an experience.

Organization of the Book

The collaborative nature of the Worlds of Journalism Study is reflected not only in the evidence presented in the following chapters but also in the way this book has come into being. The book benefited from the extensive expertise of more than forty authors who have contributed to one or more chapters, as well as from the input of other WJS members who contributed to the individual country studies.

The book is broadly separated into two sections. The first part, encompassing chapters 1 to 3, provides an overview of the conceptual and methodological aspects of the second wave of the WJS (2012–2016). The second part presents the empirical results and the concluding chapter.

Chapter 2 advances an overall understanding of the key definitions underpinning the project: journalism, journalistic culture, and the contexts of journalism. It outlines the study's overall conceptual framework in the theoretical tradition of looking at journalism as a social institution that is discursively (re)created, (re)interpreted, appropriated, and contested. This discourse produces different "worlds of journalism"—or articulations of journalistic culture—that compete in a discursive space. Further, the chapter argues that journalistic culture can be meaningfully studied by examining the way it is articulated and enacted in terms of its extrinsic dimensions (journalists' perceived influences and editorial autonomy) as well as its intrinsic dimensions (journalists' roles, ethics, and trust).

Chapter 3 introduces the methodological framework, focusing on the methodological and data-related coordination efforts, sampling, data collection, data management, and the questionnaire. The use of a common, collaboratively designed methodological framework, mostly nationally representative samples of journalists, and rigorous techniques for data collection and data checking all speak to the ambition of this project to meet the highest standards of comparative research. Given the complexity of this endeavor, however, there are also limitations, which the chapter documents for reasons of scientific transparency.

Chapter 4 reports and discusses central parameters of the full sample of journalists interviewed for the study and of the organizational contexts in which they worked. Providing an overview of the journalists' social and professional backgrounds, it highlights key variables such as gender, age and education, as well as professional experience and membership in professional organizations. Covering the organizational contexts, the chapter presents journalists' conditions of employment, journalistic specializations, newsroom organization and hierarchies, as well as ownership and publication platforms. Results indicate that, from a global perspective, journalism is still dominated by men, not only numerically but especially in terms of power within newsrooms. Journalists tend to be in their late thirties and tertiary educated and have job experience of around twelve years. However, there is substantial variation across the countries in our study, which is often related to the larger opportunity structures of the respective societies.

Chapters 5 and 6 focus on what we call the extrinsic aspects of journalistic culture. Chapter 5 focuses on journalists' perceived influences on news work. Based on a hierarchy-of-influences approach, it identifies the main sources of influence on news work based on journalists' perceptions. These influences are organized along five distinct domains: political, economic, organizational, procedural, and personal networks influences. In the comparative analysis, political influence emerged as a major denominator of differences across countries. Chapter 6 continues this discussion by investigating journalists' perceptions of their editorial autonomy in light of the factors that determine how much freedom they have in everyday reporting. The focus of this chapter is on the extent to which journalists in different countries perceive they have autonomy in selecting news topics and story angles in day-to-day news work, and under what contextual conditions similarities and differences exist. Our findings complicate long-held assumptions about editorial autonomy around the world, as we find journalistic freedom to exist in both liberal and authoritarian environments to serve different purposes.

The subsequent three chapters are concerned with the intrinsic aspects of journalistic culture. Chapter 7 examines the ways in which journalists around the world have discursively constructed normative roles and how these roles are translated into cognitive journalistic roles. The chapter argues that cross-national differences in journalists' conceptions of their cognitive roles can be meaningfully studied with regard to four central dimensions: monitorial versus collaborative and interventionist versus accommodative roles. Of these, the collaborative and interventionist roles were found to be meaningful descriptors of difference in the way journalists around the globe construct journalism's position vis-à-vis broader society.

Chapter 8 takes the discussion to the realm of journalists' professional ethics and looks at both general ethical orientations of journalists and journalists' justification of ethically controversial practices. Based on these two sets of comparative evidence, the chapter maps out similarities and differences in journalists' ethical views across countries, pinpointing universal standards as well as culturally specific practices. The chapter presents some evidence of a primary—particularly for absolutism and subjectivism—but not exclusive allegiance among journalists to an ethical orientation, indicating hybridity in the approach these journalists adopt. The allegiance is mostly influenced by the political and press-related opportunity structures in the journalists' countries and is therefore to some extent regionally distinguishable.

Still concerned with the intrinsic dimensions of journalistic culture, chapter 9 provides a comparative examination of journalists' trust in public institutions. The chapter demonstrates how levels of journalists' trust in regulative and representative institutions vary across the world, and how trust among journalists compares to trust among the general population. Connecting institutional and cultural theory explanations of trust with comparative journalism research, the chapter identifies the main contextual factors that explain differences in journalists' institutional trust around the globe. The results indicate that journalists have particularly little trust in political institutions when they work in countries that have experienced significant political, socioeconomic, and cultural transformation and are suffering from political instability.

Chapter 10 revisits many of the aspects mentioned above by emphasizing journalists' perceptions of and reflections on journalism's ongoing transformations, with a specific focus on questions about changes in aspects of work such as audiences, technology, economics, and journalism education, and an examination of the increasing precariousness of journalistic labor. The chapter further identifies cross-national patterns in the way journalists conceive of these changes and pinpoints the factors that account for these perceptions on a comparative level. The analysis suggests that a crisis of journalism narrative is very much prevalent in the Western countries of our study, and perhaps less so in the Global South.

Chapter 11, finally, highlights some of the global trajectories of journalistic culture with regard to journalists' professional roles, ethics, autonomy, perceived influences, and transformation of journalism, as well as journalists' trust in public institutions. The chapter integrates the complex findings presented in the previous chapters to identify broad similarities and differences in journalistic cultures across the globe as well as to pinpoint underlying geographic patterns. It further tests the dimensions of journalistic culture against key differences in the broader contexts of journalistic culture: politics and governance, socioeconomic development, and cultural value systems. Ultimately this comparative analysis yields a global classification of journalistic cultures consisting of four ideal-type models: monitorial, advocative, developmental, and collaborative.

Central to this understanding of different models of journalistic culture is our conceptual framework, which is discussed in depth in chapter 2.

Notes

1. Worlds of Journalism Study, http://worldsofjournalism.org/.
2. E-mail exchange with ICA Member Services, December 18, 2017.
3. International Communication Association, https://www.icahdq.org/members/group_con tent_view.asp?group=186103&id=631059.
4. World Values Survey, http://www.worldvaluessurvey.org/WVSOnline.jsp.
5. "Remapping the News of the World," ibiblio.org, http://www.ibiblio.org/newsflow/results /Newsmap.htm.
6. As a service to the academic community, the multinational data set will become publicly available for secondary data analysis in the second half of 2019, to be downloaded from the WJS project website at http://www.worldsofjournalism.org/data/data-and-key-tables-2012 -2016/.
7. Worlds of Journalism Study, http://www.worldsofjournalism.org/about/organization/.
8. The study also included Hong Kong and Kosovo, which we counted as "countries" despite their status as, respectively, a Special Administrative Region (Hong Kong) and a partially recognized state (Kosovo).

2

JOURNALISTIC CULTURE IN A GLOBAL CONTEXT

A Conceptual Roadmap

Thomas Hanitzsch, Laura Ahva, Martin Oller Alonso, Jesus Arroyave,
Liesbeth Hermans, Jan Fredrik Hovden, Sallie Hughes, Beate Josephi,
Jyotika Ramaprasad, Ivor Shapiro, and Tim P. Vos

In this chapter we lay out the broad framework that serves as the conceptual backbone to the analysis presented in this book. We concur with Michael Gurevitch and Jay Blumler (2004), who argue that while theory and conceptual clarity are central to all kinds of research, they are especially critical in comparative studies. Without a theoretical map or conceptual compass, the comparative researcher may remain "stranded in Babel" (Norris 2009, 323). Large-scale, cross-national comparative research is thus an exercise in positing a unified conceptual foundation that is also inclusive enough to do justice to the local realities within individual societies. Such an undertaking is not without problems. On the one hand, the demand for theoretical universalism may lead to measurement that is insensitive to context and formulates key concepts at such a high level of abstraction that researchers may have difficulty relating them to real-world phenomena in their countries. On the other hand, efforts to adequately accommodate the local may lead to a plethora of concepts that are so grounded in the specific that they become theoretically meaningless and thus frustrate any attempt to rise to the level of systematic conceptual comparative analysis.

Balancing this exercise is further complicated by the fact that the level at which the analysis is conducted can hide or reveal differences. What we treat as similar at one level of analysis may actually comprise a myriad of differences at more detailed levels (Kohn 1989). Journalists in the established democracies of the West, for instance, may be found to broadly share a professional ideology when studied at a macroanalytic level but may exhibit substantial differences at finer levels of analysis. The distinctive approach to news in France as compared with that in the United States and Great Britain is a case in point (Chalaby 1996). News in the Anglo-Saxon world has been historically constructed around what are perceived to be objective facts, with the most newsworthy fact placed first, while in France the organizing principle of many articles is the mediating subjectivity of the journalist. Another example is the concept of "development journalism," generally attributed to the Global South, but which is in fact differently understood at the country level. Some associate it with the idea of journalists acting as nation builders and government partners; others with watchdog journalism, constructive criticism, and sociopolitical empowerment (Romano 2005; Shah 1996).

As in the case for other multinational projects, the research team steering the Worlds of Journalism Study (WJS) was tasked with striking a healthy balance between two seemingly antagonistic demands: positing universal theoretical concepts that would be similarly understood in different cultural contexts and thus allow for meaningful comparison, and providing culturally sensitive theoretical concepts that would enable sensible conclusions about the local conditions of journalism in societies around the world. This trade-off is particularly difficult to navigate when the comparison is across sixty-seven countries from all inhabited continents, as is the case in this book. In a study of this magnitude, the sheer number of cultural peculiarities in the various societies is overwhelming: including all of them would result in a questionnaire so long as to make its administration infeasible and would still not serve journalism's full cross-cultural panoply. In the end, it was all about making reasonable compromises within a group of researchers from often distant academic galaxies, with different theoretical and epistemological cultures, and sometimes irreconcilable worldviews and understandings of research and its methodologies.

Despite these conundrums, we firmly believe that theory development is an indispensable element of comparative research. There is something to be gained because it involves researchers from around the world, in face of the fact that most journalism research, comparative or not, about a Western country or not, still carries significant Western conceptual baggage. The Western "hegemonic model of journalism" recognizes the journalist as an independent, public-spirited verifier of factual information (Nerone 2013). It assumes that the news media are independent of the state and that journalists are engaged in an antagonistic relationship with power while representing the people. In what Peter Golding (1977) termed a transfer of occupational ideology, this model was exported to the developing world and has become the professional standard against which journalism in non-Western countries is largely measured. One consequence is that journalism was sometimes cast, in some countries, mostly developing and transitional, as "needing to catch up" with the norms and practices celebrated by the West.

No less significant, journalistic cultures have mostly been studied in democratic contexts in the West. This, as well as a concentration of scholarly resources in the Northern Hemisphere, has produced a Western bias that tends to pin journalism to the idea of democracy. While few would deny the news media's centrality to democratic processes, journalism has always existed beyond democratic lands (Josephi 2013). In fact, journalism within democracy is experienced only by a minority of the world's population. A consequence of both developments—a focus on Western journalistic norms and an emphasis on journalism's link to democracy—is that journalism research may ironically have produced undemocratic scholarship as it has privileged a journalistic world that is narrower than that which resides on the ground (Zelizer 2013).

The WJS therefore deliberately chose an inclusive strategy to cope with the danger of research ethnocentrism. In developing the general theoretical framework for the project, we drew on the rich theoretical expertise and cultural experience of researchers involved in this study from across the world. In the many discussions we had during the study, a key narrative emerged: the world of journalism is populated with a splendid diversity of distinct forms—journalistic cultures—that operate in different societal contexts. In the current, rapidly changing journalism scenario in the world that is due both to digitalization and to the advance of neoliberal economic policies, each journalistic culture has found its own answers and is traversing its own path. Given this scenario, we advance, in the following pages, a common understanding of three essential conceptual areas that underpin the WJS. First, we conceptualize journalism as a discursive institution. We then turn to explaining the notion of journalistic culture, which is meant to embody the differential readings and articulations of forms of journalism in different societal contexts. Based on this foundation, we finally theorize the contextual influences on journalistic culture and outline the "conceptual roadmap" that organizes the content of this book. In the end we hope that the WJS and this book contribute meaningfully to the development of shared theoretical key concepts and to the very idea of what journalism is. We also believe that the study makes a contribution in its standardized operationalization of both theorized constructs and empirical measures; these will be described in the relevant thematic chapters in this volume.

Journalism as Discursive Institution

Most established theories in the field tend to embrace an essentialized view of journalism. These attempts to posit the core of journalism provide such a variety of definitions and attributes that they have still left unanswered the question of "what is journalism." This longstanding and sometimes heated debate, joined by both practitioners and academics, may be unresolvable: neither academics nor practitioners agree among themselves about a definition of "journalism," and there is a lack of consensus across the two groups. The core of journalism aside, there is little agreement even on the question of whether journalism is a profession, an occupation, a craft, or a trade (Zelizer 2004).

At the same time, there seems to be a normative understanding—shared by most parts of the Western world and exported to the Global South, at least normatively if not in practice—that attaches the notion of journalism to the ideas of citizenship and democracy. In this view, journalism is expected to provide surveillance of and information about potentially relevant events and their contexts; commentary, guidance, and advice; and the means for access, expression, and political participation; as well as to contribute to a shared consciousness and act as critic or watchdog to hold the government to account (Christians et al. 2009; McQuail 2000).

Little empirical evidence is marshaled to support the universality of this understanding, however. The absence of an empirically supported, coherent, and shared understanding of what journalism is becomes even more evident when one includes non-Western societies in the analysis. Because developing and transitional societies face a number of unique challenges with regard to political, economic, and social development, journalism in these societies is often expected to support the government and assist with nation building and social empowerment (Romano 2005). Several proponents of "development journalism," for example, argue that journalists have a social responsibility that includes the preservation of harmony in society and a respect for authority (Masterton 1996; Xu 2005). In many parts of the Arab and Islamic world and in sub-Saharan Africa, journalism is taking a much more active and participatory role in political discourse than in most Western nations (Hanitzsch et al. 2011; Pintak 2014). In Latin America, some of the most influential online journalists specifically reject neutrality and objectivity while at the same time embracing traditional norms of independence and fact-based truth telling (Harlow and Salaverría 2016).

Journalists and publics in the West, by way of contrast, tend to see both the social responsibility role and participatory practice as illegitimate, and more than a few would describe these as a transgression of journalism's normative and ethical core, since they seemingly tread on a professional ideal of objectivity. Are journalists outside the older democracies of the West, then, less professional than their colleagues in Europe and the United States? Not necessarily so. Available comparative evidence in the Global North impressively demonstrates that a unitary normative core does not exist across this universe of journalistic cultures (Christians et al. 2009; Waisbord 2013b; Weaver 1998a; Weaver and Willnat 2012). At the same time, professional subcultures appreciative of journalists' social responsibility and intervention in social reality, for instance, also exist in many Western contexts; one example is the movement advocating the practice of peace journalism (Lynch and McGoldrick 2005). Hence judgments about the extent to which journalists adhere to professional standards can be made meaningfully only from within their respective societies, based on criteria defined by local cultural expectations.

In the considered search for a useful theoretical perspective for the WJS, we have offloaded some of the conceptual baggage of the past, bid farewell to some common and long-held assumptions, and, most important, abandoned the idea that journalism has some kind of true "essence." This is not to say that we deny the obviously institutional character of journalism, but even with the rise of citizen and entrepreneurial journalisms, most journalistic work is still conducted within an institutional framework (Sjøvaag 2013). In our view, the conceptual tensions resulting from an emphasis on the material realities of news making, on the one hand, and a focus on journalism as practice infused with meaning, on the other, can be overcome by adopting the framework of discursive institutionalism—a perspective developed relatively recently in political science (Schmidt 2008, 2010). Building on our initial work (Hanitzsch and Vos 2017, 2018), we derived two central theoretical propositions for our work that we will develop further in the following, namely, that journalism is a *social institution* and that it is *discursively (re)created.*

Political communication researchers have long recognized journalism and the news media as a social institution (Cook 1998; Sparrow 1999). Generally, social institutions are understood as humanly devised constraints to create order and reduce uncertainty (North 1991). These constraints can include "formal or informal rules, conventions or practices, together with the organizational manifestations these patterns of group behavior sometimes take on" (Parsons 2007, 70). Social institutions influence behavior by providing the cognitive scripts, categories, and models that are indispensable for action (Hall and Taylor 1996); key to individual behavior is the "logic of appropriateness" (Cook 1998, 61). It is in this sense, Timothy Cook (1998) argues, that they can be seen as a social institution. The news media entail social patterns of behavior identifiable across organizations, which extend across space and endure over time, and which preside over a societal and/or political sector. As an institution, the news media are "an ordered aggregate of shared norms and informal rules that guide news collection" (Sparrow 2006, 155).

The institutional character of journalism is clearly visible around the world and across a wide range of news organizations. Even if journalism as an institution spreads beyond organizational contexts, it is clear that organizations form hubs in which journalistic actions are institutionalized. Although there is a trend toward shrinking newsrooms in a number of countries, with freelancers increasingly replacing employed journalists, it is safe to say that most journalists still work in organizational environments. News production decisions are subject to a chain of command that follows specific rules and conventions. Furthermore, like other institutions—such as government, education, family, and religion—journalism has obligations and responsibilities toward society. These may be seen as a tacit social contract that lends journalism its social legitimacy and guarantees its very existence. But there is no universal standard contract that uniformly applies to all parts of the world, since the relationship of journalism with society depends on specific political, economic, sociocultural, technological, and other contextual conditions.

Journalism's institutional framework is made up of rules, conventions, and practices that are limiting and enabling, constraining, and constitutive. A typical institutional framework includes formal structures (e.g., press laws or work contracts) and informal rules and procedures, such as customs, traditions, taboos, and codes of conduct. Young journalists mostly learn and understand these rules in terms of a cultural consensus as to "how we do journalism" rather than as explicit rules of conduct. The choices journalists make as part of their day-to-day work are governed less by their personal values and social dispositions than by assumptions and expectations about appropriate or legitimate modes of practice, that is, about "what a journalist's role is, what her or his obligations are, what values and commitments are appropriate" (Ryfe 2006, 205). Journalists thus work according to unspoken and often uncritically accepted norms, rules, and procedures, which are understood to be the "natural" way to gather news (Cook 1998, 75–76). Thus one might say that the institution of journalism is the shortcut through which journalists navigate the complexities and uncertainties of news making.

Journalists are socialized into this institutional framework both within the news organization and during vocational education and training (Gravengaard and Rimestad 2014; Singer 2004; Tandoc and Takahashi 2014). In this way, they develop specific idealized expectations about work and news organizations, which remain a pervasive standard against which daily practices are compared (Russo 1998). This process takes place in a specific community of practice in which the professional veterans have common goals and share a repertoire of myths and tales (Gravengaard and Rimestad 2014). Here occupational socialization works toward the preservation of an institutional mythology: the prescription that "the way we do" things becomes "the way one should do" things (Schudson 2001; Singer 2004).

Forms of ritual solidarity that call on journalists to celebrate themselves as a professional community invigorate the articulation of institutional norms. Shared interpretations of, and narratives about, journalism's key moments, such as the exposure of the Watergate scandal, feed into the collective imagination of journalists and serve to reinforce professional identity (Zelizer 1993). Together these recursive practices serve to demarcate and protect the institutional boundaries of journalism, keeping outside forces at bay (Carlson 2017; Deuze 2005). In this process, which Thomas Gieryn

(1983) referred to as "boundary work," journalists rely on narratives about their work to support their claims to cultural authority and to retain "definitional control" over what they consider legitimate practice (Carlson 2017, 79). Seth Lewis (2012) argues that such boundary work is, first and foremost, a rhetorical exercise.

Hence drawing on a growing body of work on institutional discourse, we argue that, as a social institution, journalism has no true "essence": it exists because and as we talk about it. This is where the idea of journalism as discourse can make a meaningful contribution: discourse defines and produces the objects of our knowledge. It not only governs the way things can meaningfully be talked and reasoned about but also influences how ideas are put into practice (Foucault 1980; Hall 1997). A discursive perspective allows us to de-essentialize the institution of journalism and situate it within the context of discursive constitution and of renegotiation. Central to this view is the assumption that in order to be intelligible, the norms, values, and practices of journalism are part of a wider framework of meaning—that is, of a discourse.

This discourse is never neutral or objective; it is always a space of struggle. Following Pierre Bourdieu (1998), we can characterize this space as a field of forces, as a symbolic place where journalists and other agents—by discursively activating and articulating particular values, ideas, and practices—struggle over discursive authority in conversations about the meaning and role of journalism in society. It is the place where discursive agents legitimize journalistic ideas and practices, perform boundary control and paradigm repair, and argue the fundamental questions, namely, what is journalism (and what is not), and who is a journalist (and who is not)? These discourses are omnipresent; they populate journalists' everyday experience, ranging from the most significant symbolic events (such as speeches honoring journalistic prizewinners) to the minutest aspects of daily journalistic life where praise and criticism are expressed verbally and nonverbally, directly and indirectly, intentionally and unintentionally. This is how the discourse of journalism acts as a central venue through which journalistic rules, conventions, and practices are legitimized (Carlson 2017).

Discursive power is not equally distributed across all relevant agents, however. Some journalists, news organizations, and professional ideologies have a stronger imprint on institutional discourse than others, depending on their centrality in the field. Journalistic cultures that dominate the discourse of journalism—usually associated with larger mainstream media and news of national, often political, relevance (or "serious news"; see Hovden 2016)—have the power to impose certain values and practices as institutional norms and "good practice." In this sense, the institution of journalism as it exists today in various local contexts represents the state of play in an ongoing struggle over discursive authority. Discursive work creates the institution of journalism, re-creates it as new agents are socialized, and reshapes it during discursive contestation or reflection even as more powerful players try to establish their discourse as central or final.

Owing to the dynamic nature of this jurisdiction contest, journalism as a discursive institution is in a state of constant flux, not only locally but also across the globe. The institutional framework provides journalists with a discursive repertoire that allows them to selectively activate contingent forms of journalistic values, norms, and practices in a particular space and time. At the same time it may prompt journalists to question the logic of appropriateness that their organization or society espouses. A discursive perspective treats journalism's institutional logic not as a given but as a dynamic structure of meaning that is subject to discursive (re)negotiation (Zelizer 1993). It is here that discourse has strategic functions as a site of identity formation and identity transformation.

Around the world, political, economic, technological, and other disruptions have become occasions for the reinterpretation of journalism's boundaries. In countries where journalism supports a political regime that is being undermined by political or economic liberalization, journalism as an institution may become fragmented into competing cultures that may be organizationally based. Discourses on appropriateness, and the underlying norms and practices associated with it, may openly compete. Such is the case in Mexico, where news culture still displays a hybrid character that became especially notable during that country's political and economic transition from the 1980s to the 2000s. Competing logics of appropriateness—civic, hypercommercial, and inertial authoritarian—were evident in headlines and storylines of the 1980s and 1990s and remain visible—though more muted—today, as new forms of social control, including violence, have silenced more critical journalists (Hughes 2006).

In Western democracies, where systemic political or economic shocks are relatively rare, journalism controversies or more long-term contextual changes have presented moments where discourse becomes the means of reactive paradigm repair or proactive reform. The former was the case, for instance, in the weeks following the death of Princess Diana in a car crash in 1997 during a chase by paparazzi. The journalistic paradigm was restored in media discourse by placing blame on media audiences and the paparazzi rather than on specific journalists or news organizations (Berkowitz 2000). For the mainstream media and for the tabloid press, paradigm repair involved a demonstration of how the paradigm should have worked but failed to do so in this unusual instance. Audiences were cast as being too hungry for stories about Princess Diana, and the paparazzi were identified as freelancers who sold their work to the tabloid press, not as official employees. Proactive reform, on the other hand, is often brought about through journalistic reform movements. One example is the public journalism movement in the United States, promoting journalists' involvement in the community and increased citizen participation in news and public life (Rosen 1999). Another is the more recent trend toward "constructive journalism" in northern Europe, advocating against excessive negativity in the news (Haagerup 2014). Institutional discourse thus allows for the renewal of journalism and emergence of new journalistic subcultures through contestation.

While journalists are the central discursive agents in the articulation of journalism's key norms, ideas, and practices, they enact this role in an exchange with interlocutors in broader society and by using a discursive toolkit that the broader society recognizes as legitimate. Journalists have given legitimacy to the norm of journalistic transparency by invoking the existing social discourse of governmental transparency (Vos and Craft 2016) and have also legitimized entrepreneurial journalistic practices by adapting the discourse of the already legitimate tech and startup worlds (Vos and Singer 2016). Hence journalists find themselves in discourse with agents from other social institutions, with agents within journalism, and invariably, in light of these interchanges, with their own reflecting selves. In this process, discursive agents produce the symbolic boundaries of journalism and news practice.

Journalism researchers, whatever their intentions, cannot choose to stand outside these struggles; they participate in this discourse even in their seemingly most objective moments—for instance, when choosing and justifying a sample of journalists for an interview or survey study. Journalism scholarship can be seen as a vital part of a larger, global discourse on the cultural meaning of journalism. The standing of journalism as an institution is, then, according to Meryl Aldridge and Julia Evetts (2003), not a matter of legal protections and institutional forms. It is a discourse shared and nourished by journalists, their employers, and the larger public.

The journalistic logic of appropriateness—whether consolidated within a unitary institutional framework or competing within a field of news organizations (Cook 1998; Hughes 2006)—provides journalists with discursive scripts that have emerged through an interchange among internal and external agents. The normative positions about appropriate journalistic practice in the West, for example, emerged from discursive exchanges generally rooted in shared social values, such as democracy and modernity (Schudson 2001; Vos 2012). Other societies may place greater emphasis on collective needs and social harmony (Masterton 1996; Mehra 1989). And still others may layer democracy and modernity on values normalizing social hierarchies and inequality (Blofield 2011; Hughes and Prado 2011). In this sense the discourse of journalism performs a double duty, acting as a marker of institutional boundaries and a source of professional legitimacy relative to broader society and, through a process of socialization, informing the cognitive toolkit that journalists use to think about their work.

Journalistic Culture as Discursive Articulation

The cognitive toolkit of journalists consists of a repertoire of discursive positions activated in institutional discourses. These discursive repertoires, also known as interpretative repertoires, are a key element in articulations of journalistic culture. The literature defines a discursive repertoire as a lexicon or register of terms and metaphors, and as "a culturally familiar and habitual line of argument comprised of recognizable themes, common places and tropes" (Potter and Wetherell 1987; Wetherell 1998, 400). Such repertoires are flexible discursive resources that journalists deploy as they reflect on their profession, thus rendering their work meaningful to themselves and external stakeholders. Emblematic of these rhetorical devices are journalists' conceptions of their role in society, including references to roles such as the "neutral disseminator," "watchdog," or "agent of change" (see chapter 7). In this sense discursive repertoires index journalists' occupational identities, and the absence of certain repertoires from the core of institutional values, such as roles related to journalism contributing to everyday life, speak to how normativity is construed by the professional mainstream (Charlebois 2015). In this way, discursive repertoires set the parameters of what is appropriate or acceptable action in contexts over which the institution of journalism has jurisdiction. At the core of this discourse is journalism's identity and locus in society.

It is for this reason that journalism as an institution and its relationship with society at large are never static; they are, as mentioned above, subject to discursive (re)creation, (re)interpretation, appropriation, and contestation. Ultimately this ongoing discursive struggle produces different forms of journalism—within and across countries and news organizations. These forms populate the universe of journalism; they make up the "worlds of journalism"—an idea that has obviously contributed to the very name of the study reported in this book.

We are using the notion of *journalistic culture* to denominate the differential articulations and manifestations of forms of journalism. Journalistic cultures become discernable in the way journalists think and act; they can be defined as particular sets of ideas and practices by which journalists legitimate their role in society and render their work meaningful for themselves and wider society (Hanitzsch 2007). Jackie Harrison (2000, 108) broadly describes journalistic culture as "a set of extant formulas, practices, normative values and journalistic mythology passed down to successive generations" of journalists. She argues that a journalistic culture ensures that a certain set of shared practices, values, and normative assumptions exists alongside a clear and identifiable set of skills and expectations within which journalists work.

The concept of journalistic culture enables a dynamic understanding of journalism as a discursive institution that is permanently being reconstituted and reaffirmed through a number of culturally negotiated professional values and conventions. Like any other culture, journalistic culture exists in three general states of manifestation: as sets of ideas (values, attitudes, and beliefs), as practices (of doing news), and as artifacts (news content). The empirical locus of a journalistic culture depends on the level of aggregation: journalistic subcultures or milieus, organizational or newsroom cultures, and national cultures of journalism.

Journalists who broadly share similar professional views represent journalistic milieus. Akin to the notion of subcultures, they can be loosely or tightly bound. Some are only a loosely defined strand of a "parent culture" (e.g., sports journalists), while others have a stronger institutional basis with a distinctive, coherent identity (e.g., political correspondents) (Bourdieu 1998). Such professional milieus (re)constitute themselves on the grounds of shared work conditions, assumptions, and beliefs that provide the cultural framework for journalistic practice.

In a similar vein, journalists working in the same newsroom often share a specific organizational culture, indexed through a common and tacit understanding of what it takes to be a good journalist and how news is supposed to be done (Boczkowski 2004; Harrison 2000). In an ethnographic study of a midsized U.S. newspaper, David Ryfe (2009) has impressively shown that newsroom culture can be remarkably resistant to change, for instance, when a new editor introduces changes that challenge established rules.

National journalistic cultures, finally, reflect differences between journalistic values and practices in different countries. This book is putting a spotlight on a cross-national comparative perspective, arguing that—the obvious forces of globalization notwithstanding—journalistic culture is still articulated and enacted within national spaces. News production is strongly geared toward news agendas that prioritize domestic news; media coverage primarily features national actors and interests; and journalists speak to national or local audiences. Hence the relevance of the nation for journalism's conditions of existence still holds true, despite the fact that national borders do not necessarily reflect cultural, ethnolinguistic divisions or correspond to a common sense of identity (Hantrais 1999). This is not to say, however, that the variation in journalistic cultures always neatly follows the common geographic, political, and cultural patterns, as we shall see in the following chapters.

Furthermore, a large array of studies—including our own current and previous work—has found that significant diversity exists in journalistic cultures, even within countries, and that many of these cultures have crossed national borders (Guðmundsson and Kristinsson 2017; Hanitzsch et al. 2011; Weaver and Willnat 2012). For example, the idea of journalism serving as a watchdog to hold the powerful accountable has crossed U.S. borders and gained a foothold in many parts of the world, including the Global South (Waisbord 2000).

Just as definitions of journalistic culture are invariably bound to the theoretical and epistemological perspective of the researcher, so is the choice of empirical features for a comparative analysis. In the literature, journalistic cultures have frequently been compared with regard to journalists' roles, ethical practices, professional commitment, and many other aspects (e.g., Hanitzsch et al. 2011; Patterson and Donsbach 1996; Preston 2009; Statham 2008; Weaver 1998a; Weaver and Willnat 2012). We argue that in the discourse of journalism, journalistic culture is substantively articulated and enacted in terms of journalists' perceived influences and editorial autonomy (extrinsic dimensions), as well as vis-à-vis journalists' roles, ethics, and trust (intrinsic dimensions; see fig. 2.1). We selected these five dimensions as they dominated professional, academic and public conversations about journalism at the time the study was designed. In these areas of debate, journalistic cultures articulate some of the "essential shared values" (Elliott 1988, 30) that give journalists a group identity and help to create a collective conscience for the profession (Keeble 2005).

As noted in figure 2.1, the extrinsic dimensions of journalistic culture include perceived influences and editorial autonomy. These dimensions are extrinsic as they relate to journalists' experiences of and reflections on external constraints. *Perceived influences* refer to journalists' subjective perceptions of the various forces that shape the process of news production (see chapter 5). Through studying news influences from a perceptional perspective, the emphasis is not only on the extent to which journalists are aware of influences but also on the degree to which they think these influences play an important role in their work. Journalists' perceptions therefore work as a filter through which external pressures translate into consciously experienced influence. While widely experienced pressures will often correspond to actual pressures in the real world, the previous WJS found that this is not always the case for all sources of influence or for every single journalist (Hanitzsch et al. 2010).

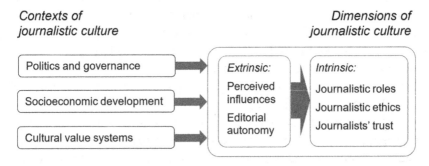

Figure 2.1 Conceptual roadmap for the comparative study of journalistic culture

Another extrinsic feature of journalistic culture is *editorial autonomy*. Often considered a normative prerequisite for institutional journalism (e.g., McDevitt 2003), editorial autonomy firmly underpins journalistic culture, not least by acting as a defining feature of professional consciousness and as a key narrative in both professional and public discourse. Conceptualized as the latitude journalists have in selecting stories and deciding which aspects of stories to stress, editorial autonomy emphasizes organizational constraints over external pressures (see chapter 6). It is sensible to expect that journalists' perceptions of influence adversely affect their perceived autonomy. In this sense, editorial autonomy "is restricted at the political, economic and organizational levels of news production, negotiated at the editorial level and exercised at the level of practice" (Sjøvaag 2013, 155).

The intrinsic dimensions of journalistic culture—journalists' roles, ethics, and trust—relate to broader articulations of journalism's relationship with society. These aspects are intrinsic as they represent key discourses of professional self-awareness in which journalists (and other institutional actors) internally negotiate the appropriateness of journalistic norms, values, and practices. *Journalistic roles* are generalized and aggregate expectations that journalists believe society deems desirable (Donsbach 2012), and which incorporate the occupational values and beliefs that individual journalists embrace as a result of their professional socialization and the internalization of normative expectations (see chapter 7). Through journalistic roles, news workers articulate journalism's identity and position vis-à-vis society and broader public expectations. As a discourse shared by journalists, these roles tend to appear as evident, natural, and self-explanatory, guarding the boundaries of journalism's professional jurisdiction (Aldridge and Evetts 2003; Schultz 2007).

Journalistic ethics, as conceptualized for this book, refer to journalists' responses to situations in which their actions can have potentially harmful consequences for individuals, groups of individuals, or society as a whole (see chapter 8). Many journalists have to make ethically relevant choices as part of their everyday work. When covering the abduction of a child, for instance, journalists need to weigh the public's right to know against the parents' right to privacy. Two aspects are of particular interest here: first, journalists' general ethical orientations, that is, their subjective dispositions informing their moral reasoning as applied in the profession; and second, their opinions about the justifiability of reporting practices that are marked as controversial in professional discourse. In some societies, for example, it is more accepted for journalists to expose the private lives of politicians and celebrities, while in other countries protection of privacy has greater value than the freedom of information. We consider the possibility that journalists' acceptance of these practices is premised to a degree on their ethical orientations, which likely serve to guide their position.

Finally, *journalists' trust* has more recently come into focus as journalists are usually seen as intermediaries between the public, on the one hand, and social institutions (such as the government, the parliament, the judiciary, and religion), on the other. In this book we define journalists' trust as the willingness of a journalist to be vulnerable to the performance of public institutions based on the anticipation that these institutions will meet journalists' expectations (see chapter 9). Journalism's stance toward social institutions became a matter of concern in journalism studies when researchers noted startling signs of a continued erosion of public trust throughout the Western world, which they attributed—at least in part—to a persistent pattern of negativity in the news (Cappella and Jamieson 1997; Gronke and Cook 2007). The first WJS indeed found a tendency among journalists around the globe to be highly skeptical especially of political parties and politicians (Hanitzsch and Berganza 2014).

For the study reported in this book, we gave priority to the way journalists around the world perceived the dimensions of journalistic culture noted above. Such an approach allowed us to launch an investigation into journalistic cultures through the eyes of journalists, by making journalists from a wide array of countries and news organizations *speak* about the way they look at the institution. Because these journalistic cultures exist within, and are shaped by, geographically, politically, and culturally different contexts, we expected to see considerable variation in the discursive creation, maintenance, and re-creation of these cultures.

It is precisely here that the WJS has a major advantage over other large, comparative projects. The participation of sixty-seven countries in this study provided us with a smorgasbord of journalistic cultures, whose diversity we were then able to map onto some of the dimensions that are well established in journalism research, as well as onto a number of new conceptual facets. Even more significantly, the truly international scope of the project allows us to move substantially beyond a predominantly Western understanding. As noted above and in the introduction to this book, the identity and contribution of journalism to society is still profoundly articulated from within Western perspectives and Western notions of democracy. Such a view emphasizes individual liberties and freedom, while other societies may give greater priority to collective needs and social harmony (Mehra 1989). Conventional studies of journalistic culture often insufficiently account for the variation in political and sociocultural value systems around the world.

Societal Contexts of Journalistic Culture

It has been a fundamental premise of the WJS that the discourse of journalism cannot be understood in isolation. Therefore, throughout this book, we address a set of potential contextual determinants of journalistic culture at the national level. There is, of course, much more to say about other factors, including the individual dispositions of journalists and the characteristics of their news organizations. Valuable as such studies are, they clearly go beyond the scope of this book.

Journalistic culture is continuously negotiated within a set of external forces, both restraining and enabling professional practice. Capturing journalism's contextualities, we will draw on the notion of *opportunity structures*, a concept originally developed to describe the political conditions shaping the likelihood of social movements, the nature of their formations, and whether and how they may have an impact on social development (McAdam 1982). Apart from Dough McAdam, researchers such as William Gamson and David Meyer (1996) have looked at political opportunity structures to understand cultural and politico-economic institutions of a society at a given point in time. We refer to the opportunity structure for journalistic culture to describe the set of external contexts within which journalists may act individually or as part of an occupational group to construct and articulate a subjective sense of professional identity, desirable editorial practice, position vis-à-vis other social institutions, editorial autonomy, and the influences with which they are confronted. This line of thought connects well with communication scholarship that has long recognized the societal level as a force that substantially shapes journalistic culture in a variety of ways, most notably with regard to the relevant political, economic, social, and cultural contexts within which journalists work (Ettema, Whitney, and Wackman 1987; Preston 2009; Shoemaker and Reese 2013).

The opportunity structures assessed in this book broadly fall into three general domains: politics and governance, socioeconomic development, and cultural value systems (see fig. 2.1). Among these three areas, the significance of the *context of politics and governance* as a major source of cross-national variation in journalistic cultures is largely undisputed (Gurevitch and Blumler 2004; Hallin and Mancini 2004; Weaver 1998a). In most developed democracies in the West, a monitorial role is at the very heart of the news media's legitimacy, grounded in a liberal pluralist understanding that sees journalism as essential to the creation and maintenance of participatory democracy (Gans 1998). This model assumes that news media are independent of the state and that journalists are agents representing the people with sufficient autonomy guaranteed by the news organizations in which they operate (Nerone 2013). From a comparative point of view, however, Western democracies, and the United States in particular, are arguably no longer home to the dominant model of journalism. The number of people exposed to journalism in China is significantly larger than the population of those consuming news in all Western countries combined. Furthermore, the United States may not always neatly exemplify the "Western model." Eroding political trust and extreme ideological polarization—a veritable breeding ground for public disaffection with mainstream news media (Hanitzsch, van Dalen, and Steindl 2018)—are pulling U.S. journalism in directions farther away from other Western societies, including many continental European countries.

Societies other than those in the Global North provide different contexts for journalistic culture to exist. In a number of developing and transitional countries, journalists and the news media are closely scrutinized and censored, and the state still maintains tight control over political news. Rather than providing a critical check on political performance, journalists are expected to cater to national imperatives, such as nation building, social harmony, economic development, and the preservation of cultural and religious values (Bartholomé, Lecheler, and de Vreese 2015; Romano 2005). Publics tend to conceive of journalists as actors in political, social, and cultural processes rather than as impartial and detached bystanders.

Political control over the media is not always exercised in a direct and explicit fashion, however. In some countries the government leverages economic disincentives to specific media outlets to silence critical voices (George 2007); in other societies political and economic powers maintain a relationship of strong clientelism with the media in order to secure favorable news coverage. In highly politicized contexts, journalists often decide to suppress norms such as independence, or the monitoring of power for the sake of their careers or the survival of their news organizations (Hughes et al. 2017a; Hughes and Márquez-Ramírez 2017). Hence different societal conditions are likely to produce distinct national cultures of journalism along the lines of differences between political systems.

Likewise, the legal and regulatory conditions also matter to the articulation and enactment of journalistic cultures. Not only will journalists have little trust in social institutions in societies heavily affected by corruption and bad governance (Hanitzsch and Berganza 2012), but they are arguably also more likely to embrace an interventionist role as they have a strong desire to change society (see chapter 7). Furthermore, journalists calibrate their ethical orientations and practices to align with the relevant legal and regulatory infrastructures. A previous study showed that in countries where journalists enjoy considerable stability and certainty with regard to media freedom and press laws, they can safely rely on established codes of conduct with few exceptions (Plaisance, Skewes, and Hanitzsch 2012). In other societies, where journalists face significant regulatory and legal uncertainty, they need to exercise greater care and base their decisions on the situational context and on personal judgment.

Socioeconomic development is the second area that we believe drives journalistic cultures in certain directions. A number of studies point to a strong association between journalists' values and practices, on the one hand, and human development and good governance, on the other (Norris 2006; Roy 2014). Arguably, a journalistic culture that strongly emphasizes the need for social reform is more likely to develop in societies that are socioeconomically less developed, such as many countries in sub-Saharan Africa, and that are going through disruptive changes, such as Egypt during and after the revolution of 2011. In societies facing problems of low human and economic development, as well as strong legal and institutional uncertainty, journalists may be more inclined to act as "agents of change" in order to fight social grievances and transform society. Also, it is reasonable to expect "brown envelope" journalism to be more pervasive in low-income countries that score high on corruption (Hanitzsch 2006; Lodamo and Skjerdal 2009). Overall, while socioeconomic development may have an impact on journalistic culture in significant and meaningful ways, a review of the literature suggests that its influence may be less profound than pressures emanating from the political context.

Finally, it makes considerable sense to understand journalistic culture as grounded in *sociocultural value systems* predominant in a society (Hanitzsch, Hanusch, and Lauerer 2016; Obijiofor and Hanusch 2011). Assertive and relentlessly critical styles of reporting, to which many audiences in developed democracies are accustomed, may seem culturally appropriate in these contexts, but such styles may be construed as displaying a disrespectful attitude toward authority in others. Proponents of an Asian values approach to journalism stress aspects of collective harmony and social stability, recommending a constructive and collaborative role to journalists to help authorities bring about national unity, economic growth, and social development (Wong 2004). In such an environment, journalistic culture is less likely to exercise its monitorial role in an overt and explicit fashion.

Research on social value systems undertaken in psychology, sociology, and political science is illuminating in this respect. Drawing on Ronald Inglehart's (1977, 2006) work, political scientists are observing a "silent revolution" entailing a shift from survival values to self-expression values in postindustrial societies. This "emancipative value change" gives rise to postmaterialist values, such as individual autonomy, self-expression, and free choice (Inglehart and Welzel 2005, 1). Over time this value drift has contributed to greater emancipation from both religious and secular-rational authority, which in turn coincided with a decline in institutional trust (Inglehart 1999) and the rise of the "critical citizen" (Norris 1999). Not only have citizens become more skeptical of social institutional arrangements, including governments, big corporations, and the news media, but they have also developed higher aspirations in terms of the social liberties they are entitled to have. As a consequence, journalistic culture is likely to emphasize a monitorial role more vigorously in countries where publics have developed a greater appreciation for emancipative values, since the authority of social institutions is no longer taken for granted as blindly as in the past (see chapter 7).

Also based on the influence of sociocultural value systems, we would expect journalists to face stronger influences and enjoy less editorial autonomy in societies that have greater tolerance for inequalities in terms of how power is distributed. Here we draw on the work of organizational psychologist Geert Hofstede (1998), who has observed significant variation across countries in the extent to which the less powerful members of organizations and institutions expect power to be distributed unequally and accept that it is. People in societies with greater tolerance for power inequalities tend to accept a hierarchical order in which individuals have their place and in which those arrangements are not subject to scrutiny and further justification. In such a cultural climate, journalists are likely to accept the authority of governments and other social institutions as a given, which may ultimately lead to less critical coverage.

Throughout this book we will use societal conditions, which create specific opportunity structures for journalism to operate within, as a contextual backdrop against which to understand cross-national similarities and peculiarities of journalistic cultures. There is much reason to believe that these factors contribute to differential articulations of forms of journalism in substantive ways, producing a variety of national cultures of journalism. Key to such an analysis was and continues to be the conviction that the study of cross-national differences is one, but not the only, way of approaching the global diversity of journalistic cultures.

A Fresh Look Into the Dynamics of Journalism

In this chapter we have argued that journalistic cultures are both discursively constituted and negotiated in a nexus of relations between discursive positions, indexed through the way journalists selectively employ discursive repertoires in conversations about journalism. This discourse is the arena where journalistic cultures produce, reproduce, and contest professional authority; it is the place where the struggle over the preservation or transformation of journalism's identity takes place. Although journalistic culture articulates itself on several levels, such as the level of newsrooms and subcultures of journalists, this book focuses on the cross-national and regional patterns of this discourse. In any attempt to map the universe of journalistic cultures, it is important to realize that all these cultures are connected in meaningful ways even as they discursively position themselves vis-à-vis other competing journalistic cultures.

Asian scholars and politicians, for instance, have advanced the Asian values approach to journalism to counter Western ideological hegemony over journalistic professionalism and to retain national, political, and cultural identities (Xu 2005). Connected to values such as freedom-with-responsibility, communalism and consensus, social harmony and self-restraint, and respect for order and authority (Loo 1996; Massey and Chang 2002), a distinctively Asian values framework was articulated to challenge the Western understanding of what it takes to be a good journalist, which was believed to undermine and erode local values systems (Kharel 1996). In this sense the Asian values discourse has become a significant site of struggle over the cultural meaning of journalism in the region, most notably in South and Southeast Asia.

This discursive jurisdiction contest takes place within newsrooms and societies but—as mentioned earlier—is now increasingly transcending organizational and national boundaries. Western models of journalism have been exported to other parts of the world (and idealized by some countries), but the Global South, based on its own historical and cultural contextualities, has presented alternative, and possibly competing, approaches (e.g., see Rodny-Gumede, Milton, and Mano 2017 for South Africa). While it is true that every society has to find its own answers to the question of what constitutes journalism and what it can meaningfully contribute to the public, the discourse of journalism has long become a global one. As a consequence, hegemonic journalistic cultures are confronted with potential alternatives on all levels—organizational, national, and global.

We believe that looking at journalism from the perspective of discursive institutionalism can help resolve a number of theoretical problems. For one, such an approach would allow us to de-essentialize the notion of journalism and treat it as a concept loaded not only with meaning but also with shifting meanings. A relational understanding of journalism puts the diversity of journalistic cultures into the spotlight and helps address inequalities in the discursive field and hence speaks to issues of power and authority. Furthermore, the discursive approach allows us to link "classic" journalism research focusing on journalists as individuals (i.e., their views, practices, and experience) to macrolevel approaches looking at journalism as an institution. In this regard, treating journalism as discourse also resolves the problem of having to draw conclusions about journalism from survey responses of journalists. As researchers, we gain access to the discourse of journalism by speaking to journalists; hence every interview we conduct invites journalists to articulate their stance in this discourse.

Finally, the perspective of discursive institutionalism enables us to conceptually account for the unfolding, and sometimes dramatic, changes in journalism's institutional environment. The discursive field, as a metaphor, paves the way for a dynamic understanding of journalism's transformation in terms of a discursive struggle between competing views about the identity and position of journalism in society. From this perspective, the discursive negotiation of journalism's boundaries can be understood as an adaptive response to journalism's ever-changing conditions (Carlson 2017). As new journalistic paradigms enter the arena, such as citizen or participatory journalism, they effectively change the discursive relations within the field and thus call for a renegotiation of journalism's social identity and contract. It is for this reason that the WJS pays particular attention to the way journalists experience this transformation and how they feel about the future of journalism (see chapter 10).

3

SURVEYING JOURNALISTS AROUND THE WORLD

A Methodological Framework

Corinna Lauerer and Thomas Hanitzsch

Because of its large scale, the Worlds of Journalism Study needed a special research approach. Planning, coordinating, and executing a study of this magnitude has proved to be demanding in many ways. While the project was not the first cross-national endeavor of its kind, its scale and complexity have called for innovative as well as sometimes unconventional answers to the challenges of research coordination and methodology. As a result, in addition to shedding new light on the global diversity of journalistic cultures, this work has broken new ground on methodological issues in comparative journalism research.

Since its beginnings in 2006, the WJS has grown from a relatively modest pilot project spanning seven countries into a massive multinational endeavor, covering more than 27,500 journalists in sixty-seven countries around the globe. In the early years the study's leaders had not anticipated such growth; there was no master plan for the project's expansion and no central source of funding to cover the expenses of researchers in all countries. Fundamentally, the study builds on the credo Robert L. Stevenson (1996) so famously referred to as "Give a little, get a lot." We interpreted this motto simply: every participating researcher who contributes a sufficiently reliable set of data from interviews with journalists to the WJS gets access to the combined comparative data set that includes all sixty-seven countries.

Researchers from all world regions were welcome to participate on the condition that they adhered to the study's key premises and methodological framework. This framework related to definitions, field procedures, and measures, collaboratively developed through extensive deliberation, as well as during four workshop gatherings. The study's leaders converted the essence of these discussions into detailed field instructions, research protocols, and memos answering frequently asked questions. Despite all these efforts, the project leaders had to deal with several unanticipated issues that arose during field research and data analysis. We managed to fix most but not all of the issues we encountered.

The main purpose of this chapter is to introduce the methodological framework of the study. We focus on project coordination, the sampling process, data collection, data management, questionnaire development, and index construction. While we worked hard to meet the highest standards of comparative research, the WJS, like most other studies, is not without imperfections. Considering the complexity of this large-scale multinational endeavor, methodological problems were bound to arise—more in some areas, less in others. As a service to future comparative researchers, and for reasons of scientific transparency, in this chapter we also discuss the major challenges we experienced along the way and document the limitations of the study.

Coordination

The first phase of the WJS (2006–2011) included twenty-one countries and resulted in several peer-reviewed international journal publications. Its success led to the idea of a second phase. After the initial planning for this wave in early 2010, the number of participating countries, and thus the extent of managerial complexity, quickly reached a level that necessitated greater sophistication in the project's coordination and management. One of the first actions of the WJS network was to implement an additional layer of regional coordination to support the central project management. Countries were pragmatically grouped into seven regions, each to be overseen by a regional coordinator: (sub-Saharan) Africa, Asia, Oceania, Central and Eastern Europe, Latin America and the Caribbean, the Middle

East and North Africa, and Western Europe and North America. Together the seven regional coordinators would form the WJS Executive Committee, which closely collaborates with the WJS Center based in Munich. As a matter of democratic principle, regional coordinators are elected in a general assembly of national principal investigators (PIs). In the elections, each country has one vote.

As the study's second wave unfolded, communication and deliberation processes were professionalized. For instance, a mailing list, a project website, and social media accounts were created, and detailed field instructions and methodological documentation were formulated. These measures, along with centralized data management and regular meetings, helped to keep methodological standards on a high level. Several problems remained, however. Researchers collaborating in the WJS typically come from various theoretical, methodological, and cultural backgrounds and tend to have different understandings of quantitative research and of the division of labor. Furthermore, communication in such a multinational group of scholars is not always easy. New communication technologies effortlessly bridge vast geographic distances, but communication habits still differ substantially from country to country. Regular meetings—held in Thessaloniki (2014), Munich (2015, 2016), Cardiff (2017), and Prague (2018)—were extremely instrumental in overcoming many of these challenges. They provided opportunities for discussing conceptual, methodological, as well as organizational matters and created a space for personal encounters, building a scholarly community and nurturing a commitment to the study.

Global Representation

Comparative researchers typically distinguish between two types of strategies for the selection of countries. The *Most Similar Systems Design* aims at comparing very similar societies that primarily differ in the outcome variable, while the *Most Different Systems Design* seeks to maximize cultural variability across the selected countries (Przeworski and Teune 1970). During the first wave of the WJS, the project compared relatively few societies that were selected systematically, deliberately using the Most Different Systems Design (Hanitzsch et al. 2011). In its second phase, the project replaced systematic selection with the principle of inclusivity and thus opened the door to researchers worldwide. While this new strategy allowed for comparisons across different geographic, political, economic, and linguistic regions, it also led to a certain degree of regional bias because inclusion of countries depended on the interest and commitment demonstrated by the national teams of researchers in the various geographic locations, as well as research infrastructure.

Owing to the global political economy of academic research, scholars from developed democracies in the West were more likely to join the project than were their colleagues from the Global South. For the most part, Western countries have a well-developed academic infrastructure with funding available to cover field expenses. Typically this privilege contributes to a strong overrepresentation of Western countries in comparative studies, which can have substantial implications for the interpretation of findings. In political science, for instance, Linda Hantrais (1999) noted that similarities or differences revealed by international comparison could result, to a substantive extent, from the choice of countries. Barbara Geddes (2003) convincingly demonstrates how case selection can affect, or even render unreliable, outcomes of a comparative study. Hence the selection of countries is a crucial step in any cross-national inquiry into journalism, as noted elsewhere (Chang et al. 2001; Hanitzsch 2009).

We dealt with the tradeoff between inclusivity and systematic country selection by actively seeking and supporting collaboration with researchers in parts of the world underrepresented in comparative studies. Much effort, for instance, went into recruiting researchers in sub-Saharan Africa, with the result that we were able to include eight countries from that region. In many cases, funding provided by Western European partners allowed us to secure collaboration with scholars from underresearched countries. Universities in Norway, for instance, covered expenses of field research in Ethiopia and Kosovo. LMU Munich, the WJS Center's host institution, provided partial funding to more than twenty countries through a formalized procedure, in which the WJS Executive Committee made decisions on financial support based on a review of funding applications submitted by national teams. In this process, we particularly prioritized regions that have to date received scarce attention from journalism researchers as a way to counterbalance the disproportional representation of European and North American societies in our sample.

When the most recent WJS wave was completed in early 2017, a total of sixty-seven countries were represented (see table 3.1). Together these societies cover almost three-quarters of the world's population. Still, European and North American countries have considerably more weight in the project than do other regions. Despite all our efforts to reach out to researchers worldwide, North, Central, and West Africa are poorly represented in the study, as are Central Asia and parts of Latin America.

Selection of News Media and Journalists

The selection of news media and journalists as specified in our *Field Manual* consisted of three steps: (1) estimating the population of journalists, (2) selecting news media organizations, and (3) choosing journalists within those organizations.[1] As the amount of relevant information for making these choices and the access to this information varied among the sixty-seven countries, researchers needed to find creative solutions to the problem of identifying news media organizations and journalists for the sample. Whichever strategy they used, the key principle was that national samples of journalists provide a reasonable representation of the respective national populations.

The WJS focused on studying professional journalists, broadly defined as those who have at least some editorial responsibility for the content they produce (Weaver and Wilhoit 1986). To qualify as a "journalist," individuals had to earn at least 50 percent of their income from paid labor for news media. In addition, they had to either be involved in producing or editing journalistic content or be in an editorial supervision and coordination position. Press photographers, for instance, generally counted as journalists, while TV camera operators counted only if they had the necessary freedom to make editorial decisions (i.e., when they did not merely follow orders from the producer). Freelancers who met the criteria were included. News media organizations that had their own news programs or news sections for which they produced original content were included as sites for the selection of journalists, as were news agencies, but radio stations that aired only music programs, for example, were not included. While this selection strategy was inclusive enough to provide a breadth of representation of journalists, it excluded a range of individuals because they did not classify as "professional" journalists according to our definition, despite the fact that many of them engage in activities in which they reproduce the discursive techniques of journalists. This group included, among others, citizen journalists and bloggers, individuals who worked in journalism as a side job, and those who were recently laid off by their news organizations.

Usually the first step in the sampling process consisted of gathering data about national media systems and populations of journalists. In some countries this information was easy to compile, as there were national lists and directories of news media readily available to the public. In many cases, however, this information was often outdated or incomplete, requiring researchers to combine several sources of data, including media directories, official or government information, data from industry associations and journalists' unions, as well as results from previous studies. In countries where the information was difficult to obtain, principal investigators provided an educated estimate of the population. These estimates were based on the national researchers' experience in the field and on leveraging the limited data available, for example, by extrapolating the population from those news media for which numbers of journalists were known. In some cases even this turned out to be challenging because the dynamic media sector created uncertainty in many ways, with media outlets closing, new ones opening, and news organizations moving locations.

The second step was to draw a systematic sample of news organizations. All research teams were encouraged to construct national samples of news media that reflect the structure of their country's media system. A common way of achieving this was by using a quota scheme that specified the composition of media outlets and news organizations in the country with respect to indicators such as media channel (newspapers, magazines, TV, radio, online, and agencies), content orientation (e.g., "quality"/broadsheet vs. popular/tabloid), audience reach (national, regional, and local), and primary ownership (public, private, or state-owned). Within these categories, investigators ideally chose news media organizations randomly or systematically.

The third and final step consisted of selecting journalists from within the sample of news media organizations and content providers. Wherever possible, researchers chose journalists randomly or systematically from newsrooms, so that every journalist in a chosen news organization had an equal or at least nonzero chance of being selected for the survey. Furthermore, according to the instructions detailed in the *Field Manual*, PIs were required to consider journalists from all editorial ranks and all kinds of news beats (including politics, culture, sports, lifestyle, and other news topics) for the sample.

As part of this strategy, we also applied a differential to the sampling process to minimize the disproportionate representation of news organizations with smaller or larger numbers of journalists. Researchers were instructed to select a greater number of journalists from larger organizations and proportionally fewer from smaller news media. What constituted a "large" or "small" organization ultimately depended on the national context. As a guiding principle, we advised researchers to select three or fewer journalists from smaller news media and five from larger organizations. This approach was employed in more than two-thirds of the participating countries.

Problems and difficulties, however, were the norm rather than the exception. Limited access to both data and journalists, as well as fast-changing conditions on the ground, led to less than ideal research settings in many countries. Several research teams had to rely on snowball sampling as a last resort (at least for a certain subgroup of respondents). In Cyprus, for instance, access to journalists was impossible in a number of news media organizations; hence respondents were approached through personal recommendations from other journalists. Freelancers were hard to identify in most of the countries. The Finnish team, for instance, used snowball sampling for freelance journalists to achieve a sufficient number of interviews in this group. In other countries, such as Sudan, an omnipresent atmosphere of physical violence, harassment, and surveillance complicated researchers' efforts to reach out to journalists and win their cooperation for the survey. As a quality control measure, we thus asked all researchers to document problems in the sampling process. In addition, they were required to compare the composition of their samples (using some basic sociodemographic measures as a reference point) with the respective national populations of journalists wherever such comparable data were available.

Given the rather substantive variation in national conditions, we needed to exercise a certain degree of flexibility in the application of the methodological framework. Several key aspects of the sampling process, however, were not open to negotiation. The minimal sample size required for each country was calculated based on a maximum margin of error of 5 percent (at a 95 percent confidence level). Samples that met this threshold were treated as being sufficiently reliable representations of the respective country's population. The vast majority of national teams of researchers were able to comply with this condition (see table 3.1). Only five countries failed to meet this criterion; hence we included them in our analyses (with necessary caution) but tagged them as "nonrepresentative" to flag the deficiency.

These countries were Bulgaria, France, Singapore, South Korea, and Turkey. It needs to be noted, however, that the margin-of-error criterion privileges countries with larger populations of journalists. In Bhutan, a country with only 114 journalists at the time of the survey, researchers had to interview almost every reporter to meet the required sample size.

Naturally, the overall sampling strategy detailed here, and international variability in the application of the common methodological framework in particular, inevitably created variance in sample sizes across countries. We accounted for these differences by giving each country exactly the same weight in all cross-national comparisons reported in this book.

Data Collection and Fieldwork

National PIs were responsible for fieldwork in their respective countries. Data collection took place between 2012 and 2015, though in four countries (Brazil, Canada, China, and Thailand) field research extended into 2016, and in Bulgaria even into January 2017. Albania was the first country to deliver data, in July 2012, closely followed by Iceland and Egypt. Owing to its late entry into the study, Bulgaria was the final country to submit data. Across the whole sample, most interviews were conducted in 2014 and 2015 (see table 3.1).

The time span between the start and end date of data collection varied among countries too, broadly depending on the interview method and local circumstances. In almost half the countries, researchers completed data collection within roughly half a year or less; it took longer than a year in about a third of the countries. Data collection was fastest in the United Kingdom, where researchers finished the whole survey in less than one month. In Mexico, by way of contrast, the national team needed twenty-seven months to complete the study.

Since the required number of interviews was relatively large, data collection in many countries turned out to be demanding and time-consuming. Journalists were often reluctant to participate in surveys, as the low response rates in various countries indicate. Several media organizations in various parts of the world had a general policy of not cooperating with journalism researchers. Moreover, several teams had to go back into the field after the

Table 3.1 Overview of samples and data collection

	Population size	Sample size	Response rate	Year(s) of data collection	Interview method(s)			
					FTF[a]	Phone	(e-)mail	online
Albania	1,200	295	95%	2012	✓	✓		✓
Argentina	5,525	363	26%	2013–2014	✓	✓		
Australia	11,000	605	90%	2012–2013		✓		
Austria	4,100	818	29%	2014–2015		✓		✓
Bangladesh	3,766	352	92%	2013	✓			
Belgium[b]	5,082	592	N/A / 37%	2012–2014	✓	✓	✓	✓
Bhutan	114	90	84%	2012–2013	✓			
Botswana	361	186	88%	2013–2015	✓		✓	
Brazil	44,915	376	35%	2014–2016		✓	✓	✓
Bulgaria[c]	5,800	263	28%	2016–2017				✓
Canada	6,500	352	22%	2014–2016		✓		
Chile	5,000	491	45%	2014–2015	✓	✓		✓
China[d]	258,000	652	68%	2012–2016	✓		✓	
Colombia	10,000	560	63%	2013–2014	✓	✓	✓	
Croatia	2,797	561	21%	2013–2014			✓	✓
Cyprus	431	204	92%	2013–2014	✓	✓	✓	
Czech Republic	1,191	291	65%	2012–2014	✓	✓	✓	✓
Denmark	7,196	1,362	19%	2015				✓
Ecuador	17,000	372	14%	2014–2015	✓		✓	✓
Egypt	10,000	400	95%	2012	✓			
El Salvador	710	250	51%	2015	✓			✓
Estonia	905	274	93%	2012–2013	✓			
Ethiopia	1,600	350	85%	2013–2015	✓			
Finland	7,726	366	50–55%	2013		✓	✓	
France[e]	35,000	228	N/A	2014–2015	✓	✓		✓
Germany	41,250	775	35%	2014–2015		✓		✓
Greece	12,000	411	57%	2015	✓		✓	
Hong Kong	11,554	471	59%	2012			✓	

(*continued*)

Table 3.1 Overview of samples and data collection (*continued*)

	Population size	Sample size	Response rate	Year(s) of data collection	Interview method(s) FTF[a]	Phone	(e-)mail	online
Hungary	8,000	389	42%	2014–2015	✓	✓	✓	✓
Iceland	350	187	53%	2012	✓			✓
India	700,155	527	≈82%	2013–2015	✓		✓	
Indonesia	41,818	663	95%	2014–2015	✓		✓	
Ireland	1,500	304	29%	2014–2015			✓	✓
Israel	3,000	341	37%	2014–2015		✓		
Italy	15,850	396	3.8%	2015				✓
Japan	25,200	747	34%	2013			✓	
Kenya	3,000	341	60%	2014–2015	✓			
Kosovo	300	206	73%	2014–2015	✓			
Latvia	600	340	72%	2013–2014	✓			✓
Malawi	330	182	48%	2014–2015	✓	✓	✓	
Malaysia	6,000	368	95%	2014	✓			
Mexico	18,400	377	57%	2013–2015	✓	✓		
Moldova	500	221	68%	2013	✓	✓		✓
Netherlands	15,000	522	10%	2014				✓
New Zealand	3,000	539	23%	2015				✓
Norway	7,750	656	36%	2013				✓
Oman	320	257	86%	2014–2015	✓		✓	
Philippines	3,500	349	52%	2015				✓
Portugal	5,750	407	55%	2013–2014			✓	
Qatar	800	412	68%	2012–2014	✓	✓	✓	
Romania	3,000	341	54%	2014–2015	✓	✓	✓	✓
Russia	200,000	390	41%	2014–2015	✓	✓	✓	✓
Serbia	8,000	407	51%	2014	✓	✓	✓	✓
Sierra Leone	350	225	75%	2014–2015	✓			✓
Singapore[f]	1,000	95	25%	2014–2015		✓		✓
South Africa	2,000	371	17%	2014				✓
South Korea[g]	29,000	355	N/A	2014	✓	✓	✓	✓
Spain	18,000	390	82%	2013–2015	✓	✓		

	Population size	Sample size	Response rate	Year(s) of data collection	Interview method(s)			
					FTF[a]	Phone	(e-)mail	online
Sudan	1,000	277	84%	2013–2015	✓		✓	
Sweden	20,600	675	36%	2013–2014				✓
Switzerland	10,000	909	27%	2014–2015			✓	✓
Tanzania	890	272	78%	2013–2014	✓			
Thailand	15,000	374	65%	2013–2016	✓		✓	
Turkey[h]	14,415	95	N/A	2014–2015	✓			✓
United Arab Emirates	600	237	70%	2013–2015	✓		✓	✓
United Kingdom	63,618	700	8%	2015				✓
United States	91,410	414	69%	2013		✓		

Source: Based on information provided by the national research teams.
[a] Face-to-face.
[b] Belgium: Flanders/Wallonia.
[c] Margin of error (MOE) = 5.9%.
[d] Data collection for print media in 2012–2013; for broadcast media, in 2015–2016.
[e] MOE = 6.5%.
[f] MOE = 9.6%.
[g] MOE = 5.2%.
[h] MOE =10.0%.

WJS Center found their data sets to be of insufficient quantity or quality. In one country, for instance, the number of interviewed journalists fell short of the required sample size after the WJS Center discovered that several respondents did not meet the study's definition of a journalist. In other countries, researchers had to deal with unforeseeable events. In Sierra Leone, for instance, data collection was interrupted due to the Ebola outbreak in 2014. Field research resumed about one year later after Sierra Leone was declared Ebola-free.

The contextual realities in participating countries required that the general methodological framework allow for several methods of data collection. Effects of different survey modes are well documented in the literature (e.g., Hantrais and Mangen 2007; Stoop et al. 2010), and methodological equivalence in this respect is generally regarded highly desirable in comparative journalism research (Hanitzsch 2008). However, several practical limitations prevented us from achieving this goal. On the one hand, conducting face-to-face interviews in all countries was simply infeasible because of limited funding. Online interviews, on the other hand, were not suited to countries with restricted internet access or where journalists did not routinely use e-mail communication. Personal interviews seemed to be a better choice under specific local circumstances, such as the omnipresent surveillance of journalists by government authorities or cultural norms that privilege oral communication over other forms of communication. In Egypt and Ethiopia, for instance, journalists would generally feel uncomfortable responding to online or telephone surveys as face-to-face encounters are the preferred form of interaction. In Scandinavian countries (and in several other nations, too), by way of contrast, online surveys are widely accepted by and routinely conducted among journalists.

As a response to the political, cultural, economic, and technological peculiarities in the countries participating in the study, national teams were free to choose the interview method, or a combination of interview modes, that best suited local conditions. The interview mode was recorded as a separate variable in the data set. Overall, investigators in twenty-six countries relied on one interview mode exclusively (table 3.1). In the remaining countries, teams combined different interview modes for a variety of reasons. The German team, for instance, started with an online survey but quickly switched to telephone interviews owing to the discouraging response rate from the online survey.

Response rates also varied considerably among countries (table 3.1). More than half the research teams managed to achieve response rates of higher than 50 percent. In about one-fifth of the countries, response rates were lower than 30 percent. In Italy, the Netherlands, and the U.K., where researchers collected data through large online surveys, response rates were extremely low, at 10 percent or less.

Data Inspection and Management

One of the most challenging aspects of the study was the inspection, filing, and management of data sets from sixty-seven countries. The WJS Center coordinated this process as a service to the entire research network.

Data screening and cleaning, which also included some preliminary data analyses, were implemented with rigor. Our data integrity check included several steps. Typically we first checked data sets for invalid or missing entries, typographical errors, incorrect use of scales, errors in filter variables, and missing information for mandatory measures. In a second step, we screened data sets for inconsistent values across related variables and sometimes even across similar countries. We also searched for systematic response sets (e.g., acquiescence bias), duplicate cases, and even manipulated data. The following examples illustrate the variety and scope of challenges we dealt with as part of this process.

In some instances, problems were easy to detect. In six countries, for example, work experience was measured through categories rather than in exact years. In two countries, a suspiciously high percentage of female journalists led to an examination that discovered incorrect numeric codes for gender. Sophisticated methods of data inspection were required to identify the cause of a problem in many other cases. A preliminary comparative analysis of mean scores and tests of bivariate relationships, for example, revealed that journalists' responses in one country showed a pattern that was diametrically the opposite of results in other societies in the region. Through careful inspection of the data we established that the respective national team had reversed numeric scales for some questions, though not for all of them.

In a few other cases, we decided to reject whole data sets for a number of reasons. In one country, for instance, the data set was returned because the national research team had used four-point scales for a large number of questions instead of five-point scales as stipulated in the core questionnaire. That team finally decided to conduct the entire survey again one year after the initial study, this time using the proper scales.

We also rejected data sets in which we found duplicate cases. In three countries, we provided national research teams with the opportunity to investigate the duplicate interviews and replace them with new respondents to meet the required sample size. In other cases, PIs did not provide any plausible explanation as to how the duplications occurred, or they did not undertake any significant effort to resolve the problem. These data sets were eventually not included in the international data file.

The extent of investigative work that went into detecting and classifying duplicate data varied from country to country. In one country, duplicate respondents were easily identified because researchers apparently duplicated not only the journalists' answers but also their supposedly unique

ID numbers. In other instances, research teams appeared to have invested considerable effort and sophistication in covering their tracks, mostly by tweaking answers here and there. Severe data manipulation by local teams was considered a serious breach of the WJS Statutes and ultimately led to immediate termination of the membership of two national research teams.

Data integrity checks were time- and labor-intensive not least because the WJS Center had to communicate back and forth with sixty-seven national research teams whenever questions and issues arose. Many data sets were revised several times until they were deemed sufficiently reliable and ready for inclusion in the multinational data set. In a final step, the WJS Executive Committee and Statistical Advisory Board reviewed the con-solidated version of the multinational data set before it was shared with all participating researchers. As the WJS community began to work with the comparative data, a few more issues were discovered and resolved, necessitating several updates of the international data set during the first months of data analysis.

For reasons of transparency, and to provide clarity to the whole research network, we codified matters related to data ownership, data sharing, and data usage in a *Data Sharing Protocol*, which the whole group adopted in July 2015.[2] As per this agreement, and as a service to the academic com-munity, key variables from the cross-national data set are being made avail-able for secondary analysis on the project's website in June 2019.[3] The web-site also contains a summary of methodological documentation provided by all country teams.

Data and Measures

At the heart of the WJS methodological framework was a common core questionnaire that contained a range of both mandatory and optional ques-tions.[4] While research teams could add some of their own questions, they were not allowed to change the meaning of any question in the core questionnaire.

We developed the questionnaire collaboratively between 2010 and 2012 in a series of meetings before the group formally adopted it. The major chal-lenge was to make enough room for relevant and timely questions while at the same time limiting the questions to a number that would not deter potential respondents from participating in the survey.

In the questionnaire, most mandatory questions pertained to key elements of the study that were in line with the framework presented in chapter 2, such as journalists' perceived influences on news work, editorial autonomy, journalistic roles, professional ethics, and perceived changes in journalism. Most of the questions on journalists' personal and professional backgrounds, conditions of journalistic labor, and relevant characteristics of the newsrooms and news organizations were mandatory, too. Several optional questions complemented the questionnaire, including journalists' trust in public institutions, and questions pertaining to journalists' personal backgrounds (including income, ethnicity, and political orientation). Research teams were free to decide whether to include these questions in their respective countries.

We distinguished between mandatory and optional questions for both pragmatic and substantive reasons. On a pragmatic level, we wanted to keep the list of key questions as short as possible based on concerns that a very long questionnaire could result in a significant number of nonresponses. Furthermore, several questions about journalists' personal backgrounds were considered potentially sensitive—in some countries more than others. Hence we did not force PIs to ask the question about political leanings in countries where journalists had limited political freedoms. Moreover, the way this question is commonly asked in international surveys—by inviting respondents to place themselves on a left-right continuum—does not necessarily provide meaningful results in every society. For example, in the case of many countries belonging to the Islamic world, political ideologies are not typically classified into "left" and "right." A similar example is the question about journalists' ethnic identification, which would cause confusion in societies where ethnicity is irrelevant or even a sensitive category. Finally, questions about journalists' incomes and religious affiliations were also marked optional owing to their very private nature.

The master questionnaire was drafted in English first and subsequently translated into the relevant local languages. As a rule, functionally equivalent translation was given priority over literal translation. National teams were instructed to use creative means to retain the original meaning of the concept in the translated version. Strict literal translations can sometimes change the meaning of a question or answer categories. To reduce the possibility of translation errors, we kept the wording of the English master questionnaire simple and avoided using culture-specific idioms (e.g., "watchdog") and normatively loaded language. National research teams were instructed to ensure sufficiently accurate translations by utilizing established techniques, such as translation-back-translation routines, or by working with multilingual experts (Van de Vijver and Leung 1997; Wirth and Kolb 2004).

Despite our best efforts to produce measures and question wordings applicable in a wide range of countries, we were still confronted with a number of issues that came up in the process of field research and during data checking. Several of these issues pertained to answer options given to journalists in the interview. Job denominations such as "reporter" or "desk editor" and the associated level of editorial responsibility, for instance, varied substantially across national contexts. In some journalistic cultures, editors have considerable editorial responsibility in the newsroom, while in other contexts, they have relatively little say on editorial matters. Another example is the categorization of media organizations according to the main type of ownership into "private," "public," and "state-owned." The Norwegian Broadcasting Corporation (NRK), for instance, is usually classified as public service broadcasting. In a strictly formal sense, however, one would have to categorize it as state-owned because the media organization belongs to the state. However, putting the NRK into the same category as Chinese state television CCTV would obviously be an inaccurate description. Furthermore, for researchers in several other countries, public ownership could also mean that a media corporation was publicly traded on the stock market. This ambiguity eventually required us to recode the ownership variable for a variety of media organizations. We also added a new category for community media that was particularly relevant for the African and South American contexts.

In addition to compiling an integrated international database from interviews with journalists, the WJS Center gathered relevant data on the national context in the broader areas of politics and governance, socioeconomic development, and cultural value systems (see chapter 2). For politics and governance, we compiled information on press freedom, democratic development, transparency, and the rule of law from the websites of Freedom House, Reporters Without Borders, the Economist Intelligence Unit (EIU), Transparency International, and the World Bank. For socioeconomic development, we gathered information about gross national income, economic freedom, and human development from the World Bank, Heritage

Foundation, and United Nations Development Programme (UNDP), respectively. In the area of cultural value systems, we compiled data on the prevalence of emancipative values and acceptance of power inequality from the World Values Survey and European Values Study, as well as from an online repository established by comparative social psychologist Geert Hofstede.[5] All this information was gathered for the year during which each country's survey was mainly conducted. This additional layer of societal-level data allowed us to properly contextualize our findings and identify the main factors behind cross-national differences across our sample of countries.

Composite Indexes

Several chapters in this book draw conclusions based on a relatively wide range of indicators. Journalists' perceptions of their roles, for instance, were measured through a complex array of eighteen statements. Discussing every single aspect of journalistic roles would clearly be a monumental task beyond the scope of this book. For reasons of parsimony, we constructed composite indexes for selected areas of analysis, including journalists' perceived influences, editorial autonomy, journalistic roles, and journalists' political trust. In constructing these indexes, which are outlined in more detail in the respective chapters, we deliberately followed a formative rather than a reflective logic, thus diverging from the standard approach used in most communication and media research.

In the standard approach, indexes are constructed in such a way that indicators are manifestations of the index, which represents a "latent" construct presumed to exist independently from research. Causality in this context means that variation in the latent construct "creates" variation in all indicators that belong to the same index. A reflective index assumes that indicators are strictly interchangeable and expects them to covary with each other; indicators should thus have the same or similar content, or they should share a common theme (Coltman et al. 2008; Jarvis, MacKenzie, and Podsakoff 2003). Furthermore, composite measures of this kind assume that relationships between the index and its corresponding indicators on the individual level of measurement can be replicated at the aggregate level

(Welzel and Inglehart 2016). Thus the validity of indexes hinges solely on a construct's internal consistency, and on configurations within cultures, which are given priority over configurations between cultures. However, as comparative researchers in psychology, the political sciences, and other disciplines increasingly argue, this logic does not hold true even for many psychological value constructs (Alexander, Inglehart, and Welzel 2012; Boyle 1991; Welzel 2013).

The formative approach to index construction, in contrast, does not assume that the indicators are all "caused" by a single underlying construct. Rather, it assumes that indicators are defining characteristics of the construct measured by the index. Causality in this context means that the construct is formed—or "caused"—by the indicators and does not exist independent of the researcher's conceptualization. Hence the direction of causality flows from the indicators to the latent construct, and the indicators, as a group, jointly determine the conceptual and empirical meaning of the construct measured by the index. Indicators need not be interchangeable; they may be correlated, but the model does not assume or require this to be the case (Coltman et al. 2008; Jarvis, MacKenzie, and Podsakoff 2003).

Dropping the assumption that indicators covary consistently across cultures does not automatically diminish the validity of an index. As Welzel and Inglehart (2016) convincingly argue, the underlying combinatory logic, assuming compositional substitutability among indicators, may contribute to a better representation of differential realities in distinct cultures (see also Boyle 1991). This may be particularly true for the concepts analyzed in this book. We have indeed little reason to assume that theoretical and empirical relationships among indicators for the indexes we use are exactly the same in cultures that differ on a variety of variables.

Political influence is a case in point. This index includes four groups of actors: politicians, government officials, pressure groups, and business representatives (see chapter 5). In some countries, the parliament may be weak or may simply not exist, which is why it might exert little or no influence on journalists. However, the government, which tends to have more power in political systems different from parliamentary democracy, may well compensate for this lack of influence. A logical consequence would be to expect the relationship between perceived government influence and influence of parliament to vary, perhaps considerably, across political systems. In such a situation, formative indexes may better represent the different realities in various cultures, particularly because they do not prioritize a certain—often Western—theoretical framework. A clear disadvantage of formative indexes, however, is that their reliability cannot be established through technical or statistical measures in a way similar to that used for establishing the reliability of reflective indexes, which are routinely checked for internal consistency. One way to overcome this deficiency is to examine how well an index relates to external or contextual measures (Bagozzi 1994; Welzel and Inglehart 2016). As our analyses in the following chapters demonstrate, our indexes perform reasonably well on this count.

Into the Future

Steering the Worlds of Journalism Study is both an exciting and a challenging venture because of its unique conceptual, methodological, and organizational nature. It was, and continues to be, an instructive endeavor in which all of us continue to learn how to practice comparative research. Despite its sometimes atrociously large managerial complexity, the project generated a wealth of information about journalists from sixty-seven countries, putting the study at the forefront of comparative communication and media research (Blumler 2017). The experiences made and lessons learned in this most recent wave of the WJS continue to serve as a substantial source of motivation to further professionalize the project as we prepare for the third wave. Ultimately we hope to turn this project into a sustainable academic endeavor to study the state of journalism around the world. The idea is to keep selected key measures of journalistic cultures in the questionnaire, while leaving sufficient space for additional measures designed to follow up on current developments in journalism worldwide. This would allow for a long-term assessment of journalistic cultures on a global scale while shedding light on the political, cultural, and socioeconomic directions in which the institution of journalism is traveling.

Notes

1. Methodological documentation, 2012–2016, Worlds of Journalism Study, http://www .worldsofjournalism.org/research/2012-2016-study/methodological-documentation/.
2. Data Sharing Protocol, Worlds of Journalism Study, July 1, 2015, http://www.worldsof journalism.org/fileadmin/Data_tables_documentation/Documentation/WJS_Data_Shar ing_Protocol.pdf.

3. Aggregated tables for key variables, 2012–2016, Worlds of Journalism Study, http://www.worldsofjournalism.org/research/2012-2016-study/data-and-key-tables/.

4. Master questionnaire, 2012–2016, version 2.5.1, Worlds of Journalism Study, http://www.worldsofjournalism.org/fileadmin/Data_tables_documentation/Documentation/WJS_core_questionnaire_2.5.1_consolidated.pdf.

5. Geert Hofstede, https://geerthofstede.com/research-and-vsm/dimension-data-matrix/.

4

PROFILES OF JOURNALISTS
Demographic and Employment Patterns

Beate Josephi, Folker Hanusch, Martin Oller Alonso, Ivor Shapiro,
Kenneth Andresen, Arnold de Beer, Abit Hoxha, Sonia Virgínia Moreira,
Kevin Rafter, Terje Skjerdal, Sergio Splendore, and Edson C. Tandoc, Jr.

As a foundation for the analyses of crucial variables in the chapters that follow, this chapter provides a comparative profile of journalists in the sixty-seven countries of the second wave (2012–2016) of the Worlds of Journalism Study. It provides answers to a fundamental question—who are the journalists?—in terms of gender, age, level of experience, education, work environment, and employment conditions. Demographic and job-related profiles of journalists are essential basics, but in a comparative examination they are additionally important because they may provide explanations that allow us to grasp the similarities and differences of media environments around the world. By combining data on a range of demographic and employment-related variables, we establish a picture of journalists and their work conditions in newsrooms worldwide.

These conditions shine an important light, for example, on who works in journalism. One recurrent aspect that has been much discussed in journalism scholarship relates to the role of women in the news, with the percentage of women and the length of time they stay in journalism varying across the globe. Belarusian investigative journalist Svetlana Alexievich, the first journalist to be awarded the Nobel Prize for Literature, for example, writes about working for "almost forty years going from person to person, from voice to voice," recording and capturing the lives of her compatriots (https://www.nobelprize.org/nobel_prizes/literature/laureates/2015/alexievich-lecture_en.html). However, Alexievich's length of service to journalism is an exception among female journalists; for several reasons, women journalists do not tend to have such long careers in journalism, and according to Carolyn Byerly (2013), women are disadvantaged in journalism across much of the world. This is among the many subjects that this chapter addresses.

Given the small number of global studies, and therefore the lack of a worldwide overview of journalists, a comprehensive profile that may also explain the relationships between demographic and employment patterns becomes considerably important. It provides benchmarks for future studies, but, more significant, it adds invaluable information to the journalism studies literature given its comparison of journalists' profiles across a large number of countries. Published in 1998, *The Global Journalist* for the first time drew together information on journalists from twenty-one countries and territories (Weaver 1998a). The update, *The Global Journalist in the 21st Century*, included thirty-three countries and regions (Weaver and Willnat 2012). The first wave of the WJS covered twenty-one nations (Hanitzsch et al. 2011). While all three of these provided some information on trends in gender distribution, age, and education, the level of representativeness of the samples varied.

Thus this study, we believe—based on the particular care to approximate the highest level of representativeness outlined in chapter 3—offers the most comprehensive picture to date of journalists across the globe. Half the journalists surveyed work in print. The average age of all journalists is 38 years, and the participation rate of women in the profession is 43 percent. Journalists are increasingly university educated, and on average they stay twelve years in the profession. Less than half of the global journalistic workforce are members of a professional association, and 80 percent are in full-time employment. As this chapter outlines, however, we find considerable variance across the globe in relation to these variables.

Backgrounds and Working Conditions of Journalists

In relation to journalists' backgrounds and work conditions, journalism scholarship has tended to focus on a range of key aspects, including gender, age, education, and newsroom composition. Most visible has been the concern with gender, particularly in terms of the numeric presence of women in journalism as well as the distribution of power within newsrooms.

Global organizations and projects have gathered information on these aspects of journalists' life and work. The International Federation of Journalists (IFJ) has been collecting data on gender and journalism for some time (see, for example, Wage Indicator Global Report 2012). Also, since 1995 the Global Media Monitoring Project (GMMP) has provided data every five years on the representation of women in the news media, in terms of both their presence in newsrooms and their representation in news content (GMMP 2015). The UNESCO report *Inside the News* (2015) has similarly addressed the challenges for women journalists in Asia and the Pacific. Finally, a large body of scholarship is available on the role of women in journalism (see, for example, Allan, Branston, and Carter 2002; De Bruin 2000; Robinson 2005; Rush, Oukrop, and Sarikakis 2005).

Typically these studies have found that women tend to be underrepresented in countries like the United States (Weaver et al. 2007) and—more generally—operating in a male-dominated environment (North 2009). Women also often leave the journalism profession early, a phenomenon that has been attributed to early burn-out syndrome (Reinardy 2009) or to structural inequalities and family-work tensions (Tsui and Lee 2012). In a study of South Korean journalism, Kyung-Hee Kim (2006) outlined the entrenched patriarchal culture, which keeps women's participation in South Korean journalism at below 25 percent.

The age of journalists has received much less attention, even though it could be an important factor affecting how journalists think about their work. Scott Reinardy (2016) found that journalists in their twenties and sixties experienced greater job satisfaction than did midcareer journalists. In their longitudinal study of American journalists, Weaver and others (2007) used age and work experience profiles as indicators of the state of the labor market. These attributes continue to be used in a similar way as indicators, particularly in North America, Europe, and Oceania, where media companies are transitioning their delivery of journalistic content to digital platforms. The resulting transformations in the companies' income and work structures have created hiring delays or led to layoffs, which can affect the age profile of journalists. As scholars have argued recently, the increasing precariousness of labor conditions and the ongoing job cuts in traditional newsrooms are deleterious to journalistic work and morale (Gollmitzer 2014; Reinardy 2016; Sherwood and O'Donnell 2018).

As far as journalism education and training are concerned, the literature emphasizes the benefit of well-schooled journalists, especially in the areas of general knowledge, writing, and ethics. In fact, on a global level, scholars have noted a considerable growth in journalism education, tied to attempts to professionalize journalism (Mellado et al. 2013). As a result, journalism scholarship has examined a range of aspects related to the tertiary training of future journalists (e.g., Deuze 2006b; Goodman and Steyn 2017; Hovden, Nygren, and Zilliacus-Tikkanaen 2016; Josephi 2010; Reese and Cohen 2000). Of importance in a comparative context is that pathways into journalism differ across countries, emphasizing either academic or nonacademic traditions (Fröhlich and Holtz-Bacha 2003).

The relationship between various aspects of journalists' backgrounds and their organizational loci has also been explored for some time. Stephanie Craft and Wayne Wanta (2004) found that female editors tend to encourage positive news reporting and are less likely than men to differentiate between male and female reporters when assigning beats. Paula Lobo and colleagues (2017, 1148) found that both organizational factors and "the traditional gender system" played important roles in Portuguese journalists' attitudes toward and perceptions about the role of gender in their work. Tracy Lucht (2016) highlighted differences in the issues male and female journalists considered salient and in how they talked about their work, with men more likely to use language that evoked professional efficacy and presence and women more likely to emphasize production and position. Edward Kian and Marie Hardin (2009) found that journalists' gender influenced how female athletes were presented in the news, with male writers more likely to reinforce gender stereotypes.

Given the considerable literature on how the various demographics and work-related conditions of journalists relate to and interact with one another and transform the institution of journalism, as well as the need for global benchmarks for these variables, this chapter presents a profile of journalists in the WJS both in the form of descriptors and as mutually and iteratively interacting variables that define the conditions of journalism in sixty-seven countries.

Measures

The demographic data collected on journalists included their gender, year of birth, education, and educational specialization as well as the number of years they had worked as journalists. For education, journalists were asked to indicate their level of completion from among the following choices: not completed high school, completed high school, college/bachelor's degree or equivalent, master's degree or equivalent, doctorate, or undertook some university studies but did not earn a degree. All those who had attended university were asked whether they had specialized in journalism or another communication field.

In relation to employment patterns, journalists were asked to identify their job titles and their position in the editorial hierarchy; their position was subsequently categorized as rank-and-file journalist (on the lowest level of the editorial hierarchy, consisting of journalists with limited authority, such as reporters and news writers), junior manager (those on the middle level who make operational decisions on a regular basis, such as desk heads, department heads, and senior editors), or senior or executive manager (those with power to shape strategic goals of their news organizations across broad divisions of the newsroom, such as editors-in-chief and managing editors). Journalists' employment situation was also assessed in terms of full-time, part-time, or freelance work. An optional question identified whether full-time and part-time respondents had permanent or temporary employment. Data were also gathered on whether respondents had any other paid jobs outside journalism, as well as whether they belonged to any organizations or associations that were primarily for people in the journalism or communications field.

Further, the questionnaire measured the medium in which journalists worked (daily or weekly newspaper, magazine, television, radio, news agency, standalone online outlet, or online version of an offline outlet), and whether they worked on various news topics or on a topic in which they had specialized. If they did specialize, they were asked to indicate this in terms of their beat. Beats were coded into three categories: hard news (politics, economy and current affairs, crime and law), mixed (local and regional news), or soft news (society and religion, science, technology, education, environment and health, culture and entertainment, lifestyle, and sports). In this chapter we focus only on the three categories of beats and not on specific topics within the beats.

For a global overview, all central tendencies reported in this and other chapters were averaged across societies. This procedure gives equal weight to every country included in this analysis regardless of population and sample size.

The Global View

The analysis across the sixty-seven countries in our study shows that about 43 percent of all journalists in the study were female (table 4.1). This result was not unexpected given prior evidence that women are underrepresented in journalism (GMMP 2015; Weaver and Willnat 2012). Still, it signifies an advance when compared with the figure of around 33 percent reported in Weaver's (1998b) first global survey. The mean age of our journalists was 38 years; the median, 36. Nearly two-thirds of journalists were between 24 and 42 years old. Journalists' average work experience was thirteen years, with a median of eleven years, indicating that most journalists enter the profession when they are relatively young.

Globally, journalists tended to be well-educated, with more than 80 percent holding a university degree. This constitutes a distinct increase over Weaver's (1998b) finding, roughly two decades before the WJS, that 63 percent of journalists in the twenty-one countries and territories in his study held a degree. It is similar, however, to the result of a more recent study by Weaver and Willnat (2012), which recorded 82 percent. In our study, 89 percent of journalists between the ages of 24 and 40 held a university degree, compared with 83 percent of journalists aged 41 and over. These figures indicate a trend toward a university-educated journalistic workforce across the world.

Despite the overwhelming percentage of journalists who held a tertiary degree, not all of them studied journalism or a related communications field. This is in line with findings from earlier studies that journalism education is not the only and sometimes not even the most dominant pathway into the profession (Weaver 1998b). Still, nearly two-thirds of university graduates in our study specialized in these fields. Out of our global sample— regardless of whether they had studied at university or not—this means that more than 60 percent of journalists had studied journalism or communication at the university level. Younger journalists were more likely to have specialized in journalism at the university level. Of those aged 24 to 40, 60 percent had studied specifically journalism, compared with only 54 percent of those aged 41 and over. This provides yet more evidence of the global trend among journalists to pursue tertiary journalism education (Goodman and Steyn 2017; Mellado et al. 2013).

Table 4.1 Key demographics of journalists across sixty-seven countries

	Female journalists	Male journalists	All journalists
Gender	43.4%	56.6%	100.0%
Age			
Weighted mean[a]	35.42	39.30	37.70
Average median	33.85	38.27	36.18
Experience			
Weighted mean[b]	10.73	13.84	12.56
Average median	9.06	12.32	10.74
Education[c]			
Completed high school	11.4%	17.2%	14.4%
College/bachelor's degree or equivalent	56.8%	54.1%	55.5%
Master's degree or equivalent	29.9%	25.6%	27.5%
Doctorate	1.3%	1.9%	1.7%
Specialized in journalism/ communication at university[d]	66.5%	57.2%	61.4%
Specializations			
Generalist[(e)]	62.2%	61.6%	61.7%
Hard news beat[f]	22.1%	23.4%	22.8%
Soft news beat[g]	14.9%	14.3%	14.7%
Membership in a professional association[h]	45.2%	48.5%	47.2%
Rank[i]			
Senior/executive manager	13.0%	18.2%	15.9%
Junior manager	25.8%	28.5%	27.2%
Rank-and-file	61.8%	53.3%	56.9%
Employment[j]			
Full-time	78.3%	81.9%	80.3%
Part-time	11.1%	8.3%	9.6%
Freelancer	9.0%	8.6%	8.8%
Other paid jobs[k]	21.5%	24.2%	23.0%

(*continued*)

Table 4.1 Key demographics of journalists across sixty-seven countries (*continued*)

	Female journalists	Male journalists	All journalists
Platform			
Print	48.7%	50.1%	49.8%
Television	23.1%	22.3%	22.6%
Radio	17.8%	16.7%	17.1%
Online	14.9%	16.5%	15.6%

Note: All percentages, mean scores, and median scores averaged across countries; gender differences significant for items as noted below.

[a] $t = -25.36$, df $= 24,036$, p $< .001$, d $= 0.320$.
[b] $t = -22.63$, df $= 23,177$, p $< .001$, d $= 0.294$.
[c] $Chi^2 = 232.86$, df $= 4$, p $< .001$, V $= .094$.
[d] $Chi^2 = 362.79$, df $= 1$, p $< .001$, Phi $= .119$.
[e] $Chi^2 = 10.31$, df $= 1$, p $< .01$, Phi $= .020$.
[f] $Chi^2 = 40.27$, df $= 1$, p $< .001$, Phi $= .040$.
[g] $Chi^2 = 8.74$, df $= 1$, p $< .01$, Phi $= .018$.
[h] $Chi^2 = 33.71$, df $= 1$, p $< .001$, Phi $= .036$.
[i] $Chi^2 = 205.51$, df $= 2$, p $< .001$, V $= .089$.
[j] $Chi^2 = 99.57$, df $= 3$, p $< .001$, V $= .061$.
[k] $Chi^2 = 7.70$, df $= 1$, p $< .01$, Phi $= .017$.

An overwhelming majority of journalists—just over eight out of ten—in our sample worked in full-time employment, with the remainder split between part-time employment and freelancing. Further, nearly one in four journalists had a second paid job outside journalism. Not surprisingly, employment outside journalism was particularly widespread among freelancers, almost half of whom did not derive their income solely from journalism. A notable percentage of part-time journalists—39 percent—had a second paid job outside journalism, compared with only 19 percent of full-time journalists.

Just under half of our study's journalists were union members. We do not have comparative figures from either Weaver's (1998a) or Weaver and Willnat's (2012) volumes because only some countries provided these data in both cases. However, from data on union membership recorded in a few studies, it appears that union membership has been declining around the world. In Australia, it dropped from 86 percent in 1998 (Weaver 1998b) to 56 percent in 2010 (Josephi and Richards 2010) and again to 48 percent in 2014 in our study. In the United Kingdom, it dropped from 62 percent in 1998 to 44 percent in our study, and in Spain from 61 percent to 41 percent for the same time span.

On the global level, most respondents in our study—57 percent—were rank-and-file journalists, followed by junior managers and senior or executive managers in that order (table 4.1). Not surprisingly, there was a clear association between journalists' rank in the editorial hierarchy and work experience. While average work experience for senior managers was eighteen years, it was only ten years for rank-and-file journalists. Similarly, senior managers were on average 44 years old, while rank-and-file journalists were about nine years younger.

Despite the rise of digital media, it appears that journalism is still a predominantly print-based occupation across the globe. In our sample, 35 percent of the journalists worked for a daily newspaper, 9 percent for a weekly newspaper, and 7 percent for a magazine. Another 23 percent worked for a television station, while slightly fewer (17 percent) worked for a radio station. Only 4 percent worked for a news agency, and 16 percent worked for an online outlet.

Finally, with regard to specialization in particular beats, such as politics, sports, and lifestyle, the majority of our journalists identified themselves as generalists, with six out of ten not specializing in a specific area of coverage (table 4.1). Just under one-quarter of all journalists worked in predominantly hard news beats, while 15 percent worked in soft news beats. Journalists specializing in soft news also appeared to face more precarious job situations; more than 84 percent of hard news journalists were in full-time employment compared with 76 percent of soft news journalists.

Among demographics, gender has frequently been discussed as a critical indicator of difference in other dimensions of news work. Indeed, our study found considerable evidence that this is the case on a global level. The findings indicate differences by gender for journalists' age, work experience, education, specialization, unionization, hierarchies, and employment conditions. Broadly speaking, this is a story of disparity. Across all sixty-seven countries combined, female journalists were on average four years younger and had three years less work experience than men. They were less likely to be members of a professional association in journalism and much less likely to be senior or junior managers than their male counterparts. While women represented 43 percent of all journalists, they represented only 38 percent of all junior and senior managers. They were also slightly less likely to be in full-time employment, that is, more of them were employed part-time and as freelancers, although slightly fewer had another paid job outside of journalism. Further, female journalists were less likely than male journalists to work on hard news beats, and somewhat more likely to work on soft news. More female journalists held a university degree, and more had specialized in journalism while at university. At the same time, the effect sizes reported in the notes to table 4.1 suggest that, if placed in the broader context of news work, gender is a relatively small factor in accounting for variance in most of these aspects.

Gender Differences Across Regions

While the global picture provides a rough indication of key findings, it also masks some considerable differences across individual countries (table 4.2). For example, while overall, women made up 43 percent of journalists in the sixty-seven countries, the country-wise range was large. Women constituted less than one quarter of the workforce in Bangladesh, Japan, and Indonesia but were a two-thirds majority in Latvia, Bulgaria, and Russia (fig. 4.1). The findings are similar for the percentage of women among junior and senior managers. Fewer than 15 percent of managers in Japan, Bangladesh, and Ethiopia were women, while more than 60 percent of women journalists held this position in Latvia, Bulgaria, and South Africa.

Closer analysis of these results shows a strong association with societal factors relating to the role of women, as measured by the Gender Development Index (GDI). A gender-sensitive extension of the Human Development Index (HDI), the GDI accounts for the human development impact of existing gender gaps in the three dimensions of the HDI: life expectancy, education, and income (Klasen 2006; UNDP 2014). The GDI shows the HDI of women as a percentage of the HDI of men and thus acts as a measure of the gender gap in a country. While the GDI has its own conceptual, methodological, and empirical problems, measures of gender development and empowerment have proven useful in previous analyses of gender in journalism (Hanitzsch and Hanusch 2012). Indeed, our comparison of gender balance across sixty-seven countries found strong correlations between the GDI and both the percentage of women journalists in a

Table 4.2 Country overview of sample properties (sociodemographic variables)

	Female journalists	Age in years			Work experience in years			University degree	Specialized in journalism/ communication at university
		Mean	(SD)	Median	Mean	(SD)	Median		
Albania	51.7%	32.54	(8.76)	31	9.36	(6.62)	8	98.0%	72.4%
Argentina	36.9%	38.75	(10.18)	37	13.83	(9.15)	12	67.7%	70.9%
Australia	55.5%	37.74	(11.27)	35	14.45	(10.99)	12	82.1%	70.2%
Austria	40.8%	43.00	(9.87)	43	17.94	(9.79)	17	63.2%	41.9%
Bangladesh	10.9%	36.67	(10.05)	35	11.56	(8.72)	9	86.8%	43.7%
Belgium	36.5%	38.16	(10.83)	36	12.64	(9.89)	10	96.3%	64.3%
Bhutan	50.0%	27.89	(3.95)	28	4.57	(2.30)	5	98.9%	23.0%
Botswana	37.6%	34.07	(7.68)	33	8.84	(7.40)	7	89.1%	81.4%
Brazil	49.2%	34.68	(11.22)	32	11.61	(9.69)	8	88.8%	90.8%
Bulgaria	64.6%	41.74	(10.40)	41.5	19.36	(9.54)	18	96.6%	60.1%
Canada	43.5%	44.51	(11.88)	44.5	18.88	(11.17)	18	93.4%	71.3%
Chile	43.2%	32.99	(8.48)	30	8.46	(7.53)	5	96.5%	86.5%
China	50.5%	33.9	(7.17)	33	9.01	(6.37)	8	99.5%	76.2%
Colombia	39.7%	35.21	(12.06)	32	11.17	(9.69)	7	89.4%	27.5%
Croatia	53.9%	44.69	(9.75)	44	19.73	(9.29)	20	71.7%	48.4%
Cyprus	42.2%	37.51	(9.09)	36	11.85	(8.47)	10.5	99.0%	80.8%

(continued)

Table 4.2 Country overview of sample properties (sociodemographic variables) (*continued*)

	Female journalists	Age in years			Work experience in years			University degree	Specialized in journalism/ communication at university
		Mean	*(SD)*	*Median*	*Mean*	*(SD)*	*Median*		
Czech Republic	43.3%	35.68	(9.44)	33.5	10.79	(8.15)	8	67.7%	47.5%
Denmark	43.1%	45.90	(11.78)	45.5	18.41	(11.89)	16	93.2%	82.2%
Ecuador	33.2%	35.22	(10.68)	32	10.04	(9.09)	7	80.1%	77.2%
Egypt	36.5%	36.73	(11.08)	35	12.00	(8.93)	10	97.3%	71.8%
El Salvador	40.4%	32.00	(9.27)	28				79.6%	81.7%
Estonia	58.4%	40.94	(11.11)	40	13.54	(9.37)	12.5	81.7%	51.5%
Ethiopia	28.9%	30.39	(6.84)	29	5.19	(4.63)	4	97.4%	55.2%
Finland	55.2%	43.40	(10.01)	42.5	17.27	(9.88)	15	74.6%	55.6%
France	45.4%	36.64	(10.81)	34	11.84	(9.81)	9	95.6%	79.2%
Germany	40.1%	45.58	(10.50)	46	19.52	(10.33)	20	75.5%	36.6%
Greece	47.0%	40.23	(9.50)	40				65.6%	56.1%
Hong Kong	44.9%	30.01	(9.05)	26	7.31	(7.5)	4	88.9%	69.1%
Hungary	47.5%	33.17	(11.03)	30	8.88	(8.09)	6	74.6%	68.3%
Iceland	35.0%	39.58	(11.44)	36	11.99	(9.52)	9	68.4%	24.9%
India	27.6%	36.52	(10.9)	34	11.04	(8.4)	9	99.2%	72.1%
Indonesia	21.5%	34.43	(7.04)	33	8.48	(5.46)	7	87.0%	33.9%
Ireland	41.9%	39.18	(11.27)	38	15.25	(10.85)	14.5	85.6%	73.0%

Israel	32.6%	42.88	(12.86)	40	15.47	(11.1)	13	73.4%	38.3%
Italy	42.4%	42.98	(10.54)	42.5	16.84	(9.79)	15	72.9%	50.1%
Japan	17.9%	41.25	(8.99)	41	16.94	(8.99)	17	99.0%	12.5%
Kenya	42.3%	31.94	(7.14)	30	6.16	(5.07)	5	90.9%	92.6%
Kosovo	45.5%	30.83	(8.99)	29	7.51	(5.98)	6	86.2%	67.0%
Latvia	72.4%	40.27	(11.08)	38	16.29	(8.93)	15	80.3%	58.5%
Malawi	35.1%	31.23	(7.79)	30	6.45	(5.42)	5	94.8%	85.9%
Malaysia	52.6%	35.46	(10.84)	32.5	9.57	(9.32)	6	82.8%	55.9%
Mexico	31.8%	38.41	(10.38)	37				86.9%	62.5%
Moldova	60.6%	30.26	(8.38)	27	7.91	(6.78)	5	81.4%	68.2%
Netherlands	39.3%	46.76	(11.06)	47.5	18.73	(10.46)	18	81.8%	57.8%
New Zealand	50.4%	43.66	(13.26)	44	17.00	(12.46)	15	85.1%	65.3%
Norway	50.4%	43.33	(11.63)	43	16.69	(11.11)	15	89.3%	64.3%
Oman	39.7%	37.88	(8.65)	37	12.60	(7.68)	11	78.7%	61.4%
Philippines	51.1%	37.86	(10.68)	37	14.10	(9.13)	13	93.6%	73.1%
Portugal	45.9%	39.00	(8.81)	39	14.65	(8.60)	14	86.2%	75.9%
Qatar	27.7%							72.7%	71.1%
Romania	62.5%	30.65	(9.79)	28	7.81	(7.16)	5	70.7%	64.7%
Russia	64.6%	32.11	(11.7)	28	11.38	(9.82)	8	82.3%	76.1%
Serbia	53.8%	40.92	(10.47)	40	15.99	(9.64)	15	68.6%	48.5%

(continued)

Table 4.2 Country overview of sample properties (sociodemographic variables) (*continued*)

	Female journalists	Age in years			Work experience in years			University degree	Specialized in journalism/ communication at university
		Mean	*(SD)*	*Median*	*Mean*	*(SD)*	*Median*		
Sierra Leone	29.1%	31.59	(7.59)	30	5.79	(3.53)	5	40.4%	48.3%
Singapore	58.9%	37.70	(11.34)	34	11.42	(9.58)	7	93.7%	39.4%
South Africa	62.1%	39.92	(11.98)	37	13.65	(10.79)	10	84.3%	69.6%
South Korea	23.7%	37.19	(8.37)	36	11.30	(8.04)	10	99.4%	46.0%
Spain	41.0%	39.23	(9.17)	38	15.91	(8.91)	15	96.7%	88.6%
Sudan	34.9%	37.34	(11.49)	35	11.41	(8.61)	9	95.2%	65.2%
Sweden	45.9%	51.32	(10.05)	52				60.5%	68.0%
Switzerland	38.5%	41.63	(10.95)	41	14.62	(9.75)	14	69.6%	37.9%
Tanzania	45.2%	27.63	(3.69)	27	6.80	(2.19)	6	99.3%	77.2%
Thailand	43.8%	37.19	(11.33)	36	7.51	(7.19)	4	81.6%	52.6%
Turkey	44.9%	32.35	(8.01)	30	9.31	(7.75)	6.5	91.1%	31.9%
United Arab Emirates	50.2%	37.73	(10.29)	36				91.8%	72.6%
United Kingdom	45.2%	43.17	(12.30)	43	18.53	(11.48)	18	86.3%	41.2%
United States	27.1%	46.91	(11.92)	49	22.74	(12.03)	24	93.7%	78.9%

Latvia	72.4		Chile	43.2
Russia	64.6		Denmark	43.1
Bulgaria	64.6		Italy	42.4
Romania	62.5		Kenya	42.3
South Africa	62.1		Cyprus	42.2
Moldova	60.6		Ireland	41.9
Singapore	58.9		Spain	41.0
Estonia	58.4		Austria	40.8
Australia	55.5		El Salvador	40.4
Finland	55.2		Germany	40.1
Croatia	53.9		Oman	39.7
Serbia	53.8		Colombia	39.7
Malaysia	52.6		Netherlands	39.3
Albania	51.7		Switzerland	38.5
Philippines	51.1		Botswana	37.6
China	50.5		Argentina	36.9
Norway	50.4		Belgium	36.5
New Zealand	50.4		Egypt	36.5
UAE	50.2		Malawi	35.1
Bhutan	50.0		Iceland	35.0
Brazil	49.2		Sudan	34.9
Hungary	47.5		Ecuador	33.2
Greece	47.0		Israel	32.6
Sweden	45.9		Mexico	31.8
Portugal	45.9		Sierra Leone	29.1
Kosovo	45.5		Ethiopia	28.9
France	45.4		Qatar	27.7
UK	45.2		India	27.6
Tanzania	45.2		USA	27.1
Turkey	44.9		South Korea	23.7
Hong Kong	44.9		Indonesia	21.5
Thailand	43.8		Japan	17.9
Canada	43.5		Bangladesh	10.9
Czech Republic	43.3			

Figure 4.1 Women journalists around the world (percentages)

Source: WJS; N = 67.

society (r = .503, p < .001) and the percentage of women managers (r = .509, p < .001, N = 66; fig. 4.2).

The most significant clusters of similar percentages of women journalists appear in Europe, with states that have emerged from the former USSR, from former Yugoslavia, as well as those in Eastern Europe characterized

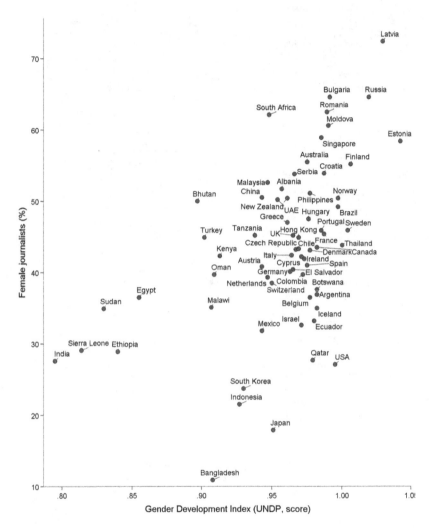

Figure 4.2 Women journalists and gender development

Source: United Nations Development Programme, WJS; N = 67.

by high percentages of women journalists. Across the region, women were in a clear majority, representing more than 60 percent of the total journalistic workforce in Latvia, Russia, Bulgaria, Romania, and Moldova, and more than 50 percent in Estonia, Croatia, Serbia, and Albania. China, the only currently communist country in the survey, had an even gender balance. Kim (2006) suggests that both Marxist and socialist feminism emphasize work as materially changing a woman's life situation. As the figures for the postcommunist societies in Eastern Europe show, this situation appears to have had a considerable impact on women's participation in the journalistic workforce. However, it should be recognized that the cataclysmic political events that occurred in that region also had much influence, introducing a young, mostly female workforce into journalism (Lukina and Vartanova 2017). Notably, the high percentage of women journalists also results in high-profile work. One of "journalism's heroic figures" (Hartley 2000, 40) is Russian investigative reporter Anna Politkovskaya; another is the documentary journalist Svetlana Alexievich, referenced earlier (Hartsock 2015). The first female television newsreader in Europe read the news in the former German Democratic Republic (GDR) in 1963 (MDR 2013), ten years before a female newsreader appeared on screen in West Germany.

Scandinavian countries, too, have a strong tradition in equity in terms of gender distribution in upper-level positions. Eastern and Nordic Europe are reported to have "crossed the one-third Rubicon" with women in the media occupying 33 and 43 percent in top management and governance jobs, respectively, in Eastern Europe, and 36 and 37 percent, respectively, in Nordic Europe (UNESCO 2015, 6). This figure compares favorably with a worldwide trend of less than 10 percent of women in a managerial position across different occupations.

Western Europe, with few exceptions, has a female participation rate in journalism ranging between 40 and 47 percent, showing a clear upward trend compared to the figures found by Weaver (1998). While numbers vary slightly across studies, the United States, on the other hand, has had "a near stagnation growth over the past 25 years," as a result of which women constitute only about one-third of the journalistic workforce (GMMP 2015, 45; Weaver and Willnat 2012; Weaver et al. 2007).

In South Korea, female journalists made up a quarter of the journalistic workforce. According to Kim (2006), this low participation is likely a consequence of the patriarchal Korean society. Female presence was even lower in Japan. Two countries in South Asia also showed notable low or meager percentages of women journalists: India had 28 percent and Bangladesh 11 percent. This is unlikely to be due to religious reasons as these two countries follow different belief systems. In fact, no distinct pattern emerged for the influence of religion across our sample. For example, in Malaysia, where Islam is practiced by around 60 percent of the population, 50 percent of the journalists were female; this percentage is comparable to the ones found in countries where the majority practice a different religion, such as Scandinavia. In Malaysia, the gender pay gap is smallest among the Asian and Pacific nations (UNESCO 2015).

Malaysia also belongs to a distinct group of Commonwealth countries that have achieved numerical gender equity among journalists. While the United Kingdom is nearing gender balance, Australia, New Zealand, South Africa, Malaysia, and Singapore already have a predominantly female workforce. A mixed picture, however, emerges for Africa, where all surveyed countries except Ethiopia are former British colonies or protectorates. The East African states of Kenya and Tanzania showed strong rates of female participation in the journalistic workforce, while some of the other African nations scored below 40 percent, and others even below 30 percent.

In Latin America, Brazil stands out with near gender equity, very likely a consequence of a former requirement of a tertiary degree to be licensed as a journalist but also due to the high number of female journalism students. Other South American countries, except Chile, record a substantially lower involvement of women in the media, possibly due to the patriarchal nature of the societies in the region (Oller Alonso and Chavero 2016). In Mexico, in particular, only one-third of journalists were female; this may partially be the consequence of the lack of safety for journalists in this country (Hughes et al. 2017a).

Overall, the past fifteen to twenty years have seen an increase of about 10 percent in women journalists worldwide. However, the conditions of female participation in the profession of journalism do not compare well with the conditions in the labor force in general (Global Gender Gap Report 2016). A number of studies have found that more women enter the journalistic profession than men, but more women than men leave in their thirties. Weaver et al.'s (2007) longitudinal study of American journalists shows this trend most pronounced for 2002. While among journalists under 25, 61 percent were women, among the 35- to 44-year olds, the figure dropped to 25 percent; the figure did go back up to about a third of the workforce among journalists 55 years and older (Weaver et al. 2007). One likely reason for the increase in female journalists globally is the fact that many more women than men have studied journalism since the 1990s (Weaver et al. 2007). Another reason may be the notion—at least in some contexts—that it is the decreasing financial attractiveness of journalism that has led to the increase in women journalists (Lukina and Vartanova 2017).

Age and Professional Experience

Weaver and Willnat (2012), in their study of thirty-three countries and regions, reported that the average age of their sample journalists was 39 years. In the sixty-seven countries of the WJS, the average age of journalists was 38 years, with a median of 36 years. The age of journalists has been considered an indication of employment patterns. Weaver et al. (2007) observed for the United States that many journalists hired during the boom period of the 1970s were still working in 2002. The authors attributed the rising median age of journalists to virtually no growth in the field of traditional mainstream journalism in the 1990s and since. In fact, our results point to a rise in the median age of journalists from 41 years in 2002 reported by Weaver et al. (2007) to 49 years in 2013, when our survey was conducted in the United States. This increase in age in the United States shows that contractions and growth in the job market can have a noticeable impact on the age pattern in the profession. It is also worth noting that journalists' median age in the United States was considerably higher than the median age of 42 found in the general U.S. labor force more broadly (ILO 2017). Overall, however, journalists' median ages showed a strong correlation with the median ages of their countries' labor forces ($r = .520$, $p < .001$, $N = 65$; see fig. 4.3).

In addition to the United States, in a small number of other countries, journalists' median age was higher than that of the general labor force. These countries include Sweden, where journalists' median age was more than ten years higher than that of the labor force, as well as the Netherlands, where the difference was just over five years. On the other hand, in a substantial number of countries, journalists' median age was at least five years younger than the median age of the labor force. These include the former Eastern bloc member countries of Moldova, Romania, Russia, Hungary, and the Czech Republic, and countries and territories in Asia, including Hong Kong, Singapore, South Korea, China, Bhutan, Thailand, and Indonesia. The group also includes the Latin American countries of Chile, El Salvador, Ecuador, and Colombia.

Given the global age patterns, differences go beyond a direct relationship between age and labor market. For example, we found that the maturity of a country's media sector and the age of journalists were related. More specifically, age and a country's level of newspaper circulation were related

Table 4.3 Country overview of sample properties (employment conditions and working patterns)

	In full-time employment	In part-time employment	Freelancer	Job outside journalism	Union member	Generalist	Hard news specialist	Soft news specialist
Albania	90.5%	8.8%	0.7%	19.2%	36.1%	53.6%	31.9%	13.6%
Argentina	58.3%	31.2%	10.5%	41.3%	36.2%	61.5%	23.7%	12.7%
Australia	88.1%	7.9%	3.0%	18.7%	47.8%	67.1%	15.1%	15.9%
Austria	77.0%	14.4%	8.3%	20.2%	49.4%	38.9%	28.5%	26.9%
Bangladesh	83.2%	13.6%	2.6%	11.9%	65.5%	83.9%	10.4%	3.8%
Belgium	74.5%	6.6%	18.1%	24.7%	62.3%	51.4%	20.6%	27.6%
Bhutan	82.8%	11.5%	5.7%	5.0%	27.9%	77.8%	20.0%	2.2%
Botswana	88.6%	1.1%	6.5%	16.3%	38.7%	74.2%	12.9%	11.8%
Brazil	59.0%	35.4%	5.1%	23.3%	40.8%	44.9%	31.7%	19.7%
Bulgaria	84.0%	4.2%	10.3%	34.2%	38.8%	56.3%	22.8%	19.8%
Canada	78.1%	3.4%	17.0%	29.3%	56.4%	49.7%	23.1%	22.5%
Chile	80.4%	10.0%	9.6%	28.5%	23.7%	59.4%	23.7%	16.8%
China	98.5%	1.2%	0.3%	8.3%	14.5%	55.2%	22.8%	11.9%
Colombia	83.2%	11.2%	5.6%	27.4%	27.8%	52.1%	22.3%	24.3%
Croatia	80.3%	1.3%	15.0%	21.0%	46.5%	85.3%	4.0%	7.7%
Cyprus	92.2%	5.9%	2.0%	11.8%	52.7%	57.8%	33.8%	8.3%
Czech Republic	85.6%	4.1%	8.6%	23.3%	7.3%	80.8%	11.8%	6.6%

Denmark	71.1%	5.4%	20.5%	17.5%	100.0%	59.2%	19.7%	20.2%
Ecuador	70.5%	23.6%	4.9%	32.0%	22.1%	55.9%	21.4%	21.7%
Egypt	83.8%	10.3%	6.0%	30.0%	54.3%	49.3%	42.3%	8.5%
El Salvador	68.8%	26.4%	4.4%	32.5%	30.7%	71.6%	17.6%	9.4%
Estonia	93.4%	4.8%	1.5%	18.0%	24.3%	75.9%	8.7%	12.9%
Ethiopia	93.7%	1.7%	4.3%	15.3%	16.3%	75.1%	9.4%	15.4%
Finland	78.1%	3.6%	17.5%	13.2%	91.3%	52.1%	25.3%	18.9%
France	78.9%	4.8%	14.1%	18.9%	27.7%	75.6%	8.9%	13.4%
Germany	74.5%	7.9%	17.7%	17.2%	53.4%	40.1%	15.6%	33.1%
Greece	87.9%	12.1%	0%	22.5%	71.6%	46.9%	34.4%	18.2%
Hong Kong	88.1%	8.3%	0%	13.9%	19.4%	48.9%	42.3%	6.4%
Hungary	61.4%	26.1%	9.6%	39.3%	23.5%	64.2%	13.8%	20.4%
Iceland	89.8%	4.8%	5.3%	23.2%	82.7%	70.4%	13.2%	13.2%
India	87.5%	10.0%	2.1%	11.6%	36.3%	57.9%	25.0%	15.5%
Indonesia	69.2%	8.2%	17.2%	37.5%	69.5%	66.6%	25.0%	4.8%
Ireland	81.5%	3.3%	12.5%	19.6%	64.7%	36.5%	26.3%	20.2%
Israel	68.3%	11.5%	12.4%	36.6%	50.5%	35.0%	36.7%	21.5%
Italy	62.9%	4.8%	32.3%	27.5%	100.0%	67.7%	16.4%	15.9%
Japan	100.0%	0.0%	0.0%	2.0%	3.8%	47.3%	36.4%	3.1%
Kenya	80.5%	11.1%	6.9%	46.8%	63.0%	63.9%	23.9%	11.2%

(continued)

Table 4.3 Country overview of sample properties (employment conditions and working patterns) *(continued)*

	In full-time employment	In part-time employment	Freelancer	Job outside journalism	Union member	Generalist	Hard news specialist	Soft news specialist
Kosovo	86.4%	8.7%	2.9%	15.2%	46.6%	60.6%	20.2%	13.8%
Latvia	87.1%	4.4%	8.2%	17.4%	26.6%	74.7%	13.9%	8.3%
Malawi	84.1%	7.7%	1.1%	30.4%	76.4%	79.4%	12.6%	6.0%
Malaysia	92.1%	4.1%	0.8%	16.9%	51.9%	67.8%	19.5%	9.2%
Mexico	83.5%	10.4%	5.6%	34.8%	25.2%	78.5%	17.2%	3.8%
Moldova	86.4%	11.3%	2.3%	33.0%	29.2%	62.9%	30.5%	6.4%
Netherlands	41.7%	16.9%	36.9%	32.7%	34.5%	39.1%	22.7%	36.5%
New Zealand	87.0%	6.1%	6.3%	23.8%	33.5%	62.2%	16.6%	18.3%
Norway	72.6%	4.7%	18.8%	25.9%	100.0%	63.0%	12.2%	22.1%
Oman	55.3%	25.7%	17.1%	40.9%	59.1%	52.2%	36.4%	11.1%
Philippines	87.1%	3.5%	6.7%	38.3%	62.1%	53.6%	36.9%	9.0%
Portugal	91.6%	0.2%	6.6%	11.9%	39.0%	54.3%	14.1%	23.0%
Qatar	63.1%	21.6%	13.1%	28.8%	23.2%	33.7%	54.5%	11.8%
Romania	87.4%	11.1%	1.5%	27.6%	22.0%	76.2%	14.7%	9.1%
Russia	77.2%	14.9%	7.9%	34.4%	20.1%	56.9%	24.9%	17.4%
Serbia	91.2%	2.5%	6.1%	17.9%	43.0%	64.6%	20.2%	13.6%

Sierra Leone	65.2%	20.5%	10.3%	22.1%	79.2%	71.0%	15.7%	12.0%
Singapore	98.9%	0.0%	1.1%	3.2%	34.0%	55.8%	16.8%	26.3%
South Africa	79.7%	4.9%	13.8%	29.6%	43.5%	76.0%	14.6%	8.1%
South Korea	96.9%	2.8%	0.3%	4.5%	87.8%	9.0%	65.1%	10.1%
Spain	85.6%	5.1%	9.2%	12.8%	41.1%	67.2%	13.4%	15.2%
Sudan	81.5%	6.2%	12.3%	26.6%	78.5%	38.0%	41.5%	20.4%
Sweden	74.4%	7.3%	17.0%	12.6%	68.9%	34.1%	39.4%	15.5%
Switzerland	57.1%	35.2%	7.7%	21.3%	56.8%	52.2%	21.6%	20.0%
Tanzania	72.8%	16.2%	11.0%	31.6%	89.3%	89.3%	7.4%	2.6%
Thailand	66.5%	13.7%	18.2%	39.7%	45.3%	71.8%	15.8%	12.2%
Turkey	91.5%	1.1%	6.4%	11.6%	31.6%	50.5%	23.3%	17.4%
United Arab Emirates	88.7%	8.6%	1.8%	16.5%	43.5%	47.6%	32.1%	17.9%
United Kingdom	74.0%	6.9%	16.6%	26.7%	43.8%	47.1%	23.6%	27.8%
United States	98.8%	0.2%	0.7%	14.3%	52.2%	79.3%	11.3%	7.1%

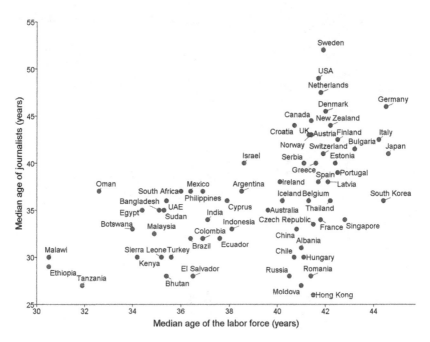

Figure 4.3 Median age of journalists and overall labor force

Source: International Labour Organization, WJS; N = 66.

(WAN-IFRA 2014) for the thirty-eight countries in our sample where such data were available (r = .496, p < .001). Countries with an early development of mass-circulation newspapers (Hallin and Mancini, 2004) and a broad readership as measured by newspaper circulation (WAN-IFRA 2014) in the second half of the twentieth century tend to have older journalists. Conversely, countries where the media market developed only in the second half of the twentieth century or where the media sector has considerably grown in past decades tend to have younger journalists. Despite significant media transformations in the twenty-first century, the impact of an early establishment of the media is still evident in the age profile of journalists.

Journalists were younger also in countries where a politically cataclysmic event has led to a renewal of the journalistic workforce. Russia, Romania, and Kosovo, where the median age of journalists was below 30, are examples; these countries underwent considerable changes in their media markets following the collapse of communism and the break-up of Yugoslavia, respectively (table 4.2).

The picture of the relationship between age and experience differs noticeably from the one for age and gender. As noted, countries with long-established media tend to have older journalists, who tend to be men. However, there was no clear opposite pattern. While some countries with a high percentage of female journalists, such as Russia and Romania, have a young workforce, no distinct pattern of female journalists being younger can be established more broadly.

Almost all the older journalistic cohorts are found in North America and Western Europe, where journalists had overall the highest average median age of 44 years. In these countries, journalists also had the most experience, with a median of seventeen years. In the Mediterranean countries, which are characterized by a later development of the press, journalists were five years younger in terms of their median age (39 years). Correspondingly, they possessed less experience, with an average median of thirteen years and a range of medians between fifteen years for Italy and Spain and nine years for France (table 4.2). Arguably, the late development of the media sector due to years of military dictatorship in some Mediterranean countries, and the subsequent new expansion of the job market, had a determining effect on the age of the journalistic workforce.

Africa, overall, had a young journalistic workforce with an average median age of 31 years. Not surprising, then, the professional experience of journalists was quite brief in most African countries, with a low average median of six years. Several countries—Malawi, Kenya, and Sierra Leone—had a median of five years for professional experience. Journalists in Latin America could also be considered young, with an average median age of 33 years, and average median experience of eight years. The differences between countries are considerable, with a median of twelve years of experience for Argentinian journalists, and of only five years for Chilean journalists. The Middle East also presents as a cluster, with an average median age of 37 years and average median work experience of eleven years. In this cluster, Israel had the oldest journalist population, at a level similar to Western liberal democracies. In Egypt, Oman, and the United Arab Emirates, journalists' average age was very similar to that found in the Mediterranean countries.

The picture in Asia was considerably varied for age and work experience. A cluster emerged only for Southeast Asia. The average median age was 35 years, with a range from 37 years in the Philippines to 33 years in Malaysia and Indonesia. The most experienced journalists were in Japan and the Philippines. In many countries in Asia, journalists were young and did not stay long in the job. The lowest median years of professional experience were found in Thailand and Hong Kong, at four years. In Hong Kong, Celia Tsui and Francis Lee (2012) found that many journalists left after only a few years in the profession. The median years of professional experience in Malaysia, Indonesia, Singapore, and China were not much higher, ranging from only six to eight years. The South Asian countries of India and Bangladesh both had a median of nine years in this respect.

As we contended earlier, the history of a country's press has a lasting impact on the age structure of the journalistic workforce. The media situation in the countries of the Commonwealth is a case in point. Ireland, Canada, Australia, South Africa, and New Zealand were the dominions and India the colony that took part in the Empire Press Union meeting in 1909. The average median age of 39 years and median work experience of thirteen years in this cluster of countries provides support for the argument that a press fostered early continues to influence the configuration of a country's journalism institution.

Geographical and historically shaped clusters are discernible for the average age of journalists. With the projected growth of journalism particularly in Asia, it can be assumed that the average age of journalists there will drop because a younger workforce will populate the profession. On the other hand, the trend in the United States and Europe, where the market is contracting, is toward an older workforce, as a comparison with Weaver (1998b) and Weaver and Willnat (2012) shows. Countries whose media are in a growth phase have a younger workforce. Journalists in the BRICS countries had an average median age of 33 and average median work experience of nine years. These states can be taken as representative of the relationship between journalists' age and a growth spurt in the market. China, India, and Brazil are among the seven most prominent newspaper markets; in 2015 China and India alone accounted for 62 percent of the average global daily print circulation (WAN-IFRA 2016).

Journalists' age and years of professional experience are also a reflection of employment conditions. In North America, Oceania, and Europe, where relatively high salaries and labor laws had helped build a lifelong commitment to journalism, journalists are now forced to leave the industry because of increasingly precarious financial situations of media organizations. A survey of 225 Australian journalists who had been made redundant between 2012 and 2014 found that 68 percent had worked in journalism for more than twenty-one years (Sherwood and O'Donnell 2018). Also, young cohorts are not the result only of recent media development or growth spurts. They can also be a manifestation of a lingering dissatisfaction with working in journalism and with its pay scales, leading to a "revolving door" syndrome. Hong Kong, with a median of four years of professional experience, is a prime example of a "high degree of turnover within the journalistic profession" (Chan, Lee, and So 2012, 26).

In other parts of the world, low pay and fragility of the job market can prompt journalists not to stay in the job for long. In Chile, where journalists' "average income is very low" (Mellado 2012, 389), journalists were also young (median of 30 years), and their years of professional experience were few (median of five years). Europe, and in particular postcommunist countries, such as Romania and Moldova, is not immune to this phenomenon; the countries here struggle to find economic stability. In Romania and Moldova, median professional experience was five years. Poor working conditions and poor pay were also present in Kenya (median experience of five years), where journalists are often tempted by "illegal incentives to survive" (Ogong'a 2010, 149); the circumstances often force these journalists to accept such illegal incentives as bribes to make ends meet. In Thailand, where median professional experience was four years, "many reporters did not regard journalism as a long-term career, but as a chance to broaden their experience before going on to further study" (McCargo 2000, 55). Other scholars have similarly indicated that journalism is often considered a transitional phase in young people's working lives in East Asia (Heuvel and Dennis 1993).

Education and Professional Specializations

The differences among countries in the percentage of journalists who held a tertiary degree appear to be mostly due to the numerous pathways to becoming a journalist. Some European countries have had a tradition of traineeships or nonacademic courses at highly selective journalism schools; these are not considered tertiary education (Fröhlich and Holtz-Bacha 2003; Deuze 2006b). As a result, the nations that stand out as having an unexpectedly low percentage of degree holders (below 70 percent) include Austria, Iceland, Switzerland, and Sweden, which all belong to a group of countries where "a formal journalism education is not required to become a journalist" (Bonfadelli et al. 2012, 325). We also see some evidence of this in Germany, where three-quarters of the journalists held a tertiary degree, but only just over one-third had specialized in journalism or communication (table 4.2). Only one country in the survey, Sierra Leone, provides no easy access to colleges or universities, resulting in only four of ten journalists having completed a degree. University education appears to be widespread in China, Cyprus, Tanzania, India, South Korea, Bhutan, and Japan, where at least 99 percent of journalists held a degree. In another eighteen countries, at least 90 percent of journalists had been educated at university. Overall, we found considerable variance across countries in terms of the percentages of university-educated journalists who had actually specialized in journalism. Less than 50 percent of journalists had specialized in journalism in eighteen countries, which include such diverse societies as Colombia, Germany, Iceland, Indonesia, and South Korea. At the same time, specialization can be quite high in some countries; for example, 93 percent of the journalists in Kenya had specialized. At the other end, in Japan only 12 percent had specialized.

An analysis of the gap between the percentage of university graduates and the percentage of those who specialized in journalism does tell us something about the dominant pathways into journalism across the globe. The results somewhat reflect the categorizations developed earlier by Romy Fröhlich and Christina Holtz-Bacha (2003) and Mark Deuze (2006b), which relate to systems that focus predominantly on university education, standalone journalism schools, or vocational on-the-job training. We found the most substantial gap in Japan and Bhutan, where 99 percent of journalists held a degree but only 12 and 23 percent, respectively, had specialized in journalism or communication. This indicates a system where journalism education continues to be primarily conducted in the workplace (Josephi 2017; Kim 1976). In the United Kingdom, where until recently on-the-job training had been the dominant form of education in journalism, we found that only four out of ten journalists had studied journalism at university, despite the fact that, overall, 86 percent were university graduates. Specializing in journalism appears to be very popular in countries like Brazil, Spain, Chile, Kenya, Malawi, Denmark, El Salvador, Cyprus, and Botswana, where at least 80 percent of journalists focused on journalism or communication in their studies.

Whether journalists are assigned to a particular area of coverage also varied considerably across countries. Journalism seems to be the least compartmentalized into beats in Tanzania, where nine out of ten respondents said they worked across a range of topics and issues. Other countries with a high percentage of generalized work include Croatia, Bangladesh, and Malawi. Specialization appears to be much more common in South Korea, Qatar, Sudan, and Israel, where at least 60 percent worked on a specific beat. Some European countries—Netherlands, Austria, Germany, Sweden, Greece, and the UK—also had more than 50 percent of their journalists work on a beat. By far the largest numbers of journalists specializing in hard news were in South Korea and Qatar, where more than half of journalists worked in this area. Only three other countries (Hong Kong, Egypt, and Sudan) had percentages over 40 percent (table 4.2).

Soft news, that is, beats that focus on audiences as consumers, is significantly more likely to be practiced in advanced economies, with at least one-quarter of journalists working on soft news in the Netherlands, Germany, the UK, Belgium, and Austria. In Bhutan, Tanzania, Japan, Mexico, and Bangladesh, however, less than 4 percent of journalists reported working on such news. The correlation between gross national income and the percentage of journalists specializing in soft news is significant and very strong ($r = .445$, $p < .001$, $N = 66$), suggesting that the more economically developed a society is, the more likely its media will focus on soft news, such as lifestyle or entertainment. This relationship is consistent with recent arguments in the literature that point to broader societal trends toward economic security as a reason for the rise in lifestyle journalism. For example, Folker Hanusch and Thomas Hanitzsch (2013) have argued that in many postindustrial societies, where economic resources are secure, people have more options and flexibility to shape their lifestyles, in line with the move from survival values to self-expression values (Inglehart 1997). This change in values, they argue, contributes to a rise in lifestyle coverage in the news.

Employment Conditions and Working Patterns

While globally nearly four in five journalists were in full-time employment, journalists in some countries also faced precarious situations. An extreme example is the Netherlands, where only four out of ten journalists had full-time employment; one-third of the journalists here worked as freelancers, which likely has consequences for salaries (Vinken and IJdens 2013). High percentages of freelancers were found predominantly in Western countries; Italy stands out with around one-third of its journalists working as freelancers (table 4.3). In Denmark, Norway, Germany, Belgium, Finland, Canada, the UK, and Sweden, the figures ranged between 20 percent and 17 percent. In some countries, however, freelancing may not be as precarious an employment condition as it seems. In Germany, for example, a sizable minority of journalists, particularly in broadcasting, work as so-called *feste freie Journalisten*, a description that denotes freelancers who work regularly for the same organization and often receive a regular monthly income (Meyen and Springer 2009). Nevertheless, it would appear that the economic crisis of journalism across these highly developed media markets is indeed related to a higher percentage of the journalistic workforce working as freelancers. These developments do not appear to be as strong for journalists in Japan, Singapore, China, South Korea, and Ethiopia, to name a few countries, where the vast majority were employed full-time. We also found low percentages of full-time employed journalists in Oman, Switzerland, Argentina, and Brazil, where the figures range between 55 and 59 percent. In these countries, however, the larger percentage of journalists were part-time workers rather than freelancers. Still, these figures on part-time and freelance employment in a range of countries are evidence of a relatively insecure work environment.

As discussed earlier, in many countries journalists combine journalistic work with other jobs, even when they work full-time as journalists. While globally just under one-quarter of journalists had a job outside journalism, the proportion was considerably higher in developing economies (table 4.3). In Kenya, for example, at least four out of ten journalists had a second job outside journalism. In the economically more advanced regions of South and East Asia, however, journalists were much less likely to have a second job—for example, fewer than 10 percent of journalists had a second job outside journalism in China, Japan, Singapore, and South Korea. Overall, these figures point to a link between national economic indicators and the likelihood of journalists having a second job that is outside journalism. Our understanding of the situation is confirmed by statistical analysis: we found a negative correlation between countries' gross national income and the percentage of full-time journalists who also have jobs outside journalism ($r = -.415$, $p < .001$, N = 66; fig. 4.4).

We found the largest percentages of journalists who worked full-time but supplemented their income with another paid job in Kenya, Oman, Argentina, Thailand, and Indonesia. The opposite was the case for Spain,

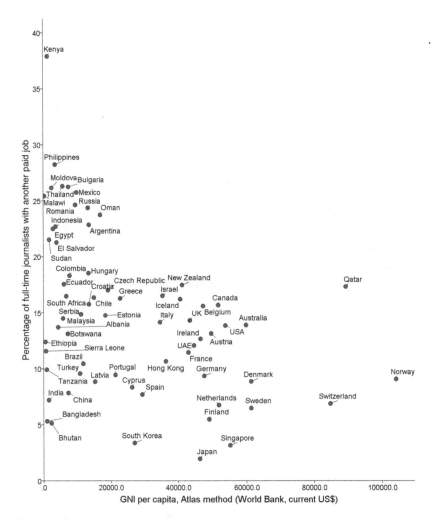

Figure 4.4 Full-time journalists with additional paid job and economic development

Source: World Bank, WJS; N = 67.

Sweden, India, China, Finland, South Korea, and Japan, where less than 10 percent of full-timers had a paid job outside journalism. At the same time, it is important to point out that income may not be the sole reason for holding a second job outside journalism. In some cases, journalists take another job for journalistic prestige rather than economic need. In

Ecuador, for example, some senior managers of national media organizations hold other positions owing to their social reputation. These positions include appointments at universities, as well as political or business positions, and are thus more a case of wielding influence in society than of precariousness (Oller Alonso and Chavero 2016).

Analysis of journalists' employment conditions also reveals that journalists in Europe were more likely than those elsewhere to occupy permanent positions. Of the seventeen countries with at least 90 percent of employed journalists with permanent contracts, ten are in Europe. However, Oman, Australia, the Philippines, Israel, Bhutan, Botswana, and South Africa also score high on this front. Only in Colombia (47 percent) and Kosovo (30 percent) did less than half the employed journalists have permanent contracts. Kosovo's media market experienced a full restart after the end of the NATO intervention in 1999. Since then, most journalists and editors have had temporary contracts of either a few months or a year, which are typically renewed rather than turned into permanent contracts (Andresen, Hoxha, and Godole 2017).

Unionization is an important aspect of labor conditions in journalism. We found that in several countries, especially in the Nordic countries of Denmark, Norway, Sweden, and Finland, almost all the surveyed journalists were union members. This was also the case in Italy. In most other countries, journalists' unions or associations have only a moderate foothold. In Japan and the Czech Republic, membership was less than 10 percent. Filip Láb and Alice Němcová Tejkalová (2016) consider the longstanding distrust in professional organizations responsible for the disinterest in joining a journalistic association in the Czech Republic. Few other countries displayed such low membership.

Among postcommunist societies, too, few had membership numbers as low as those in the Czech Republic; however, in countries in this group where a high percentage of women journalists was present (these include Russia, Romania, Estonia, Latvia, and Moldova), union membership ranged between 20 and 30 percent. The countries that resulted from the breakup of the former Yugoslavia, by comparison, had somewhat higher union membership, around 45 percent.

Canada and the United States both had just over 50 percent of their journalists in unions. Latin America emerges as a relatively coherent cluster, where membership ranged from 24 percent in Chile to 41 percent in Brazil. African countries such as Tanzania, Sierra Leone, Sudan, and Malawi reported high percentages of union membership. In Malawi, membership was above 75 percent, but this was offset by low membership in Botswana and, especially, in Ethiopia. Neither Asia nor Europe presents a unified picture of union membership.

In Europe and North America, the drop in union membership is seen as a direct result of the transformation in the media sector, where the digital impact on news production and distribution has significantly altered the work of journalists. In an increasingly deregulated industry, which has also experienced fragmentation of the occupation, it is becoming more and more difficult for unions to represent journalists. The unions themselves are acutely aware of the changing "status of the journalist, the perception of the journalist occupation, permanent employees, and freelancers" (Bittner 2011, 10). The unions recognize that their organizational structures have not kept up with changes in the industry, notably in those countries that have been strongly affected by developments in their media industries. Still, in some countries, unlike the situation in earlier years, self-employed and freelance journalists and even unemployed journalists can be union members, a concession in the face of the decline in the number of the "journalistic core clientele" (Bittner 2011, 11).

Even if figures show that, for example, in the United States, those "covered by collective agreements earn up to 27 percent more than their nonunionized counterparts" (IFJ 2016), unions find it hard to attract freelance and young journalists. From among journalists in our study who were younger than 36 years, 40 percent belonged to an association, whereas among their older colleagues, 55 percent were union members. Marginally fewer female journalists (45 percent) than male journalists (49 percent) held membership in unions. While unions warn that nonmembership in their associations negatively influences wage negotiations, the gender gap in salaries, legal protection, and other conditions, such as pension payments, diversification in journalistic work, and fragmentation of the editorial workforce, may make it less likely that younger journalists become part of a distinct professional body.

Conclusion

The picture of an "average" journalist that emerges from our data is this: male, in his late thirties, holding a university degree most likely in journalism or communication studies, employed full-time, and with work experience of about twelve years. This snapshot, however, hides a vast array of variations. After all, 43 percent of journalists were women, an increase of about 10 percent compared to Weaver's first global report on journalists (Weaver 1998b), and the participation of women in the journalistic workforce keeps rising. When we look at the distribution of countries where women journalists were in a majority or at least were equal in number to male journalists, distinct regional clusters become visible. States that have emerged from the former Soviet Union and its Eastern European allies as well as from the collapse of Yugoslavia are characterized by high percentages of women journalists, pointing to a more significant inclusion of women in the workforce that has continued beyond the communist era. While this has also translated into a higher percentage of women in top management and governance jobs in journalism than anywhere else in the world, remuneration has remained considerably below that of other countries. Cultural and societal traditions emerge as the most likely factors affecting female representation in the journalistic workforce. Importantly, when one looks at the global map, no distinct pattern emerges with regard to the influence of dominant religions.

A noticeable difference in the employment pattern of female and male journalists becomes apparent when we examine age ranges and seniority. More women than men enter the profession, but their participation drops sharply in the 35–45 and 45–55 age-groups. While the former can be attributed to women turning to family responsibilities, the latter attrition indicates that for women, journalism is far less of a lifelong attraction than it is for men. This attrition rate is also reflected in seniority within the newsroom, where men tend almost consistently to be in higher positions than women.

The average age of journalists around the globe was 38 years and the average median age 36 years, figures that have remained relatively stable over the past decade (Weaver and Willnat 2012) but mask a great diversity among countries. The age of journalists is an indication of employment patterns, and this is particularly evident in North America and Europe. Given the methodological decisions of the WJS—outlined in chapter 3—many young start-ups were not included in our sample, and our results are thus somewhat newsroom-centered. However, the age structure reveals a more profound underlying factor influencing the nature of newsroom cohorts. There is a strong correlation between the maturity of a country's media sector and the age of journalists. Societies with a well-established press and wide readership in the second half of the twentieth century tend to have older journalists.

Professional experience, more than age and education, emerges as the most robust indicator of the stability and standing of the journalistic profession. On the one hand, there is a clear correlation between age and years of professional experience, with older journalists having many years of professional experience, helped by good employment conditions and salaries. Still, countries with low median years of professional experience are present on all continents. In some cases, a young cohort is the result of only recent media development in the country, but in most instances, low pay and poor working conditions create a situation whereby journalists do not remain in the job long. In many countries where journalists have low median years in the job, they have to resort to a second job to make ends meet. In other cases, young age and short professional experience can signal a somewhat contested position of journalism in that country and point to a structure of journalistic work where a young and fluid workforce is led by a small group of older and experienced journalists. Countries that have such a workforce configuration tend to concentrate on hard news, whereas in wealthier countries with an early and well-established mass media, more journalists work in soft news.

The world over, there is a definite move toward a fully tertiary-educated journalistic workforce, and young journalists mainly enter the profession with a degree in hand. On average, 85 percent of journalists had a university degree, an increase of more than 20 percent compared to the first global report on journalists (Weaver 1998b). Overall, two-thirds of working journalists had studied journalism and/or other communication subjects, with this being true especially for younger journalists. Women were generally more likely to have attended university and also more likely to have specialized in journalism or communication in their university education. University-based journalism education, which grew exponentially from the late 1980s onward before leveling out two decades later (Berger and Foote 2017), and which schools women predominantly, has had a noticeable influence on employment patterns. The effect of tertiary journalism education on the journalistic workforce needs further research.

The decline in union membership seems to be the most precise indicator of the changes occurring in journalism. It points not only to the fragmentation of the journalistic profession but also to the declining centrality of the newsroom (see chapter 10). In Europe and North America, the drop in union membership is seen as a direct result of the transformations in the media sector, where the digital impact on news production and distribution has had a significant impact on the work of journalists. In an increasingly deregulated industry, it is becoming ever more difficult for unions to represent journalists. With the changes in the status of journalists and the shifts in the perception and nature of the profession, it is harder for journalists to see themselves as part of a coherent professional body.

5

PERCEIVED INFLUENCES

Journalists' Awareness of Pressures on Their Work

Thomas Hanitzsch, Jyotika Ramaprasad, Jesus Arroyave, Rosa Berganza,
Liesbeth Hermans, Jan Fredrik Hovden, Filip Láb, Corinna Lauerer,
Alice Tejkalová, and Tim P. Vos

Journalists, news organizations, and journalism as an institution do not operate in a vacuum. A fundamental premise of the Worlds of Journalism Study is that the discourse of journalism cannot be understood in isolation from its various contexts. In other words, journalism is, to a considerable extent, an outcome of a multitude of restraining and enabling forces. Following some early work in the 1960s (Dexter and White 1964), journalism researchers have in recent years begun to pay increasing attention to this nexus of influences, most notably to factors stemming from political, economic, and organizational contexts (e.g., Hughes and Márquez-Ramírez 2017; Shoemaker and Vos 2009; Shoemaker and Reese 1996, 2013).

These influences materialize in different ways, sometimes in the form of draconian measures constraining press freedom, and at other times in a subtle fashion, as economic considerations in the newsroom. The story of Can Dündar, a prominent journalist and the former editor-in-chief of the Turkish opposition daily *Cumhuriyet*, is an example of direct restrictions on press freedom. In October 2016 Dündar was shot on his way to the courthouse, where he was to face a charge of "revealing state secrets." Shouting "traitor," the gunman fired two bullets at him. Dündar survived the assassination attempt and received a five-year sentence the same day. The verdict was the court's decision on a criminal complaint filed by

President Recep Tayyip Erdoğan, who was dissatisfied with *Cumhuriyet* exposing Turkish military support of Syrian rebels, a claim the government had denied. After the assassination attempt, Dündar said: "I don't know who the attacker is, but I know who encouraged him and made me a target."[1]

Turkey is listed as number 157 among 180 countries in the Reporters Without Borders World Press Freedom Index of 2018. However, political pressures also exist in Finland, a country with what is considered a free press and that has topped the index since 2010. In November 2016 Finnish public broadcaster YLE ran several stories about Terrafame, a taxpayer-funded mining company that had awarded a business contract to Katera Steel, owned by Prime Minister Juha Sipila's uncles and cousins. Sipila, a former businessman, sent a series of emails to YLE complaining about its coverage of the issue. Shortly afterward, YLE appeared to have stopped its critical reporting about Katera Steel.[2]

Economic imperatives, too, are gaining ground in many media outlets, particularly in lifestyle and consumer media, and are thus creating their own set of pressures. An unnamed beauty editor of an Australian fashion magazine spoke of instances where key advertisers asked for editorial favors: "They will ask how much—we call it love—'how much love are you going to give this brand in a year?' It's up to us to decide what we think is fair" (Hanusch, Hanitzsch, and Lauerer 2017).

As the examples above demonstrate, the daily work of journalists takes place in a complex nexus of occasionally conflicting contextual forces. Journalistic culture is the space where the relative impact and relevance of these influences are discursively articulated. This chapter presents an analysis of how journalists reflect on the various sources of influences on the news, how these perceptions differ across societies, and which factors drive cross-national differences. As we demonstrate in this chapter, the influences journalists perceive on their work can be meaningfully classified into five larger domains: political, economic, organizational, procedural, and personal networks. From among these five domains, political, economic, and organizational influences emerged as the strongest indicators of differences among national journalistic cultures. Journalists in non-Western, less democratic, and socioeconomically less developed countries perceived these influences on the news to be stronger than did journalists from countries characterized by greater freedoms and socioeconomic development.

Conceptualizing Perceived Influences on News Work

Researchers have conceptualized the contextual forces that limit and enable news production in terms of a hierarchy of influences. Early models commonly distinguished between individual, organizational, and institutional levels (e.g., Ettema, Whitney, and Wackman 1987), while recent work tends to envisage a slightly more complex array of forces. Perhaps most widely known is Pamela Shoemaker and Stephen Reese's (1996, 2013) hierarchy-of-influences approach that organizes sources of influence on journalism into five hierarchically nested layers: the levels of the individual, routine practices, media organization, social institutions, and social systems. Though of U.S. origin, this classification of the driving forces of news production into a hierarchy of influences has proved to be empirically productive in a variety of cultural contexts (e.g., Pintak 2010; Relly, Zanger, and Fahmy 2015; Zhong and Newhagen 2009) and in comparative work in particular (e.g., Hanitzsch and Mellado 2011; Reese 2001).

While a growing scholarly consensus toward a common classification of influences echoes the work of Shoemaker and her colleagues, there is still little agreement on the relative importance of these levels. Early gatekeeping research suggested that individual factors reign supreme in the process of news production (Flegel and Chaffee 1971; White 1950), but other evidence points to a rather modest influence of journalists' individual predispositions (Kepplinger, Brosius, and Staab 1991; Patterson and Donsbach 1996). Instead, organizational factors have been found to have a greater influence in shaping news production mostly through ownership, editorial supervision, decision-making and management routines, as well as news routines, and the allocation of time and editorial resources (Altheide 1976; Breed 1955; Fishman 1980; Gans 1979; Schlesinger 1978; Tuchman 1978; Weaver et al. 2007).

Several studies indicate the newsroom environment is an important source of influence and a strong predictor of journalists' professional views (Hanitzsch, Hanusch, and Lauerer 2016; Shoemaker et al. 2001; Weaver et al. 2007). At the same time, researchers and journalists have long recognized the power of political factors, economic imperatives, and media structures (Bagdikian 1983; Preston and Metykova 2009; Whitney, Sumpter, and McQuail 2004). Consistent with this view, the societal level has emerged from the literature as an exceptionally important source of influence in all multilevel analyses of the previous wave of the WJS (Hanitzsch and Berganza 2012; Hanitzsch, Hanusch, and Lauerer 2016; Plaisance, Skewes, and Hanitzsch 2012; Reich and Hanitzsch 2013).

Clearly, even though these views are based on research, conclusions about the relative strength of these influences represent the theory-building efforts of academics as "outsiders." Journalists may not fully perceive and thus not completely articulate the real power (relative strength) of some of these sources of influence because these influences are part of a reality that they take for granted. In the realities of journalistic practice, the way these influences come to bear on the process of news production has a discursive element. Journalists and news organizations constantly negotiate the power of these influences in daily news work (Carlson and Lewis 2015). In the process of professional socialization, however, many of these influences tend to be normalized to the extent that journalists conceive of them as the evident and "natural" way of doing journalism (Shoemaker and Vos 2009). As a result, journalists' subjective perceptions of news influences may not fully map onto the theoretical schematas mentioned above.

Here again, the results of the first wave of the WJS warrant consideration. Based on a Principal Component Analysis of survey data from eighteen countries, the study identified six distinct domains of perceived influence: political, economic, organizational, procedural, professional, and reference groups (Hanitzsch et al. 2010). Journalists perceived organizational, professional, and procedural factors as being far more influential than political and economic influences. In that study it was reasoned that editorial management absorbs and filters political and economic pressures and redistributes them as organizational influences to subordinate journalists.

Toward a Comparative Index of Influences on News Work

This chapter is based on survey measures of how journalists perceive influences from nineteen potential sources. Tables A.1 and A.2 in the appendix list these sources, along with the corresponding descriptive statistics. In the questionnaire, we introduced the list of influences using the following wording: "Here is a list of potential sources of influence. Please tell me how much influence each of the following has on your work." Journalists were given five options to answer the question, ranging from "extremely influential"

(5) to "not influential" (1). We further collapsed the nineteen sources of influence into a parsimonious set of meaningful indexes: political influences, economic influences, organizational influences, procedural influences, and personal networks influences.[3] The composite measures are based on theoretical rather than technical or statistical considerations, resulting in formative rather than reflective indexes (see chapter 3 for a methodological discussion). For each of the five indexes, we calculated a mean score reflecting the average score across all indicators that belong to the same index. A value of 5 points indicates the maximum perceived influence, and a value of 1 indicates no influence at all.

The first index, *political influences*, comprises the sources that originate from the political context, including politicians, government officials, and pressure groups. While the connection between these three groups of actors seems sufficiently intuitive, the inclusion of business representatives requires further explanation. Here we reason that people acting within the world of business—such as entrepreneurs, industrialists, protagonists of trade associations, and industrial lobbyists—may primarily pursue economic interests, but in most interactions with journalists, these interests are voiced and asserted in the political arena (Winters 2011). Representing, advocating, and imposing the interests of business and trade are inherently political acts with political implications. These activities may have only indirect economic implications, if any, for the news organization for which a journalist works.

Furthermore, in many countries, political and business elites are strongly intertwined, making it hard for journalists to make clear distinctions between them every time. Results from our previous study did indeed point to a strong link between business representatives and the larger concept of political influence (Hanitzsch et al. 2010).

Economic influences, the second index, refer to pressures in the newsroom related to economic and commercial concerns. These influences originate from a variety of sources that we measured through "profit expectations" of media companies and "advertising considerations" within the newsroom, and through "audience research and data" (indicator wording in the questionnaire). These factors, as well as their immediate consequences in the newsroom, reflect the fact that most media companies are profit-oriented endeavors that compete in a market economy. Economic influences are thus often seen as the single largest influence on news production, especially where news organizations' primary goal is making a profit (Bagdikian 1983; Ettema and Whitney 1994). Even when that is not the case (such as for noncommercial and public service media), the high costs of modern news production and distribution introduce economic criteria at every stage, from selection to distribution (Whitney, Sumpter, and McQuail 2004).

The third index, *organizational influences,* includes pressures stemming from the hierarchical structures that govern decision-making processes and management routines of newsrooms and media organizations. The organized nature of news production is an essential feature of modern journalism, which puts the individual journalist "within the constraining boundaries of a fairly elaborate set of organizational control structures and processes" (Sigelman 1973, 146). Influence in the organizational domain is exercised on two important levels: within the newsroom (supervisors and higher-level editors, as well as editorial policy) and within the media organization (managers and owners). Obviously, the dimension of organizational influence transcends the traditional division between the newsroom and the larger structure of the media organization.

The fourth index captures what we have labeled *procedural influences* in publications from the earlier wave of the study (Hanitzsch et al. 2010, 15). These sources of influence relate to the various operational constraints journalists face in their daily tasks. The constraints usually materialize in the form of limited resources in terms of time and space, represented in our study through "time limits" and "available news-gathering resources" (questionnaire wording). Procedural influences relate to something journalists have or do not have but certainly need in order to perform their job properly. Access to information is such a "must have," too. Furthermore, journalism ethics and media laws and regulation—though they may not seem as tangible as lack of time, resources, and access—also have practical consequences for news production. Journalism ethics and professional codes of conduct dictate a journalistic practice that is normatively desirable; these norms, however, may vary in influence in reality. Media laws and regulation are, in contrast, much more consequential for journalists, depending on how strongly they are instituted in a society (Shoemaker and Vos 2009). Made and enforced by the political system, media laws and regulations provide a space within which journalists can operate without facing legal consequences. Journalists are not necessarily aware of the political component of all these legal imperatives; more important to them are the practical and legal consequences certain illegal or unethical practices may have for their work.

Personal network influences constitute the fifth and final dimension. This index combines several factors, internal and external, most strongly related to journalists' interactions with other people. Among the significant reference groups in the journalists' professional domain are their peers on the editorial staff and their colleagues in other media. These groups are relevant because, just as in many other occupational fields, reputation as a value for journalists largely depends on the recognition their work receives from peers rather than from their consumers (the audience). Journalists monitor their colleagues as they compete with them, or as a means of self-ascertainment. Hence peer recognition is the central currency of professional reputation, and it determines a journalist's "value" in the job market. Apart from their professional bonds, journalists maintain close social relationships through which they often develop an approximate sense of the audience. This noninstitutional component of the personal networks index relates to the potential influence of "friends, acquaintances, and family" (questionnaire wording) on a journalist's work.

In the following sections we use the five indexes developed here rather than the individual sources of influence as measured in the original questionnaire. This allows us to present complex data relationships in a parsimonious fashion. As outlined in chapter 3, the indexes were constructed based on theoretical rather than statistical considerations. The *political influences* index combined pressures from "politicians," "government officials," "pressure groups," and "business representatives," while *economic influences* included references to "profit expectations," "advertising considerations," and "audience research and data." The index for *organizational influences* averaged journalists' perceived pressures from the "managers of the news organization," "supervisors and higher editors," "owners of news organizations," and "editorial policy." *Procedural influences* combined five sources, namely, "information access," "journalism ethics," "media laws and regulation," "available news-gathering resources," and "time limits." Finally, *personal networks influences* referred to "friends, acquaintances, family," "colleagues in other media," and "peers on the staff."

Perceived Influences: The Big Picture

To assess the relative strength of the five domains of influence on a global level, we considered the mean scores and their distribution (reported in

Table 5.1 Perceived influences across countries

	N	Mean[a]	F[b]	Eta²
Procedural influences	27,249	3.75	65.08	.136
Organizational influences	27,011	3.30	83.68	.170
Economic influences	26,646	2.74	83.37	.172
Personal networks influences	27,211	2.62	42.15	.093
Political influences	26,803	2.25	116.71	.224

[a] Weighted.
[b] df = 66; all p < .001.

table 5.1 and illustrated in fig. 5.1). We found that the dimensions are arranged in a hierarchical structure in which journalists see procedural and organizational influences as much more powerful in their work than influences from personal networks or economic and political factors. This result reaffirms a pattern extracted from the first wave of the study (Hanitzsch et al. 2010; Hanitzsch, Hanusch, and Lauerer 2016) and replicates findings from other, similar studies (e.g., Shoemaker et al. 2001; Weaver et al. 2007). It is also a reminder that the hierarchy of influences model that places social systems atop the hierarchy is simply a catalog of influences arranged by relative abstraction rather than a statement about their relative influence (Shoemaker and Reese 1996).

More specifically, journalists around the world perceive procedural factors to be the strongest set of influences on news work. Arguably, the strength of this dimension resides in the fact that it is composed of influences closely related to key processes of journalistic work and is experienced unmediated by journalists. Particularly, limited access and time to do news work is a tangible influence affecting journalistic work fundamentally and immediately. Despite their high perceived strength overall, procedural influences vary substantially by country. The eta-squared measure indicates that differences in the national contexts account for almost 14 percent of the overall variance in procedural influences, a moderate effect. Figure 5.1 demonstrates that across the sixty-seven societies, the average scores are nearly normally distributed; there is no hint of any substantive country clusters.

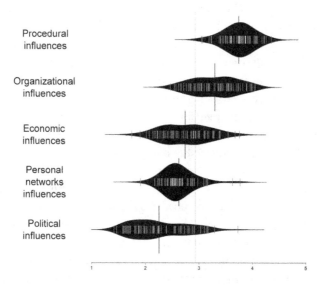

Figure 5.1 Journalists' perceived influences across countries (distribution of country means)

Source: WJS; N = 67.

Note: Scale: 5 = "extremely influential" . . . 1 = "not influential."

Not surprisingly, organizational influences were perceived as the second-strongest influence on journalistic work in all sixty-seven countries. News organizations maintain a grip on their journalistic staff through a clear chain of command and supervision, through editorial policy, and through the cultivation of a distinct newsroom culture. While their struggle for autonomy keeps journalists alert about any encroachments and, to some extent, protects them from certain external influences, such as politics and business, it leaves them defenseless against organizational forces. Levels of organizational influence vary significantly across countries, with national differences accounting for 17 percent of the overall variance. The double-peaked (bimodal) distribution of country averages suggests some qualitative differences between groups of countries that deserve further inspection, and which will be discussed later in this chapter.

Economic influences scored the third highest on average, though journalists perceived these forces to have only some or little influence. The global analysis points to considerable differences among countries; the amount of variation accounted for by cross-national differences is slightly higher (17 percent) than for organizational influences. Again, a double-peaked distribution of average scores calls for examining cross-national patterns. Similar to economic influences, the influence of personal networks was, on a global scale, perceived to be only moderate by most respondents. The countries differ on this dimension, too, but to a smaller extent than for the other four domains. However, family members and friends, as well as colleagues and peers, are perceived to have a larger impact on news work than system-related country-level structures.

Political influences, lastly, make up the domain of influence that has, in the view of journalists, the least power to shape the daily work of newsmakers. The extent to which political factors matter, however, depends strongly on the national context. The political forces domain, from among the five influence domains, exhibits the greatest variation across nations, with country differences accounting for almost one-quarter of the overall variability in the data. Therefore perceived political influences are a key marker of differences in journalistic cultures around the globe. The bimodal distribution of average scores across the sixty-seven countries, as shown in figure 5.1, clearly points to substantive differences between at least two different groups of countries, which we will explore further in the following sections.

The relatively moderate perceived importance of political and economic factors may well be counterintuitive. Given the overwhelming evidence for the existence of political and economic influence reported in large parts of the academic literature, some of which we have cited above, the objective power of political and economic influences can hardly be denied. These influences have real and often critical consequences in everyday news work. Hence the low perceived importance of political and economic factors—compared to other sources of influence—does not mean that these forces have little relevance to the production of news. To the contrary, it is quite possible that these factors are actually more powerful in reality than journalists' perceptions suggest.

We believe that the inconsistency between journalists' perceptions of influences and their impact as discussed in much of the journalism literature is reflecting the epistemological schism between "objective" and "real-existing" influences, on the one hand, and perceived influence, on the other (Reich and Hanitzsch 2013). Objective influences do exist in the real world; they have real power, and they make a practical difference in the work of journalists. Perceived influences, in contrast, refer to journalists' subjective perceptions of these forces, which may not necessarily correspond to the objective power of influences. Journalists' perceptions may thus only partly represent the reality of news making. This is an important caveat to keep in mind in interpreting the findings of this study.

Some explanations for why the objective reality of these influences may not be clearly evident to journalists are proffered. As we pointed out in our analyses from the first wave of the study, these influences may not necessarily appear as evident to all journalists equally (Hanitzsch et al. 2010). Let us return to the examples mentioned in the introduction to this chapter: not all journalists in Turkey live as dangerously as Can Dündar, who survived an assassination attempt, but they may do so when they start reporting too critically on security-related issues. Similarly, not all Australian journalists may be asked for editorial favors by advertisers in the way a beauty editor from a fashion magazine (quoted earlier) said she was. Journalists might also tend to consciously negate, and thus not acknowledge as easily, political and, even more so, economic influences as part of a professional ideology according to which journalism is supposed to operate independently of political and economic interests.

Presumably political and economic pressures appear to be less important in journalists' perceptions because these influences are further removed from their daily practice than, for example, the influence of norms and routines. Political and economic influences are likely less tangible and much more clandestine. Their significance is masked by organizational and procedural influences that have a much stronger grip on journalists' everyday practice. Rank-and-file journalists, we believe, rarely experience political and economic influences in a direct and immediate fashion. We think that the power of political and economic influences is anticipated and absorbed by the organization's news management, and these influences are subsequently filtered, negotiated, and redistributed to individual journalists, where they are finally internalized and thus appear as organizational and procedural influences (Hanitzsch et al. 2010). News organizations are therefore likely to function in many cases as a mediator of external interests and pressures rather than as a buffer protecting journalists from direct exposure to these influences. We will return to these issues in the concluding section of this chapter.

Strong ties between political and economic influences, on the one hand, and organizational imperatives, on the other, are particularly common in

Latin America, where many major news organizations belong to longstanding dynasties well connected to the world of politics (Waisbord 2000). Whereas in other parts of the world this would constitute a serious conflict of interest, Latin American journalists accustomed to this situation have learned to accept this linkage as the norm (Arroyave and Barrios 2012; Waisbord 2009). Still, journalists who question this linkage will suffer reprisals, as in the case of Carmen Aristegui, Mexico's most prominent radio personality. In 2011 she was dismissed after publicly commenting on then-president Felipe Calderón's possible alcohol problems. While her employer reinstated her only a few days later following public protests,[4] four years later she was again abruptly fired after she exposed a corruption scandal involving President Enrique Peña Nieto. Her dismissal eventually opened a national debate about corruption and helped anticorruption legislation that was working its way through Congress.[5] In this and many other cases, political and economic pressures are intertwined with organizational influence.

Differences Across Countries

As noted above, cross-national differences in our study were especially large with regard to political, economic, and organizational influences. In the following section we explore these differences further to extract general patterns of global similarities and differences. Table 5.2 reports a country-wise breakdown of average scores and standard deviations for the five domains of influence. Readers specifically interested in national differences for the various individual sources of influence may want to consult tables A.1 and A.2.

The extent to which journalists perceive political influences on their work to be weak or strong generally reflects differences between political systems and tends to follow international geographical divides. European nations dominate the top twenty countries where journalists perceived the least political influence; Canada, Israel, Japan, New Zealand, and the United States also belong to this group. Typically, journalists report relatively little political influence in developed democracies, that is, political systems that grant journalists high levels of press freedom and political liberties.

Table 5.2 Perceived influences—differences between countries

	Political influences		Economic influences		Organizational influences		Procedural influences		Personal networks influences	
	Mean	(SD)	Mean	(SD)	Mean	(SD)	Mean	(SD)	Mean	(SD)
Albania	1.88	(0.83)	2.79	(0.92)	3.14	(0.90)	3.87	(0.61)	2.30	(0.79)
Argentina	2.26	(0.94)	2.49	(1.02)	3.46	(0.95)	3.58	(0.65)	2.78	(0.78)
Australia	2.25	(0.84)	2.50	(0.98)	3.10	(0.84)	4.07	(0.55)	2.47	(0.76)
Austria	1.58	(0.64)	2.22	(0.87)	2.57	(0.78)	3.46	(0.68)	2.27	(0.66)
Bangladesh	2.15	(1.13)	2.90	(0.95)	3.43	(1.08)	3.65	(0.85)	2.23	(1.03)
Belgium	1.68	(0.80)	2.08	(0.89)	2.77	(0.84)	3.54	(0.70)	2.47	(0.72)
Bhutan	3.18	(0.96)	3.19	(0.89)	3.61	(0.92)	3.61	(0.91)	3.63	(1.05)
Botswana	2.82	(1.12)	3.01	(1.11)	3.89	(0.98)	4.36	(0.63)	2.50	(1.05)
Brazil	2.09	(0.93)	2.78	(1.05)	3.44	(0.86)	3.71	(0.68)	2.67	(0.78)
Bulgaria	2.01	(1.10)	3.12	(0.98)	3.41	(0.92)	3.95	(0.71)	2.63	(0.77)
Canada	1.65	(0.81)	1.90	(0.76)	2.81	(0.94)	3.88	(0.66)	2.31	(0.76)
Chile	2.17	(1.11)	2.71	(1.16)	3.52	(1.01)	3.62	(0.74)	2.51	(0.92)
China	2.91	(0.78)	3.10	(0.78)	3.55	(0.73)	3.59	(0.63)	2.69	(0.73)
Colombia	2.56	(1.17)	3.09	(1.17)	3.70	(1.14)	3.59	(0.79)	2.60	(1.07)
Croatia	2.15	(1.25)	2.75	(1.19)	3.04	(1.16)	3.88	(0.75)	2.69	(1.07)

(continued)

Table 5.2 Perceived influences—differences between countries (*continued*)

	Political influences		Economic influences		Organizational influences		Procedural influences		Personal networks influences	
	Mean	(SD)	Mean	(SD)	Mean	(SD)	Mean	(SD)	Mean	(SD)
Cyprus	1.72	(0.81)	2.57	(1.17)	3.90	(0.96)	3.81	(0.80)	1.91	(0.70)
Czech Republic	1.64	(0.78)	2.48	(0.94)	3.19	(0.90)	4.09	(0.62)	2.88	(0.87)
Denmark	1.98	(0.83)	2.22	(0.89)	3.00	(0.84)	3.44	(0.69)	2.38	(0.75)
Ecuador	2.79	(1.20)	2.99	(1.09)	3.60	(0.95)	3.83	(0.68)	2.80	(1.12)
Egypt	2.64	(1.09)	3.28	(0.92)	3.54	(0.92)	3.94	(0.81)	2.65	(0.98)
El Salvador	2.81	(1.16)	3.16	(1.18)	3.99	(0.91)	3.81	(0.68)	2.57	(1.01)
Estonia	1.72	(0.71)	2.53	(0.99)	2.91	(0.91)	3.77	(0.62)	2.59	(0.76)
Ethiopia	3.15	(1.18)	2.86	(1.01)	3.82	(1.02)	3.75	(0.78)	2.55	(0.91)
Finland	1.97	(0.82)	2.27	(0.73)	2.83	(0.70)	3.83	(0.60)	2.54	(0.68)
France	1.47	(0.57)	2.17	(0.81)	2.66	(0.79)	3.59	(0.71)	2.50	(0.72)
Germany	1.58	(0.63)	2.58	(0.96)	2.86	(0.90)	3.60	(0.64)	2.41	(0.70)
Greece	1.91	(1.04)	2.63	(1.03)	3.17	(1.13)	3.76	(0.74)	2.25	(0.88)
Hong Kong	2.25	(0.87)	2.31	(0.93)	3.30	(0.90)	3.23	(0.72)	2.56	(0.78)
Hungary	1.98	(0.99)	3.11	(0.98)	3.40	(0.99)	3.74	(0.69)	2.92	(0.83)
Iceland	1.61	(0.74)	1.75	(0.80)	2.47	(0.76)	3.77	(0.63)	2.65	(0.77)
India	2.54	(1.06)	3.38	(0.99)	3.64	(1.00)	4.05	(0.75)	2.58	(1.08)

Indonesia	2.30	(0.97)	3.01	(0.90)	3.36	(0.87)	3.74	(0.63)	2.79	(0.87)
Ireland	2.14	(0.93)	2.34	(0.88)	2.98	(0.85)	3.91	(0.60)	2.53	(0.74)
Israel	1.71	(0.85)	2.38	(1.02)	3.06	(1.13)	3.67	(0.77)	2.48	(0.87)
Italy	1.63	(0.79)	2.34	(0.96)	2.67	(0.99)	3.51	(0.67)	2.18	(0.75)
Japan	1.87	(0.75)	2.60	(0.76)	3.28	(0.78)	3.40	(0.57)	2.68	(0.68)
Kenya	2.62	(0.92)	3.54	(0.88)	3.90	(0.85)	4.10	(0.68)	2.98	(0.91)
Kosovo	2.16	(1.10)	2.50	(1.02)	3.06	(1.07)	3.76	(0.72)	2.31	(1.04)
Latvia	1.42	(0.62)	2.46	(0.94)	2.84	(0.88)	3.49	(0.79)	2.47	(0.78)
Malawi	2.87	(1.05)	3.40	(0.85)	4.05	(0.80)	4.27	(0.60)	3.17	(0.97)
Malaysia	3.29	(0.84)	3.38	(0.85)	3.64	(0.78)	3.87	(0.66)	3.15	(0.90)
Mexico	2.53	(1.05)	2.90	(1.09)	3.78	(1.00)	3.73	(0.69)	2.42	(0.98)
Moldova	1.83	(0.91)	2.90	(1.03)	3.15	(0.98)	3.88	(0.69)	2.52	(0.88)
Netherlands	1.89	(0.80)	2.41	(0.94)	2.85	(0.80)	3.05	(0.69)	2.50	(0.72)
New Zealand	2.02	(0.92)	2.52	(0.99)	3.04	(0.88)	3.88	(0.66)	2.63	(0.81)
Norway	1.82	(0.68)	2.02	(0.84)	2.62	(0.61)	3.54	(0.59)	2.51	(0.57)
Oman	3.03	(0.74)	3.26	(0.69)	3.54	(0.69)	3.61	(0.68)	2.86	(0.96)
Philippines	2.39	(0.94)	2.98	(0.91)	3.61	(0.77)	4.08	(0.57)	2.55	(0.74)
Portugal	1.60	(0.80)	2.35	(0.97)	3.18	(0.83)	3.83	(0.61)	2.49	(0.87)
Qatar	2.65	(0.94)	2.94	(0.99)	2.71	(1.03)	3.07	(0.88)	2.84	(0.91)
Romania	1.80	(0.94)	2.86	(1.02)	3.01	(0.99)	4.03	(0.70)	2.65	(0.91)
Russia	2.24	(0.78)	2.68	(0.99)	3.52	(0.81)	3.23	(0.75)	2.56	(0.82)

(continued)

Table 5.2 Perceived influences—differences between countries (*continued*)

	Political influences		Economic influences		Organizational influences		Procedural influences		Personal networks influences	
	Mean	(SD)	Mean	(SD)	Mean	(SD)	Mean	(SD)	Mean	(SD)
Serbia	2.13	(1.07)	2.93	(1.03)	3.36	(0.97)	3.76	(0.75)	2.63	(0.91)
Sierra Leone	2.73	(1.02)	3.39	(0.92)	4.00	(0.88)	4.22	(0.66)	2.85	(0.98)
Singapore	2.91	(0.94)	2.95	(0.90)	2.98	(1.02)	3.19	(1.15)	2.88	(0.90)
South Africa	2.39	(0.96)	2.91	(0.92)	3.57	(0.81)	4.19	(0.60)	2.65	(0.85)
South Korea	2.67	(0.90)	3.26	(0.83)	3.55	(0.79)	3.77	(0.51)	3.09	(0.65)
Spain	2.23	(0.93)	2.85	(1.00)	3.39	(1.01)	3.78	(0.62)	2.42	(0.78)
Sudan	3.16	(1.42)	3.68	(0.98)	3.73	(0.87)	4.23	(0.73)	2.91	(1.15)
Sweden	1.67	(0.60)	2.34	(0.92)	2.94	(0.76)	3.50	(0.62)	2.42	(0.60)
Switzerland	1.88	(0.68)	2.19	(0.77)	2.54	(0.72)	3.38	(0.65)	2.42	(0.63)
Tanzania	2.55	(0.56)	2.14	(0.82)	4.05	(0.56)	3.87	(0.42)	2.18	(0.40)
Thailand	3.73	(0.86)	3.76	(0.69)	3.96	(0.70)	3.96	(0.53)	3.77	(0.80)
Turkey	3.03	(1.20)	2.42	(1.00)	2.92	(1.06)	3.41	(0.67)	2.36	(0.78)
United Arab Emirates	3.10	(1.23)	3.27	(1.10)	3.74	(0.96)	3.96	(0.79)	3.14	(1.11)
United Kingdom	2.05	(0.82)	2.72	(0.92)	3.20	(0.85)	3.80	(0.71)	2.65	(0.78)
United States	1.93	(0.83)	2.23	(0.76)	3.37	(0.93)	4.06	(0.65)	2.70	(0.81)

Among the Western countries in the study, Australia and Spain had the highest scores on political influence, setting them somewhat apart from the other Western nations and—somewhat surprisingly—in close proximity to Russia.

For Spain, this finding may be less surprising than it seems at first sight. The country's media system is closely linked with political powers, historically and especially since the democratic transition. Broadcasting media, both public and private, are tightly regulated through a government licensing system, and regional and local media strongly depend on advertising revenues from public institutions (Berganza, Herrero-Jiménez, and Arcila-Calderón 2016). In Australia, there is a notoriously high concentration of media ownership, and, during the time of our survey, there was considerable debate in the country about the federal government's inquiry into media regulation and media reform in 2011 and 2012. The inquiry, and subsequent government plans to establish a statutory body to police the media, was criticized by many media organizations as a politically motivated attempt to intervene in journalistic freedoms (Flew and Swift 2013). Except for these two countries, however, our results point to a robust association between democratic development and lower perceived power of political influences on news production.

Russia, too, deserves special mention here. As indicated, Russian journalists reported, on average, political influence levels equal to those reported by Australian and Spanish journalists. Counterintuitive as this result may be, because one may expect the score to be higher for Russia, it may be a good example of how news management absorbs and redistributes political pressures to working journalists in the form of organizational influence.

After Vladimir Putin rose to power, Russian TV networks became owned by the state or by companies that functioned as corporate arms of the government (Specter 2007). Two of the three main nationwide TV networks, Channel One and Russia TV, are controlled by the state. Energy giant Gazprom owns several television channels (notably, TNT and NTV), radio stations, and print outlets (including *Izvestia*, until 2008). Anna Kachkayeva, former dean of the Faculty of Media Communications at the Moscow-based Higher School of Economics, calls it a system of contacts and agreements between the Kremlin and the heads of television networks: "There is no need to start every day with instructions. It is all done with winks and nods. They meet at the end of the week, and the problem, for

TV and even in the printed press, is that self-censorship is worse than any other kind. Journalists know—they can feel—what is allowed and what is not" (Specter 2007). The report by Freedom House in 2016 concludes that the nationalistic tone of the dominant Russian media continued to drown out independent and critical journalism.[6]

Journalists in African countries, in Turkey (where our study was conducted before the failed coup attempt of 2016), in the Gulf states, and in large parts of East, South, and Southeast Asia report relatively strong political influences. In these regions, more often than not journalists work under conditions of heavy political interference in freedom of the press and tight restrictions on freedom of speech. As we will see in the following chapters, these settings tend to produce a culture of journalism that copes with these pressures in its own way, a culture that helps journalists survive in an often hostile environment. Political influence is also seen as high to moderate in most parts of Latin America, with El Salvador emerging on top of the list in terms of influence strength. Among all Asian countries in this study, only Japan deviates from the overall pattern, as journalism there has broadly followed a Western paradigm since the end of World War II.

Geographical divides also matter with regard to economic influences on journalism. The perceived power of economic imperatives is smallest in the Scandinavian countries, in North America, and in Belgium, France, Switzerland, and Austria. Except for the United States, these countries maintain strong public service broadcasting institutions. Scandinavian societies are exemplary of this type of media system, where the state has a strong role in regulating and funding the media industry. Public service media are not limited to the broadcasting sector alone; the state also provides subsidies for print outlets in all countries but Iceland. Ahva et al. (2017) therefore see low levels of economic pressure as a distinctive feature of Nordic journalism. In these societies, the impact of commercialization and competition is mitigated through public regulation and funding. Furthermore, there are obvious similarities between Scandinavia, Estonia, and Latvia. The two Baltic countries have instituted a strong public service broadcasting media, and some of the significant commercial media organizations there are owned by Swedish and Finnish media houses.

The low levels of economic influence reported by U.S. journalists, at least in comparison to other countries in the sample, is notable because complaints about strong commercialization and the increasing power of economic imperatives are particularly rampant in the literature on American journalism (McChesney 1999). While their media outlets are overwhelmingly commercially supported, U.S. journalists experience this influence only indirectly and rarely acknowledge it (Beam, Weaver, and Brownlee 2009). Given the strong normative firewall between commercial considerations and news decisions, journalists find acknowledging a breach difficult (Artemas, Vos, and Duffy 2018; Coddington 2015). This, again, reminds us that perceptions about influences should be treated with a certain degree of caution. Journalists' interview responses may not fully reflect the material conditions on the ground, but they make apparent the way in which the power of these influences is articulated in institutional discourse.

Our results also show a noteworthy split for Europe that largely follows the geographic divide between Western and Eastern Europe. Journalists reported stronger economic influences in Eastern Europe; these factors were perceived as being remarkably potent in Bulgaria and Hungary. After almost three decades of political-economic transition in Eastern Europe, tight control of the media by the state has been replaced by the now omnipresent power of market forces, but without a long tradition of a business-news firewall. At the same time, journalists in Western European countries feel their work is less influenced by economic pressures than do their colleagues in other parts of the world.

Economic influence is seen as particularly pronounced in Asia (most specifically in Thailand, India, Malaysia, and South Korea), in the Gulf region, and in most parts of Africa. Pressures stemming from corporate profit expectations, advertising considerations, and market research are particularly strong in El Salvador and Mexico, as well as in Colombia and Ecuador. As Silvio Waisbord (2009, 393) argues, political and economic influences often appear heavily intertwined in Latin American journalism. Presidents and governors have the habit of manipulating the allocation of lucrative advertising contracts and a wide array of business opportunities "in order to court support from private media, feed the ambitions of sycophantic moguls, and prop up their own media empires."

A clear regional pattern also emerges from a cross-national analysis of perceived organizational influences on the news. Again, most pronounced is a division along the lines of Western and non-Western countries. Influences stemming from within the newsroom (editorial policy, supervisors, and higher editors) and from within the media organization (managers and owners) are seen as particularly powerful in Africa, Latin America, Russia, and most parts of Asia, including the Gulf region. Arguably, this pattern can be placed in the context of cross-cultural research on how workplace-related inequalities are generally perceived in a given society. Geert Hofstede (2001), for instance, noted that individuals from non-Western regions are more likely to accept power inequalities in organizations. Thus it seems reasonable to assume that in these societies, one may find a stronger and more pronounced hierarchy within the newsroom and the media organization, in which senior journalists and those in managerial positions have much more authority in shaping operational decisions and long-term editorial policy. We think that such a hierarchical structure and greater acquiescence to this structure are likely explanations for the stronger perceived organizational influence in non-Western countries.

Organizational cultures in other societies, by way of contrast, seem to institute a much flatter editorial hierarchy and a more egalitarian organization of journalistic labor. This is particularly true of the Nordic countries as well as of Canada, Australia, New Zealand, and most parts of Western Europe. In these countries, organizational influence was seen as exceptionally weak. This finding again resonates with Hofstede's (2001) comparative work, which generally points to lower acceptance of power inequalities in Western countries, most notably in Scandinavia. The contextual analysis presented in the following section supports this conclusion.

Among the Western societies included in the study, Spanish journalists reported the strongest levels of organizational influence. This finding puts Spain in close proximity to Latin America, where interactions between journalists tend to be less egalitarian and editorial hierarchies much stricter. Overall, it is worth noting that similarities between Spanish and Latin American journalists seem to be a general finding of this study, as the subsequent chapters will demonstrate (e.g., chapters 7 and 11).

Qatar does not follow the overall trend; here journalists reported relatively little organizational influence on their day-to-day work. We believe that a reasonable explanation for this finding is the relatively large proportion of journalists interviewed in Qatar who worked for Al Jazeera. These journalists reported significantly less organizational influence than did their counterparts in other newsrooms in the country. Although the government of Qatar owns the television network, journalists working for the network enjoy considerable editorial freedom. The fact that Al Jazeera journalists perceive organizational influence as relatively weak—as compared with journalists from other countries in this part of the world—is thus likely the result of an organizational culture that, according to Mohamed Zayani and Sofiane Sahraoui (2007), emphasizes independent thinking and individual initiative more than do other news media in the region.

The cross-national pattern for procedural and personal network influences is less clear-cut and does not seem to entirely follow the more common geographical, political, or cultural groupings. Generally, journalists perceived procedural influences to be stronger in the Anglo-Saxon world (notably, Australia and the United States), in Africa and India, in Southeast Asia, and in several Eastern European countries. Procedural influences appeared less powerful in large parts of continental Western Europe, in Latin America, and in a few other countries, such as Japan, Turkey, and China.

For personal networks, journalists from most parts of Asia, Eastern Europe, and Russia reported high levels of influence. The perceived influence of peers and colleagues as well as friends, acquaintances, and family turned out to be much less pronounced throughout continental Western Europe, Canada, and Australia. The pattern was mixed for Africa and Latin America. Interesting as these differences are, a detailed discussion of them requires a focused, fine-grained analysis that is beyond the scope of this book.

To gain a better idea of potential cross-national configurations, we mapped the cross-national similarities and differences onto a two-dimensional plot. We limited this analysis to political, economic, and organizational influences, as these emerged as the most meaningful signifiers of cross-national difference. Figure 5.2 shows a country map based on an application of Multidimensional Scaling.[7] The interpretation of the plot is rather straightforward; spatial proximities on the map represent similarities between countries across political, economic, and organizational influences.[8]

Overall, figure 5.2 exhibits a pattern that points not only to differences between Western and non-Western countries, as well as between developed and developing nations, but also to some more fine-grained disparities within these larger groups. To the right side of the figure are the continental Western European nations that cluster together owing to relatively weak influences from the political, economic, and organizational domains. These countries maintain strong public service media institutions; journalists and large parts of the population consider the media as a public good. In many regions, such as Scandinavia and France, public funding is not limited to public service broadcasting channels alone; it is also provided to print media

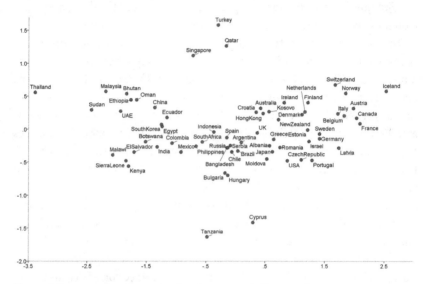

Figure 5.2 Journalists' perceived influences—differences between countries

Source: WJS; N = 67.

Note: Multidimensional Scaling plot based on Euclidean distances using Alscal.

outlets. Australia, Britain, and the United States are located at the left fringe of this particular cluster of countries on the map, underscoring their unique status in the Western world.

The two Baltic nations of Estonia and Latvia are close to the cluster of Western European countries (Estonia, in particular, mimicking the Scandinavian example), as are many societies in Eastern Europe, most notably the Czech Republic, Croatia, Romania, Moldova, Albania, and Kosovo. Broadly speaking, the transformation of media systems in Central and Eastern European countries has resulted in the Westernization of journalism but not necessarily in the homogenization of journalistic cultures in the region. Journalism in this region is traversing different paths, as our results clearly show. Bulgaria, Serbia, and Hungary exhibit a pattern distinctly different from that in the other countries, especially in terms of stronger perceived economic and organizational influences. These three countries are in close proximity to Russia in terms of the strength of these influences.

The left side of figure 5.2 is occupied solely by countries from the non-Western world. This includes all African and most Asian countries, as well as the three Gulf countries. Here journalists perceive all domains of influence on the news as being generally strong. Heavy perceived political influence seems to be a distinctive feature in these journalistic cultures. The similarities among African countries—with the exception of Tanzania, which is a clear outlier—are particularly striking. Most journalists across the continent said they operated under heavy organizational and political constraints. Differences among East, Southeast, and South Asian countries are slightly larger by comparison, with journalists in Bangladesh, Indonesia, and the Philippines most similar to their colleagues in the Western world. Thailand, a country oscillating between parliamentary democracy and military rule for decades, occupies a unique space to the far left of figure 5.2, with journalists consistently reporting enormous pressures from nearly all domains of influence.

Notably, figure 5.2 provides evidence that Japan and Hong Kong represent regionally distinct journalistic cultures, which underlines their rather exclusive position in the larger Asian context. Although mainland China is gradually gaining control over Hong Kong's uniquely cosmopolitan press environment, the British cultural legacy is still visible in the local journalism culture. Japan, in contrast, adopted a Western approach to journalism when media outlets across the country fell under the control of U.S. Headquarters after the Second World War. Since then, Japan has instituted an exceptionally strong public broadcasting organization in the form of Nippon Hōsō Kyōkai (NHK), which has a potent grip on public discourse. Further, political changes in the 1990s increased the power of journalists to report even more independently (Sugiyama 2000).

Japan and Hong Kong are not the only examples of hybrid journalistic cultures. Turkey, Qatar, and Singapore occupy unique positions at the top of figure 5.2, relatively far removed from all other countries included in the study. In terms of perceived influences on the news, journalism in these three countries seems to combine characteristics from journalistic cultures in both Western and non-Western societies in ways that create a work environment characterized by weak organizational and stronger political influence.

Another interesting observation from figure 5.2 is that despite their obvious similarities, journalistic environments in Latin America broadly split into two subgroups. One cluster of countries consists of Colombia, Ecuador, El Salvador, and Mexico, where perceived political, economic, and organizational pressures combined tend to be considerably higher than in the second group. Journalistic cultures in Argentina, Brazil, and Chile, by contrast, appear to be much more Westernized, with relatively lower levels of such influence. Still, the Latin American countries are proximate to one another and with Spain, indicating similarities between the region and Spain. The cultural bonds between Spain and its former colonies seem to pull these journalistic cultures in similar directions; much more than we found to be the case for Britain and its fallen colonial empire. Journalism in Brazil, a Portuguese colony for more than three centuries, seems to follow this path, too.

Contextualizing Perceived Influence on News Work

As noted above, the examination of differences and similarities among countries points to a number of factors underpinning journalists' perceptions of news influences. These factors broadly fall into the three societal contexts of journalistic culture outlined in chapter 2: politics and governance, socioeconomic development, and cultural value systems. In this section we examine these factors more closely, using contextual measures provided by international institutions, such as Freedom House, the World Bank, and the World Values Survey. These measures are strongly interrelated, often with correlations greater than r = .80. Societies scoring high in terms of quality of democracy, for instance, tend to grant greater freedom to the media, give more authority to the law to constrain individual and institutional behavior, exercise more transparency, fight corruption more, and have higher levels of human and economic development (see table A.8 in the appendix).

Table 5.3 reports correlations between journalists' perceived influences and relevant contextual factors. With the exception of procedural constraints, all domains of influence are related to press freedom as measured by both Freedom House and Reporters Without Borders. Associations are particularly strong for political and economic pressures, suggesting that, across countries, journalists' perceptions of the strength of these influences correspond well with external measures of media freedom. Press freedom, however, may well work as an intermediary in the journalists' perceptual structure of influences on the news. As the correlations reported in table 5.3 indicate, journalists' perceptions of influence—particularly those stemming

Table 5.3 Correlates of perceived influences on news work
(correlation coefficients)

	Political influence	Economic influence	Organizational influence	Procedural influence	Personal networks influence
Press freedom (FH)[a]	−.782***	−.691***	−.593***	−.082	−.408***
Press freedom (RSF)[b]	−.651***	−.644***	−.505***	−.066	−.279*
Democracy[c]	−.691***	−.649***	−.546***	−.046	−.401***
Rule of law[d]	−.481***	−.584***	−.633***	−.320**	−.154
GNI per capita[e]	−.412***	−.608***	−.701***	−.484***	−.216
Transparency[f]	−.439***	−.621***	−.630***	−.378**	−.161
Human development[g]	−.576***	−.630***	−.718***	−.479***	−.261*
Emancipative values[h]	−.543***	−.619***	−.502***	−.146	−.207
Acceptance of power inequality[i]	.511***	.606***	.571***	.144	.307*

Notes: Pearson's correlation coefficient. ***$p < .001$; **$p < .01$; *$p < .05$; N = 67 unless otherwise indicated.
[a] Freedom House; Freedom of the Press Index; scale reversed.
[b] Reporters Without Borders; World Press Freedom Index; scale reversed.
[c] Economist Intelligence Unit; EIU Democracy Index; N = 66.
[d] World Bank; percentile rank.
[e] World Bank; Atlas method, current US$; N = 66.
[f] Transparency International; Corruption Perceptions Index.
[g] UNDP; Human Development Index; N = 66.
[h] Scores calculated based on WVS/EVS data; N = 58.
[i] Geert Hofstede, https://geerthofstede.com/research-and-vsm/dimension-data-matrix/; N = 51.

from the political, economic, and organizational domains—are mainly driven by democratic performance.

Figure 5.3 provides a good illustration of the relationship between perceived political influence and quality of democracy as measured annually by the Economist Intelligence Unit. Journalists in democratic societies clearly perceive less political influence on their work, which is consistent with other studies that point to the importance of the political context for journalistic freedoms (Hallin and Mancini 2004; Hanitzsch and Mellado 2011; Soloski 1989). The location of countries in figure 5.3 does not follow a straight line, however, indicating that similar political conditions do

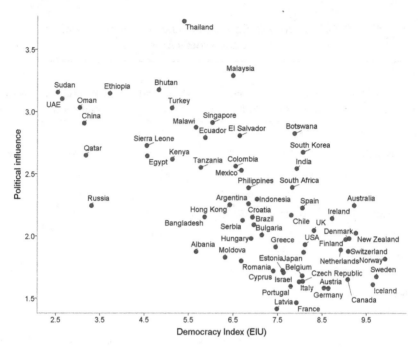

Figure 5.3 Journalists' perceived political influences and quality of democracy

Source: Economist Intelligence Unit, WJS; N = 66.

not necessarily coincide with similar levels of perceived influence. The comparison between Botswana and France, both scoring high on the Economic Intelligence Unit democracy index but different in perceived influence, is a case in point.

From table 5.3 we can see that perceived political influences are less pronounced in societies that are socioeconomically well developed, where populations have greater appreciation for emancipative values, and where power inequalities are less tolerated, though correlations tend to be slightly weaker. These findings need to be put in the context of a long-term cultural drift, or "emancipative value change," which emphasizes the importance of individual autonomy, self-expression, and free choice (Inglehart and Welzel 2005). In societies where people have a strong preference for emancipative values, journalists tend to have emancipated themselves from all kinds of authority, including political actors and government institutions.

Thus journalists would consider overt and strong political influence to be a transgression of institutional boundaries. At the same time, journalists face stronger political influences in societies that have more tolerance for inequalities in terms of how power is distributed (Hofstede 1998). Hence our analysis suggests that, as was argued in chapter 2, cultural and social value structures do indeed shape journalistic cultures considerably; overall, however, political factors seem to have greater weight in the equation.

Correlations for economic and organizational influences broadly show a similar pattern, perhaps with the difference that economic influences are more strongly related to human and economic development, transparency (or the absence of corruption), and the extent to which people embrace emancipative values. Organizational influences on the news are most strongly associated with human and economic development, the rule of law, and transparency. The overall pattern shows that journalists perceive pressures in all three domains of influence as stronger in less democratic and socioeconomically less developed countries as well as in societies with less appreciation for emancipative values and a greater tolerance for power inequality. Procedural influences are mainly related to social and economic development; journalists feel less constrained by operational pressures such as limited resources, information access, and media laws in countries that score higher on economic well-being and human development.

Human development, finally, is the only contextual factor that is significantly related to journalists' perceived influence on all five levels. The United Nations Development Programme (UNDP) measures human development from various indicators of life expectancy, education, and per capita income.[9] Our results reinforce the conclusion that as far as perceived influences on the news are concerned, differences between journalistic cultures significantly track along established classifications of developed and less developed countries, broadly mapping onto a divide between Western and non-Western societies.

Conclusions

In this chapter we have examined perceived influences on the news—the first extrinsic dimension of journalistic culture—based on journalists' responses to a set of standardized questions. The purpose was not to gather data on such influences as they objectively exist, which would have required a different research strategy, but to get a sense of how journalists perceive these pressures in everyday news work and how influences are discursively articulated. Relying on journalists' perceptions and recollections of influences on their work has obvious disadvantages. Their answers to the survey may be tailored to what respondents believe researchers want to hear from them, or to what journalists consider normatively desirable. Furthermore, because survey questionnaires typically elicit interview responses to a fixed set of questions using predefined answer options, responses may be an effect of the research protocol and not fully represent objective realities on the ground. At the same time, however, as researchers we also take journalists' interview responses for what they are: reasonable perceptions of a social and professional reality.

Keeping these caveats in mind, we identified five major domains of influence: political, economic, organizational, procedural, and personal networks. In the following chapters we consider these measures as contextual configurations, among others, that produce a diversity of journalistic cultures. The analysis for this chapter revealed that across the five domains, procedural and organizational influences mattered more in the view of journalists than influences from the political, economic, and personal networks domains. We do not believe, however, that the weak political and economic pressures reported by journalists necessarily reflect a hierarchy of influences as it exists on the ground. Journalists may not want to acknowledge the influence of these domains. They may not be equally or directly exposed to these influences. They may not be fully aware of them, or they may even systematically underestimate the power of these forces. Analyzing the global pattern of influences on the news, we argue that political and economic influences may be internalized by editorial management and transformed into organizational and procedural influences. However, it is impossible to test this hypothesis with the data set at hand. Hence the possible transformation of external influence into internal constraints through editorial routines is an issue that merits further attention from researchers.

As indicated above, the celebrated ideal of editorial independence may well encourage many journalists to deny or dismiss the unpleasant reality of economic imperatives in the newsroom. This, of course, has interesting implications in its own right. It is difficult to solve the problem of economic influence (or find an appropriate response to it) when journalists deny or dismiss the problem's very existence. Hence the low levels of political and economic pressures that journalists reported may be seen as a defensive discursive strategy to maintain the institutional boundaries of journalism in a time when they have become alarmingly porous.

The extent to which journalists perceive political, economic, and organizational influences on the news as weak or strong emerged as the strongest indicator of cross-national differences. This is particularly true for political influences—a finding that resonates with the literature on the relationship between media systems and the political environment (Hallin and Mancini 2004). Overall, we found a pattern that reflects the differences between political systems and tracks along familiar geographical divides. Disparities between countries map neatly onto common classifications of Western and non-Western countries, as well as developed and developing nations. While there were notable variations within these groups, perceived influences on the news tend to be stronger in non-Western, less democratic, and socioeconomically less developed countries.

From a classic modernization approach, the finding mentioned above may invite some readers to think that parts of the "less developed" world still need to "catch up" with journalistic standards established in the West as it pertains to issues discussed in this chapter. However, we suggest an alternative reading. The idea of journalism as an institutional endeavor that is independent of external forces may be a noble, viable, and proper ambition in most Western countries—albeit an ambition that likely outpaces reality—but cultural norms and professional realities are clearly different in other parts of the world. Ultimately, journalistic cultures need to strike their own balance between editorial independence, on the one hand, and cultural norms and social realities, on the other.

Notes

1. Samuel Osborne, "Turkish Journalist Survives Assassination Attempt Before Receiving 5 Year Sentence for 'Revealing State Secrets,'" *Independent*, May 6, 2016, http://www.inde pendent.co.uk/news/world/europe/turkish-journalist-survives-assassination-attempt -before-receiving-5-year-sentence-for-revealing-a7017816.html.

2. Richard Milne, "Finnish PM's Emails Land Him in Press Freedom Row," *Financial Times*, November 30, 2016, https://www.ft.com/content/ab69edbc-b71e-11e6-ba85-95d1533d9a62.

3. It is worth noting, however, that two of the five indexes—procedural influences and personal networks influences—slightly deviate from the way we conceptualized them in our previous study, mostly because of some modifications of the indicators (Hanitzsch et al. 2010).

4. Edgar Sigler, "Los 17 días que 'condenaron' a MVS," *Expansión*, August 22, 2012, http://expansion.mx/negocios/2012/08/22/los-17-dias-que-condenaron-a-mvs.

5. Elisabeth Malkin, "In Mexico, Firing of Carmen Aristegui Highlights Rising Pressures on News Media," *New York Times*, March 27, 2015, https://www.nytimes.com/2015/03/29/world/americas/in-mexico-firing-of-carmen-aristegui-highlights-rising-pressures-on-news-media.html.

6. Freedom House, Freedom of the Press Report, Russia, 2016, https://freedomhouse.org/report/freedom-press/2016/russia.

7. Multidimensional Scaling is a statistical technique that represents multivariate similarities (or differences) between empirical observations as spatial proximities in a space of low dimensionality. In figure 5.2 locations of countries on the map represent relative similarities among them with respect to journalists' perceptions of political, economic, and organizational influences.

8. Goodness of fit: Stress1 = .07; R^2 = .98. The statistical properties point to a solution that represents multidimensional similarities reasonably well, according to Borg and Groenen (1997).

9. United Nations Development Programme, Human Development Reports, 2015, Technical Notes, http://hdr.undp.org/sites/default/files/hdr2015_technical_notes.pdf.

6

EDITORIAL AUTONOMY

Journalists' Perceptions of Their Freedom

Basyouni Hamada, Sallie Hughes, Thomas Hanitzsch, James Hollings,
Corinna Lauerer, Jesus Arroyave, Verica Rupar, and Sergio Splendore

A comparative understanding of journalists' editorial autonomy is important both to journalism as a profession and to our comprehension of the
contribution journalism can make to society. The extent to which journalists control their professional activity includes the freedom they have in
selecting stories they deem newsworthy and in emphasizing certain aspects
in their stories. In this process of control, a core feature of journalists'
professional consciousness, namely, autonomy, which has a prominent
place in both professional and public discourse, is exercised. Journalists
around the world voice support for editorial autonomy as a protection
against state and other forms of outside intrusion or interference in the
editorial news-making process.

During the inquiry into the British press's behavior following the *News
of the World*'s phone-hacking scandal in 2011, the president of the International Federation of Journalists, Jim Boumelha, argued that journalistic
autonomy should be protected through a "conscience clause" in labor contracts. He posited that far too often, "journalists face the choice of either
undertaking work with which they are not comfortable or face the pros-
pect of losing their job."[1] In 2005 Mexican journalist Marco Lara Klahr,
speaking in favor of editorial autonomy from a democratizing country
where acceptance of power inequalities in society is comparatively high
(Hofstede 2001), criticized newsroom socialization processes that normalized submissiveness to editorial supervisors and media owners in his

country: "Mexican media have a decision-making pattern that is substantially vertical. We reporters are trained to follow orders." This becomes problematic, he added, "when there are ethical, intellectual, or ideological implications to following an order."[2]

From U.S. scholar John Merrill (1974) to Epp Lauk and Halliki Harro-Loit (2016) in Finland and Estonia, contemporary journalism studies scholars writing from a liberal tradition recognize journalistic autonomy as essential for the practice of authentic journalism, and to vigorous and self-assured journalists. A hallmark of professionalism around the world, autonomy's core insistence is one of self-rule without interference from politics and business; it works on the collective level to create a normative bulwark against interference from external influences (Carlson 2017). Not surprisingly, editorial autonomy, defined as control over work, is deeply built into Western normative discourses of journalistic legitimacy and independence. In this view, journalists as individuals and journalism as an institution need to be autonomous in order to execute their function in a democracy. Beyond longer-established democracies, journalists who wish to encourage democratization in their societies have adopted autonomy as a professional ideal (Waisbord 2000). Others have adapted the concept to fit workplaces where recent market-based economic reforms have liberalized the media's economic environment without changing political influences on the press (Li 2012). As we will see in this chapter, journalists in many societies face considerable limits on their freedom to select stories and emphasize certain aspects of stories. These boundaries range from governments prioritizing economic development, social harmony, or national security to de facto power holders such as criminal organizations and subnational political chieftains imposing their agendas on the news.

The objective of this chapter, then, is to compare journalists' articulations of editorial autonomy across the globe. We are interested in both the extent of editorial autonomy journalists recognize while producing news and the potential influences that may foster or limit this freedom. Journalists operate within a multidimensional environment of influences that can affirm or obstruct journalistic autonomy. In terms of the level at which these influences exert themselves, we focus on news organizations because both internal and external interests that potentially challenge journalistic autonomy are constantly negotiated within organizational structures (Hanitzsch et al. 2010; Hughes et al. 2017a; Örnebring et al. 2016; Sjøvaag 2013). Adapting concepts used in the sociology of structure and agency, as well as of collective action, we examine the restraining and enabling aspects of context; that is, the opportunity structure (McAdam 1982) of the subjective experience of autonomy. The main questions this chapter addresses, therefore, are to what extent journalists in different countries perceive they have autonomy in selecting news topics and story angles in day-to-day news work, and under what contextual conditions do similarities and differences exist in these perceptions.

The short answer is that journalists around the world perceive relatively high levels of editorial autonomy, with the exception of those working in a handful of countries within the most closed, that is, authoritarian political systems. In general, journalists in countries exhibiting greater levels of political liberalism perceive higher levels of editorial autonomy, and vice-versa. Further, higher levels of perceived autonomy are strongly associated with support for emancipatory values and with lower acceptance of power inequalities in society. Counter to critical political economic approaches, neither economic development nor economic liberalism in a society was associated with perceived autonomy. Human development in a society, however, was found to be related to perceived autonomy.

While our study finds that the political system in a country strongly influences perceived professional autonomy in all kinds of societies, similar to the finding of several cross-national studies (Hallin and Mancini 2004; Preston and Metykova 2009; Reich and Hanitzsch 2013), Katrin Voltmer (2013) has argued that the wider cultural context and historically embedded practices and memory of a society also influence perceptions of workplace autonomy. Thus editorial autonomy is an important, but contingent, experience for journalists in many countries around the globe.

Studying Editorial Autonomy

The notion of editorial autonomy can refer to both the independence of the journalistic profession as a whole—or "external autonomy"—and the freedom of individual journalists to do their daily work, which Gunnar Nygren (2012, 79) refers to as "internal autonomy." Arguably the two are interrelated, and journalism scholars emphasize the importance of journalistic autonomy at both levels, proposing that it nurtures a shared sense of professional identity and institutional independence. Not surprisingly, autonomy has a prominent place in journalism's professional imagination worldwide and is arguably negotiated in the workplace constantly. It is widely acknowledged as a fundamental requirement for professional journalistic practice and is commonly seen as a defining characteristic of journalism in the sense of a professional undertaking (Deuze 2005; McDevitt 2003; McLeod and Hawley 1964; Weaver 1998b). More widely, and not just in journalism, autonomy has been shown to positively influence job satisfaction and to buffer employees' health against the damaging effects of high workload and a time-stressed occupation. Further, autonomy promotes creativity and productivity (Falk and Kosfeld 2006; Lopes, Lagoa, and Calapez 2014; Ryan and Deci 2000).

In this study we focus on internal autonomy as an extrinsic dimension of journalistic culture (see chapter 2), defining editorial autonomy, in the tradition of David Weaver and colleagues (2007), as the latitude journalists have in selecting stories and deciding which aspects of them to emphasize. We consider editorial autonomy as a set of normative discourses as well as of reporting practices aimed at ensuring independence from external and internal influences. Within the liberal view of press performance, control over key occupational tasks is an indication of journalists' independence from forces that seek to exploit their work to advance particular gains (Hallin and Mancini 2004; McQuail 1992).

These potential forces can impinge on editorial autonomy at the institutional, organizational, or individual level. Using a sociology of work perspective, Henrik Örnebring and colleagues (2016) located the workplace at the meso level, which acts as an intermediary between influences on the institutional and individual levels. Based on an extensive literature review, Helle Sjøvaag (2013, 155) shows how the different levels are interwoven; journalistic autonomy is restricted by structures "at the political, economic, and organizational levels of news production, negotiated at the editorial level, and exercised at the level of practice." Relying on Anthony Giddens's (1984) theory of the duality of structure and agency, Sjøvaag argues that autonomy is not a static concept. It is continuously negotiated within economic and organizational opportunity structures, which both enable and restrain journalistic autonomy. Drawing on a body of work in sociology (Gamson and Meyer 1996; Giddens 1984; McAdam 1982), we use the notion of "opportunity structure" to refer to the complex set of external, organizational, and normative influences within which a journalist may act individually or as part of an occupational group to construct a subjective sense of occupational autonomy. Accordingly, journalists in this study construct subjective editorial autonomy from a location within the organization, which is, in turn, embedded in discursive and material societal contexts that may or may not be accepted without question within the journalist's professional worldview, or consciousness.

As an idealized editorial norm, autonomy became embedded in the editorial routines of Western-based global media companies, in the liberal ideology of a free press, as well as in journalism training materials, all of which traversed borders uneasily in the era of accelerated globalization after the 1950s, and arguably more intensely during the so-called wave of political liberalization after 1973 (Thompson 1995). As Western journalistic norms were disseminated through international education, organizations and media corporations, state-led "democracy building" efforts, or armed intervention, journalists in a range of contexts appropriated the concept of editorial autonomy and then adapted it to local circumstances. In many countries, journalists have traditionally been expected to provide support to authorities and to political, economic, and social development.

Editorial autonomy thus has become a central concept in contemporary journalistic culture beyond its originating societies in the West, but for different reasons and in different ways. On the one hand, the liberal normative model assumes that news media are relatively autonomous from the state and that individual journalists are agents representing the people, with independence guaranteed by the news media in which they operate (Nerone 2013). In countries where this is the case, it remains generally unquestioned among journalists, educators, and mainstream politicians that autonomous journalism and journalists are essential for participatory democracy (Gans 1998). On the other hand, in countries where the general pattern is that political media are closely censored and the state maintains tight control over political news, there is no editorial autonomy in any recognizable Western form. Journalists are considered integral parts of political, social, and cultural processes, and they are expected to cater to national imperatives, such as nation building, social harmony, economic development, or preservation of cultural and religious values (Bartholomé, Lecheler, and De Vreese 2015). In these cases editorial autonomy is at times associated with modernity or democratic aspirations within propagandistic public communication frameworks (Saether 2008) and at other times has coexisted with ethnic or ideological frameworks that seem incongruous with its original meaning (Relly, Zanger, and Fahmy 2015).

Between the fuzzier, but still clearly distinguishable, liberal and authoritarian poles is an increasing number of countries that are classified as electoral democracies and democratic-authoritarian hybrids where editorial autonomy has been appropriated as desirable (Coronel 2003). But the conditions for exercising this autonomy are unevenly experienced across geographic territories as well as across story topics and subjects. There are countries or regions within which the liberal ideal of editorial autonomy overlays realities where private news media owners, state media directors, advertisers from the private sector or the state, or de facto power figures such as criminal organizations, local strongmen, and rogue security forces dictate news agendas (Hughes et al. 2017a, b). Informal rules of clientelistic exchange and de facto power hierarchies have prevailed over formal constitutional liberalism in these contexts (Guerrero and Márquez-Ramírez 2014b).

Research on autonomy and general working conditions of journalists since the turn of the century suggests that the ability to exercise editorial autonomy around the world varies, as the globalized ideal collides with alternative normative traditions and unevenly hospitable contextual conditions. Thus while the norm of editorial autonomy has global reach, it is clearly a malleable, challenged, and context-dependent concept that has extended beyond the liberal democratic contexts in which it originated. Given its importance to journalistic professionalism and practice, we are therefore interested in measuring the degree to which editorial autonomy is present globally, as well as the reasons for these journalists' perceptions about their ability to exercise autonomy.

It is important to remember that, given some of the obvious limitations of survey research, the study did not investigate the actual or objective autonomy journalists experience in the real world but instead examined editorial autonomy as journalists perceive it. Clearly an assessment of the real-world autonomy of news workers would have required a different methodological strategy. Indeed, as previously noted, there is some evidence pointing to substantive differences between editorial autonomy as a normative ideal and journalistic freedom as a matter of reality (Hughes et al. 2017a; Willnat, Weaver, and Choi 2013). In this sense, autonomy may to some degree become built into the professional mythology, or *illusio*, of journalists, to use Pierre Bourdieu's term (Bourdieu and Wacquant 1992). As journalists learn what is appropriate and acceptable, they often perceive that they have more autonomy when in fact they are subscribing to the organizational or corporate viewpoint (Harrison 2000). We nevertheless believe that treating perceived editorial autonomy as an ontological object has a number of advantages. Autonomy is arguably a construction that primarily exists in subjective, relativistic terms. Capturing journalists' perceptions of autonomy renders visible the invisible, thus making it accessible to the researcher. Further, we believe that disqualifying journalists' ability to realistically, if not perfectly, gauge their ability to act exaggerates the limitations of our method. Indeed, survey evidence shows that Mexican and Colombian journalists were clearly able to distinguish levels of editorial autonomy they experienced depending on the material power or cultural authority of the actors in society they were covering, including members of organized crime, the armed forces, and politicians (Hughes et al. 2017a).

In this study the operational definition of editorial autonomy incorporates two important features, both of which are concerned with journalists' working routines. The first aspect relates to the freedom journalists have in terms of which story or topic to cover; the second aspect captures journalists' liberty in selecting story angles, sources, and narrative frames. Respondents were invited to respond to two questions: "Thinking of your work overall, how much freedom do you personally have in selecting which news stories you work on?" and "How much freedom do you personally have in deciding which aspects of a story should be emphasized?" Journalists were asked to choose between five answer categories: "complete freedom" (5), "a great deal of freedom" (4), "some freedom" (3), "little freedom" (2), and "no freedom at all" (1). For further analyses, the two individual measures were subsequently combined into a perceived editorial autonomy index by averaging the two variables across respondents. The resulting index was assumed to follow a formative rather than a reflective logic of measurement (see chapter 3).

The study operationalized the societal opportunity structure for exercising editorial autonomy in two ways. The first is perceptual: it asked journalists to identify the level of importance they attribute to possible influences on work from various sources, as discussed in chapter 5. The second is not: it uses objective, country-level measures such as political performance, level of human development, and cultural beliefs about the appropriateness of power inequalities.

Perceived Editorial Autonomy Around the World

Table 6.1 reports the global key information (mean scores and tests for country differences) for our two measures of editorial autonomy and an index averaging the two items. The table shows that, with a weighted mean score of 3.81, journalists report considerable autonomy within their news organizations in the sixty-seven countries of the Worlds of Journalism Study.[3] Although consistent with previous comparative evidence (Hanitzsch at al. 2012; Reich and Hanitzsch 2013; Weaver and Willnat 2012), this result stands in stark contrast to critical political-economic perspectives. The latter points to a deterioration of editorial autonomy in journalism based on increasing competition, concentration of ownership and/or corporate control, commercialization, as well as the exclusion of journalists from allocative decisions (Bagdikian 1983; Glasser and Gunther 2005; McManus 2009; Mastrini and Becerra 2011). The result also conflicts with facile interpretations of liberal-authoritarian continuums, where those working in less-free press systems must feel they have less editorial autonomy.

One reason for the inconsistency between comparative evidence and the thrust of critical economic discourse relates to the often-incommensurable perspectives of journalistic insiders and outsiders. As the works cited earlier—along with many similar studies—reveal, there is hard evidence for shrinking journalistic freedoms in the context of the economization of news production at a time of collapsing business models and pressures to produce more stories across multiple technological platforms. As journalists become professionally socialized into an organizational, or corporate, viewpoint,

Table 6.1 Perceived editorial autonomy—indicators and index

	N	Mean[a]	F[b]	Eta^2
Freedom in selecting stories	27,115	3.77	58.63	.125
Freedom in emphasizing story aspects	27,118	3.85	68.98	.144
Editorial autonomy (index)	27,274	3.81	77.34	.158

[a] Weighted.
[b] df = 66; all p < .001.

they may not be fully aware of these pressures. Similarly, unwritten rules or formal limitations on autonomy in state media companies may also be normalized. Limited editorial autonomy may thus become "naturalized" in day-to-day news work to the extent that the boundaries of journalistic freedom are taken for granted as an inevitable feature of news production. Journalists may then feel they have a great deal of autonomy simply because, within the limits of corporate or state media imperatives, they still enjoy considerable freedom in choosing stories and determining story angles. This is because news production capitalizes enormously on journalists' story ideas and individual creativity, for which a degree of intellectual liberty is essential. Furthermore, as journalists subscribe to a corporate or state-influenced logic, news decisions dictated by economic, political, and other external factors may begin to appear to them as their own choices. Even given this caveat, however, there are strong indications in about half the investigated countries that editorial autonomy has declined in recent years (see chapter 10).

The two aspects of editorial autonomy were, on average, very similar from a global point of view. As table 6.1 indicates, journalists around the world feel they have slightly more freedom in emphasizing aspects of stories than they have in story selection. This suggests that journalists have somewhat more control over stories that have already been chosen than over larger news agendas. In the newsroom context this certainly makes sense, as the selection of stories is often a hierarchical or collective decision, while journalists tend to have more leeway to emphasize aspects they think fit best into the story narrative when they write the story.

Also, the two aspects of editorial autonomy were highly correlated. Nonetheless, the autonomy to select story topics and the freedom to emphasize story aspects are more strongly correlated in some countries than in others. Generally, correlation coefficients were larger than $r = .50$ for all but five countries, and for forty-eight societies they were greater than $r = .60$. This speaks to the overall robustness of the editorial autonomy index that combines the two measures. The correlation between the two aspects of editorial autonomy was greater than $r = .80$ for Ecuador, Ethiopia, Serbia, Tanzania, Thailand, and Turkey but particularly weak for China ($r = .18$) and for the three Gulf states (Oman: $r = .23$; Qatar: $r = .31$; UAE: $r = .25$). The different strengths of the relationship between the two aspects of autonomy seem to reflect different approaches to editorial management and decision making. In some news cultures, stronger hierarchies may give journalists a great deal of freedom with regard to a given news item while they may have less leverage in selecting the topics and stories they cover. Other news cultures, by way of contrast, may cultivate a more egalitarian approach in which journalists are more or less autonomous with regard to both story selection and story emphasis (Dimmic 1978).

As noted above, journalists' sense of autonomy is generally relatively high across the globe. Among sixty-seven countries, the average autonomy score was higher than 3.5 in fifty-six nations and even greater than 4.0 in twenty-one countries—all on a scale ranging from 1 to 5, with the value of 5 indicating "complete freedom." Furthermore, in forty countries—a majority of societies included in our study—the autonomy scores ranged from 3.7 to 4.1. Journalists in these countries reported a great deal of editorial autonomy, with little variation between their societies. This observation is further corroborated by figure 6.1; country mean scores show a unimodal distribution, with most countries clustering in a relatively small segment of the scale.

Differences Across Countries

Despite these similarities, we can also see notable differences in journalists' perceived editorial autonomy between societies, as the F tests reported in table 6.1 suggest.[4] The values of eta squared, denominating the proportion of variance in editorial autonomy and its constituents that is due to national differences, suggest that overall, the national level accounts for considerable variability in journalists' responses, particularly for the editorial autonomy index, where country differences account for almost 16 percent of the variation. This amount of variance is substantive, pointing to significant differences among the countries. If we examine the two aspects of editorial autonomy specifically, we can see that country differences are slightly larger for journalists' freedom to select story topics than they are for their perceived freedom to emphasize story aspects.

Table 6.2 and figure 6.2 present a breakdown of country differences for our editorial autonomy index. Obviously, the general pattern of cross-national variation in journalists' perceived autonomy does not always follow the common regional, political, and economic classifications. Two general observations can be made, however. On the one hand, journalists

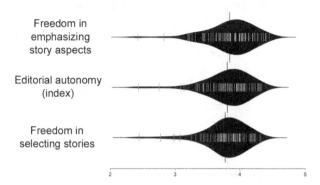

Figure 6.1 Journalists' perceived editorial autonomy across countries (distribution of country means)

Source: WJS; N = 67.

Note: Scale: 5 = "complete freedom" . . . 1 = "no freedom at all."

in developed democracies in the Western Hemisphere, notably journalists in the Anglo-Saxon world, tend to report that they have more editorial autonomy. In these societies the idea of journalism's institutional independence from other powers is built deeply into the notion of democracy and the press-state relationship. Editorial autonomy is usually protected through formal regulatory design, ethical norms, and sometimes—as Jim Boumelha's quote opening the chapter illustrates—labor contract clauses. Journalists report lower levels of editorial autonomy, on the other hand, in politically more authoritarian countries, where press freedom is often limited and governments maintain a strong state-run media. In transitional societies, such as Bulgaria and Romania, journalists' sense of editorial autonomy might appear to be strong, while their everyday practice reflects a very different experience.

This general pattern is not without exception. For example, journalists in Italy, Norway, and France report lower levels of editorial autonomy than do their colleagues in many non-Western countries. Italian journalism, for instance, is commonly characterized by a high degree of political parallelism, requiring journalists to follow editorial policy strictly (see Cornia 2014). Thus the limited autonomy reported by Italian journalists was likely the result of political pressures they felt, as well as their perceptions of a corrupt environment (Pellegata and Splendore 2017).

Table 6.2 Perceived editorial autonomy—differences between countries

	Freedom in selecting stories		Freedom in emphasizing story aspects		Editorial autonomy (index)	
	Mean	(SD)	Mean	(SD)	Mean	(SD)
Albania	3.74	(0.89)	3.74	(0.96)	3.74	(0.82)
Argentina	3.94	(0.89)	4.02	(0.91)	3.98	(0.83).
Australia	3.94	(0.77)	4.05	(0.76)	3.99	(0.69)
Austria	3.91	(0.66)	4.20	(0.65)	4.06	(0.58)
Bangladesh	3.77	(1.12)	3.86	(1.00)	3.82	(0.96)
Belgium	3.76	(0.79)	3.92	(0.75)	3.84	(0.67)
Bhutan	3.71	(0.73)	3.32	(1.02)	3.51	(0.78)
Botswana	3.66	(1.13)	3.76	(1.08)	3.71	(1.01)
Brazil	3.51	(0.90)	3.59	(0.87)	3.55	(0.82)
Bulgaria	4.16	(0.75)	4.28	(0.76)	4.22	(0.69)
Canada	4.01	(0.67)	4.14	(0.66)	4.08	(0.59)
Chile	3.74	(0.91)	3.77	(0.86)	3.75	(0.83)
China	2.98	(0.67)	3.20	(0.92)	3.09	(0.62)
Colombia	4.23	(0.95)	4.14	(0.95)	4.18	(0.90)
Croatia	4.10	(0.87)	4.20	(0.81)	4.15	(0.78)
Cyprus	4.22	(0.72)	4.27	(0.61)	4.24	(0.61)
Czech Republic	3.90	(0.84)	3.99	(0.81)	3.95	(0.75)
Denmark	3.76	(0.90)	3.93	(0.87)	3.85	(0.81)
Ecuador	3.86	(1.02)	3.86	(1.04)	3.86	(0.98)
Egypt	3.32	(1.12)	3.43	(1.17)	3.38	(1.06)
El Salvador	3.63	(0.97)	3.64	(1.01)	3.63	(0.92)
Estonia	4.15	(0.76)	4.40	(0.63)	4.27	(0.60)
Ethiopia	3.41	(1.08)	3.47	(1.07)	3.44	(1.02)
Finland	3.83	(0.64)	3.93	(0.62)	3.88	(0.56)
France	3.71	(0.79)	3.78	(0.80)	3.74	(0.73)
Germany	3.93	(0.88)	4.20	(0.86)	4.06	(0.79)
Greece	3.92	(0.88)	4.00	(0.83)	3.96	(0.79)
Hong Kong	3.07	(0.87)	3.21	(0.75)	3.14	(0.71)

	Freedom in selecting stories		Freedom in emphasizing story aspects		Editorial autonomy (index)	
	Mean	(SD)	Mean	(SD)	Mean	(SD)
Hungary	3.66	(0.90)	3.69	(0.92)	3.68	(0.85)
Iceland	4.17	(0.76)	4.23	(0.73)	4.20	(0.68)
India	3.90	(0.94)	3.93	(0.97)	3.92	(0.89)
Indonesia	3.46	(0.82)	3.52	(0.78)	3.49	(0.71)
Ireland	3.70	(0.84)	3.85	(0.82)	3.78	(0.76)
Israel	4.18	(0.93)	4.45	(0.83)	4.32	(0.81).
Italy	3.49	(1.04)	3.71	(1.00)	3.60	(0.94)
Japan	3.55	(0.73)	3.63	(0.69)	3.59	(0.65)
Kenya	3.71	(0.89)	3.70	(0.95)	3.69	(0.86)
Kosovo	3.91	(0.86)	4.00	(0.83)	3.95	(0.78)
Latvia	4.19	(0.65)	4.40	(0.61)	4.30	(0.57)
Malawi	3.82	(0.99)	3.83	(0.97)	3.82	(0.92)
Malaysia	3.44	(0.94)	3.45	(0.93)	3.44	(0.86)
Mexico	4.05	(0.96)	4.09	(0.93)	4.07	(0.86)
Moldova	4.00	(0.92)	4.08	(0.92)	4.04	(0.84)
Netherlands	4.31	(0.71)	4.36	(0.66)	4.34	(0.62)
New Zealand	3.99	(0.73)	4.03	(0.75)	4.01	(0.67)
Norway	3.60	(0.85)	3.85	(0.71)	3.72	(0.69)
Oman	3.25	(1.14)	3.45	(0.93)	3.35	(0.81)
Philippines	4.01	(0.75)	4.03	(0.75)	4.02	(0.70)
Portugal	3.99	(0.76)	4.23	(0.74)	4.11	(0.66)
Qatar	2.78	(1.28)	2.83	(1.21)	2.75	(1.06)
Romania	4.07	(0.90)	4.09	(0.96)	4.08	(0.85)
Russia	3.72	(0.95)	3.82	(0.95)	3.77	(0.88)
Serbia	3.80	(1.00)	3.94	(1.01)	3.87	(0.96)
Sierra Leone	3.69	(1.11)	3.81	(1.05)	3.75	(0.99)
Singapore	3.65	(0.68)	3.56	(0.74)	3.61	(0.65)
South Africa	3.79	(0.89)	3.85	(0.90)	3.82	(0.81)
South Korea	3.39	(0.75)	3.27	(0.74)	3.33	(0.70)

(*continued*)

Table 6.2 Perceived editorial autonomy—differences between countries (*continued*)

	Freedom in selecting stories		Freedom in emphasizing story aspects		Editorial autonomy (index)	
	Mean	(SD)	Mean	(SD)	Mean	(SD)
Spain	3.96	(0.89)	4.09	(0.83)	4.03	(0.78)
Sudan	3.75	(1.21)	3.68	(1.23)	3.71	(1.05)
Sweden	3.99	(0.78)	4.07	(0.74)	4.02	(0.72)
Switzerland	3.88	(0.67)	4.06	(0.67)	3.97	(0.59)
Tanzania	2.44	(0.82)	2.43	(0.86)	2.44	(0.82)
Thailand	3.77	(1.08)	3.80	(1.01)	3.78	(1.01)
Turkey	3.96	(1.12)	3.92	(1.12)	3.95	(1.06)
United Arab Emirates	3.68	(0.89)	3.23	(1.18)	3.44	(0.85)
United Kingdom	3.90	(0.86)	4.04	(0.85)	3.97	(0.79)
United States	4.24	(0.65)	4.34	(0.66)	4.29	(0.58)

The context-dependent nature of editorial autonomy is even more visible when we examine the situation in democracies where journalists who attempt to exercise autonomy are violently suppressed. A study by Miguel Garcés and Jesús Arroyave (2017) showed a strong relationship between perceived editorial autonomy and aggression against journalists. Specifically, in Colombia, where antipress violence has political origins, journalists have gained substantial freedom as a result of the peace process, which started in 2012. According to data published by the National Center for Historical Memory, the number of journalists killed has dropped sharply since then.[5] In Mexico, where journalists face extreme threats from criminals and unrestrained state governors, conditions are clearly different (Durazo Herrmann 2010; Gibson 2012). Hughes et al. (2017a) found that Mexican journalists perceive a great deal of occupational freedom unless they are reporting and publishing news about criminal organizations, the armed forces, and some politicians, especially outside Mexico City. In the Philippines, too, the situation is best described as regionally uneven. The People Power Revolution

Country	Score		Country	Score
Netherlands	4.34		Belgium	3.84
Israel	4.32		Malawi	3.82
Latvia	4.30		South Africa	3.82
USA	4.29		Bangladesh	3.82
Estonia	4.27		Thailand	3.78
Cyprus	4.24		Ireland	3.78
Bulgaria	4.22		Russia	3.77
Iceland	4.20		Chile	3.75
Colombia	4.18		Sierra Leone	3.75
Croatia	4.15		France	3.74
Portugal	4.11		Albania	3.74
Romania	4.08		Norway	3.72
Canada	4.08		Sudan	3.71
Mexico	4.07		Botswana	3.71
Germany	4.06		Kenya	3.69
Austria	4.06		Hungary	3.68
Moldova	4.04		El Salvador	3.63
Spain	4.03		Singapore	3.61
Philippines	4.02		Italy	3.60
Sweden	4.02		Japan	3.59
New Zealand	4.01		Brazil	3.55
Australia	3.99		Bhutan	3.51
Argentina	3.98		Indonesia	3.49
Switzerland	3.97		Malaysia	3.44
UK	3.97		Ethiopia	3.44
Greece	3.96		UAE	3.44
Kosovo	3.95		Egypt	3.38
Czech Republic	3.95		Oman	3.35
Turkey	3.95		South Korea	3.33
India	3.92		Hong Kong	3.14
Finland	3.88		China	3.09
Serbia	3.87		Qatar	2.75
Ecuador	3.86		Tanzania	2.44
Denmark	3.85			

Figure 6.2 Journalists' perceived editorial autonomy around the world (mean scores)

Source: WJS; N = 67.

Note: Scale: 5 = "complete freedom" . . . 1 = "no freedom at all."

in 1986, which ultimately led to the resignation of Ferdinand Marcos and the restoration of democracy, gave rise to a media system that vigorously maximized and protected its political liberties. Yet rankings place the Philippines consistently among the most dangerous countries for working journalists (Tandoc 2017); Filomeno Aguilar, Meynardo Mendoza, and Anne Candelaria (2014) note that journalists are especially vulnerable when contesting local power holders. Both cases—Mexico and the Philippines—suggest greater attention needs to be paid to local conditions because subnational variation is often submerged in national-level aggregate data (Hughes et al. 2017b; Hughes and Márquez-Ramírez 2018).

Within-country variation may come from other sources as well, such as international exposure and ideological polarization that is reflected in the media system. As the standard deviations reported in table 6.2 indicate, there is considerable disparity in journalists' reported autonomy, particularly in many of the countries with overall limited journalistic freedom to select stories and angles (notably Egypt, Ethiopia, Oman, Qatar, and the UAE). Among these societies, the greatest variation in perceptions of editorial autonomy is in Qatar, the home of the international Al Jazeera television network, which is among the media organizations enjoying the highest level of editorial independence in the Middle East (Hamada 2008), despite the fact that it is nominally a state-run channel (see also chapter 5).

Egyptian journalists, too, experience editorial autonomy at levels that vary widely. This variation likely reflects the uneasy state of journalism in a country that oscillates between democratic ambitions and an authoritarian legacy. The interviews in Egypt were conducted during the presidency of Mohammed Morsi, a man who was democratically elected by a small margin of votes. Journalists and media organizations, whether or not they supported Morsi, enjoyed exceptional levels of press freedom, "as voices opposing rule by the military, the Muslim Brotherhood, or actors from the Mubarak era, found ways to be heard" (Sakr 2013, 20). The overall increase in editorial freedom reported by Egyptian journalists (see chapter 10) does not seem to have transpired equally into the country's newsrooms, as the low average scores in table 6.2 indicate. Journalists working for printed media reported substantially higher levels of editorial autonomy, consistent with the behavior of the Egyptian press during the protests.

Generally, variations in journalists' perceptions of editorial autonomy within Western Europe appear more subdued when compared to the professional experience of autonomy globally. Journalists reported the highest levels of editorial freedom in the Netherlands, Israel, Latvia, the United States, and Estonia. Interestingly, the Baltic, Central, and East European countries included in our study, with the notable exception of Hungary, seem to broadly follow the pattern found in most Western countries. This is most likely a result of a longer adaptation process of journalistic cultures to Western European standards, which were brought to these countries through journalism training and textbooks as well as through European trade associations,[6] international media corporations, and foreign capital and media ownership. Furthermore, as discussed previously, the high level of reported editorial autonomy in newer democracies and hybrid systems indeed offers empirical evidence that aspirations for autonomy have been appropriated as part of country-level liberalization processes (Coronel 2003).

Overall, the cross-national variation in perceived editorial autonomy does not seem to map neatly onto common geographical patterns beyond the blunt comparison of Western countries with the rest of the world. In Western legacy democracies, journalistic autonomy grew out of liberal press system philosophies. Higher levels of perceived editorial autonomy seem to be associated with higher levels of political liberalism, or democratic performance. The increasing diversification within political regime categories during the twenty-first century and the way this has played out across different types of media demand more examination. Thus the next section aims to shed light on the contextual aspects shaping journalists' sense of editorial autonomy.

The Opportunity Structures for Perceived Editorial Autonomy

Table 6.3 reports bivariate correlations between country-level means for editorial autonomy, on the one hand, and selected contextual indicators as well as journalists' perceptions of influences (see chapter 5), on the other. Democratic development, as measured by the Economic Intelligence Unit's (EIU) Democracy Index, has the strongest, statistically significant relationship with mean levels of perceived editorial autonomy. The more politically liberal a country is, the more editorial autonomy journalists from that country are likely to report. This finding is very much in line with a number of

Table 6.3 Correlates of perceived editorial autonomy
(correlation coefficients)

	Editorial autonomy
Press freedom (FH)[a]	.484***
Press freedom (RSF)[b]	.407***
Democracy[c]	.522***
GNI per capita[d]	.071
Economic freedom[e]	.153
Human development[f]	.306*
Emancipative values[g]	.385**
Acceptance of power inequality[h]	−.357*
Political influences	−.506***
Economic influences	−.262*
Organizational influences	−.312*
Procedural influences	.130
Personal networks	−.249*

Notes: Pearson's correlation coefficient. ***p < .001; **p < .01; *p < .05; N = 67 (countries) unless otherwise indicated.
[a] Freedom House; Freedom of the Press Index; scale reversed.
[b] Reporters Without Borders; World Press Freedom Index; scale reversed.
[c] Economist Intelligence Unit; EIU Democracy Index; N = 66.
[d] World Bank; Atlas method, current US$; N = 66; current US$.
[e] Heritage Foundation; Index of Economic Freedom; N = 65.
[f] UNDP; Human Development Index; N = 66.
[g] Scores calculated based on WVS/EVS data; N = 58.
[h] Geert Hofstede, https://geerthofstede.com/research-and-vsm/dimension-data-matrix/; N = 51.

studies pointing to the supremacy of political factors in shaping journalistic autonomy (Hallin and Mancini 2004; Hanitzsch and Mellado 2011; Soloski 1989). Furthermore, analyses in the previous World of Journalism Study arrived at very similar conclusions (Reich and Hanitzsch 2013).

Figure 6.3 presents an illustration of this relationship. Western countries cluster in an area of the chart where both editorial autonomy and democratic development are high. Moving further to the left, we see another, larger group of countries consisting of many new and several old democracies.

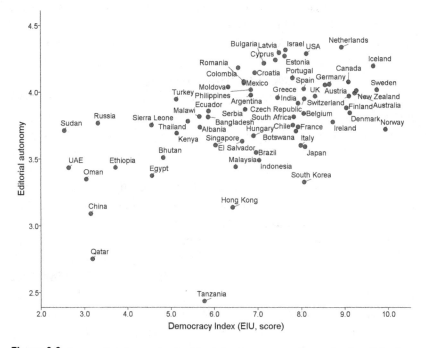

Figure 6.3 Journalists' perceived editorial autonomy and perceived political influences

Source: WJS; N = 67.

In these societies, most of which the EIU index flags as "flawed democracies," journalists report higher degrees of autonomy than their colleagues in countries scoring lower in that index. Societies that are politically more restrictive are located on the left side of figure 6.3; here, journalists on average seem to have less control over the content they produce.

Democratic development permeates the organizational environment through political influence, to which some editorial positions may be more exposed than others. Journalists in the higher echelons of the editorial hierarchy usually absorb political pressures and incentives. These journalists filter the influences and render them into editorial policy and inducements, which are passed on to subordinates (Hanitzsch et al. 2010; Sjøvaag 2013). In the previous chapter we saw a strong negative correlation between democratic development and journalists' perceptions of political influence.

Table 6.3 shows that these political influences have consequences in terms of journalists' sense of editorial autonomy. Journalists tend to report more freedom to select story ideas and angles when they work in societies that grant them greater political liberties.

The relationship between editorial autonomy and societal-level economic factors is much less pronounced. Neither economic development nor economic freedom is substantially related to journalists' perceived autonomy. However, journalists' perceptions of economic influence at the organizational level (profit expectations, advertising considerations, and audience research) do indeed show a significant, albeit weak, relationship with perceived editorial autonomy. Arguably, the relationship between editorial autonomy and its economic contexts is more complex and multifaceted than can be captured by a simple correlation coefficient.

As discussed in the previous chapter, these results run somewhat contrary to a number of studies, particularly in Western democracies, which argue or find that economic imperatives are the most important influence on journalists' work or news quality (Bagdikian 1983; McChesney 1999; Picard 2014). Based on the perceptions and reports of more than 27,500 journalists interviewed for this study in both Western and non-Western countries, it may be said that economic factors seem to be less intrusive than the studies above suggest. This finding points to at least two interpretations. Either economic influences do have relatively little power in the newsroom, or journalists are not particularly good at recognizing them. The first explanation does not mean that there are no attempts to address economic interests in the newsroom, for example, by management or by advertisers, but many of these attempts may simply be unsuccessful.

Overall, we tend to accept the latter explanation. As with political influences, economic imperatives may be absorbed and filtered by editorial management, and subsequently translated into primarily organizational constraints. Journalists have become socialized into the corporate view to the extent that they have learned to accept these influences and their consequences, in terms of restricted editorial autonomy, as a natural way of doing news. Furthermore, outside the Western world, it is also true that economic forces may pertain less to journalists in state-owned media or in societies where the state is the primary advertiser in private-sector media and where it maintains a relationship of clientelism with media owners (Guerrero and Marquez-Ramirez 2014b; Hughes and Lawson 2004; Hallin and Papathanassopoulos 2002). Both potential explanations call for deeper investigations of organizational processes. To understand why journalists perceive economic influences to be of less relevance, we need observational studies to assess how economic interests come to bear on news production, or how they are resisted by journalists in newsrooms around the globe.

Organizational influences seem to have slightly greater power in the newsroom, as our comparative analysis indicates. Journalists feel they have more editorial autonomy when they face less influence stemming from supervisors, higher-level editors, the management, and media owners, as well as from editorial policy. Clearly the relationship between perceived editorial autonomy and organizational influences rests empirically at the newsroom level. However, we think that contextual factors—notably those related to culture and general social values—also need to be taken into account. In several comparative studies, organizational psychologist Geert Hofstede (1998, 25) has noted some substantive cross-national variation in the extent to which the less powerful members of organizations expect and accept that power is distributed unequally. At the societal level, such acceptance of power inequalities is significantly associated with perceived editorial autonomy, as table 6.3 and figure 6.4 reveal. Journalists tend to perceive

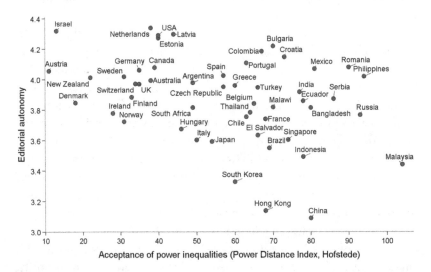

Figure 6.4 Journalists' perceived editorial autonomy and acceptance of power inequalities

Source: Geert Hofstede, https://geerthofstede.com/research-and-vsm/dimension-data-matrix/, WJS; N = 51.

less control over the content they produce in countries where inequalities in the distribution of power are generally more accepted than in others. Hence cultural notions about the appropriateness of power inequalities do indeed, at the macro level, shape the opportunity structure in which journalists operate.

Furthermore, influences stemming from personal networks—journalists' peers and colleagues, as well as their relatives and social communities— are related to perceived editorial autonomy, too. Camaraderie in the newsroom may be a strong force to assimilate journalists into existing newsroom norms, attaching editorial freedom to the acceptance of one's role in the organization. Another interpretation found in studies of journalists in societies where antipress violence is high is that journalists rely on one another to stay safe (González de Bustamante and Relly 2015; Hughes et al. 2017a). Hence group support enhances journalists' perception of control over work tasks, though the effect may run in the opposite direction, too. A shared sense of restricted editorial autonomy may well breed solidarity among journalists confronted with similar impediments on their work. Solidarity among Colombian journalists, for instance, has remained high over decades, as they learned that collaborative reporting helped prevent kidnappings, and joint publication lessened the likelihood of reprisals (Barrios and Arroyave 2007).

Finally, we found journalists' editorial autonomy to be significantly related to human development and the presence of emancipative values. Journalists tend to have greater control over the content they produce when they work in societies with higher levels of human development and a stronger appreciation of emancipative values. This result is very much in line with research indicating a strong association among editorial autonomy, human development, and good governance (Norris 2006; Roy 2014). It can also be related to Amartya Sen's (1999) notion of development as freedom, which suggests that individual freedoms are strongly connected to social development via institutional arrangements. A similar argument, based in a social values perspective, is made by Ronald Inglehart and Christian Welzel (2005), who have observed a long-term cultural drift that emphasizes the importance of individual autonomy, self-expression, and free choice. This emancipative value change has engendered emancipation from authority; over time, citizens have developed high aspirations to the social liberties to which they feel entitled. This is particularly relevant for journalism. In societies where people have a strong preference for emancipative values, any attempt to restrict editorial autonomy would trigger instant and strong resistance from journalists.

An important caveat for the present WJS is that it did not fully cover a number of contextual factors that have gained relevance fairly recently, including pressure from organized crime, rogue security forces, and subnational level political figures. Other significant developments are the rapidly growing role of social media and cross-platform publication within the same media outlet. Facebook, Twitter, and other social media platforms have become integral tools in journalistic work in many countries, but this happened only after the questionnaire for the current survey was designed in 2010 and 2011. Likewise, pressure to produce stories more rapidly and in forms that cross platforms also increased. We think it is likely that future studies will show that these developments have a significant impact on perceived autonomy. The impact might notably take the form of journalists having less time to produce stories and being exposed more directly to audience feedback, both positive and negative, including harassment and hateful comments (Brambila and Hughes 2019), and using social media to establish themselves as a brand (Hanusch and Bruns 2017). Further, for this book we have not explicitly measured differences in perceived autonomy within countries that may result from individual-level characteristics such as gender, ethnic minority status, years of experience, position of authority in the newsroom, or employment in different types of media, which some research has found important (Weaver et al. 1996; Hughes et al. 2017a).

Conclusions

Defined as an extrinsic dimension of journalistic culture, editorial autonomy is typically seen as a defining feature of professional consciousness and acts as a key narrative in both professional and public discourse about journalism. In this chapter we have conducted a comparative investigation into the extent to which journalists around the world feel they are autonomous in day-to-day news work. Our analysis has particularly focused on journalists' freedom, defined as the latitude they have within the organizational constraints of routine news production, in selecting story topics and emphasizing key aspects of a story.

Overall, in the vast majority of the sixty-seven societies investigated, journalists reported that they enjoy considerable editorial autonomy—a finding that runs counter to assumptions and assertions of weak journalistic freedom, which are common in the literature. The variation we discovered among the countries in the study suggests, however, that strong editorial autonomy is not a universal feature of journalistic cultures around the world. Cross-national differences broadly relate to—among other variables— democratic performance, human development, the presence of emancipative values, and the acceptance of power inequalities. These contextual influences are filtered through editorial organizations, which absorb external influences and translate them into internal imperatives and constraints. Assuming that editorial autonomy is related to actual control over work tasks, the opportunity structure for enacting editorial autonomy thus depends on how much leeway newsroom managers and editors have to translate liberal philosophies about the role of the press and support for equality in society into actual newsroom practices.

Journalists in Western democracies tend to have greater editorial autonomy than their colleagues in other societies; however, the demarcation and differences are not clear-cut enough to be reduced to a simple Western/ non-Western classification. There are a number of noteworthy exceptions to this pattern related to the fact that many nondemocratic regimes (e.g., China) do allow some journalistic freedom at the local level, while some developed democracies (e.g., Israel) are notorious for restricting press freedom.[7] Additionally, governments in other countries have developed more sophisticated measures of media control by putting an invisible leash on the watchdog, such as the practice of calibrated coercion in Singapore (George 2007), or through clientelistic advertising relationships (Guerrero and Márquez-Ramírez 2014b). As many studies have concluded (and Latin American journalists overwhelmingly recognize), there are no independent media in the strictest sense; all news media are shaped, constrained, informed, subject to diverse interests, and part of a network of relationships (Cheung and Wong 2016; Hughes et al. 2017a; Nossek and Rinnawi 2003).

Following Sallie Hughes et al. (2017a), we therefore argue that editorial autonomy is situational, contextually dependent, and historically contingent. Journalistic freedom exists in both liberal and authoritarian cultures to serve different purposes. In liberal democracies, editorial autonomy is considered a fundamental asset to ensure that individuals and institutions that are supposed to serve the public remain transparent and are held accountable. In other contexts, a different vision is articulated, one that conceptualizes journalism as serving the state's development agenda. Asian and African journalists, for example, have their own values that shape the role of news media and of individual journalists primarily to help forge public consensus for strong governments in pursuit of economic growth and social development (see chapter 7). In many authoritarian societies that have transitioned to democracy during the lifetimes of the journalists in our study, the expression of relatively high levels of autonomy, despite many forms of outside influence, may be considered aspirational or indeed a latent comparison on the part of journalists to the working conditions in previously more constrained circumstances. Qualitative and ethnographic observation studies are needed to better interpret the meaning of these responses.

As we have noted above, the high levels of editorial autonomy we have found among journalists from most of the countries included in the WJS stand in contrast to common criticisms that suggest prevalence of low levels of editorial autonomy, attributed often to the growing importance of economic factors. We believe a major reason for this dissonance is the fact that we did not study autonomy as it is actually exercised on the ground. Rather, the analysis presented in this chapter is based on journalists' perceptions of and self-reports on editorial autonomy. Further, when gauged in relative terms, responses may reflect journalists' tacit comparisons of economic pressures to other influences such as death threats or orders from bosses to please a local politician. As journalists are socialized into the professional norms and realities of news work, restrictions on their autonomy may become normalized to the extent that they appear as a "natural" feature of news production—the perimeter of what is professionally desirable practice. Benchmarks for journalists in countries that liberalized in the late twentieth century may be based on the experience of more constrained periods, in comparison to which the current experience may appear relatively highly free. Hence journalists may not fully recognize those boundaries as undue limits imposed on their work. Arguably, then, the high levels of reported journalistic freedom reflect in part the normative superiority of editorial autonomy in journalists' professional consciousness and the aspirations they hold to be considered professionals and part of an international professional community.

Our findings and data interpretations open a number of avenues for future research, as do trends that have intensified since the study was planned. Among our interpretations that need empirical examination are those related to the level of difference (or similarity) within societies and divergences from the general pattern of political liberalism driving editorial autonomy. Empirical questions include: How much of the intra-society differences and divergences from the liberal-authoritarian trendline is explained by regional and topical unevenness in autonomy to report and then to actually publish the news? How much do new actors such as unrestrained local strongmen or criminal and terrorist organizations explain this variation? Do norm diffusion and the formation of transnational professional communities indeed explain why journalists in newer democracies sometimes report higher levels of perceived autonomy than those in longer-established democracies, or does the reason have more to do with historical memory and referents?

Intensified trends that need examination include so-called democratic reversal and backsliding that have occurred in the past decade. In this context, how are mainstream journalists in many democracies and democratic-authoritarian hybrids experiencing the impact of political polarization, populism, and nationalism on their autonomy? Another trend that should be examined is the rise in multifaceted forms of risk. A multitude of questions can be asked to address this trend. What financial, physical, or digital risks do journalists perceive in their jobs, are they trained or otherwise prepared to respond to those risks, and what are the consequences of the risks in terms of workplace autonomy, journalism practice, and their own emotional and physical well-being? How do more than a decade of layoffs and increased labor informality in many developed countries affect the autonomy of journalists who have survived these cuts but seen salaries lowered and workloads increase? Yet another trend begging examination is the digital transition in journalism. How do digital journalism practices, including greater proximity to audiences through social media, increased workloads associated with cross-platform publishing, and the intensified pressures to produce "click-bait" sensationalism in legacy news outlets, influence perceptions of autonomy as well as practice?

This chapter presented an outline of how journalists perceive their ability to control their work product in countries around the world and in broad-brush strokes has identified some of the key reasons for country-level differences in levels of perceived editorial autonomy globally. The findings have generated many avenues to reach beyond the political regime explanation for autonomy, which, while important, needs to be pried open so we have a more complete understanding of what conditions allow journalists to act on their conscience and contribute meaningfully to their communities and world.

Notes

1. "Leveson Report on UK Media Ethics Draws Mixed Reactions," IFEX.org, December 3, 2012, https://ifex.org//united_kingdom/2012/12/04/.

2. Fidel Samaniego, "Los reporteros estamos formados para complir órdenes," El Universal .mx, December 6, 2005, http://archivo.eluniversal.com.mx/nacion/132883.html.

3. For the purpose of a global assessment of editorial autonomy, each country was given exactly the same weight in the analysis.

4. F tests were used to statistically test for differences between countries (i.e., between country mean scores) on a given target variable (i.e., editorial autonomy).

5. Centro Nacional de Memoria Histórica, http://www.centrodememoriahistorica.gov.co/. Chapter 10 also reports an increase in editorial autonomy over the past five years for Colombian journalists.

6. E.g., the European Federation of Journalists (EFA), European Broadcasting Association (EBU), and European Journalism Training Association (EJTA).

7. Reporters Without Borders, Israel, https://rsf.org/en/israel.

7

ROLE ORIENTATIONS

Journalists' Views on Their Place in Society

Thomas Hanitzsch, Tim P. Vos, Olivier Standaert, Folker Hanusch,
Jan Fredrik Hovden, Liesbeth Hermans, and Jyotika Ramaprasad

When the United Nations addresses the role of journalism in the world, it typically stresses journalism's capacity to foster democracy, dialogue, and development. The news media give people access to the information they need to make critical decisions about their lives, argued Secretary-General Ban Ki-moon in his message for the World Press Freedom Day in 2012. The media "holds leaders accountable, exposes corruption, and promotes transparency in decision-making."[1] These are standards recognizable around the world for the roles journalists should seek to perform in society. They are seemingly universal; but it would be misguided to assume that journalists everywhere agree with these norms or value them in similar ways. Democracy may be a touchstone in places in the West, but development may be journalism's raison d'être in parts of the Global South. This chapter explores the roles of journalism, finding areas of agreement and disagreement on how the world's journalists think about their societal roles and examining factors that might explain commonalities and differences.

Journalists are mostly place based and thus likely tailor their role to the particular local situations they face. If roles are locally stimulated and defined, then a rich variety of journalistic roles is possibly present around the world. At the same time, journalists in different parts of the world do at times face similar situations even within their local conditions. Does this lead to role similarity, a convergence, a shared understanding of the journalistic role? For U.S.-based journalist and media observer Tom Rosenstiel

(2016), the role of journalists is "to watch for public malfeasance, stealing, corruption, lawbreaking, private enrichment, rewarding friends, and abuse of power. Even in the era of declining trust in media, this role—the journalist as investigator—still gets high marks." However, do journalists in parts of the developing world, when faced with these abuses of power, also call for an investigator role? For Ghanaian journalist Mahama Haruna (2009), journalism must be "well-focussed on development issues, educating the public and entertaining instead of turning itself into an instrument of blackmail, intimidation, tyranny and an agent of confusion, conflicts, anarchy and chaos." Thus, even when confronted with similar challenges, journalists might think about their roles in ways that are situated within local, historical contexts.

This chapter examines the interpretative repertoires journalists employ when they think about journalism's place in society. We survey journalistic roles as markers of journalism's professional identity, focusing on tensions arising from a coexistence between institutional universality and global cultural diversity. An institution implies a shared set of norms, practices, and outlooks (Parsons 2007). This chapter puts this assumption of shared roles to the test to look not only for common but also for diverging roles; it also goes a step further to assess role hierarchies for similarities and differences. The results of this analysis have implications for how we think about journalism as a social institution.

Our results indicate that the professional ideology of journalists, as represented in journalists' answers to what they believe journalism's social role should be, still coalesces around key traditional values despite the field's transformation. Many classic concepts—informer, reporter, watchdog—continue to have widespread traction, indicating that even today these journalists generally conceptualize roles in terms of a political outlook. Further, analyses of journalists' responses about their own professional aspirations reveal that cross-national differences emerge across four role dimensions: monitorial, collaborative, interventionist, and accommodative roles. Among these, the monitorial role enjoyed the strongest global support. For the collaborative and interventionist roles, countries were most strongly divided in the importance they ascribed to these roles. An interventionist role was more strongly supported in less developed countries and societies facing disruptive changes, while a monitorial role was embraced more often in countries with democratic conditions and a strong presence of emancipative values. Finally, a collaborative role was associated with lower levels of democracy, and the accommodative role received greater support in more developed and stable countries.

Normative Roles of Journalists Around the World

Journalists define their social roles in various ways, helping them place their work within a framework of meaning (Aldridge and Evetts 2003). Perceptions and articulations of journalistic roles have long been a central focus of journalism studies, whether these studies focus on a single country or are comparative in nature. As we live in a time when journalistic ideals have become more ambivalent and liquid (Koljonen 2013), the study of journalistic roles has become even more dynamic and relevant. Consistent with the overarching theoretical framework laid out in chapter 2, we conceptualize journalistic roles as discursively constituted. As structures of meaning, they set the parameters of what is appropriate and desirable in the institutional context of journalism. Journalistic roles are never static; they are subject to discursive (re)creation, (re)interpretation, appropriation, and contestation. In the context of struggles over professional jurisdiction, the discourse of journalistic roles legitimizes certain norms, ideas, and practices and delegitimizes others. At the core of this discourse is journalism's identity and locus in society (Carlson 2017; Hanitzsch and Vos 2017, 2018).

Journalists generally articulate and enact journalistic roles on four analytically distinct levels: normative and cognitive role orientations, and practiced and narrated role performance (Hanitzsch and Vos 2017). These categories capture conceptually distinct ideas: what journalists ought to do, what they want to do, what they do in practice, and what they think or say they do. Journalistic orientations may not always, and certainly not fully, translate into real practice, especially when external factors constrain journalists' editorial autonomy. A number of studies in fact point to a "gap" between the roles journalists aspire to and the roles they execute in practice (Mellado and Van Dalen 2014; Tandoc, Hellmueller, and Vos 2013). At the same time, however, there is substantive evidence of a robust relationship between journalists' attitudes and practices (Kepplinger, Brosius, and Staab 1991; Patterson and Donsbach 1996; Van Dalen, de Vreese, and Albaek 2012).

For the Worlds of Journalism Study, we paid particular attention to role orientations, by which we mean discursive constructions of the institutional values, attitudes, and beliefs regarding the position of journalism in society. As indicated above, these orientations can be normative and cognitive. Normative roles indicate what is generally desirable to think or do in a given context (Schmidt 2008). Norms appear external to individual journalists; they encompass generalized and aggregate expectations that are deemed desirable in society (Donsbach 2012). Normative roles speak to how journalists are expected to meet journalism's social aspirations and ideals.

Fred Siebert, Theodore Peterson, and Wilbur Schramm's (1956, 1) premise that journalism's normative core "always takes on the form and coloration of the social and political structures within which it operates" still seems plausible today. This is because normative roles are generally discursively negotiated between journalists and actors within other social institutions (Vos 2016). Articulated from within Western notions of democracy, most normative approaches emphasize individual liberties and freedom. Many societies in the Global South, however, may prioritize collective needs and social harmony (Mehra 1989). In developing and transitional countries, journalists are often expected to act in the capacity of nation builders, partners of the government, and agents of empowerment (Romano 2005). From a comparative point of view, conceptualizations of normative roles need to account for such diversity—by including roles that emphasize socioeconomic development and partnership with government as well as roles related to the management of self and everyday life (Hanitzsch and Vos 2018).

Hence normative roles of journalists refer to the ways journalism should serve society. These expectations are articulated both in professional discourse and in broader conversations about the desirable place of journalism vis-à-vis the broader public. The WJS provides us with an unprecedented opportunity to examine the global panoply of journalists' normative roles. Typically, survey researchers mention a number of specific roles to journalists and ask them to indicate the extent to which they feel these roles are important. While we adopted a similar technique for cognitive roles (discussed later in this chapter), we used a more flexible strategy for the study of normative roles. During each interview we invited respondents to name, using their own words, the three most important roles journalists should play in their countries. This way we were able to capture journalists' interpretative repertoires by which they describe journalism's place in society.

This strategy produced a wealth of complex data. Overall, we compiled more than 70,000 entries from 20,638 respondents. Not all journalists responded to the question, some mentioned fewer than three roles, and several named more than three. In an attempt to reduce complexity, we eliminated responses that were not related to journalistic roles specifically but to professional standards and practices more broadly, such as mentions of "neutrality," "impartiality," "accuracy," "objectivity," and "honesty." We then inductively coded the remaining 45,046 entries into forty-one distinct normative roles, following a dictionary informed by both the academic literature (e.g., Hanitzsch and Vos 2018) and the coding experience itself. It took us several iterations to arrive at a sufficiently consistent method of coding.

Figure 7.1 presents a visualization of the forty-one roles in terms of their relative importance. Larger words indicate that the interviewed journalists mentioned these roles more frequently. Since some roles were mentioned frequently and others infrequently, creating a large difference in roles mentioned, we applied a square-root transformation to the frequencies. This allows us to also visualize the roles less prominently featured by the interviewed journalists.

The results clearly show that it is still the "classic" role concepts—journalists acting as "informers," "reporters," "watchdogs," "investigators," "monitors," and "educators"—that dominate the global imagination of journalists consistently across all sixty-seven countries. These six normative

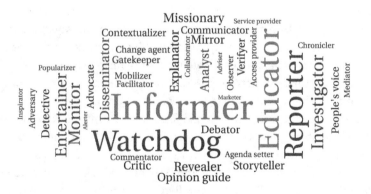

Figure 7.1 Visualization of roles mentioned by journalists

Note: Word cloud based on square-root-transformed frequencies; N = 45,047.

roles account for half the total number of answers. Furthermore, normative roles closely related to the news media's contribution to political discourse continue to reign. Thus, in the view of the journalists, certain normative roles, mostly those related to news media's contribution to political discourse, reign at the top of the hierarchy, possibly representing a longstanding professional premise, despite the fact that journalism as a social institution is in a phase of ongoing transformation. These findings are notable in that traditional concepts still dominate journalists' interpretative repertoires despite the diversity of global norms and stand in contrast to journalism's growing relevance for and contribution to everyday life and the management of self (Eide and Knight 1999; Hanusch and Hanitzsch 2013). Roles such as "service provider," "marketer," "adviser," and "inspirator" are still largely underplayed. Professional and public discourse tends to brand these roles as the unworthy "other," often placed in the context of increasing commercialization in the media, which is why many journalists may have found it hard to acknowledge them as normatively desirable roles (Hanitzsch and Vos 2018).

These responses thus impressively demonstrate that journalists around the world still see their normative roles primarily in the political arena. In all sixty-seven countries, political roles constitute more than 80 percent of the roles mentioned. The monitorial capacity of journalism as an institution to hold ruling powers to account is slightly more pronounced in democratic societies, but it also resonates in less democratic contexts. A large number of journalists in China, for instance, mentioned the "collaborator" role (33 percent), yet many of them also subscribed to the idea of journalists acting as "monitors" (35 percent). This finding is not necessarily a contradiction. Party leaders have actively promoted a media watchdog role to reassert control over a partly dysfunctional bureaucracy. By calling individual transgressors to account, watchdog journalism may even strengthen the party's legitimacy for policing the political, economic, and social boundaries of an authoritarian market society (Zhou 2000).

From among the frequently mentioned roles, it is only the "educator" role that journalists in non-Western countries mentioned more often than did their colleagues in the Western world (22 percent vs. 12 percent, respectively). Journalists in many Asian and African countries, most notably in Indonesia and the Philippines, as well as in Botswana, Kenya, and Sierra Leone, strongly emphasized a pedagogical role, through which journalists raise public awareness and knowledge about social issues (Statham 2007). Germany was the only Western country where a notable proportion of journalists (27 percent) mentioned the "educator" role, using the German term *Aufklärung*, a notion that also carries a meaning usually connected to "enlightenment."

While figure 7.1 reflects the dominant discourse about the kind of roles that publics expect journalists to perform in society, it also pinpoints a number of roles rarely mentioned in both the academic literature and public conversation. Examples are roles related to the development of public opinion, such as the journalist as "opinion guide," "commentator," "analyst," or "debater"; roles related to enabling "people's voice" by giving a voice to the socially disadvantaged (Janowitz 1975; Ramaprasad and Kelly 2003); and roles such as the "chronicler," who records recent history to be stored in collective memory, and "mediator," who strives to reduce social tensions and mediate between rival groups (McQuail 2000).

Further, many journalists, especially in non-Western countries, articulated a normative duty for intervention in social processes and for a more constructive attitude toward ruling powers. Emblematic of the social intervention role is the "change agent," a role also expressed by journalists in other studies (Chan, Pan, and Lee 2004; Hanitzsch 2011; Pintak 2014). Journalists who play the change agent role do not only report on social grievances; they also actively promote measures to remedy social problems and thus drive political and social reform. This normative duty was reported particularly from Bangladesh, India, and Ethiopia. In these and several other countries, journalists also emphasized the importance of a "facilitator" role, which refers to a journalistic approach foregrounding the media's constructive support of the government's efforts to achieve commonly shared social goals, such as social and economic development (Romano 2003; Wong 2004). In some political contexts, such as in China, this stance may ultimately lead to acceptance of government objectives, embodied in the role of the "collaborator."

Overall, this first analysis demonstrates that the normative core of journalism around the world is still invariably built on the news media's contribution to political processes and conversation, while other areas, such as the management of self and everyday life, remain marginalized. At a time when, in many parts of the world, the institution of journalism faces existential challenges and calls for reinvention (Waisbord 2013b), its fundamental institutional ideology, as articulated by journalists, still seems to be surprisingly intact. However, the question about the extent to which these normative premises are reflected in journalists' cognitive roles remains. The sections that follow address this question.

Cognitive Roles of Journalists: Monitorial, Collaborative, Interventionist, and Accommodative

Cognitive roles of journalists express the institutional values, attitudes, and beliefs journalists embrace as a result of their occupational socialization. While normative roles articulate a framework of desirable practice, cognitive roles represent journalists' own professional aspirations and ambitions. As a discourse shared by journalists, these roles tend to appear as evident, natural, and self-explaining; they act as markers of professional identity (Aldridge and Evetts 2003; Schultz 2007). In this capacity, cognitive roles often serve to maintain the boundaries of professional jurisdiction: between journalists working for institutional news media, on the one hand, and producers of user-generated content who merely reproduce the discursive techniques of journalism, on the other.

An overview such as this cannot do justice to the large body of research on cognitive roles. Early studies in the United States cultivated a distinction between neutral and gatekeeper vs. participant and advocate roles (Cohen 1963; Janowitz 1975). David Weaver and G. Cleveland Wilhoit (1996) suggested a classification into four roles—disseminator, interpreter, adversarial, and populist mobilizer—which would become influential for the field. The application of their questionnaire to a variety of countries culminated in two seminal collections documenting the professional attitudes of journalists around the world (Weaver 1998a; Weaver and Willnat 2012). Both volumes point to substantial cross-national differences in journalists' role orientations, which clearly speaks against the idea of a universal understanding of journalistic roles institutionalized in journalism globally.

The previous WJS arrived at very similar conclusions, finding major differences in the extent to which journalists want to involve themselves in social matters (Hanitzsch et al. 2011). In this chapter, we argue that cross-national differences in cognitive journalistic roles are primarily related to the way journalists emphasize four general role dimensions in their work: monitorial, collaborative, interventionist, and accommodative roles.

The *monitorial role* sits at the heart of journalism's identity in all developed democracies, but also in many less democratic societies. This role is broadly grounded in the ideal of journalism acting as "Fourth Estate," with journalists voicing criticism, holding those in power to account, and, in so doing, creating a critically minded citizenry (Christians et al. 2009;

Hanitzsch and Vos 2018). The legitimacy of journalists to act in a monitorial role is most strongly anchored in journalism's institutional position vis-à-vis political authorities. Journalists may exercise this function in a more or less active fashion. They might act as critical observers of institutional conduct (e.g., political decisions), responding to transgression as they become aware of it. Or, they may also proactively investigate and scrutinize government claims and gather information about issues they consider suspicious (Meyen and Riesmeyer 2012; Weaver and Wilhoit 1996). Watchdog journalism is even more assertive; journalists who embrace this mode provide an independent critique of society and its institutions (McQuail 2000). An important function of monitorial journalism is the mobilization of citizens to participate in political activity (Weaver et al. 2007). Journalists may act as agents of empowerment (Romano 2003) by framing the news "in a way that invites people into civic activity and political conversation" (Rosen 2000, 680).

A *collaborative role* is quite different from the monitorial role. In this role, journalists act as partners of the government and support it in its efforts to bring about development and social well-being (Hanitzsch 2007; Hanitzsch and Vos 2018). This role dimension calls on journalists to support authorities in defense of the social order against threats of crime, conflict, and natural emergencies (Christians et al. 2009). In this capacity, journalists may actively defend the government and its policy through acting as "propagandists" (Pasti 2005, 99) or as "agitators" (Wu, Weaver, and Johnson 1996, 544). As facilitators, journalists may voluntarily assist the government in its efforts to maintain social harmony and advance socioeconomic development (George 2013; Wong 2004), an approach that often emphasizes nation building and the preservation of national unity (Pintak and Nazir 2013; Romano 2003). Furthermore, journalists may see it as their responsibility to provide legitimacy to the government by explaining political decisions to the people and guiding public opinion (Lee 2001), for example, in the tradition of the Mexican *oficialista* (Hallin 2000, 99). In such a "mouthpiece" role, journalists remain markedly paternalistic toward "the people"; they ostensibly "improve communication" between officials and citizens (Chan and So 2005, 73), thus ultimately contributing to the consolidation of power inequalities in society.

An *interventionist role* is characterized by a strong disposition of journalists to pursue a particular mission and promote certain values. Interventionist journalists are typically involved, socially committed, and motivated to engage themselves in social affairs (Hanitzsch 2007). They tend to conceive of themselves as "participants" in political life rather than as objective bystanders. Journalists may act as advocates of particular groups and causes, missionaries for certain values and ideologies, facilitators of national development, and agents for change. Journalists may consider themselves as spokespeople for specific societal groups and their causes, or—more generally—for the socially disadvantaged (Ramaprasad and Kelly 2003). Identification with a particular group is at the core of advocacy journalism, with journalists acting as campaigners, as "lobbyists," as a "voice for the poor" (Pintak and Nazir 2013, 649). Journalists acting as "missionaries" often propagate particular ideals, values, and ideologies (Köcher 1986) or support specific causes, such as the preservation of Arabic culture or the interests of Palestinians (Ramaprasad and Hamdy 2006). Especially in transitional and developing societies, journalists also advocate for social change and drive political and social reform (Chan, Pan, and Lee 2004; Hanitzsch 2011; Pintak 2014). As agents of change, they typically emphasize quality of life, social equity, citizen participation in public life, and human development (Romano 2005). In such a capacity, journalists try to change society to what it might become, rather than just mirroring social reality (Wasserman 2013).

The *accommodative role* is, among all four role dimensions discussed here, most strongly oriented toward audience members as consumers, notably—though not exclusively—through providing orientation for the management of self and everyday life. Journalists who embrace an accommodative role strive to provide their audiences with the sort of information that appeals the most to the public. This role could take the form of consumer journalism, featuring various kinds of commercial products and leisure-time activities, or more generally provide help, advice, guidance, and information about the management of everyday life through "news-you-can-use" content (Eide and Knight 1999; Underwood 2001). This role of journalism has become important at a time and in places where identity work has become an individual exercise and traditional social institutions fail to provide collective orientation in an increasingly multioption society (Hanitzsch and Vos 2018; Hanusch and Hanitzsch 2013). In this role, journalists not only contribute to affect regulation (e.g., by providing entertainment and relaxation content) but may also stimulate rewarding social and cognitive experiences that contribute to emotional well-being in more complex and sustainable ways, for example, by fostering a sense of insight, meaning, and social connectedness (Bartsch and Schneider 2014).

The four role dimensions outlined above provide, we believe, a useful framework to account for the global diversity of journalistic roles. Each of these dimensions captures a variety of distinct journalistic roles that at the same time share a certain approach. The interventionist dimension, for instance, includes roles such as the advocate, missionary, facilitator, and agent of change. What these four roles have in common is a strong journalistic disposition toward involvement and social commitment. Furthermore, we argue that the way the role dimensions relate to one another reveals a theoretical structure of a higher order. The monitorial role, for instance, is likely to be inversely related to the collaborative role. Journalistic cultures that strongly embrace a monitorial understanding may arguably not be very inclined to provide unconditional support to the government. The underlying theoretical link, we believe, is the concept of power distance, defined here as the positioning of journalism vis-à-vis the power centers in society (Hanitzsch 2007). Journalistic cultures that value distance from authorities are more likely to embrace a monitorial role, while journalists who are or feel close to power centers in society may tend to see themselves as collaborators or partners of authorities.

Likewise, an interventionist role, which calls on journalists to transform society, may often be at odds with an accommodative role, which strongly appeals to the taste of the audience. The underlying theoretical link seems to be the source of journalists' determination of communication goals. Self-determined journalists define those goals (e.g., a better society) in their own intellectual and professional terms, while other journalists may ground communication goals more strongly in perceptions of audience demands. Pierre Bourdieu (2005, 42) has suggested that both approaches result from tensions between the "intellectual" and "commercial" poles of the journalistic field. At the intellectual pole, the journalistic logic is strongest, with journalists and media organizations forming public debate rather than merely reflecting it. On the other side of the field, societies tend to construe journalism's contribution as a service to the audience, though not necessarily because of commercial motives. Journalists embracing an accommodative role thus emphasize the needs and desires of the audience, or what they believe them to be. Interventionist journalists, by way of contrast, depart from their own, personal and professional, aspirations and provide their audiences with the content that they believe is critical to achieving social transformation.

These two higher-order theoretical dimensions, greater versus smaller power distance and self-determination versus audience determination, open up a relational space onto which we believe we can meaningfully map the cross-national diversity of journalistic roles. In such a "coordinate system," we expect the four role dimensions to correspond to vectors pointing in different directions.

Three qualifications are in order, however. First, we are not suggesting that theoretically linked role dimensions are mutually exclusive. The opposite of interventionism, for instance, is not an accommodative understanding but one that emphasizes detachment and noninvolvement (Hanitzsch 2007). Likewise, the opposite of a collaborative approach is not monitorial but rather adversarial journalism. Second, in the day-to-day routine of editorial work, journalists typically subscribe to multiple roles, often simultaneously. Hence the above dimensions correspond to ideal types of journalistic roles; they are a necessarily parsimonious representation of a reality that is far more complex on the ground. Rather than subscribing to a single journalistic role in its pure form, journalists, we assume, discursively position themselves on a continuum between these ideal-type role dimensions. Third, the four dimensions outlined above represent differences in journalistic roles at the aggregate level of societies and may not replicate well at the individual level—a phenomenon often observed in cross-national comparisons (Welzel and Inglehart 2016).

The results presented in this chapter are based on journalists' subjective assessments of the importance of eighteen specific professional roles. In the interview, the statements representing these roles were introduced to the journalists with the following question: "Please tell me how important each of these things is in your work." Respondents were then asked to rate the importance of these roles using a scale ranging from 5 ("extremely important") to 1 ("unimportant"). Tables A.3 and A.4 in the appendix present an overview of journalists' responses to the role statements, averaged by country and accompanied by standard deviations. A detailed discussion of all aspects of journalistic roles is beyond the scope of this book given the number of countries in the study. For such analysis, we suggest, a more targeted comparison of perhaps a few rather than many countries would be more insightful. For this chapter we constructed four indexes based on the above theoretical considerations. Like other composite variables created for this book, these indexes are formative, not reflexive (see chapter 3).

In technical terms, we computed the four role indexes by averaging the journalists' responses to all indicators that belong to the same index (that is, to the same role dimension). This strategy allowed us to retain the original scale of measurement, with a value of 5 pointing to maximum importance and a value of 1 representing no importance at all. Together the four indexes contain thirteen of the eighteen role indicators. The *monitorial role* index was built from four statements: "Provide political information," "Monitor and scrutinize politics," "Monitor and scrutinize business," and "Motivate people to participate in politics." The *collaborative role* index includes two indicators: "Support government policy," and "Convey a positive image of political leaders." The *interventionist role* index is composed of four statements: "Advocate for social change," "Influence public opinion," "Set the political agenda," and "Support national development." The *accommodative role* index is based on three indicators: "Provide entertainment and relaxation," "Provide news that attracts largest audience," and "Provide advice, orientation, and direction for daily life."

Global Trends: Monitorial Role Is Most Highly Regarded

Table 7.1 presents an overview of journalists' average responses to the eighteen key aspects of journalistic roles along with overall mean scores for the four role indexes. Consistent with the previous WJS (Hanitzsch et al. 2010) and other comparative surveys (Weaver 1998a; Weaver and Willnat 2012), the professional principles of realism, analysis, inclusiveness, and detachment seem to be canonical around the world. Across all investigated countries, journalists most highly regarded roles such as "Report things as they are," "Provide analysis of current affairs," "Let people express their views," and "Be a detached observer."

Notably, journalists tend to embrace the detached observer role even in societies in which we found a relatively high regard for an interventionist or collaborative role. Table A.4 in the appendix, which reports a breakdown of average scores for all sixty-seven countries, demonstrates that this is particularly the case in several non-Western countries, such as Oman and Thailand. This finding points to a—sometimes latent, sometimes acute—conflict between a professional understanding journalists were trained into, on the one hand, and a reality of journalistic practice, on the other. The ideal of journalists acting as detached observers and objective bystanders has been developed in newsrooms in advanced industrialized societies

Table 7.1 Journalistic roles across countries

	N	Mean[a]	F[b]	Eta²
Report things as they are	27,142	4.50	63.66	.134
Provide analysis of current affairs	27,023	4.08	53.98	.117
Let people express their views	26,906	3.98	64.61	.137
Be a detached observer	26,773	3.97	65.47	.139
Provide political information	26,779	3.71	55.37	.120
Monitor and scrutinize politics	26,767	3.70	73.98	.155
Advocate for social change	26,729	3.61	126.46	.238
Provide news that attracts largest audience	26,997	3.52	106.08	.206
Monitor and scrutinize business	26,767	3.50	61.96	.133
Support national development	26,417	3.45	206.02	.340
Provide advice, orientation, and direction for daily life	26,911	3.37	60.73	.130
Influence public opinion	26,670	3.36	112.30	.218
Motivate people to participate in politics	26,670	3.15	61.36	.132
Provide entertainment and relaxation	26,800	3.10	57.26	.124
Set the political agenda	26,409	2.95	81.38	.169
Be an adversary of the government	25,701	2.48	76.25	.162
Support government policy	26,382	2.21	298.77	.428
Convey a positive image of political leaders	26,435	2.10	205.41	.340
Monitorial role	27,213	3.51	77.46	.158
Interventionist role	27,208	3.35	207.62	.335
Accommodative role	27,300	3.33	96.93	.190
Collaborative role	26,732	2.16	306.27	.431

[a] Weighted.
[b] $df = 66$, except for "Be an adversary of the government": $df = 65$; all $p < .001$.

and has subsequently been exported to large parts of the non-Western world through institutional transfer, training, and education, as well as the diffusion of occupational ideologies (Golding 1977; Herscovitz 2004). Owing to the economic and cultural hegemony of Western media corporations, the availability of Western capital and funding, and the presence of media assistance programs, these values have become the global gold standard of news production. Journalists in the Global South obviously discursively emphasize these ideals, even when they may not be able to put them into practice (Mwesige 2004).

Aspects that relate to a collaborative or facilitative understanding of journalism's role in society, however, received very weak support from journalists. Around the world, journalists demonstrated relatively little appreciation for the statements "Convey a positive image of political leaders" and "Support government policy." In contrast to the more canonical roles reported earlier, the importance of supporting government policy and giving positive coverage to politicians is a controversial issue globally, as indicated by the large amount of cross-national variance we found (43 percent and 34 percent, respectively). Surely it would be hard to come across positive references to these roles in journalism textbooks; hence journalists may find it difficult to articulate or admit support for them even when they are enacted in professional practice, given the expectations they might feel audiences and interviewers have of them.

Likewise, journalists in a vast majority of countries found an adversarial role relatively unappealing. The statement "To be an adversary of the government" received support in just a few countries, such as Egypt, Kosovo, and Thailand. Arguably, an adversarial understanding is journalism's response to political and social ruptures that often create a strong public sentiment against the government. Egypt is a case in point. The surveys with Egyptian journalists were conducted in 2012, at a time when Muslim Brotherhood leader Mohamad Morsi was elected fifth president of Egypt by a slight margin. Public opinion and the country's intellectual elite were divided over his presidency at a time of heightened political polarization. The news media, enjoying unprecedented freedoms after the 2011 revolution, became a battleground for both revolutionary and counterrevolutionary forces (Alexander and Aouragh 2014). In June 2013 massive public protests, supported by highly adversarial media coverage, finally led to Morsi's removal from office by General Abdel Fattah el-Sisi.[2]

Space does not allow for a detailed discussion of cross-national similarities and differences for all eighteen aspects of journalistic roles measured by the WJS. In the following, we will thus focus our analysis on the four role dimensions, monitorial, collaborative, interventionist, and accommodative. Table 7.1 reveals a clear hierarchy of these journalistic roles around the world. The monitorial role was most highly regarded across the globe, though we found considerable cross-national variation (national differences account for 16 percent of the variance). At the same time, the unimodal distribution of mean scores in figure 7.2 does not suggest strong differences between groups of countries.

The finding is clearly different for the collaborative role. As noted earlier, the collaborative role is indeed little appreciated by journalists worldwide. The extent to which journalists think that supporting government policy and conveying a positive image of political leaders is an important aspect of their job, however, varies considerably between countries, as figure 7.2 illustrates. The distribution of country means is bimodal (or double-peaked), pointing to the existence of two larger clusters of societies. In a bigger group of countries, journalists strongly and fairly consistently disapprove of the collaborative role, while in another, smaller group of societies, this role seems to have some notable appeal to those working in the news media.

The interventionist and accommodative roles are seen as almost equally important by journalists globally. Cross-cultural variation is much greater (34 percent) for the interventionist role than for the accommodative role (19 percent). As figure 7.2 shows, the distribution of country means for the interventionist role yields a notable bimodal distribution. Societies are broadly split into two groups—one in which journalists are strongly motivated by an interventionist attitude, and another in which this

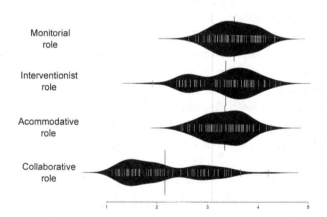

Figure 7.2 Journalistic roles across countries (distribution of country means)

Source: WJS; N = 67.

Note: Scale: 5 = "extremely important" . . . 1 = "unimportant."

aspect is much less pronounced. We explore the four role dimensions and country-wise differences in them in the following section.

A Global Map of Journalists' Professional Views

For the sake of parsimony, we base the following analysis of cross-national similarities and differences on the four higher-order role dimensions identified above. Taken together, these roles—along with their empirical indicators—yield a relational space that seems to cover a great deal of the relevant cross-cultural differences in journalistic roles. In such a universe of professional dispositions, it makes sense to interpret journalists' preferences for certain roles in relation to other roles. One methodological strategy to take advantage of relative dispositions is to center country mean scores for each of the four roles on the overall mean across all four dimensions. This technique has proved useful in a large number of cross-cultural comparisons using self-reported data (Fischer 2004; Hofstede 1980). Technically, centering converts "raw" country mean scores ("mean" in table 7.2) into relative mean scores, so that each centered value indicates the extent to which journalistic culture in a given country embraced a certain role more strongly than it did others.[3] Since centering can eliminate substantive information from the data (Fischer 2004), we interpreted centered scores in conjunction with the respective noncentered index scores. Table 7.2, therefore, reports both types of information.

Figure 7.3 provides an intuitive sense of the relative similarities and differences among the sixty-seven countries. Generated by the software tool *Visual CoPlot*, the map visualizes similarities and differences among countries in relation to the four role dimensions.[4] Since the figure was generated from centered mean scores, the origin of the four vectors (the role dimensions) represents the overall average (grand mean) for all countries across all role dimensions. Hence the location of a country reflects a national hierarchy of journalistic roles relative to role hierarchies in other societies. This way the logic of centering is applied to national aggregates of journalists' responses. Each centered average score indicates the extent to which journalists in a national journalistic culture embrace a certain role more strongly than they embrace others.

Table 7.2 Journalistic roles—differences between countries

	Monitorial role			Collaborative role			Interventionist role			Accommodative role		
	Mean	(SD)	Centered mean	Mean	(SD)	Centered mean	Mean	(SD)	Centered mean	Mean	(SD)	Centered mean
Albania	2.81	(0.86)	-0.22	2.14	(0.99)	-0.88	3.51	(0.72)	0.49	3.63	(0.76)	0.61
Argentina	3.66	(0.86)	0.57	2.22	(0.98)	-0.87	3.51	(0.86)	0.42	2.98	(0.95)	-0.11
Australia	3.25	(1.01)	0.53	1.57	(0.74)	-1.15	2.65	(0.90)	-0.07	3.41	(0.90)	0.69
Austria	3.31	(1.12)	0.62	1.31	(0.57)	-1.38	2.54	(0.80)	-0.15	3.60	(0.83)	0.91
Bangladesh	3.58	(0.84)	0.12	2.87	(1.17)	-0.59	3.79	(0.78)	0.33	3.60	(0.87)	0.14
Belgium	3.15	(1.03)	0.62	1.50	(0.66)	-1.03	2.57	(0.81)	0.04	2.88	(0.89)	0.36
Bhutan	3.88	(0.73)	0.44	2.93	(1.12)	-0.50	3.36	(0.83)	-0.07	3.57	(1.06)	0.14
Botswana	4.09	(0.83)	0.45	2.81	(1.20)	-0.83	3.76	(0.81)	0.12	3.90	(0.99)	0.26
Brazil	3.39	(0.90)	0.49	1.83	(0.90)	-1.07	3.32	(0.81)	0.42	3.05	(0.88)	0.15
Bulgaria	3.47	(0.98)	0.46	1.54	(0.80)	-1.46	3.66	(0.80)	0.66	3.35	(0.99)	0.34
Canada	3.59	(1.06)	1.05	1.26	(0.52)	-1.28	2.66	(0.91)	0.12	2.64	(0.91)	0.11
Chile	3.56	(1.09)	0.30	2.31	(1.13)	-0.95	3.72	(0.98)	0.46	3.45	(1.05)	0.19
China	3.18	(0.85)	-0.21	3.47	(1.01)	0.07	3.40	(0.73)	0.00	3.55	(0.76)	0.15
Colombia	3.94	(0.92)	0.30	2.71	(1.10)	-0.92	4.11	(0.76)	0.47	3.79	(0.96)	0.15
Croatia	4.31	(0.60)	1.05	1.87	(1.18)	-1.40	3.87	(0.78)	0.61	3.00	(0.91)	-0.26
Cyprus	3.23	(1.15)	0.37	2.04	(1.13)	-0.82	3.66	(0.86)	0.80	2.50	(1.04)	-0.35

Czech Republic	3.01	(0.95)	0.47	1.43	(0.70)	−1.12	2.73	(0.88)	0.19	2.99	(0.95)	0.45
Denmark	3.89	(0.61)	1.32	1.17	(0.37)	−1.40	2.76	(0.82)	0.19	2.47	(0.69)	−0.10
Ecuador	3.76	(0.89)	0.20	3.02	(1.21)	−0.53	3.87	(0.84)	0.32	3.57	(0.93)	0.01
Egypt	4.02	(0.70)	0.46	2.61	(1.14)	−0.95	4.00	(0.71)	0.44	3.61	(0.81)	0.05
El Salvador	3.92	(0.78)	0.36	2.74	(1.09)	−0.82	4.11	(0.74)	0.54	3.49	(1.01)	−0.08
Estonia	3.26	(0.98)	0.25	1.66	(0.77)	−1.34	3.43	(0.73)	0.42	3.67	(0.83)	0.67
Ethiopia	3.67	(0.87)	−0.07	3.41	(1.13)	−0.33	3.72	(0.79)	−0.02	4.16	(0.82)	0.42
Finland	3.36	(1.02)	0.70	1.23	(0.44)	−1.43	2.86	(0.76)	0.20	3.19	(0.75)	0.53
France	3.50	(0.84)	1.05	1.23	(0.52)	−1.22	2.44	(0.90)	−0.01	2.63	(0.86)	0.18
Germany	3.03	(1.24)	0.40	1.26	(0.53)	−1.37	2.44	(0.81)	−0.18	3.77	(0.78)	1.15
Greece	3.64	(0.98)	0.82	1.57	(0.85)	−1.25	3.18	(0.87)	0.36	2.88	(1.05)	0.07
Hong Kong	3.64	(0.77)	0.80	1.83	(0.96)	−1.01	2.93	(0.75)	0.10	2.95	(0.75)	0.11
Hungary	3.05	(1.26)	0.02	2.15	(1.23)	−0.89	3.24	(0.92)	0.20	3.70	(0.92)	0.67
Iceland	2.90	(1.05)	0.67	1.11	(0.30)	−1.13	1.90	(0.79)	−0.33	3.02	(0.86)	0.79
India	3.60	(0.84)	0.12	2.91	(1.19)	−0.56	3.71	(0.81)	0.24	3.66	(0.95)	0.19
Indonesia	3.60	(0.64)	0.09	3.21	(0.75)	−0.29	3.53	(0.65)	0.03	3.68	(0.64)	0.17
Ireland	3.26	(0.98)	0.62	1.44	(0.66)	−1.20	2.78	(0.90)	0.14	3.08	(0.86)	0.44
Israel	3.40	(1.08)	0.34	1.65	(0.95)	−1.40	3.83	(0.95)	0.77	3.34	(0.97)	0.29
Italy	3.12	(1.00)	0.68	1.35	(0.67)	−1.08	2.43	(0.79)	0.00	2.84	(0.99)	0.40

(continued)

Table 7.2 Journalistic roles—differences between countries (*continued*)

	Monitorial role			Collaborative role			Interventionist role			Accommodative role		
	Mean	(SD)	Centered mean	Mean	(SD)	Centered mean	Mean	(SD)	Centered mean	Mean	(SD)	Centered mean
Japan	4.01	(0.62)	0.95	1.65	(0.64)	−1.41	3.38	(0.70)	0.33	3.18	(0.73)	0.12
Kenya	3.52	(0.93)	0.05	2.94	(1.10)	−0.54	3.75	(0.87)	0.27	3.70	(0.97)	0.22
Kosovo	3.39	(0.98)	0.07	2.47	(1.12)	−0.85	3.78	(0.82)	0.46	3.63	(0.99)	0.31
Latvia	3.27	(1.05)	0.38	1.63	(0.83)	−1.26	3.53	(0.74)	0.64	3.14	(1.04)	0.24
Malawi	4.13	(0.75)	0.26	3.20	(1.25)	−0.67	4.13	(0.71)	0.26	4.02	(0.84)	0.15
Malaysia	3.48	(0.76)	−0.03	3.36	(1.03)	−0.15	3.53	(0.72)	0.01	3.70	(0.78)	0.18
Mexico	4.03	(0.73)	0.37	2.69	(1.04)	−0.97	4.22	(0.73)	0.56	3.70	(0.92)	0.04
Moldova	3.28	(1.03)	0.27	1.89	(0.82)	−1.11	3.58	(0.83)	0.57	3.28	(0.97)	0.27
Netherlands	2.75	(0.94)	0.20	1.58	(0.61)	−0.97	2.49	(0.76)	−0.06	3.37	(0.79)	0.82
New Zealand	3.39	(1.06)	0.75	1.42	(0.70)	−1.23	2.74	(0.96)	0.09	3.03	(0.93)	0.39
Norway	2.93	(1.05)	0.42	1.44	(0.60)	−1.08	2.85	(0.89)	0.34	2.84	(0.78)	0.32
Oman	3.37	(0.63)	−0.18	3.33	(0.87)	−0.22	3.75	(0.60)	0.20	3.76	(0.69)	0.20
Philippines	4.04	(0.77)	0.60	2.61	(1.00)	−0.84	3.85	(0.70)	0.41	3.26	(0.86)	−0.18
Portugal	3.71	(0.88)	0.94	1.51	(0.77)	−1.26	3.14	(0.85)	0.36	2.73	(0.86)	−0.04
Qatar	2.62	(1.12)	−0.54	3.33	(1.00)	0.17	3.43	(0.98)	0.27	3.26	(0.95)	0.10

Romania	3.18	(1.10)	0.19	1.79	(0.84)	-1.19	3.53	(0.87)	0.55	3.44	(0.95)	0.46
Russia	3.02	(0.84)	0.05	2.02	(1.00)	-0.95	3.33	(0.77)	0.36	3.51	(0.79)	0.54
Serbia	3.65	(1.01)	0.42	1.96	(1.09)	-1.27	3.90	(0.87)	0.66	3.42	(1.05)	0.19
Sierra Leone	3.84	(0.67)	0.13	3.01	(1.04)	-0.70	4.12	(0.65)	0.40	3.89	(0.72)	0.18
Singapore	3.19	(0.94)	0.05	3.13	(1.20)	-0.01	3.15	(0.88)	0.01	3.08	(0.88)	-0.06
South Africa	3.38	(1.06)	0.40	1.87	(0.99)	-1.10	3.17	(0.91)	0.20	3.48	(0.91)	0.50
South Korea	3.98	(0.67)	0.92	2.07	(0.76)	-0.99	3.46	(0.66)	0.40	2.73	(0.73)	-0.33
Spain	4.00	(0.79)	0.85	2.00	(0.87)	-1.15	3.53	(0.78)	0.38	3.07	(0.84)	-0.08
Sudan	4.32	(0.81)	0.36	2.86	(1.49)	-1.11	4.43	(0.60)	0.47	4.25	(0.78)	0.28
Sweden	3.93	(0.73)	1.36	1.20	(0.40)	-1.37	2.56	(0.88)	-0.01	2.60	(0.70)	0.02
Switzerland	3.34	(0.96)	0.72	1.39	(0.55)	-1.22	2.50	(0.77)	-0.11	3.22	(0.81)	0.61
Tanzania	3.85	(0.48)	0.41	2.10	(0.58)	-1.34	4.34	(0.49)	0.90	3.47	(0.39)	0.03
Thailand	3.95	(0.57)	0.10	3.65	(0.81)	-0.21	3.91	(0.55)	0.06	3.90	(0.62)	0.05
Turkey	3.66	(0.73)	0.50	1.98	(1.06)	-1.18	3.86	(0.77)	0.71	3.12	(0.98)	-0.04
United Arab Emirates	3.13	(1.14)	-0.52	4.20	(0.98)	0.54	3.46	(1.01)	-0.19	3.82	(0.95)	0.17
United Kingdom	2.99	(1.12)	0.48	1.41	(0.66)	-1.10	2.57	(0.91)	0.06	3.08	(0.92)	0.57
United States	3.97	(0.71)	1.24	1.51	(0.84)	-1.23	2.38	(0.89)	-0.35	3.07	(0.84)	0.34

As seen in figure 7.3, the representation of empirical similarities and differences among countries supports the theorized relationships between the four role dimensions and the underlying theoretical structure of these dimensions. The angle between two vectors represents the correlation between role dimensions; hence the monitorial role is inversely related to the collaborative role, and the interventionist role is negatively associated with the accommodative role. As reasoned above, a higher-order theoretical structure underpins the relationships between the four indexes. On the horizontal axis, the relationship between a monitorial and a collaborative role maps onto greater versus smaller power distance. A monitorial attitude corresponds to larger power distance, as journalists tend to see themselves

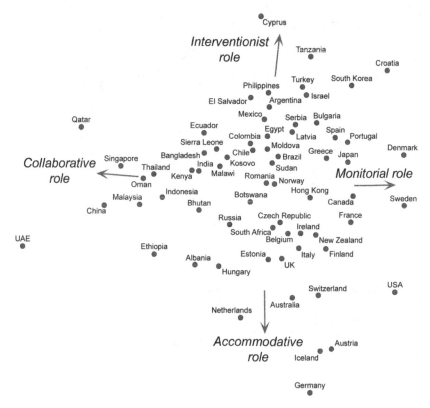

Figure 7.3 Journalistic roles—differences between countries

Notes: Coplot based on centered mean scores; coefficient of alienation: .15; average of correlations: .89; N = 67.

as critical watchdogs holding powers to account. For journalists following a collaborative approach, power distance is smaller, as they conceive of themselves as partners of authorities with whom they would work to achieve commonly shared goals (e.g., national development or unity). The vertical axis, representing an emphasis on an interventionist versus an accommodative role, is conceptually connected to the determination of communication goals. Journalists in contexts with a strong emphasis on the accommodative role, such as in large parts of continental Western and Central Europe, tend to see themselves as providing a service to the audience (audience determination). Journalistic cultures in Latin America, however, place greater emphasis on journalism's autonomy to determine its communication goals (self-determination). In other words, in societies with an emphasis on self-determination, journalists report according to what they believe is crucial *for* their audiences, while in societies that emphasize audience determination, journalists prioritize content that is needed or desired *by* their audiences.

Cross-national proximities in figure 7.3 do not point to clearly delimited clusters of countries, however, as cultural similarities seem to be a matter of degree. Countries to the left of the map, where power distance tends to be smaller, are slightly more coherent, while societies on the other side of the figure seem to be more disparate. Generally, countries located on the left side represent politically restrictive environments. In the quadrant located to the lower right (between the arrows representing monitorial and accommodative roles), we find societies that tend to be socioeconomically more developed than the countries in the quadrant to the upper left (between the vectors for the interventionist and collaborative roles). Despite the large differences between Western countries noted in several previous studies (e.g., Köcher 1986; Patterson and Donsbach 1996), journalistic cultures in these societies actually form a relatively coherent cluster here. Most Western journalistic cultures share an aversion to an overt collaborative and interventionist approach; they differ mostly in the relative emphasis placed on a monitorial versus an accommodative role. Overall, the differences in the prioritization of journalistic roles in Western countries shrink to relative similarity when positioned vis-à-vis global diversity.

As mentioned above, monitorial and accommodative roles do not necessarily contradict each other; journalistic cultures can embrace both a monitorial and an accommodative role at the same time. U.S. journalism is a case in point, as its location in figure 7.3 indicates. The drama and conflict built into the critical coverage of politics—the result of monitorial journalism—is highly appealing to a substantive proportion of the audience (Bennett 2016). In other words, there is little reason to think that monitorial and watchdog news are inherently unattractive to audiences. Overall, the importance of the monitorial role is undisputed among journalists in all Western countries. A major source of difference, however, is the extent to which journalistic cultures stress an accommodative role over an interventionist approach. Journalists in Spain, Portugal, and Greece, for instance, have a greater appreciation for the interventionist role compared to their colleagues in other Western societies. Other disparities include those between journalists in Western European countries, which have a strong tradition of media regulation and public service broadcasting; these seem to be related to different readings of the notion of "public service." German, Austrian, and Icelandic journalists, for instance, place their public mission more centrally in the context of detachment, objectivity, and "reporting things as they are" (see table A.4). Their Danish and Swedish colleagues, in contrast, define their duties more in their own terms—looking at journalism as an institution critically contributing to the exercise of democracy.

Our analysis also provides further evidence for the existence of multiple paradigms under the larger conceptual umbrella of development journalism, thus challenging the idea of a single, unitary mode of journalism aspiring to contribute to national development (Edeani 1993; Kalyango Jr. et al. 2017; Shah 1996). From figure 7.3 we can identify three distinct modes of development journalism: collaborative, interventionist, and monitorial.

The collaborative paradigm—sometimes discussed under the label of developmental journalism (Kunczik 1988; Ogan 1982)—frames development journalism as a practice in which journalists and state authorities work together as partners with the ostensive goal of bringing about socioeconomic development. Typically exercised in contexts where government maintains tight control over the media, its main responsibility is to publicize government policies, projects, statements, and activities (Edeani 1993). In a number of Asian contexts, the collaborative paradigm is culturally connected to the promotion of social harmony and consensus (Wong 2004).

Singapore is emblematic of this approach, which the city-state's founding father, Lee Kuan Yew, neatly summarized in a speech given in 1971 at the International Press Institute in Helsinki: "Freedom of the press, freedom of the news media, must be subordinated to the overriding needs of the integrity of Singapore, and to the primacy of purpose of an elected government." Over time, open censorship in Singapore has been largely replaced by self-censorship, achieved through economic disincentives against noncooperation with the state. Through "calibrated coercion," Singapore's government has achieved effective media control by way of creative legislation and by exercising fine political judgment to maintain a press system that balances government interests, the profit motives of publishers, the professional needs of journalists, and the public's demand for information (George 2007). Nicholas Frisch, Valerie Belair-Gagnon and Colin Agur (2017) have observed a similar tendency, which they refer to as "media capture," in Hong Kong after its handover to China.

The interventionist paradigm of development journalism calls on journalists to drive social reform and defend certain social, cultural, or national values (e.g., in parts of the Islamic world). Through a strong sense of professionalism, journalists assume a critical responsibility toward the citizenry and help audience members to be not only well informed but also meaningfully educated, motivated, inspired, and moved into action (Edeani 1993; Kalyango Jr. et al. 2017). In this context, journalists may act as agents of empowerment, foregrounding concepts of quality of life, social equity, citizen participation in public life, and human development (Romano 2005). In figure 7.3, the interventionist branch of development journalism is exemplified by the Philippines. Notably driven by the pioneering work of Nora C. Quebral, Filipino scholars have been at the forefront of promoting development communication as a distinctive area of inquiry since the 1970s. Since then, development journalism has found an institutional stronghold at the University of the Philippines Los Baños, which established a Department of Development Journalism, and another Department of Development Broadcasting and Telecommunication.

The monitorial paradigm of development journalism, finally, combines elements of social interventionism with a strong monitorial component. As figure 7.3 indicates, this approach is typical for many transitional democracies, including postcommunist societies in Eastern Europe. The monitorial branch of development journalism most strongly emphasizes a watchdog role that calls on journalists to highlight problems and weaknesses in government policies and performance, thus allowing for corrective action (Romano 2005). Based on a separate analysis of South African journalists, De Beer et al. (2016) argue that such blending of monitorial and "classic" development journalism powerfully challenges a long-held traditional dichotomy propagated by liberal and developmental media theory, according to which journalists should be either watchdogs or developmental journalists but not both at the same time (see also Hanusch and Uppal 2015, for a similar argument based on surveys with Fijian journalists). The evidence collected through the WJS clearly demonstrates that—in the eyes of journalists—it is indeed possible for the media to fulfill both roles. Notably, journalists in Spain, Portugal, and Greece come close to this paradigm, although it may sound slightly unconventional to group these societies under the label of development journalism. Nevertheless, such a classification becomes plausible considering the specific histories of these three southern European countries, which shook off their authoritarian heritage only in the 1970s.

Monitorial and Collaborative Roles

As noted above, the monitorial role tends to be emphasized more strongly in Western societies than in the non-Western world (see table 7.2). The power of a monitorial approach in journalism is clearly related to democratic governance and the extent to which societies maintain political freedom. Monitorial journalism is most pronounced in Sweden and Denmark—countries that continue to lead international democracy and political freedom rankings (e.g., Economist Intelligence Unit 2016; Freedom House 2015)—as well as in the United States, where the watchdog function of the press is grounded in a liberal pluralist understanding, which envisions the media as essential to the creation and maintenance of a democratic republic. Historically, this has contributed to an unshakable and almost sacred normative commitment to journalism as the Fourth Estate, providing a necessary check on the government (Brennen 2000).

The monitorial role is less emphasized by journalistic cultures in Africa (in Ethiopia and Kenya most notably), in the Gulf region (Oman, Qatar, and the United Arab Emirates), and in large parts of East, South, and Southeast Asia (particularly in China, Malaysia, and Singapore). In these societies, journalists enjoy little political freedom—obviously a prerequisite for the practice of monitorial journalism. This conclusion is also supported by the fact that Japan, South Korea, and Hong Kong, where journalists and the news media enjoy considerable freedom relative to other countries in the region, are the only Asian countries where the monitorial role is fairly appreciated. The results also show that growing restrictions on civil rights, political liberties, and press freedom are taking their toll on Russian and Hungarian journalists, as their relatively low mean scores on the monitorial role dimension indicate. Press freedom in Russia, as reported by Freedom House and Reporters Without Borders, has seen a continued decline since 2000, when Vladimir Putin was elected president.[5] Although less dramatic, we observe a similar tendency in Hungary, a member state of the European Union. The country's press freedom ratings have continued to fall particularly since Viktor Orban, leader of the national-conservative Fidesz party, returned to power in 2010.

Journalists from Turkey, on the other hand, reported a relatively strong appreciation for the monitorial role when the survey was conducted in 2014 and 2015, although the situation has likely changed after the failed coup in 2016 and the widespread crackdown and detention of journalists that followed. Furthermore, journalistic cultures in South America seem to be divided on the importance of monitorial journalism. Journalists in Argentina and Brazil—two countries suffering from political and economic crises leading to massive street protests against the government—place greater emphasis on the monitorial role than do their colleagues in Chile, Colombia, and Ecuador. This result is consistent with earlier findings suggesting that, especially during moments of political tension, Latin American journalists have a more critical attitude (Mellado et al. 2012; Waisbord 2000).

Overall, a monitorial role is much more pronounced among journalists in countries that provide them with greater media freedom and democratic liberties as well as in societies where emancipative values play a more significant role. This role can thrive best in societies where journalists enjoy greater editorial autonomy and experience smaller political, economic, and organizational influence. Table 7.3 reports a series of correlation analyses on the contextual level for each of the four role dimensions. The results clearly indicate that while democracy is not a precondition for journalism to exist, journalists need political and media freedom for a monitorial role to be practical. Figure 7.4 convincingly illustrates the close relationship between the prevalence of the monitorial role and democratic performance. Furthermore, the strong relevance of sociocultural value orientations as shown in table 7.3 is also consistent with results from a previous study (Hanitzsch, Hanusch, and Lauerer 2016). The global drift toward "emancipative values" is believed to give rise to postmaterialist values

Table 7.3 Correlates of monitorial, collaborative, interventionist and accommodative roles (correlation coefficients)

	Monitorial role	Collaborative role	Interventionist role	Accommodative role
Press freedom (FH)[a]	.657***	−.687***	−.172	.296*
Press freedom (RSF)[b]	.499***	−.552***	−.174	.311**
Democracy[c]	.679***	−.659***	−.195	.249*
Rule of law[d]	.429***	−.298*	−.437***	.279*
Transparency[e]	.438***	−.263*	−.507***	.281*
GNI per capita[f]	.313*	−.165	−.444***	.246*
Human development[g]	.427***	−.337**	−.282*	.201
Emancipative values[h]	.570***	−.533***	−.432***	.363**
Political influences	−.492***	.699***	−.010	−.362**
Economic influences	−.553***	.585***	.159	−.272*
Organizational influences	−.342**	.415***	.294*	−.435***
Procedural influences	−.016	−.028	.119	−.051
Personal networks	−.300*	.519***	−.262*	−.115
Editorial autonomy	.355**	−.502***	.030	.237

Notes: Pearson's correlation coefficient. ***p < .001; **p < .01; *p < .05. Scores for roles centered. N = 67 unless otherwise indicated.
[a] Freedom House; Freedom of the Press Index; scale reversed.
[b] Reporters Without Borders; World Press Freedom Index; scale reversed.
[c] Economist Intelligence Unit; EIU Democracy Index; N = 66.
[d] World Bank; percentile rank.
[e] Transparency International; Corruption Perceptions Index.
[f] World Bank; Atlas method, current US$; N = 66.
[g] UNDP; Human Development Index; N = 66.
[h] Scores calculated based on WVS/EVS data; N = 58.

such as individual autonomy, self-expression, and free choice and, ultimately, to promote greater emancipation from authority (Inglehart and Welzel 2005). Clearly, maintaining distance between journalism and social institutions central to the exercise of power (such as the government and political parties)—in other words, greater emancipation from authority—is at the heart of monitorial journalism.

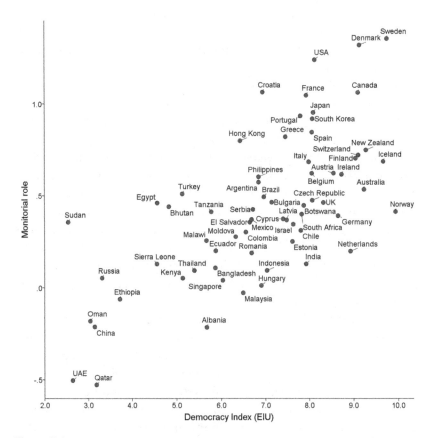

Figure 7.4 Relevance of monitorial role and democratic development

Source: Economist Intelligence Unit, WJS; N = 66.

Note: Mean scores for monitorial role centered.

The global spread of the collaborative role broadly shows a picture opposite to the one for the monitorial role, the former being less pronounced in most Western developed democracies, in large parts of East Europe, and in Japan. Supporting government policy and providing a positive image of political leadership is most strongly appreciated by journalists in countries that are socioeconomically less developed, in political climates that tend to restrict journalistic freedom, or in societies that combine both conditions. Ethiopian journalism is a case in point. The country is among the socioeconomically least-developed nations in the sample. Ethiopian authorities actively promote development journalism as the "official" reporting style for state media, effectively co-opting journalists to support not only national development but also government decisions (Skjerdal 2011). Likewise, journalists in China, Russia, and the three Gulf states are forced into a collaborative role in a political climate that leaves them with limited freedoms.

The situation is slightly different in Southeast Asia, where journalists also hold the collaborative role in relatively high regard. In Singapore and Thailand, journalists' stronger emphasis on a collaborative role is likely driven by a political culture unconducive to journalistic autonomy, while in Indonesia, the primary motivation may rest with journalists' responsibilities for publicly shared development goals, such as socioeconomic well-being and national unity. In many, if not all, countries in the region, the collaborative role resonates well with the idea of journalism being driven by "Asian values," which stress government-media partnerships to "promote the larger good of social harmony and stability together with economic growth and development" (Wong 2004, 37).

Altogether the collaborative role is much more emphasized by journalists in countries where the state constrains media freedom and political liberties, with journalists being less likely to act as watchdogs in a politically more restrictive climate. As the results reported in table 7.3 demonstrate, the appreciation for a collaborative role is stronger in countries where journalists face considerable political, economic, and organizational pressures and where personal networks play an important role as a source of influence. Figure 7.5 provides a strong illustration of this point in its depiction of the relationship between the prevalence of a collaborative role and press freedom as measured annually by Freedom House. Like in many other analyses reported in this book, however, the relationship is not deterministic. The locations of countries in the figure do not follow a straight line, which indicates that similar levels of media freedom do not necessarily coincide with a similar prevalence of a collaborative role. The comparison between Sudan and the United Arab Emirates is a case in point. Both countries score low in terms of press freedom but are different with regard to the dominance of the collaborative role. Furthermore, correlation coefficients point to a stronger emphasis on a collaborative role in societies less dominated by emancipative values. It is important to note, however, that with the data at hand, we are unable to quantify the true impact of a specific factor, such as press freedom, on journalistic culture in the presence of strong

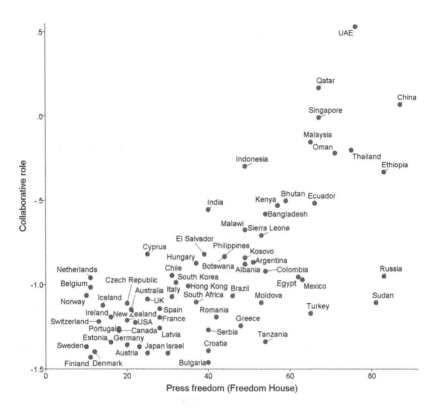

Figure 7.5 Relevance of collaborative role and press freedom

Source: Freedom House, WJS; N = 66.

Notes: Higher values indicate smaller press freedom; mean scores for collaborative role centered.

intercorrelations between contextual measures. In our sample, the Economist Intelligence Unit's Democracy Index is powerfully associated with Freedom House's annual Press Freedom measure (r = −.92, p < .001, N = 66) and with emancipative values (r = .78, p < .001, N = 57), while the World Bank's Rule of Law measure highly correlates with Transparency International's Corruption Perceptions Index (r = .94, p < .001, N = 67). Hence journalistic cultures do not necessarily depend on a single external influence but on a combination of factors that together foster specific national preferences for journalistic roles. This view of journalistic cultures, again, underscores the importance of historical and institutional contexts for the emergence and prioritization of journalistic roles.

Interventionist and Accommodative Roles

The interventionist role of journalists is, in relative terms, more strongly embraced in socioeconomically less developed countries. Consistent with previous research (e.g., Edeani 1993; Ramaprasad 2001), advocacy for social change, influencing public opinion and the political agenda, as well as the support of national development are media functions that journalists find important in many African contexts. A strong emphasis on interventionism is also a defining element of Latin American journalism, where it resonates with a journalistic heritage that championed journalism as advocacy and active interpretation of political reality (Waisbord 2000). Despite a notable move toward more independent and objective news, journalism in Latin America has historically been rooted in a tradition of ideological attachment and outright opinionated coverage.

Furthermore, our data point to a trend of journalistic interventionism being more strongly articulated in societies that are going through disruptive changes and where the political climate is permissive of journalists playing a more proactive role in political discourse. This is clearly visible throughout Eastern Europe, where societies have experienced a process of profound political, economic, and cultural transformation. Other examples are the European Union member states Greece, Portugal, and Spain, which were, at the time the surveys were conducted, in the midst of a severe economic crisis.

Different contexts seem to incubate distinctive approaches to interventionism. Journalists in Croatia, for instance, report a similar preference for an interventionist role as do their colleagues in Ecuador, despite strikingly different journalistic contexts. Journalists in Croatia combine an interventionist attitude with a strong monitorial component, while their Ecuadorian counterparts tend to blend journalistic interventionism more closely with a collaborative approach. Especially the latter example suggests a more general pattern in the comparative picture: if the impulse to political and social intervention coincides with a climate of tight political restrictions, journalists tend to displace an interventionist attitude and replace it with a stronger emphasis on a collaborative role. Journalists in Ethiopia and the United Arab Emirates are strongly inclined to advocate for social change and support national development, but in a political culture that leaves little space for dissent, they place less emphasis on setting the political agenda and influencing public opinion.

On the whole, the interventionist role seems to be strongly related to socioeconomic development, the quality of the institutional framework in a country, and the prevalence of emancipative values. As the results reported in table 7.3 demonstrate, journalists are more willing to take on an interventionist role in less wealthy societies and in countries where the influence and authority of law are relatively weak. Of all the contextual relationships, the correlation is strongest for transparency. Journalists are keener to embrace an interventionist role in societies that are less effective in fighting corruption. In societies facing problems of low human and economic development as well as strong legal and institutional uncertainty, journalists tend to be more willing to act as "agents of change" in order to fight social grievances and transform society—provided that the state does not substantively restrict media freedom and political liberties.

The accommodative role, finally, is most strongly articulated by journalists in most parts of the Anglo-Saxon world, namely, in Australia, Great Britain, Ireland, New Zealand, and the United States, but not in Canada. These are countries that broadly belong to the liberal or North Atlantic model (Hallin and Mancini 2004), in which journalism operates in a politically and economically deregulated environment and thus tends to be firmly market driven. Canada does not follow this trend, mostly because its journalists are regionally divided in their role orientation: journalists working for Anglophone media find the accommodative role significantly more appealing than those working for Francophone news outlets. Geneviève Bonin et al. (2017) found this to be a consistent trend among French-speaking journalists around the world. Francophone journalists identify more strongly with a politicized role rather than one that focuses on audience needs.

The roles of "providing entertainment and relaxation," "providing news that attracts the largest audience," and "providing advice, orientation, and direction for daily life" found considerable traction among journalists in Central Europe (Austria, Czech Republic, Germany, and Switzerland), Belgium, and the Netherlands as well as in many Nordic countries (Finland, Iceland, and Norway). Using the classification Daniel Hallin and Paolo Mancini (2004) have established, these countries belong to the North/Central European model of media systems that stands in the tradition of democratic corporatism. In these societies the news media tend to be seen as a social institution for which the state has a responsibility, while at the same time journalists enjoy a great deal of freedom. Overall, the importance of the accommodative role alongside a high appreciation for the monitorial approach among journalists in this part of Europe powerfully demonstrates that critical watchdog journalism can successfully coexist with an approach that emphasizes the needs and desires of the audience.

An accommodative role also resonated in Russia, where journalists score exceptionally low on the importance of the watchdog role yet they were not particularly keen to embrace an outright collaborative role. A strong emphasis on an accommodative role may be a reasonable way out of often conflicting expectations. Under conditions of tightening political control, it is arguably much safer for journalists and media organizations to steer clear of potentially dangerous territory by implementing a stronger market orientation—that is, by appealing to the "taste" of the audience through news that emphasizes entertainment and issues of everyday life, providing content such as celebrity, consumer, and service news. Here again we were particularly struck by the similarities between Russian and Hungarian journalists. Although the political situation in Hungary is by no means comparable to that in Russia, Hungarian journalists seem to have chosen similar strategies in coping with a sometimes hostile political environment.

Journalists in Portugal, Spain, and all of Latin America placed relatively little emphasis on the accommodative role. This, again, points to remarkable similarities between journalistic cultures in the Hispanic and Lusophone world. These regions are historically connected through centuries of colonial rule. Daniel Hallin and Stylianos Papathanassopoulos (2002) argue that in both regions, the conflict between liberal democratic and authoritarian traditions continued through most of the twentieth century. A greater prevalence of clientelism, in which access to social resources is controlled by patrons and delivered to clients in exchange for deference and various kinds of support, has made it more difficult for journalists to develop a sense of a public interest connected to society as a whole rather than to particular social groups.

Conclusions

As we have shown in this chapter, the normative core of journalism is still linked to journalism's political obligations. Journalists around the world cling to interpretative repertoires that broadly link the news media to the promotion of political self-governance by articulating support for such journalistic roles as being an informer, a watchdog, and a disseminator. Meanwhile, journalists express some support for being entertainers, popularizers, and advisers, but these roles have far less traction with journalists as normative goals than other roles. The domain of everyday life, while a seemingly important location for the management of daily life and a focus of much journalistic work (Eide and Knight 1999; Hanusch and Hanitzsch 2013; Hanitzsch and Vos 2018), is not a strong normative anchor for the institution of journalism as a whole, though it is the case in specific areas of journalism (e.g., lifestyle news).[6]

Overall, our results show that journalists around the world not only share a common understanding of how journalism should serve society but also have professional identities that seem to withstand, or ignore, the changing contexts of their practice. Despite a lack of rigid professional boundaries, journalists still tend to coalesce around a common normative framework of practice (Carlson 2017). In times of uncertainty, the professional ideology of journalism, as articulated by journalists, shows astonishing signs of consolidation around its key values (Wiik 2009).

For cognitive roles, the data show a clear role hierarchy around the world. The monitorial role is at the very top of the hierarchy, although more dominant in the Western than in the non-Western world. Meanwhile the collaborative role is located firmly at the bottom of the hierarchy, albeit valued more in the non-Western than the Western world. The interventionist and accommodative roles find similar levels of support around the world, with the former more strongly supported in less developed countries and countries facing disruptive changes, and the latter garnering greater support in more developed and stable countries. Global diversity is also apparent within the bounds of seemingly similar journalistic traditions. While journalists in the Western world are strongly supportive of the monitorial role, they are nevertheless divided by orientation into the accommodative versus the interventionist role. Likewise, development journalism is refracted through differing orientations toward the collaborative, interventionist, and monitorial roles. This reminds us that development and democracy are not mutually exclusive bases for journalism.

That being said, the data presented in this chapter show that democratic conditions and the strong presence of emancipative values favor journalistic cultures embracing a monitorial role. Lower levels of democracy, meanwhile, are associated with a collaborative role. These results provide further support for the importance of the political context as a major source of cross-national variation in journalistic cultures, an argument found in much comparative journalism research (Gurevitch and Blumler 2004; Hallin and Mancini 2004; Weaver 1998a). Taken as a whole, the monitorial role finds the strongest support around the world, but political, economic, social, and cultural factors all illuminate global diversity in journalistic roles. This lends support to the basic proposition that social systems leave an imprint on journalistic roles (Siebert, Peterson, and Schramm 1956; Vos 2016), but it also points to global similarities, particularly in terms of a monitorial role, that transcend local contexts (Hanitzsch et al. 2011).

This chapter aids in the theorization and conceptualization of journalistic roles. In some journalistic cultures it is common for journalists to collaborate *with* those in power, while in other societies, journalists are monitorial *of* those in power. Hence the underlying theoretical structure is based on how power distance is valued (Hanitzsch 2007). Likewise, in some journalistic cultures, journalists are interventionist *in* social affairs, driven by self-determination, while in other countries, journalists are accommodative *to* their audiences, driven by audience determination. Here the underlying structure is based on the locus of determination. Role orientation, then, is a matter of how journalists think about their social purpose and to whom and how they direct their ambitions.

This chapter used a slightly different nomenclature to identify journalists' cognitive roles from that used in previous studies. We do this advisedly, mindful of using concepts with familiarity, resonance, and parsimony (Gerring 1999). The monitorial and collaborative roles have a recognizable denotation tied to existing scholarship (e.g., Christians et al. 2009; Hanitzsch et al. 2011). Those meanings are tapped here. The interventionist role is derived from previous work by Thomas Hanitzsch (2007) that conceptualized interventionism as a theoretical dimension of journalistic roles. That meaning is fleshed out here as a journalistic role focused on the pursuit of a journalistic mission and the promotion of certain social values. The accommodative role, meanwhile, is largely a new label. We believe it captures a theoretically coherent cognitive role, while avoiding excess meaning from previous terms in the roles literature, such as populist mobilizer (Weaver and Wilhoit 1997). The accommodative role, still underarticulated in normative terms, is nevertheless a distinct role, often dealing with matters of everyday life.

Further studies should devote greater attention to this journalistic role, and they need to spell out the theoretical links between the various forms of journalistic roles (between normative and cognitive roles, for instance) and investigate the causal mechanisms by which journalists are enacting their role orientations in everyday news work. In the following chapters we will thus explore the extent to which journalistic roles drive journalists' understandings of ethical conduct and trust in public institutions.

Notes

1. United Nations, World Press Freedom Day, 2012, https://www.un.org/sg/en/content/sg/statement/2012-05-03/secretary-generals-message-world-press-freedom-day.
2. Freedom House, Freedom of the Press Report, Egypt, 2013, https://freedomhouse.org/report/freedom-press/2013/egypt.
3. To obtain centered scores, we proceeded as follows: We first computed "raw" country mean scores for the four indexes of journalistic roles ("mean" in table 7.2). Then we calculated the average mean for every country by averaging the four raw means. Finally we subtracted the average mean from each of the four raw means, again for each country separately. The resulting scores average to zero for every country, which has the advantage that it removes potential acquiescence bias from the data, that is, the general tendency of respondents in some countries to respond more positively or negatively to a given survey question regardless of its content.
4. CoPlot is an adaptation of multidimensional scaling (MDS), which we used in chapter 5 to visualize cross-national differences for perceived influences on news work. Like MDS, CoPlot is a method for the graphical analysis of multivariate data. The advantage of CoPlot over similar techniques is that it enables simultaneous analysis of both observations (in our case countries, or national journalistic cultures) and variables (i.e., the four role indexes) in one model (Bravata et al. 2008). The software tool *Visual CoPlot* was developed by David Talby and Adi Raveh (http://davidtalby.com/vcoplot/). In our analysis, the coefficient of alienation, indicating the loss of information arising from the transformation of multidimensional data into two dimensions, amounts to .15, and correlations between vectors average to .89. This points to a reasonable empirical solution (Bravata et al. 2008).
5. Reporters Without Borders, World Press Freedom Index, 2018, https://rsf.org/en/ranking.
6. Lifestyle journalists in our sample have a significantly higher appreciation for the accommodation role than do their colleagues in other areas of journalism.

8

ETHICAL CONSIDERATIONS

Journalists' Perceptions of Professional Practice

Jyotika Ramaprasad, Thomas Hanitzsch, Epp Lauk, Halliki Harro-Loit,
Jan Fredrik Hovden, Jari Väliverronen, and Stephanie Craft

In India, a journalist (who was promised confidentiality) reflects on an ethical dilemma she faces in her daily practice: "Many times, many times, many times. People wanted to give me money or a bribe to publish, but I just very politely, I declined."[1] This journalist's dilemma is not unique. On a day-to-day basis journalists are required to make decisions of an ethical nature as they go about covering the news, whether about engaging in paid news, as in the case above, or, as illustrated by the following case, reporting on a story that is not fully verified.

Sunil Tripathi, a 22-year-old student at Brown University in the United States, had been missing for a month before the Boston Marathon bombing in April 2013. To find him, his family had set up a Facebook page with his photograph. When the FBI released photos of two suspects, a Reddit user posted Tripathi's picture next to that of one of the suspects and made comparisons.[2] A sequence of online posts, tweets, and retweets followed, including from journalists (Kang 2013). Concerned about consequences, the family took down the Facebook page, but this only served to fuel more online activity. A few days later, after the real suspects were identified, Tripathi's body was found in the Providence River, a case of suicide. Some journalists apologized to the family, but Tripathi's reputation was destroyed, and his family had gone through a nightmare.

Journalism is often posited rather straightforwardly as a "moral calling," a profession that, when well executed, fulfills "human telos, or natural purpose," that is, "the good of a whole virtuous life" that includes promoting the common good (Borden 2010, 54). Journalism is also, however, a profession whose practice is often affected by a host of factors, both within the institution of journalism and at the societal level. Given these contexts, the question of the common good is rarely an easy negotiation, within the community of journalists as well as between journalists and various societal agents (see chapters 5 and 7). This situation is exacerbated today because "ethical journalism has rarely been under such sustained pressure, both political and commercial" (White 2017, 4).

Within this framework, we understand journalism as a continuously changing discursive institution that builds its legitimacy and sets its boundaries through constant negotiation with the larger society (see chapter 2). Journalists and news organizations bring their own perspectives, from which vantage point they continuously interact among themselves and with external agents, who in turn have their own ideologies and agendas. It is within this discursive practice that journalistic conventions and practices are legitimized or delegitimized, including in the realm of journalistic ethics wherein ethical principles and professional practices are defined and articulated.

The conditions journalists have to negotiate are not universal; instead, they are heavily informed by "the particular historical circumstances of [their] country" (Richards 2010, 180; also see Gamson and Meyer 1996; McAdam 2010; Shoemaker and Reese 2013). As these differ across nations, so do the results of the discursive processes. This plurality of outcomes is represented in the notion of journalistic culture. One of the key ways in which this culture is articulated is through professional ethics. It is said of ethics in general, and is likely true of journalism ethics too, that "only some ethical knowledge is global—most is local, and appropriately so" (Flanagan, Sarkissian, and Wong 2008, 19; also see Plaisance 2011). Thus, for example, while what is deception rests on negotiated meanings within an occupation (Lambeth 1992; Lee 2004; Luljak 2000), it is also determined by such meanings within a country. As Seow Ting Lee (2004, 116) points out, journalistic deception "as defined by American journalists is likely to differ from the journalistic deception constructed by Japanese or Brazilian journalists." Bala Musa and Jerry Komia Domatob (2007, 320) make a similar argument: "When First World and Third World journalists say they are committed to truth, freedom, and the common good, they each have different understandings of these concepts or pursue them through different means."

We focus on ethics practice and orientation as sites in which national-level similarities and differences might materialize. This chapter draws a comparative picture of journalists' general ethical orientations in sixty-six countries,[3] as well as their positions on the justifiability of controversial practices in sixty-seven countries. Recognizing that ethical orientations and news-gathering practices are part of the discursive process that does not occur in a vacuum, the chapter explores the relationship between these two manifestations of journalistic culture and contextual factors. At the societal level, these contextual factors, or opportunity structures (McAdam 2010), are related to politics and governance, socioeconomic development, and cultural value systems. At the professional level, they are journalists' perceived autonomy, influences, and roles. In a relatively new approach, the chapter also explores how journalists' ethical orientations might relate to their perception of the justifiability of specific news-gathering practices.

As we will show, absolutism was the most preferred ethical orientation globally. Regionally, the Global North was most aligned with absolutism, which in turn was related to higher freedoms and the monitorial role and to lower societal and professional influences. These characteristics, and thus the Global North, with its greater freedoms and fewer influences, were related to greater approval of controversial news-gathering practices. The Middle East and North Africa were aligned with subjectivism, which was associated in turn with lower freedoms, greater influences, and a collaborative role, as well as lower approval of controversial practices. Situationism and exceptionism did not display strong regional patterns.

Conceptualizing and Measuring Journalistic Ethical Orientations and Controversial News-Gathering Practices

Unlike our dual focus on practices and orientations, comparative studies of journalism ethics typically focus only on the way journalists perceive news-gathering practices that are often assumed to be controversial within the profession (i.e., *justification of reporting practices*). Surveys of journalists around the world widely use this approach, as documented, for instance, in Weaver and Wilhoit (1986, 1996), Weaver (1998a), Weaver and Willnat (2012), and Weaver et al. (2007). These works have served as a significant source for research into questionable journalistic practices, and we too turn to them for guidance on this aspect of journalistic cultures.

Among the controversial news-gathering practices that have long been debated in professional ethics are issues of deception, loyalty to various stakeholders, and journalists' autonomy and truth telling (Christians, Rotzoll, and Fackler 1991; Harro-Loit 2015; Klaidman and Beauchamp 1987). When journalists pay for confidential information, their autonomy and truth telling are at stake (Boynton 2008; Sanders 2003). When they engage in deception, such as using hidden cameras, claiming to be someone else, or gaining employment in a firm or organization to gather inside information, they are engaging in a deliberate intention to mislead (Christians, Rotzoll, and Fackler 1991). And when journalists use confidential business or government documents without permission, they are making a loyalty choice (Brevini, Hinz, and McCurdy 2013; Harro-Loit 2015; Vanacker 2016) between the public's right to know and possibly the nation's safety and corporate security.

For the manifestation of journalistic culture in beliefs/ideas, we turn to Donelson Forsyth's (1980) taxonomy of *ethical orientations*. Forsyth created a parsimonious typology of people's intuitive moral philosophies, using a general ethics position perspective. He based his explanation for variations in morality and moral judgment on the distinction between an ethics of idealism (concern for consequences) and an ethics of relativism (concern for principles). Combining various degrees of idealism and relativism, Forsyth identified four distinct ethics positions: absolutism (rules are to be followed at all times), situationism (the situation decrees the most ethical solution), exceptionism (rules are generally accepted but may be waived if circumstances demand it), and subjectivism (moral judgments should depend primarily on one's own personal values). Situationists are high, and exceptionists low, on both counts. Absolutists are high in idealism and low in relativism, while subjectivists are high in relativism and low in idealism. Forsyth, Ernest O'Boyle, and Michael McDaniel (2008, 815) suggest that people intuitively make judgments about right and wrong based on their personal ethical posture "developed over a lifetime of experience in confronting and resolving moral issues."

Lawrence Kohlberg and Richard Hersh's (1977) stage theory of moral growth provides some insight into how ethical positions may develop over time. According to the authors, people move from the preconventional, through the conventional, to the postconventional stage wherein "the choice is based on principles that supercede conventions," and people are able "to use more adequate and complex reasoning patterns to solve moral problems" (Kohlberg and Hersh 1977, 57). Thus it may be inferred that, at this stage of moral growth, people may be more willing at times to disregard the Forsythian absolutist ethical approach, defined solely by convention—an approach that founds judgment on inviolate moral principles—and be more willing to engage in actions that deviate from convention. In our case, for ethical orientations, this means that journalists may not always subscribe to an absolutist professional orientation. It also means that journalists may be willing to approve of controversial news-gathering practices. For example, investigative journalists now and then defend the use of deceptive practices by saying that professional ends—acquiring important information or publishing a story that the public needs—justify deceptive means (Braun 1988; Elliot and Culver 1992; Lambeth 1992). Thus ethical dilemmas often arise, requiring journalists to decide what to prioritize when professional objectives (see chapter 7) conflict with ethical conventions.

Forsyth's concept of ethics as an individual-level psychological construct, a cognition that guides behavior, parallels the thinking of many other scholars (Coleman and Wilkins 2002; Forsyth and Nye 1990; Klaidman and Beauchamp 1987; Plaisance and Skewes 2003). As already noted, however, journalists are not autonomous moral agents (Voakes 1997). Instead, their professional ethics are subject to a dynamic and complex mix of factors and thus discursively formulated, rendering unrealistic a theoretical model that focuses on personal values alone as the foundation for journalists' ethics decision making (Voakes 1997; see also Meyers 2010).

In this context the comprehensive review of studies by James Hollings, Thomas Hanitzsch, and Ravi Balasubramanian (2017) is useful; it provides various internal (professional) and external (societal) factors that affect journalists' ethical beliefs about controversial practices. This review is evidence of a rich literature, one where much consideration and identification of contextual factors is present, in both theoretical and post-hoc explanatory concluding sections, but also where there is a lack of use of a consistent set of relational variables, particularly macrolevel opportunity structures, within or across studies to test empirically for national differences (e.g., Lee 2005; Mellado 2012; Sanders et al. 2008; Weaver1998a; Weaver and Willnat 2012; Weaver et al. 2007).

In contrast to the long tradition of research in news-gathering practices, the application of ethical orientations as defined by Forsyth is more recent in journalism studies (Hanitzsch 2007; Hanitzsch, et al. 2011; Juntunen 2010; Plaisance 2006; Plaisance, Skewes, and Hanitzsch 2012). This literature is therefore even less likely to offer studies examining a consistent set of contextual factors. We did, however, find one empirical examination of the relationship between ethical orientations and macrolevel (ideological, cultural, and societal) as well as professional (perceived autonomy and economic influence) structures. Here, Patrick Plaisance, Elizabeth Skewes, and Thomas Hanitzsch (2012) found these structures to be critical factors in explaining ethical orientations globally.

In our study we use a consistent set of societal and professional factors and test them empirically for both practices and orientations as contexts journalists have to negotiate in their discursive work. The societal factors we consider are press freedom, democracy, corruption, human development, emancipative values (see chapter 2), and Geert Hofstede's (2001) cultural dimension of uncertainty avoidance. Among the professional factors we consider are perceived autonomy, perceived influences, and journalistic roles. Autonomy is defined as the freedom to select stories and to emphasize story aspects. Perceived influences (political, economic, organizational, procedural, and personal networks) and journalistic roles (monitorial, collaborative, interventionist, and accommodative) are conceptualized and empirically derived through formative modeling (see chapters 5 and 7, respectively). We also examine the relationship between orientations and practices. In one study that specified this relationship (Hollings, Hanitzsch, and Balaubramanian 2017), journalists' ethical orientations predicted their likelihood of justifying controversial news-gathering practices.

Within the Worlds of Journalism Study's methodological framework, the four *ethical orientations* were measured by four statements, each followed by a 5-point Likert scale eliciting journalists' level of agreement. The statements were: "Journalists should always adhere to codes of professional ethics, regardless of situation and context" (absolutism); "What is ethical in journalism depends on the specific situation" (situationism); "What is ethical in journalism is a matter of personal judgment" (subjectivism); and "It is acceptable to set aside moral standards if extraordinary circumstances require it" (exceptionism). Given the journalism context of this study, these orientations represent journalists' general professional ethics. Thus, for example, we speak of absolutism not in terms of Forsyth's universal moral rules but in terms of "codes of professional ethics."

To study journalists' evaluations of potentially *controversial news-gathering practices*, we asked our respondents to evaluate the justifiability (always justified, justified on occasion, and would not approve under any circumstances) of various controversial news-gathering practices. In this chapter we focus on the following five: paying people for confidential information (a practice that calls into question journalists' autonomy and truth telling); using confidential business or government documents without authorization (a loyalty choice); being employed in a firm or organization to gain inside information; using hidden microphones or cameras; and claiming to be somebody else (all deceptive practices).[4]

Journalists' Ethical Orientations Around the Globe

Absolutism, or adherence to codes of ethics at all times, had the highest mean score, indicating that journalists in the sixty-six countries strongly endorsed this orientation (table 8.1 and fig. 8.1). Situationism had the second highest mean; almost two-thirds of the country means indicated some

Table 8.1 Ethical orientations across countries

	N	Mean[a]	F[b]	Eta^2
Journalists should always adhere to codes of professional ethics, regardless of situation and context	26,909	4.47	50.68	.109
What is ethical in journalism depends on the specific situation	26,713	3.13	30.518	.069
What is ethical in journalism is a matter of personal judgment	26,720	2.65	47.521	.104
It is acceptable to set aside moral standards if extraordinary circumstances require it	26,541	2.70	50.216	.110

[a] Weighted; all p < .001.
[b] df = 65.

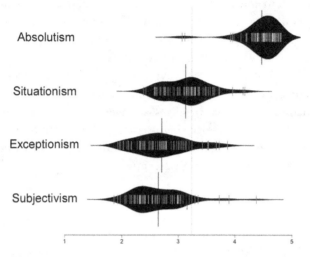

Figure 8.1 Journalists' ethical orientations across countries (distribution of country means)

Source: WJS; N = 66.

Note: Scale: 5 = "strongly agree" . . . 1 = "strongly disagree."

measure of agreement (means above the midpoint of 3). Comparatively, both subjectivism and exceptionism had less appeal as ethical approaches; most country means indicated some degree of disagreement.

Thomas Hanitzsch et al. (2011) also found considerable consensus among countries about following universal ethical principles, and much less consensus on having flexibility that allows for personal latitude. Still, in our study, of all journalists who strongly agreed that ethical codes should always be followed, about 43 percent also agreed (strongly agree and agree) that ethics depend on the specific situation, 29 percent agreed that ethics are a matter of personal judgment, and 27 percent agreed that moral standards could be set aside in extraordinary circumstances. Thus our journalists were not singularly aligned with any one orientation; they combined their orientations, albeit to different degrees.

National contexts explained a moderate amount of variance (10–11 percent) for absolutism, subjectivism, and exceptionism, and a smaller amount for situationism (7 percent) (table 8.1). To explore this variance comparatively, we employed *Visual CoPlot* in a way similar to how we used it for chapter 7 (see fig. 8.2).[5] Country mean scores were centered for responses to the four statements to minimize acquiescence bias (see table 8.2 for centered means by country). In essence this means, for example, that journalists in Sudan score lower on absolutism than journalists in the United States, even if the former more often agree that it is important to follow the codes. This is because the Sudanese journalists (in contrast to their U.S. colleagues) tend to rely on exceptionist and relativist orientations almost as often as on absolutist ones. Thus the countries are located on the coplot in terms of their *relative* emphasis on the four ethical orientations. Our solution has acceptable "fit," with a coefficient of alienation of .17 and an

Figure 8.2 Journalists' ethical orientations—differences between countries

Notes: Coplot based on centered mean scores; coefficient of alienation: .17; average of correlations: .85; N = 66.

Table 8.2 Ethical orientations—differences between countries

	Absolutism			Situationism		
	Mean	(SD)	Centered mean	Mean	(SD)	Centered mean
Albania	4.43	(0.82)	0.98	3.47	(1.12)	0.02
Argentina	4.38	(0.98)	1.40	2.76	(1.48)	−0.23
Australia	4.67	(0.59)	1.58	2.98	(1.46)	−0.11
Austria	4.64	(0.61)	1.66	3.03	(1.23)	0.05
Bangladesh	4.66	(0.66)	1.35	3.24	(1.45)	−0.08
Belgium	4.39	(0.70)	1.21	3.29	(1.26)	0.11
Bhutan	4.72	(0.52)	0.81	4.14	(0.92)	0.23
Botswana	4.80	(0.50)	1.54	3.23	(1.60)	−0.03
Brazil	4.40	(0.82)	1.48	2.76	(1.30)	−0.16
Canada	4.51	(0.80)	1.38	3.15	(1.39)	0.02
Chile	4.49	(0.94)	1.50	2.73	(1.52)	−0.26
China	4.51	(0.71)	1.46	2.82	(1.17)	−0.23
Colombia	4.52	(0.99)	1.55	2.60	(1.56)	−0.37
Croatia	4.69	(0.66)	1.70	2.57	(1.55)	−0.42
Cyprus	4.54	(0.70)	1.53	2.75	(1.42)	−0.26
Czech Republic	4.33	(0.91)	0.87	3.37	(1.26)	−0.08
Denmark	3.98	(1.11)	0.83	3.02	(1.29)	−0.13
Ecuador	4.79	(0.58)	1.45	2.93	(1.56)	−0.41
Egypt	4.56	(1.01)	1.22	2.85	(1.53)	−0.49
El Salvador	4.71	(0.63)	1.40	3.19	(1.57)	−0.11
Estonia	4.49	(0.73)	1.40	3.23	(1.29)	0.15
Ethiopia	3.11	(1.53)	−0.01	3.27	(1.45)	0.14
Finland	4.65	(0.59)	1.74	2.60	(1.36)	−0.30
France	4.46	(0.76)	1.17	3.11	(1.38)	−0.18
Germany	4.60	(0.64)	1.64	3.15	(1.32)	0.19
Greece	4.53	(0.67)	1.46	2.69	(1.33)	−0.39
Hong Kong	4.32	(0.76)	0.95	3.30	(1.01)	−0.08
Hungary	4.30	(0.85)	1.05	3.29	(1.31)	0.05
Iceland	4.35	(0.83)	1.43	2.42	(1.17)	−0.50
India	4.10	(1.26)	0.65	3.64	(1.32)	0.19

Subjectivism			Exceptionism		
Mean	(SD)	Centered mean	Mean	(SD)	Centered mean
2.89	(1.28)	−0.56	3.01	(1.19)	−0.44
2.54	(1.48)	−0.44	2.27	(1.36)	−0.72
2.23	(1.23)	−0.86	2.49	(1.22)	−0.60
2.31	(1.07)	−0.68	1.95	(1.02)	−1.03
2.98	(1.46)	−0.34	2.38	(1.41)	−0.93
2.32	(1.12)	−0.86	2.73	(1.25)	−0.45
3.35	(1.21)	−0.56	3.43	(1.24)	−0.48
2.23	(1.45)	−1.03	2.77	(1.53)	−0.48
2.21	(1.10)	−0.71	2.31	(1.17)	−0.61
2.16	(1.13)	−0.97	2.70	(1.30)	−0.43
2.34	(1.34)	−0.66	2.41	(1.44)	−0.58
2.31	(0.94)	−0.74	2.55	(1.08)	−0.49
2.75	(1.64)	−0.22	2.02	(1.33)	−0.95
2.60	(1.54)	−0.39	2.09	(1.42)	−0.90
2.05	(1.30)	−0.96	2.69	(1.33)	−0.32
2.61	(1.24)	−0.85	3.52	(1.14)	0.06
2.47	(1.21)	−0.68	3.12	(1.29)	−0.03
3.05	(1.53)	−0.29	2.60	(1.57)	−0.74
3.30	(1.49)	−0.04	2.63	(1.54)	−0.70
2.80	(1.52)	−0.51	2.53	(1.48)	−0.78
2.27	(1.23)	−0.81	2.33	(1.26)	−0.75
2.59	(1.48)	−0.54	3.53	(1.40)	0.41
2.40	(1.24)	−0.51	1.97	(1.15)	−0.93
2.55	(1.20)	−0.75	3.06	(1.28)	−0.24
2.08	(1.05)	−0.89	2.03	(1.04)	−0.94
2.33	(1.26)	−0.74	2.75	(1.26)	−0.33
3.01	(0.99)	−0.36	2.87	(1.00)	−0.51
2.48	(1.26)	−0.77	2.91	(1.32)	−0.33
2.42	(1.26)	−0.50	2.49	(1.16)	−0.43
2.99	(1.44)	−0.47	3.08	(1.51)	−0.37

(*continued*)

Table 8.2 Ethical orientations—differences between countries (*continued*)

	Absolutism			Situationism		
	Mean	(SD)	Centered mean	Mean	(SD)	Centered mean
Indonesia	4.77	(0.46)	1.73	2.67	(1.34)	−0.37
Ireland	4.37	(0.89)	1.10	3.28	(1.38)	0.01
Israel	4.29	(1.22)	1.18	3.09	(1.70)	−0.02
Italy	4.62	(0.74)	1.77	2.57	(1.48)	−0.27
Japan	4.21	(0.77)	0.86	3.44	(0.97)	0.09
Kenya	4.69	(0.65)	1.16	3.56	(1.31)	0.03
Kosovo	4.76	(0.58)	1.46	3.22	(1.29)	−0.08
Latvia	4.66	(0.75)	1.34	2.98	(1.38)	−0.34
Malawi	4.70	(0.65)	1.39	3.00	(1.53)	−0.31
Malaysia	4.40	(0.74)	0.80	3.72	(1.04)	0.11
Mexico	4.73	(0.58)	1.23	3.36	(1.44)	−0.14
Moldova	4.48	(0.74)	1.29	3.35	(1.36)	0.16
Netherlands	4.30	(0.91)	0.79	3.61	(1.30)	0.10
New Zealand	4.64	(0.65)	1.35	3.24	(1.41)	−0.04
Norway	4.68	(0.61)	1.37	3.17	(1.33)	−0.15
Oman	4.19	(1.13)	0.50	3.61	(1.11)	−0.08
Philippines	4.60	(0.75)	1.17	3.34	(1.42)	−0.09
Portugal	4.60	(0.67)	1.71	2.58	(1.38)	−0.31
Qatar	3.92	(1.18)	0.90	2.81	(1.44)	−0.22
Romania	4.50	(0.75)	1.43	3.11	(1.45)	0.04
Russia	3.95	(1.10)	0.74	3.49	(1.39)	0.28
Serbia	4.67	(0.76)	1.76	2.62	(1.43)	−0.29
Sierra Leone	4.80	(0.53)	1.04	3.53	(1.41)	−0.23
Singapore	3.06	(1.69)	0.08	3.14	(1.32)	0.15
South Africa	4.54	(0.85)	1.50	2.77	(1.51)	−0.27
South Korea	4.36	(0.75)	1.55	2.38	(0.96)	−0.43
Spain	4.39	(0.83)	1.57	2.58	(1.37)	−0.24
Sudan	4.79	(0.77)	0.54	4.17	(1.30)	−0.08
Sweden	4.58	(0.58)	1.00	3.30	(1.27)	−0.28
Switzerland	4.50	(0.73)	1.43	3.24	(1.24)	0.17

Subjectivism			Exceptionism		
Mean	(SD)	Centered mean	Mean	(SD)	Centered mean
2.24	(1.24)	−0.80	2.47	(1.27)	−0.57
2.64	(1.32)	−0.63	2.78	(1.37)	−0.49
2.31	(1.58)	−0.80	2.75	(1.65)	−0.36
1.86	(1.22)	−0.98	2.31	(1.38)	−0.53
2.77	(1.05)	−0.57	2.96	(1.05)	−0.38
2.79	(1.45)	−0.74	3.09	(1.44)	−0.45
2.53	(1.37)	−0.76	2.66	(1.43)	−0.63
2.90	(1.35)	−0.42	2.75	(1.29)	−0.57
2.54	(1.48)	−0.77	2.99	(1.45)	−0.31
3.24	(1.16)	−0.36	3.06	(1.23)	−0.55
3.00	(1.50)	−0.50	2.93	(1.46)	−0.58
2.39	(1.29)	−0.80	2.54	(1.26)	−0.65
2.99	(1.32)	−0.52	3.14	(1.33)	−0.37
2.63	(1.36)	−0.66	2.63	(1.35)	−0.65
2.86	(1.29)	−0.45	2.55	(1.26)	−0.77
3.72	(1.09)	0.03	3.24	(1.25)	−0.45
3.00	(1.38)	−0.43	2.78	(1.35)	−0.65
1.98	(1.12)	−0.91	2.40	(1.24)	−0.49
3.04	(1.45)	0.02	2.33	(1.31)	−0.70
2.27	(1.25)	−0.80	2.39	(1.29)	−0.67
2.67	(1.35)	−0.54	2.72	(1.43)	−0.49
2.41	(1.40)	−0.49	1.93	(1.21)	−0.98
2.99	(1.52)	−0.77	3.72	(1.31)	−0.04
2.71	(1.20)	−0.27	3.03	(1.35)	0.05
2.36	(1.39)	−0.68	2.49	(1.49)	−0.55
2.33	(1.03)	−0.48	2.16	(0.94)	−0.65
2.14	(1.15)	−0.68	2.17	(1.18)	−0.65
4.38	(1.16)	0.13	3.67	(1.63)	−0.58
2.93	(1.28)	−0.65	3.53	(1.17)	−0.06
2.17	(1.05)	−0.89	2.36	(1.12)	−0.71

(*continued*)

Table 8.2 Ethical orientations—differences between countries (*continued*)

	Absolutism			Situationism		
	Mean	(SD)	Centered mean	Mean	(SD)	Centered mean
Tanzania	4.19	(0.72)	0.75	3.18	(0.90)	−0.26
Thailand	4.76	(0.49)	0.64	3.95	(1.06)	−0.16
Turkey	4.40	(0.74)	1.45	2.90	(1.25)	−0.05
United Arab Emirates	4.75	(0.66)	1.19	3.72	(1.30)	0.17
United Kingdom	4.56	(0.73)	1.17	3.49	(1.29)	0.09
United States	4.66	(0.65)	1.82	2.67	(1.44)	−0.17

average of correlations of .85 (Bravata et al. 2008). In our analysis we use regions rather than countries for the sake of parsimony, and also because contextual factors could be similar within geographical regions, and thus negotiations over them could result in similarities in orientations. The six regions we use are the Global North (North America and Western Europe) and Australia/New Zealand; Eastern Europe, former Yugoslavia and former Soviet republics; the Middle East and North Africa; Latin America; sub-Saharan Africa; and Asia (the latter three regions are at times referenced together below as the Global South).

Hanitzsch et al.'s (2011) map reproduced Forsyth's (1980) theoretical grid reasonably well, dividing sample countries more or less into the four cells of absolutism, situationism, subjectivism, and exceptionism. In this study we found that a triad better captures the relative priorities of countries, given the proximity of the situationism and exceptionism vectors on the coplot. Consequently, in this analysis we find it useful at times to look at situationism and exceptionism in combination; journalists likely see a similarity between deviating from absolutism for a "situation" and deviating from it for an "extraordinary circumstance." Because of this close alliance between situationism and exceptionism, strong examples of the two were difficult to find; the two orientations were strongly intertwined in nearest-fit countries, such as Denmark. On the other hand, we found strong

Subjectivism			Exceptionism		
Mean	(SD)	Centered mean	Mean	(SD)	Centered mean
3.19	(1.11)	−0.24	3.19	(1.11)	−0.25
3.90	(1.01)	−0.22	3.87	(0.97)	−0.25
2.38	(1.10)	−0.57	2.12	(1.12)	−0.83
3.08	(1.47)	−0.47	2.67	(1.51)	−0.88
2.74	(1.27)	−0.65	2.79	(1.29)	−0.61
1.93	(1.07)	−0.92	2.11	(1.18)	−0.73

examples for absolutism (high idealism, low relativism) to the left of the graph and for subjectivism (low idealism, high relativism) at the top of the graph. Where we find a relatively clear pattern of affiliation of a geographical group of countries to an ethical orientation, we offer possible explanations from the literature.

The clearest affiliation between an orientation and a region was for subjectivism and countries of the Middle East and North Africa (top edge of the graph), namely, Oman, Egypt, Qatar, and Sudan (an Arabized country; see Sharkey 2008), and to a smaller extent the United Arab Emirates. This region's high emphasis on subjectivism, combined with the low emphasis of the Global North on this orientation, explains the small bimodality apparent in the distribution of the uncentered subjectivism means in figure 8.1. These countries have low press freedom and highly authoritarian governments (see table A.8 in the appendix), circumstances that may lead to a relativistic orientation due to the need for journalists to be adaptable (Plaisance, Skewes, and Hanitzsch 2012). In these countries, as compared with countries in other WJS regions, news organizations are often said to lack professionalism, and journalists to have insufficient media skills (El Issawi and Cammaerts 2015; Pintak and Ginges 2009). There is also an absence of a uniform understanding of journalistic values; for example, payment for news coverage is prevalent here (El Issawi and Cammaerts 2015;

Pintak and Ginges 2009). Such conditions allow for personal judgment to surface.

Next, the group of countries that emphasize absolutist codes most strongly (toward the left of the graph) come from the Global North (including Australia) and to some extent from the countries of the former Yugoslavia (see also table 8.2). The United States, Italy, Serbia, Finland, Croatia, Portugal, Austria, and Germany are all examples of countries where absolutism was strongly emphasized. At the same time, not all Global North and former Yugoslav countries affiliated with this orientation.

Overall, the tendency of journalists was to combine orientations. Most Latin American countries, for example, nestle in almost a straight line in the broad V created by the absolutism and subjectivism vectors, directly across from the situationism and exceptionism vectors. As a group, with the exception of Brazil and Chile, which are mostly absolutist, these countries combine code adherence with personal judgment, to different degrees. As we move from the angle formed by the two vectors toward the outer edges of the V, the countries increasingly take on absolutist and subjectivist characteristics. Colombia was relatively the most absolutist and Ecuador relatively the most subjectivist in this group, but in absolute terms they were both high on these traits as compared with El Salvador, for example. The location of these countries vis-á-vis absolutism and subjectivism may be explained somewhat by journalists' concern for their own physical safety (Solheim 2017) as well as the prevalence of a mixed level of professionalism (Waisbord 2000). According to Silvio Waisbord (2000, xiv), in Latin America, while "ideals of professional and factual reporting have gained currency and informed journalistic work," the interest in facticity is not consistent and continuous. What is clear about these Latin American countries is their antisituationist and antiexceptionist position. As a group, they are defined more by this stance than by a common affiliation to an orientation. The farther the countries are from the center of the graph, the more they hold this oppositional position.

In a somewhat similar manner but with a little less consistency, the sub-Saharan countries, with the exception of Tanzania, are antisubjectivist (at the bottom of the graph). Lying as they are between the absolutism and situationism/exceptionism vectors, these countries combine the two orientations to different degrees. Some countries from the Global North share the antisubjectivist space with the sub-Saharan countries and similarly exhibit different degrees of affiliation to absolutism and situationism/exceptionism.

To varying degrees they combine low subjectivism with strong absolutism (United States, Italy, and Portugal, to the left of the graph), with situationism (Germany, Estonia, and Moldova, to the lower middle), or with situationism and exceptionism (some Eastern and Western European countries as well as Canada, to the near right of the graph). Even farther to the right of the graph, among the countries that represent greater situationist and exceptionist tendencies, we identified a geographically disparate set of countries, including Sweden, Denmark, the Netherlands, Russia, India, Bhutan, and Japan. Finally, as we move farther away from situationism/exceptionism toward subjectivism, we find many East Asian countries, including Thailand, Malaysia, Hong Kong, and the Philippines. These countries manifest a mix of the three orientations to different degrees. In these broad groupings of countries by orientation, some exceptions were apparent. Tanzania occupied a completely different space from that of other sub-Saharan countries, being mostly subjectivist. Both Ethiopia and Singapore were outliers in the space between exceptionism and subjectivism but closer to exceptionism.

In a larger perspective, the most striking pattern in ethical orientations followed a not unfamiliar geographical arrangement. As we move from left to right on the map, toward a weaker emphasis on the need for following professional codes, we see fewer countries from the Global North, or Eastern Europe and the former USSR and Yugoslavia, and instead more countries from the Middle East and North Africa, as well as Asia. While some countries adjacent on the coplot are not necessarily geographically proximate and are highly variable in press and political freedoms and in emancipative and cultural values, most adjacencies are based on North-South groupings. We will return to the discussion of the contextual factors that may explain adherence to the four ethical orientations later in this chapter.

Journalists' Justification of Controversial News-Gathering Practices

The *American Journalist* series (Weaver and Wilhoit 1986, 1996; Weaver et al. 2007) found temporal changes in the acceptability of controversial practices over three waves of surveys. More recently Willnat and Weaver (2014) noted a greater reluctance in 2013 as compared with 1992 and 2002 to endorse certain practices. This was particularly true for the practice of paying people for confidential information. At the same time, over time some findings remained consistent. "Claiming to be somebody else" was consistently considered the least justifiable (lowest percentage agreement), while a majority of journalists consistently deemed "getting employed to gain insider information" and "using confidential business or government documents without authorization" justifiable (Weaver and Wilhoit 1986, 1996; Weaver et al. 2007).

Overall results in the current study are somewhat similar. In our case, while "using hidden microphones or cameras" had the highest approval rating (10 percent said it is always justified and 57 percent said it is justified on occasion), it was followed by "using confidential business or government documents without authorization" and "getting employed in a firm or organization to gain inside information," in that order. Overall, a majority of journalists indicated that these practices are justified always or on occasion. "Paying people for confidential information" had the lowest justifiability rating globally, with "claiming to be somebody else" placed just above it. Approval for these two practices was 42 and 48 percent, respectively (see table 8.3 and fig. 8.3).

At the same time, approval levels differed considerably by country, indicating disagreement among journalists in different parts of the world. As the chi-square tests and moderate but robust effect sizes reported in table 8.3 indicate, cross-national differences are somewhat more pronounced for the practice of using hidden recording devices and using confidential documents without authorization, while differences are less marked for paying people and getting employed in a firm to gain inside information. Reflecting this, figure 8.3 shows that country differences, especially for paying people for confidential information, are somewhat less pronounced than for the use of hidden recording devices and use of confidential information.

The practice of "using confidential business or government documents without authorization" is related to the public's right to know, on one hand, and to the complicated issue of the use of leaked information by journalists, on the other (Vanacker 2016). In the United States, journalists are generally willing to accept controversial practices that target newsmakers, in a bid to show their loyalty to their audiences (Lee 2004). In our study, in terms of the percentage of journalists who consider the practice justifiable, the

Table 8.3 Ethical practices across countries

	N	Always justified	Justified on occasion	Not approve	Chi²	Cramer's V
Using hidden microphones or cameras	26,665	9.6%	56.9%	33.4%	6835.53	.358
Using confidential business or government documents without authorization	26,532	13.1%	51.9%	34.9%	6407.62	.347
Getting employed in a firm or organization to gain inside information	26,361	8.7%	45.9%	45.3%	4913.00	.305
Claiming to be somebody else	26,634	6.7%	41.1%	52.2%	5962.02	.335
Paying people for confidential information	26,210	5.8%	35.8%	58.5%	4298.82	.286

Notes: Percentages weighted across countries; df = 132, p < .001.

Figure 8.3 Journalists' justification of ethical practices across countries (distribution of country percentages)

Source: WJS; N = 67.

Note: Average percentage of respondents saying "always justified" or "justified on occasion."

top-twenty-five list featured, with the exception of Japan, South Korea, Turkey, Brazil, and the Czech Republic, only Western liberal democracies (see table 8.4). Thus journalists in Western countries are more likely to place their loyalty with the public than with authority. Countries from the Global South and the Middle East and North Africa occupied the last nineteen spots. Many of these nineteen countries have strict government control in political and media spheres; Qatar, the UAE, Singapore, and China are all authoritarian countries or flawed democracies (EIU 2015) and have nonfree press systems (Freedom House 2015; also see table A.8). These countries also have high public acceptance of inequality.[6] Where governments particularly and businesses, too, possibly represent figures of authority with powers to sanction, journalists may choose not to confront. For this practice, the middle ranks in terms of percent approval were occupied mostly by Eastern European countries and countries of the former Soviet Union and Yugoslavia.

As we move from the loyalty choice practice of using confidential documents to deceptive practices, in the following order—undercover employment, undercover recording, undercover identity—the Global North countries move farther and farther down toward the middle of the list of sixty-seven countries (and some closer to the lower end), and the countries of Eastern Europe and former Soviet/Yugoslav republics move increasingly upward, indicating greater approval on their part of these practices than in the Global North countries. This trend continues for paying people for confidential information, resulting in Eastern Europe, former Soviet/Yugoslav republics, and some Asian countries placing at the top of the list, indicating their greater willingness to approve of a practice that compromises their autonomy and truth telling. With a few exceptions, Latin American, African, and Middle Eastern/North African countries remain toward the lower end of the list (indicating less approval) across the practices. Qatar (rated not free in press freedom, Freedom House, 2015) was either last or second to last across the five practices, and Tanzania (rated partly free) alternated in these positions across four practices. On the other hand, Sweden (free in all respects) ranked at the top for three of the five items, was fourth for "claiming to be someone else," and was twenty-fifth for "paying people." China ranked first for "paying people" and second for undercover identity.

Table 8.4 Ethical practices—differences between countries ("always justified" and "justified on occasion")

	Pay people for confidential information	Use confidential documents	Use hidden recording devices	Undercover employment	Claim to be somebody else
Albania	73.1%	68.6%	81.4%	70.9%	46.8%
Argentina	30.1%	72.5%	61.7%	40.7%	42.2%
Australia	28.4%	76.2%	42.4%	30.9%	13.4%
Austria	44.6%	80.0%	66.4%	70.4%	48.6%
Bangladesh	50.5%	46.2%	57.7%	42.0%	33.9%
Belgium	33.0%	79.4%	83.4%	78.7%	56.0%
Bhutan	71.6%	69.3%	70.1%	56.2%	49.4%
Botswana	32.6%	57.8%	64.1%	49.5%	31.2%
Brazil	19.8%	77.9%	88.0%	36.4%	56.7%
Bulgaria	51.7%	75.2%	86.2%	63.7%	56.7%
Canada	34.2%	89.9%	85.1%	65.2%	38.7%
Chile	35.9%	71.1%	64.7%	46.1%	48.6%
China	81.9%	38.1%	81.3%	54.2%	86.3%
Colombia	14.8%	22.7%	34.4%	15.5%	20.2%
Croatia	42.4%	74.5%	59.2%	61.0%	46.9%
Cyprus	35.8%	72.8%	48.5%	57.4%	60.3%
Czech Republic	59.1%	80.5%	89.6%	77.2%	66.5%
Denmark	21.1%	90.9%	95.1%	80.9%	70.4%
Ecuador	31.9%	36.7%	47.2%	34.9%	31.2%
Egypt	49.3%	50.5%	47.7%	51.5%	38.4%
El Salvador	26.2%	48.0%	42.9%	33.9%	31.7%
Estonia	55.8%	68.3%	63.8%	56.9%	62.7%
Ethiopia	28.4%	22.5%	39.3%	34.0%	40.4%
Finland	41.4%	84.1%	70.2%	77.2%	64.6%
France	38.2%	94.6%	88.0%	72.6%	59.4%
Germany	56.1%	77.6%	54.9%	73.8%	49.9%
Greece	37.9%	77.5%	42.4%	38.4%	36.3%
Hong Kong	49.7%	74.5%	78.8%	64.5%	71.8%

(*continued*)

Table 8.4 Ethical practices—differences between countries ("always justified" and "justified on occasion") (*continued*)

	Pay people for confidential information	Use confidential documents	Use hidden recording devices	Undercover employment	Claim to be somebody else
Hungary	49.6%	56.9%	71.9%	61.2%	56.7%
Iceland	35.1%	84.1%	77.9%	38.5%	36.4%
India	53.4%	49.9%	75.0%	41.2%	49.5%
Indonesia	64.3%	52.2%	83.8%	60.8%	30.7%
Ireland	52.1%	91.7%	88.0%	82.8%	44.5%
Israel	56.0%	65.1%	84.7%	65.6%	58.3%
Italy	38.7%	76.5%	76.6%	51.7%	60.2%
Japan	48.2%	91.8%	71.0%	39.9%	22.9%
Kenya	56.7%	51.2%	85.3%	63.5%	43.2%
Kosovo	43.1%	58.9%	63.4%	53.4%	35.9%
Latvia	40.9%	75.6%	91.2%	75.2%	78.3%
Malawi	45.6%	49.4%	63.2%	62.4%	38.3%
Malaysia	49.9%	33.8%	57.2%	42.9%	37.9%
Mexico	29.1%	58.5%	59.6%	42.8%	41.4%
Moldova	55.0%	67.0%	85.8%	65.7%	83.2%
Netherlands	42.8%	84.4%	84.3%	87.9%	54.0%
New Zealand	35.7%	83.4%	74.9%	50.5%	25.9%
Norway	26.8%	90.1%	93.7%	71.1%	67.5%
Oman	51.7%	57.2%	48.2%	53.3%	60.3%
Philippines	29.7%	67.8%	64.0%	30.9%	24.7%
Portugal	48.6%	78.3%	80.6%	64.4%	58.6%
Qatar	9.4%	7.3%	8.9%	9.3%	5.6%
Romania	58.8%	60.5%	86.7%	61.8%	87.2%
Russia	68.7%	65.4%	86.4%	77.2%	67.2%
Serbia	47.5%	62.9%	48.2%	49.9%	36.3%
Sierra Leone	52.2%	44.6%	79.8%	80.5%	55.1%
Singapore	21.5%	46.7%	55.4%	36.3%	33.0%
South Africa	21.3%	75.3%	77.5%	47.8%	39.7%
South Korea	61.9%	85.9%	68.6%	64.1%	85.9%

	Pay people for confidential information	Use confidential documents	Use hidden recording devices	Undercover employment	Claim to be somebody else
Spain	39.8%	81.8%	54.9%	52.2%	46.8%
Sudan	40.4%	42.0%	31.3%	38.8%	33.9%
Sweden	49.0%	96.5%	98.1%	95.0%	85.1%
Switzerland	28.5%	82.9%	66.6%	63.2%	49.8%
Tanzania	4.4%	4.4%	9.7%	37.6%	1.5%
Thailand	46.4%	46.4%	62.0%	43.9%	43.2%
Turkey	46.2%	79.6%	60.0%	48.9%	77.7%
United Arab Emirates	25.2%	22.7%	23.6%	19.1%	28.4%
United Kingdom	52.9%	81.3%	78.4%	74.9%	46.4%
United States	12.7%	75.8%	63.8%	37.4%	11.6%

Correlates of Journalists' Ethics

Thus far the results indicate patterns of similarity and of differences in journalists' ethical orientations and practices around the world. Generally, it appears that the main differences follow familiar sociogeographical divides, in particular between the Global North and the rest of the world, with a few marked exceptions. In this section we therefore explore empirically how opportunity structures relate to journalists' ethical orientations and justification of selected reporting practices. Of considerable importance for journalism ethics are the external societal factors of levels of press freedom and democratic performance, of corruption and human development, of emancipative values in society, and of adherence to certain cultural values. In addition, we investigate the relationships between journalistic ethics and the internal professional factors of perceived influences, editorial autonomy, and journalistic roles. Finally, we relate practices to orientations.

The correlations reported in table 8.5 lend some additional support to our initial reading of the distinction between the Global North and the rest of the world and also provide evidence of how ethics are subject to various societal-level opportunity structures and professional-level factors.

Table 8.5 Correlates of ethical orientations and practices (correlation coefficients)

	Ethical orientations			
	Absolutism	Situationism	Subjectivism	Exceptionism
Press freedom (FH)[a]	.414***	−.064	−.515***	−.069
Press freedom (RSF)[b]	.321**	−.019	−.460***	−.017
Democracy[c]	.426***	−.101	−.517***	−.058
Transparency[d]	.104	.172	−.292*	.001
Human development[e]	.273*	.039	−.252*	−.185
Emancipative values[f]	.144	.087	−.431***	.097
Uncertainty avoidance[g]	.398**	−.250	−.145	−.240*
Political influences	−.433***	.046	.533***	.091
Economic influences	−.280*	.032	.397**	.007
Organizational influences	−.232	−.080	.223	.179
Procedural influences	.183	−.164	−.183	.025
Personal networks influences	−.317**	.077	.330**	.093
Editorial autonomy	.368**	.037	−.417***	−.165
Monitorial role	.341**	−.281*	−.327**	.013
Interventionist role	.082	−.254*	.197	−.121
Collaborative role	−.397***	.141	.355**	.139
Accommodative role	.044	.413***	−.266*	−.110

Absolutism

Situationism

Subjectivism

Exceptionism

Notes: Pearson's correlation coefficient. ***p < .001; **p < .01; *p < .05. Scores for ethical orientations and roles centered; N = 66/67 (orientations/practices) unless otherwise indicated.
[a] Freedom House; Freedom of the Press Index; scale reversed.
[b] Reporters Without Borders; World Press Freedom Index; scale reversed.
[c] Economist Intelligence Unit; EIU Democracy Index; N = 65/66.
[d] Transparency International; Corruption Perceptions Index.
[e] UNDP; Human Development Index; N= 65/66.
[f] Scores calculated based on WVS/EVS data; N = 57/58.
[g] Geert Hofstede, https://geerthofstede.com/research-and-vsm/dimension-data-matrix/; N = 50.

| | | Controversial reporting practices | | |
Pay for confidential information	Use confidential documents	Use hidden recording devices	Undercover employment	Claim to be somebody else
−.103	.752***	.463***	.499***	.173
−.203	.609***	.327**	.444***	.109
−.155	.734***	.469***	.384**	.106
−.196	.551***	.230	.294*	.080
−.084	.629***	.271*	.250*	.208
−.169	.673***	.403**	.452***	.196
−.036	−.663***	−.504***	−.495***	−.279*
.256*	−.576***	−.306*	−.331**	−.120
.004	−.581***	−.369**	−.360**	−.264*
.048	−.147	−.058	−.112	−.211
.208	−.291*	−.066	−.173	−.072
.072	.542***	.395***	.294*	.195
−.172	.723***	.344**	.327**	.141
.012	−.160	−.136	−.056	.118
.027	−.679***	−.360**	−.450***	−.217
.181	.182	.200	.281*	.018
−.023	.337**	.107	.044	.042
.218	−.014	.132	.142	.074
−.163	−.483***	−.498***	−.398***	−.248*
.030	−.036	.219	.208	.120

Absolutism, the preferred orientation, correlated strongly with high levels of press freedom and with a functional democracy. Further, journalists aligning with this perspective were more likely to come from societies where individuals have a tendency to avoid uncertainty and ambiguity. These are prevalent societal features in the Global North, where the history of journalistic professionalism is the longest (e.g., Waisbord 2013b; Slattery 2014).

Journalists strongly aligning with ethical absolutism, for instance, came from societies where uncertainty is less accepted, a characteristic more typically found in Global North countries (Hofstede 2001). Plaisance, Skewes, and Hanitzsch (2012), too, found that journalists were less likely to be flexible in following ethics codes where they had more certainty in the legal framework in their country. A study of general ethical orientations similarly found that countries with a nonrelativistic orientation were more likely to have high uncertainty avoidance (Forsyth, O'Boyle, and McDaniel 2008).

Further confirmation of our regional distinction comes from absolutist journalists' responses to questions about their autonomy, influences they feel, and roles they play. What they report are traits of journalism in the Global North. Journalists with an orientation to adhere to codes perceived they had greater autonomy and felt smaller political, economic, and organizational influence and little influence from personal networks. Further, absolutist journalists (as compared with journalists from other orientations) were more likely to play a monitorial role and less likely to be collaborative (support government policy and provide a positive image of political leaders). For Global North countries, then, there was considerable coalescing of evidence to support the finding of an absolutist orientation.

A subjectivist orientation was more pronounced in countries with lower levels of press freedom and democratic quality. Subjectivists were also more likely to come from countries with low human development ratings, high corruption ratings, and low emancipative values. These are features mostly prevalent in the Middle East/North Africa and the Global South, and in fact it was the Middle East/North African countries that most subscribed to this orientation. Forsyth, O'Boyle, and McDaniel (2008) found similarly that the Middle East leaned more toward relativistic ethics than did the West. In a low-freedom environment, the professional position of journalism tends to be more insecure. In fact, greater subjectivism was correlated with lower levels of reported professional autonomy and higher levels of influence from political, economic, and personal networks (the correlation with these influences was highest for this orientation). The finding on personal networks is particularly indicative of highly subjectivist journalists' use of personal judgment in their ethics decision making. The personal and the professional often mix in many of these countries where group harmony is important and personal networks carry much influence, so that personal distance from work-related matters, in our case reportage, highly valued in the West, may not have similar currency. Further, subjectivism was related negatively to the monitorial and accommodative roles and positively to the collaborative role, features more likely to be prevalent in controlled countries.

We found the remaining two ethical orientations—situationism and exceptionism—largely unrelated to the societal and professional factors in table 8.5. Among professional factors, the only significant correlations were between situationism and a greater preference for an accommodative role and less pronounced monitorial and interventionist roles. As noted earlier in the discussion of the coplot, in our study situationism and exceptionism represent ethical orientations that journalists combine with either subjectivism or absolutism, in different ways in different parts of the world. The different combinations explain why no significant correlations were found between journalists' situationist and exceptionist orientations and the conditions for politics and media in their respective countries.

Overall, national conditions relating to the news media seem to have a greater impact on journalists' preference for an absolutist versus a subjectivist orientation than they have on their preference for situationist and exceptionist orientations. Our findings suggest that journalists have a less flexible ethical toolkit in countries where they enjoy greater certainty in the political-legal environment and where they have greater autonomy.

We see a somewhat similar picture if we turn our attention to the right side of table 8.5, which reports associations between journalists' justification of controversial practices of reporting and contextual factors.[7] Three of the five practices (using confidential documents without authorization, using hidden recording devices, and investigating undercover) exhibited relatively similar relationships. Journalists were more likely to consider these reporting techniques as justified in countries scoring higher in terms of the societal factors of press freedom, democratic development, transparency (low corruption), human development, and emancipative values. Further, journalists tended to approve of these practices more strongly when they enjoyed greater editorial autonomy and faced lower political, economic, and organizational pressures. The strong association between journalists' justification of these three controversial reporting methods, particularly of using confidential documents without authorization, and the prevalence of certain journalistic roles is telling in this respect. In countries where journalists have a greater preference for the monitorial role, they were more likely to think that using confidential documents is justifiable at least on occasion (see fig. 8.4). At the same time, support for the collaborative role correlated negatively with the proportion of journalists who felt that the practice of using confidential documents was justified in their country. The essence of a collaborative role is alignment with government, that is, supporting its policies and providing a positive image of political leaders, whether from coercion or conditioning or free will; journalists who accept

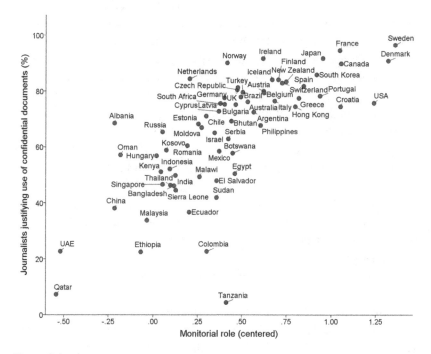

Figure 8.4 Journalists' use of confidential documents and relevance of monitorial role

Source: WJS; N = 67.

Note: Mean scores for monitorial role centered.

this role are unlikely to use confidential government documents without authorization. Correlations were considerably smaller for the practices of claiming to be someone else (negatively related with political and organizational influences) and paying people for information (positively correlated with economic influences).

Table 8.5 also indicates that justification of controversial reporting practices is related in part to two of the four ethical orientations. Specifically, four of the five practices (the exception being paying people) were negatively correlated with the prevalence of a subjectivist orientation. Countries that were largely subjectivist came from the Middle East and North Africa, where, given strict controls, journalists may be wary of using practices that entail deception and require making a loyalty choice between persons/institutions with authority and getting the story for the public. On the other hand, journalists in countries where professional ethics are more closely aligned with an absolutist orientation were more approving of the loyalty practice of using confidential documents. This finding casts an interesting light on a key assumption in this line of research: that the five practices are "controversial." Journalists are more likely to justify four of the five reporting methods in journalistic cultures that are opposed to the idea that decisions about what is ethical practice should be a matter of personal judgment. Hence the controversial quality of these reporting methods may be less a perception or belief within the professional community and more an attribution made by discursive agents from outside the institution of journalism, such as scholars, politicians, and members of the audience.

Overall, our analysis suggests that the five reporting practices investigated in this chapter are predominantly the privilege of journalists in the Global North. A more nuanced analysis of the other contextual factors also indicates some differences between the five practices, findings that we can divide into three groups. The first, most strongly linked to the Global North, comprises the use of governmental and business documents without authorization, which has the strongest correlations with journalistic, political, and personal freedoms, relative autonomy from political, economic, and organizational influences, and adherence to emancipative values and professional codes of conduct, conditions that allow choice between loyalties. The second—with substantively weaker correlations pointing in the same direction and with very few nonsignificant relationships (but including such a correlation with absolutism)—consists of using hidden cameras and being an undercover employee. The third, with the fewest correlations, is composed of claiming to be someone else and paying for confidential information.

What explains these findings? The fact that three of the five practices tend to vary in much the same way with regard to contextual factors is a reminder that these practices share a common trait in being associated with "investigative" methods. They are controversial, first and foremost, for those in power. Moreover, they represent a style of journalism that has been developed and become more accepted (and possible) in democracies in the Global North (see de Burgh 2000). In contrast, in countries in the Global South and the Middle East and North Africa, this style of journalism is less prevalent. Here journalists are less likely to be independent and more likely to be polite, obedient, and responsible, that is, more collaborative than monitorial in their relationship with their governments, and more influenced by political entities and personal networks (see chapters 5 to 7). These regions appear to be characterized by a collectivistic culture that prioritizes group harmony and accepts higher inequality (Hofstede 2001).

Conclusions

Based on an understanding that journalistic cultures are discursively created, the inductive approach used in this chapter offers a way to free journalism ethics from its hegemonic baggage of Western, and particularly U.S., beliefs about values within the journalism profession. We find hybridity in journalists' ethical orientations rather than a singular adherence to any one orientation (Kraidy 2002; Lauk 2008), as well as regional disparity in both orientations and acceptance of practices. To different degrees, in different regions, journalists combined absolutism with situationism, subjectivism, and exceptionism. Fackson Banda (2008) explains succinctly that hybridity in Africa, a mostly collectivistic region, is the consequence of a conflagration between the "meta-ethical narrative of national unity and development" and the influence of the liberal ethical imperative. This chapter adds a number of other contextual factors to our understanding of ethical hybridity.

Still, some dominant allegiances were evident. Based on deontology—the idea that it is our duty to do what is right—absolutism appeals to journalists because of their normative belief that journalism is about truth telling. Exceptions to this founded on a seemingly unprofessional basis, such as the use of personal judgment or ignoring moral standards to allow for extraordinary circumstances, will have less currency with journalists. Our results indicate this. Absolutism was the preferred orientation across the sixty-six countries.

Regionally, countries in the Global North were the ones most associated with absolutism, albeit with some exceptions. Contextual factors that seed this orientation were the various democratic and journalistic freedoms, emancipative values, and the cultural value of uncertainty avoidance. Much discursive power lies in the hands of journalists in such free countries; somewhat unconstrained, most of these journalists privilege absolutism as an ethical orientation. Allegiance to subjectivism, which was least accepted by journalists, was more evident in the countries of the Middle East and North Africa, where opportunity structures are characterized by limited political and press freedoms, more corruption, and less adoption of emancipative values.

These two orientations were the mirror opposite in their relationship with internal professional factors: absolutism was correlated negatively with political, economic, and personal networks influence and positively with a monitorial role and editorial autonomy, while subjectivism was correlated positively with these influences and with a collaborative role and negatively with autonomy. While absolutism and subjectivism evidenced clear regional patterns and contextual impacts, this was not the case with the other two orientations. The situationist and exceptionist orientations were supported in more Global South countries, but they also drew support in a considerable mix of other countries, thus not allowing any definite generalizations. Because these two orientations were closely aligned (see fig. 8.2), countries in their proximity were considerably intertwined in their orientations.

With regard to controversial practices, journalists in countries that score higher in freedom and emancipative values and in which they experience greater autonomy and fewer internal pressures as well as play a greater monitorial role are also more likely to think that using confidential documents without authorization, using hidden recording devices, and investigating undercover are justified. Many of these are countries of the Global North.

In fact, the acceptance of controversial practices is negatively correlated with the prevalence of a subjectivist orientation, found more often in the countries of the Middle East and North Africa.

Considerable scholarship in media ethics has called for or theorized macrolevel universal ethical norms (Christians 2014; Christians, Ferré, and Fackler 1993; Christians et al. 2008). Such a deductive exercise may not, however, withstand empirical scrutiny, which finds that most knowledge of ethics is multidimensional and pluralistic because it is grounded in the local (Plaisance 2011). Journalists adopt professional ethical orientations owing to the circumstances of their political, economic, and cultural environment and the strictures defined for their profession in their country in terms of roles and editorial autonomy. They are less likely to embrace an absolutist orientation where they have to deal with the vagaries of an uncertain environment and consequently embrace adaptability. It is apparent, then, that there is no universal application of certain ethical orientations and practices in journalism.

We have dealt with aggregated country scores rather than individual journalists in this chapter, so it seems best to interpret both aspects of ethics—professional orientations and acceptance of controversial practices—as expressing some of the same underlying opportunity structures that journalists are a part of, rather than one leading to the other. Interesting as these results are, they capture links between ethical orientations and journalistic practices only on the societal level. Orientations of journalists and their justification of certain reporting methods are likely connected to one another through mechanisms working on the individual level. A fruitful avenue for future studies may thus be analyses that try to establish causal links between ethical orientations and practices using individual-level data, along the lines of Hollings, Hanitzsch, and Balasubramanian's (2017) study, or through multilevel analysis.

Researchers exploring journalists' ethics in the future may also want to consider using a framework of risk, as suggested by Hollings, Hanitzsch and Balasubramanian (2017) and articulated in considerable detail by them. As these authors suggest, this could provide a theoretical approach that might make for a more cohesive interpretation of the various independent findings in journalism ethics research. For journalists, accepting a certain ethical orientation or practice is an exercise in risk taking, and it is becoming increasingly so even in freer countries, given ease of distribution and access due to technology. These risks include earning the wrath of the public and one's community, of the power elite, whether government, business, or social powerbrokers, and even of one's family and friends. In addition, these choices may have legal, financial, and social consequences and may harm journalists' and their families' physical and emotional security, the latter a major cause of concern. Using a measure to assess perceptions of both personal and professional risk in the practice of journalism and of journalism ethics at the level of the individual journalist may provide a new and useful direction to this trajectory of research.

Finally, a study using as large a quantitative questionnaire as ours could not easily add qualitative questions to elicit reasons and explanations from journalists. Future studies that focus only on ethics may want to use a mixed method so that the voice of journalists themselves is provided to more comprehensively explain quantitative findings.

Notes

1. Personal communication, July 26, 2014.
2. Reddit (https://www.reddit.com/) is one of the largest websites in the world, attracting more than seventy million unique visitors and about five billion page views per month.
3. Bulgaria was not included because of translation issues.
4. The questionnaire contained ten mandatory questions about reporting practices, of which we included five in this chapter. Among those not included, four had very little variation across countries, with an overwhelming majority of journalists rejecting them: "Exerting pressure on unwilling informants to get a story," "Making use of personal documents such as letters and pictures without permission," "Publishing stories with unverified content," and "Accepting money from sources." Another practice was prone to misinterpretation due to its wording: "Using re-creations or dramatizations of news by actors."
5. CoPlot is a method for the graphical analysis of multivariate data that enables simultaneous analysis of observations (in our case, country averages) and variables (the four ethical orientations) on a two-dimensional map (Bravata et al. 2008; also see chapter 7). *Visual CoPlot* was developed by David Talby and Adi Raveh; http://davidtalby.com/vcoplot/.
6. Qatar is not part of Hofstede's database (https://geert-hofstede.com/china.html). Within a range from 0 to 100, a higher number equates with greater acceptance of power inequalities.
7. To obtain correlations, we first calculated, for each country, the percentage of those respondents who considered the respective reporting practice justified (always or on occasion). These percentages were subsequently correlated with contextual factors.

9

TRUST

Journalists' Confidence in Public Institutions

Arjen van Dalen, Rosa Berganza, Thomas Hanitzsch,
Adriana Amado, Beatriz Herrero, Beate Josephi, Sonja Seizova,
Morten Skovsgaard, and Nina Steindl

Journalists are important intermediaries between public institutions—such as the government, parliament, and judiciary—and their audiences, linking ordinary citizens to the authorities who are supposed to represent them and who govern their lives (Mishler and Rose 2001). Since most people have limited direct experience with these institutions, journalists and the content they produce are vital to the level of public satisfaction with democracy and governance. In this context, the news media can play either a constructive or a destructive role. A persistent pattern of negativity in the news, for instance, can contribute to public disdain for political actors (Cappella and Jamieson 1997; Moy, Pfau, and Kahlor 1999). At the same time, journalism can also create and consolidate people's trust in social institutions (Norris 2011).

In this sense the extent to which journalists trust the public institutions in their respective societies is an essential feature of journalistic culture. It is a marker of how journalists in a given context position themselves vis-à-vis larger structures of power and authority. In many journalistic cultures a certain degree of skepticism is deeply built into journalism's professional ideology, articulated in the monitorial role of the news media (see chapter 7). However, several researchers have expressed the concern that journalists' skepticism has gone too far and is thus instigating cynicism among citizens. Belgium and the Netherlands provide examples of skepticism that are concerning; journalists and politicians here regard each other with cynicism and distrust (Brants et al. 2010; Van Aelst et al. 2008). In many other countries in the Western world, where journalists' role as watchdogs is key to the professional paradigm, studies point to eroding public trust in public institutions (e.g., Mair 2006; Torcal and Montero 2006), for which the news media are often held responsible. Journalists appear to be walking a tightrope between exercising a healthy amount of skepticism and entertaining an attitude of overt cynicism.

In a speech given to graduating journalism students, *New York Times* journalist and three-time Pulitzer Prize winner Thomas Friedman (2005) argued that striking a proper balance between skepticism and cynicism is essential to being a good journalist. He reminded his audience of the critical difference between skepticism and cynicism: "Skepticism is about asking questions, being dubious, being wary, not being gullible, but always being open to being persuaded of a new fact or angle." Cynicism, on the other hand, is about already having the answers—or thinking one does—about a person or an event. Friedman illustrated the difference thus: "The skeptic says, 'I don't think that's true; I'm going to check it out.' The cynic says: 'I know that's not true. It couldn't be. I'm going to slam him.'"

Frequently journalists are among the first to become aware of institutional misconduct, and, not rarely, they become victims of a corrupt system. This can further erode journalists' trust in the institutional fabric of their societies as these institutions are supposed to protect them from violence and harassment. The situation in Serbia, where media freedom has declined substantially in recent years, is a case in point. Media organizations most critical of the government face heavy political pressure and are subjected to frequent arbitrary financial and administrative inspections.[1] In a 2017 interview Nedim Sejdinovic, president of the Serbian Journalists' Association NDNV, indicated that "such things happen when the authorities usurp all the institutions and put them in the service of their party oligarchy. . . . In such situations, you as a victim cannot distinguish between those who threaten you and those who should protect you."[2]

If trust in public institutions is a marker of journalism's professional self-positioning vis-à-vis the larger power structures in society, and if this has consequences for journalists' reporting and, as a result, for public confidence in politics and governance, then we think it is all the more important to study journalists' institutional trust within a comparative assessment of journalistic cultures. This chapter examines the extent to which journalists around the world have trust in public institutions and the contextual factors that may account for differences in this trust across journalistic cultures. Further, the chapter investigates the degree to which journalists' institutional trust matches such trust held by the public.

The results show that journalists around the world have more confidence in regulative institutions (the judiciary, military, and police) than in representative ones (parliament, government, political parties, and politicians in general). They appear to have particularly low trust in politicians and political parties, which is a strikingly consistent pattern across different nations. On a comparative level, journalists' political trust is related to democratic performance and prevailing journalistic roles, but these relationships often show a nonlinear pattern. Trust is higher among journalists working in the democratic-corporatist media system, where journalists have high levels of autonomy, while it is lowest in countries that have recently undergone major political, economic, and cultural transformations, including several post-communist countries and transitional democracies in South America. Furthermore, in liberal democracies journalists tend to have more political trust than do the general populations, while in non-Western countries we found an opposite pattern.

Journalists and Trust in Public Institutions

Studies of public trust are generally rooted in theories of public engagement (Easton 1965; Putnam 1993), which assume that "the greater the level of trust within a community, the greater the likelihood of cooperation. And cooperation itself breeds trust" (Putnam 1993, 171). Three theoretical assumptions about trust inform most definitions. First, theorists emphasize that trust is based on past experiences that lead to expectations about (and an assessment of) how another person or institution will perform in the future (Misztal 1996; Rotter 1967; Vanacker and Belmas 2009). Second, this process involves risk and uncertainty because outcomes or intentions of actors are not fully known, which makes trust particularly essential where verification is most difficult. Third, trust reduces social complexity by generalizing expectations about future behavior (Luhmann 1979). Thus trust is a psychological state comprising the intention to accept vulnerability based on positive expectations of a trustee's future actions, which cannot be controlled by the trustor (Mayer, Davis, and Schoorman 1995; Rousseau et al. 1998). For this chapter we define journalists' trust as the willingness of a journalist to be vulnerable to the performance of public institutions based on the anticipation that these institutions will meet the journalists' expectations. As outlined in chapter 2, we treat journalists' institutional trust as a form through which journalists indicate their position vis-à-vis larger society.

Like all forms of trust, institutional trust depends on the reference object. These objects can be classified in various ways. One way is to distinguish between trust in institutions and trust in individuals or aggregates of individuals. Thomas Hanitzsch and Rosa Berganza (2014), for instance, found that in a number of countries journalists have substantial trust in political institutions, such as the parliament or the government, but have little confidence in the individuals serving these institutions.

In this chapter we also distinguish between *representative institutions*, which are responsible for democratic representation and political decision making, and *regulative institutions* that implement these decisions (Walter-Rogg 2005). In the following sections we refer to the government, the parliament, and political parties as representative institutions, and to the police, military, and judiciary as regulative institutions. A major focus of this chapter is journalists' trust in representative political institutions.

The decline of public trust in these representative institutions, at least in Western societies, can be read as a symptom of citizens' growing dissatisfaction with, and shrinking participation in, politics. Both these issues are problematic for democratic performance and for a political system that cannot function without citizens' participation and trust in political institutions (Mishler and Rose 2001; Norris 1999; Torcal and Montero 2006). As several authors have pointed out, higher levels of trust in representative institutions positively correlate with subjective evaluations of bureaucratic efficiency and can foster a sense of good governance and increase institutional effectiveness (Knack and Keefer 1997; Morrone, Tontoranelli, and Ranuzzi 2009; Rice and Sumberg 1997).

Political scientists have established a variety of factors that may contribute to differences in public trust across societies. Two schools of thought dominate the discussion—institutional and cultural. *Institutional theories* argue that trust is endogenous; it is seen as a consequence of institutional performance (Mishler and Rose 2001). In this rationally grounded perspective, the erosion of trust is rooted in the failure of public institutions to meet citizens' expectations (Lühiste 2006). Among the aspects of institutional performance that were found to be most relevant to public trust are bad governance, corruption, and the general quality of democracy (Grosskopf 2008; Kotzian 2011; Kunioka and Woller 1999; Slomczynski and Janicka 2009).

Cultural theories, on the other hand, argue that public trust is exogenous and deeply rooted in culture. In this view, trust in public institutions is an extension of social (or interpersonal) trust, learned early in life and, much later, projected onto public institutions (Hudson 2006; Mishler and Rose 2001). The more people trust each other in a given society, the more they trust political institutions. Another line of argument builds on the work of Ronald Inglehart (1977, 2006), who has observed a "silent revolution" entailing a shift from survival values to self-expression values in postindustrial societies. This "emancipative value change" gives rise to postmaterialist values such as individual autonomy, self-expression, and free choice (Inglehart and Welzel 2005, 1). This value change most notably entails greater emancipation from authority, which—according to Inglehart (1999)—contributes to an erosion of institutional trust and gives rise to the "critical citizen" (Norris 1999; see chapter 2).

While many studies have investigated the ways in which the news media contribute to either a growing or an eroding sense of trust in public institutions, relatively few have looked at the mindset of those who routinely cover these institutions. Early studies that investigated journalists' and politicians' perceptions of one another in Belgium, Denmark, Germany, Italy, and Spain, as well as in the Netherlands and the United Kingdom, found a tendency toward political cynicism among political reporters (e.g., Brants et al. 2010; Mancini 1993; Van Aelst et al. 2008; Van Dalen, Albaek, and de Vreese 2011). Based on data of the second phase of the Worlds of Journalism Study, Alice Tejkalová et al. (2017) found that journalists tend to have greater trust in their own institution—the media—than in political and regulative institutions.

Based on an examination of data collected through the first WJS, Hanitzsch and Berganza (2012, 2014) found that journalists had little trust in political parties and politicians, pointing to a generally cynical attitude in journalists with regard to political actors. This finding was strikingly consistent across all countries studied. These scholars also found that journalists in Western nations had more trust in public institutions than did their colleagues in the non-Western world. Journalists were more trusting of public institutions in countries where they enjoyed greater press freedom and faced less corruption, when they worked in state-owned news organizations, and when they worked in societies where people tend to trust each other. Comparing journalists' trust assessments with those of the larger public, the study discovered an interesting pattern. In Western countries, either journalists turned out to be more trustful than the general population, or trust levels did not differ significantly between the two groups. In most non-Western countries, however, journalists exhibited significantly less political trust than did the public.

In the following section we first report our findings about journalists' trust in representative and regulative institutions and then present our analysis of the patterns in representative trust around the world. All analyses are based on journalists' responses to the question: "Please tell me how much you personally trust each of the following institutions." Journalists could choose answers on a scale ranging between 1 ("no trust at all") and 5 ("complete trust"). In essence we measured institutional trust among journalists in a way similar to the measure used in large-scale comparative surveys inquiring into institutional trust among the public, such as the World Values Survey and the European Values Study.

The Big Picture: Who Do Journalists Trust?

Table 9.1 and figure 9.1 report the average levels of trust in seven public institutions among journalists from all fifty countries where this question was asked.[3] The table shows that, in general, journalists around the world have limited trust in these institutions. For all institutions, average trust falls between 2.0 ("little trust") and 3.0 ("some trust"). The differences in the size of eta squared, denominating the variance accounted for by country, demonstrates that trust among journalists varied across societies depending on the type of public institution involved.

The average level of trust in regulative institutions was close to the neutral midpoint of the scale. Journalists around the world placed their highest trust in three regulative institutions: in decreasing order, the judiciary, the police, and the military. Cross-national differences are especially large for the judiciary and the police, with eta squared values of .25 and .22,

Table 9.1 Trust in institutions among journalists around the world

	N	Mean[a]	F[b]	Eta²
Judiciary/the courts	19,109	3.00	129.50	.250
Military	18,644	2.93	82.23	.175
Police	19,134	2.82	109.86	.220
Parliament	18,915	2.74	117.72	.234
Government	19,058	2.67	83.19	.177
Politicians in general	19,052	2.28	86.13	.182
Political parties	18,811	2.23	71.46	.155

[a] Weighted; all p < .001.
[b] df = 49, except for political parties and military (df = 48).

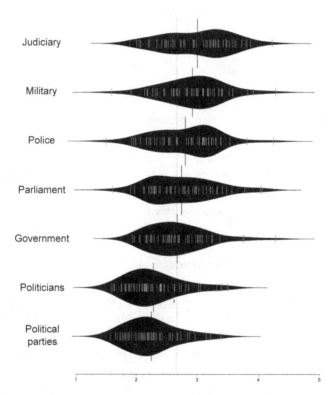

Figure 9.1 Journalists' trust in public institutions around the world (distribution of mean scores)

Source: WJS; N = 50.

Note: Scale: 5 = "complete trust" ... 1 = "no trust at all."

respectively. These figures demonstrate that trust in regulative institutions varied widely across countries. Table A.5 in the appendix reports a countrywide breakdown of average levels of trust in each of the institutions above.

In the case of representative institutions, journalists had relatively little trust in their parliaments and governments, with mean scores of 2.74 and 2.67 on a 5-point scale, respectively. Further, politicians and political parties appeared at the bottom of the ranking, with average scores of 2.28 and 2.23, which indicate a significant lack of confidence among journalists in these institutions. Although differences among societies are large, with the country level accounting for about 18 percent and 16 percent of the overall variation, our results unequivocally point to dramatically low levels of journalists' trust in politicians and political parties. This finding is not only strikingly consistent across the countries, as table A.5 indicates, but is also in line with results of previous studies (Hanitzsch and Berganza 2014).

Figure 9.1 shows that for politicians and political parties, the country means are distributed over a narrow range of the scale (with the exception of Bhutan, where journalists were strongly trusting of these political institutions, a finding that is discussed further below). The low level of trust journalists have in these two institutions is a striking commonality among countries. Journalists around the world agree that politicians and political parties are less trustworthy than other institutions. These results may be both a reason for optimism and a source for concern. One the one hand, a certain lack of trust—in other words, an attitude of "healthy" skepticism—indicates a critical stance of journalists toward authority, which, at least from a traditionally Western normative point of view, is a desirable attitude needed to hold parties and politicians to account. On the other hand, journalists' lack of confidence in these institutions could also breed public cynicism toward political authority, which can seriously undermine democracy.

In summary, journalists have less trust in representative institutions than in regulative institutions. In the United States, this pattern is clearly evident (see table A.5). Here journalists have very little faith in representative institutions and political actors, a finding in line with the low, and steadily declining, levels of political trust among the public (Gronke and Cook 2007). At the same time, U.S. journalists' average levels of trust in regulative institutions are higher than the neutral midpoint of the scale for each of the three regulative institutions. Sweden and Argentina are the only two countries where journalists have about the same level of trust in regulative institutions as they have in representative institutions.

Patterns of Political Trust Around the World

The previous section identified large cross-national differences in journalists' levels of trust in public institutions. For the following analyses, we combined journalists' evaluations of three representative political institutions—government, parliament, and political parties—in an index labeled "political trust." In technical terms, we computed the political trust index by averaging journalists' responses to the questions asking about trust in these three institutions. This strategy allowed us to retain the original scale of measurement, with a value of 5 pointing to complete trust and a value of 1 representing no trust at all. Figure 9.2 illustrates the differences in journalists' political trust around the world (also see table A.5). Journalists in Bhutan, India, and Oman report the highest levels of political trust. Journalists' faith in political institutions is also strong in countries that have democratic corporatist media systems (Belgium, Germany, Netherlands, Sweden, and Switzerland), and where corruption is low and a strong public service ethos is present (Hallin and Mancini 2004). This confirms findings from an earlier study (Hanitzsch and Berganza 2012). Canada and Estonia, too, are among the countries with the highest levels of trust.

The United States is a notable exception to the pattern of high levels of trust among developed countries. As noted above, journalists are not unique in their skepticism toward political institutions. U.S. citizens, too, have little faith in the government, Congress, and political parties compared to levels found in other Western countries (Putnam 2001). Hence journalists here operate within a cultural climate of public disdain for political institutions. In addition, these journalists' relative lack of political trust is arguably related to the powerful position of the watchdog approach in American journalistic ideology, which puts a strong emphasis on critical scrutiny of authorities (Kovach and Rosenstiel 2001; see chapter 7). This professional attitude, which has historically gone through several cycles of muckraking and investigative journalism (Feldstein 2006), was aptly summarized by *Boston Globe* journalist Bob Anglin more than thirty years ago: "Show me a reporter with a respect for authority, and I'll show you a lousy reporter"

Bhutan	3.65		Ecuador	2.53
India	3.47		Tanzania	2.48
Oman	3.47		Portugal	2.44
Sweden	3.18		Argentina	2.40
Malaysia	3.18		Philippines	2.38
Singapore	3.15		Russia	2.36
Belgium	3.09		Iceland	2.36
Switzerland	3.04		Indonesia	2.35
Bangladesh	2.97		Spain	2.35
Germany	2.96		South Korea	2.31
Netherlands	2.94		Israel	2.29
El Salvador	2.94		Mexico	2.28
Botswana	2.89		Chile	2.25
Estonia	2.74		USA	2.20
Ethiopia	2.69		South Africa	2.16
Kenya	2.65		Hungary	2.15
Canada	2.65		Albania	2.07
Australia	2.63		Moldova	2.07
Malawi	2.63		Czech Republic	2.06
Austria	2.62		Bulgaria	2.06
Denmark	2.59		Kosovo	2.05
Ireland	2.58		Brazil	2.05
UK	2.54		Greece	2.04
Sierra Leone	2.54		Serbia	2.04
Latvia	2.53		Romania	1.81

Figure 9.2 Journalists' political trust across countries (mean scores)

Source: WJS; N = 50 (for military and political parties: N = 49).

Note: Scale: 5 = "complete trust" . . . 1 = "no trust at all."

(cited in Nyhan 1986, 30). At the other end, certain circles of the nation's political establishment celebrate a hostile attitude toward the news media. Furthermore, the United States has a long tradition of politicians questioning the legitimacy of critical media organizations and accusing the press of biased reporting (Ladd 2012). Journalists and politicians, it seems, are caught in a downward spiral of cynicism and distrust—which arguably had not yet reached its lowest point when our survey was conducted.

In contrast, journalists in Bhutan have the highest levels of trust in political institutions. There are a number of reasons for the strong political trust expressed by Bhutan's journalists, the most important being that the country is one of the world's youngest democracies (Geringer de Oedenberg 2013). Democracy came by royal decree rather than a popular uprising, and the kingdom held its first national elections in 2008. The second national elections, in 2013, brought the opposition party, which had only two members in the first convocation of parliament, to power. Given this history, Bhutan's institutions may be experiencing a "honeymoon period" during which citizens'—and journalists'—excitement with democracy breeds high levels of confidence in public institutions. A similar—though short-lived—tendency was found in other societies that have transited from authoritarianism to liberal democracy, "directly following the foundation of democracies when they are less likely to break down" (Bernhard, Reenock, and Nordstrom 2003, 406; Mishler and Rose 1997). Furthermore, corruption is comparatively rare in Bhutan. In Transparency International's Corruption Perceptions Index for 2015, the country ranked third highest in Asia after Singapore and Japan, performing better in terms of transparency than several developed countries, including Portugal, Poland, and Spain.[4]

Journalists in the younger democracies, particularly in Eastern and Central Europe (Albania, Czech Republic, Greece, Hungary, Kosovo, Moldova, Romania, and Serbia) appear to have relatively little political trust. Like Bhutan, these countries have introduced democracy relatively recently, but what sets them apart from the Bhutanese case (where democracy was given by the king) is that their transition to democracy has been, and still is, much more complicated. Political ruptures and growing social inequalities have left the countries' representative institutions in a state of fragility in many cases. The precarious state of institutions is often indicated through widespread corruption, which Transparency International has reported for Albania, Kosovo, and Moldova. Other countries have recently gone through a severe financial crisis, for example, Greece, or exhibit a tendency toward authoritarian resurgence, such as Hungary under President Victor Orbán. Yet another group of countries, including Serbia and Kosovo, are recovering from armed conflict.

We will illustrate this pattern with two examples. Our first example is Brazil, where journalists have very little trust in their political institutions. Both broader Brazilian (and Latin American) culture as well as specific journalistic culture in Brazil may account for this finding. Similar to other Latin American countries (Lodola and Seligson 2012; Zechmeister 2014), Brazil tends to have an extremely low level of social trust. According to a

2014 population survey, only slightly more than 7 percent of Brazilians think that most people can be trusted.[5] Further, although the economy has improved and poverty has been reduced significantly in the past two decades, Brazil's political institutions remain weak and have repeatedly fallen victim to bad governance and a system of exchange of favors (quid pro quo). Moreover, the country's media system is historically organized around strong clientelism with solid ties between political and media actors; hence partisan models of media and journalism have developed in an almost "organic" fashion (Hallin and Papathanassopoulos 2002; Waisbord 2012, 2013a, 2013b).

Even lower levels of political trust were reported by journalists in Serbia, one of the Southeast European countries that emerged from the violent breakup of Yugoslavia in the 1990s. An overall climate of public disdain for political institutions and increased violence against journalists likely contribute to a situation in which Serbian journalists have very little confidence in the government, the parliament, and political parties. The collapse of the old regime was marked by a disintegration of institutions, moral devastation, impoverishment of large segments of the population, and substantial refugee movements (Bieber 2003). Almost thirty years of political, social, and economic ruptures, fragile democratic institutions, as well as low economic performance and high corruption have created extreme socioeconomic inequalities, according to Eurostat, with the consequence that citizens' lives have not improved much.[6] As a result, citizens have generally very little confidence in the country's political institutions.[7] The Serbian government has been undermining media freedom and pluralism in recent years while formally complying with conditions to meet the criteria for joining the European Union under its enlargement framework. At the same time, political pressure and threats against journalists are widespread despite recently adopted media laws that have the purported aim to protect media pluralism (Huszka 2017).

Contextualizing Political Trust Among Journalists Around the World

The discussion above points to a variety of contextual factors that may explain why political trust among journalists varies from one country to another. At the same time, the in-depth description above of countries with high or low levels of trust showed that causes may be complex and multi-dimensional. To assess the impact of contextual factors, we conducted a series of bivariate analyses between country means of journalists' trust in political institutions and selected contextual variables related to the three domains of societal influence outlined in chapter 2: politics and governance, socioeconomic development, and cultural value systems. In addition, we looked at relationships between journalists' political trust and other aspects of journalistic culture.

A superficial reading would suggest that most correlations reported in table 9.2 contradict a rationally grounded institutional explanation, which argues that better performance of institutions generates trust in them. In the table we find no significant linear relationship between journalists' political trust, on the one hand, and the contextual factors of press freedom, democracy, the rule of law, and economic performance, on the other. The level of transparency—i.e., the absence of corruption—is the only contextual factor that is significantly related to political trust. As pointed out earlier, journalists have less political trust in countries where governments are less effective in combating corruption. This is the case, for instance, in Kosovo, Moldova, and Brazil. At the same time, journalists typically report higher levels of political trust in developed democracies that occupy top positions in transparency rankings, such as Sweden, Germany, and Switzerland (table A.8 in the appendix).

Transparency aside, there was no linear relationship between the performance of political institutions and journalists' trust. This finding indicates that the inherent dichotomy between democracy and authoritarianism, to paraphrase Ivan Krastev (2011), may not always provide for a sufficient explanation of political trust. Rather than being a linear association, the relationship between institutional performance and journalists' political trust exhibits a nonlinear pattern, in which journalists' political trust tends to be strongest in developed democracies (e.g., Northern Europe) as well as in many societies with authoritarian tendencies (e.g., Oman, Malaysia, and Singapore). At the same time, we found political trust to be substantially lower in most transitional contexts and new democracies.

Figure 9.3, which illustrates the relationship between democratic performance (as reported by the Economist Intelligence Unit) and journalists' political trust, lends support to this view. The distribution of countries in the figure broadly follows a U-shaped curve, where the lower central section of the curve is populated by countries with medium levels of democratic

Table 9.2 Correlates of political trust among journalists
(correlation coefficients)

	Political trust
Press freedom (FH)[a]	−.026
Press freedom (RSF)[b]	−.027
Democracy[c]	−.076
Rule of law[d]	.220
Economic growth[e]	.167
Transparency[f]	.313*
Human development[g]	−.086
Social trust[(h)]	.421**
Emancipative values[i]	.179
Political influences	.390**
Economic influences	.134
Personal networks influences	.236
Editorial autonomy	−.196
Monitorial role (centered)	−.074
Interventionist role (centered)	−.451**
Collaborative role (centered)	.438**

Notes: Pearson's correlation coefficient. **p < .01; *p < .05; N = 50 unless otherwise indicated.
[a] Freedom House; Freedom of the Press Index; scale reversed.
[b] Reporters Without Borders; World Press Freedom Index; scale reversed.
[c] Economist Intelligence Unit; EIU Democracy Index; N = 49.
[d] World Bank; percentile rank.
[e] World Bank; growth of real GDP; N = 49.
[f] Transparency International; Corruption Perceptions Index.
[g] UNDP; Human Development Index; N = 49.
[h] WVS/EVS data; N = 44.
[i] Scores calculated based on WVS/EVS data; N = 43.

performance and the lowest levels of political trust among journalists. These include new democracies in Eastern and Central Europe, several Latin American countries, as well as Indonesia and the Philippines. In the top right corner we find countries that belong to the democratic corporatist type of media system, where democratic institutions seem to perform

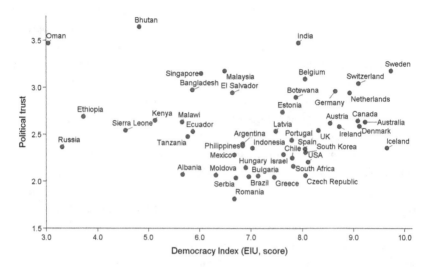

Figure 9.3 Journalists' political trust and democratic development

Source: Economist Intelligence Unit, WJS; N = 49.

well and journalists show high confidence in political institutions. The upper left quadrant has Bhutan and Oman, two countries where journalists appear to have robust confidence in politics, despite weak institutional performance.

The relationship between journalists' political trust and human development, which itself is strongly correlated with democratic performance in our sample (r = .68, p < .001, N = 49), broadly follows a similar, nonlinear pattern. The confidence journalists have in their political institutions tends to be higher in countries that perform well in terms of human development, but it is low in societies with mediocre values in the UN Development Programme's Human Development Index (see table A.8). In countries with lowest human development, journalists have more faith in politics. Examples include the African countries of Ethiopia, Kenya, Malawi, Sierra Leone, and Tanzania. These results point to the fact that the global similarities and differences in journalistic cultures may be more complicated than a developmental view would suggest. Certain important aspects of journalistic culture, such as the extent to which journalists have confidence in public institutions, are not unequivocally related to contextual measures of institutional performance in a linear fashion.

In line with cultural explanations of institutional trust, we expected journalists' trust levels to be higher in countries where citizens generally tend to trust one another and where emancipative values are less pronounced than in other societies. The results reported in table 9.2 lend some support to the expected relationship between social trust among citizens and political trust of journalists at the societal level. Journalists do indeed have more trust in political institutions when they work in social contexts in which citizens have a higher inclination to trust other people.[8] This is another finding that strongly supports the general argument advanced in this book. Journalists' professional orientations and practices need to be understood against the backdrop of the cultural environment within which they operate. Journalists have learned to trust other people as part of their socialization in a culture where such mutual trust is cultivated, and, to a considerable extent, they extend this trust to political institutions. In other words, a cultural environment of strong interpersonal trust strengthens journalists' political trust. A context of widespread public cynicism toward political institutions, on the other hand, creates a greater distance between political actors and the institution of journalism.

The prevalence of emancipative values in a society, on the other hand, has only a weak influence on journalists' political trust. A look at the distribution of countries is illuminating. The large majority of countries follow a linear trend of journalists having greater confidence in political institutions in societies that have a stronger appreciation for emancipative values (see table A.8). However, some countries contradict this pattern. Journalists in Bangladesh, India, Malaysia, and Singapore report very high levels of political trust, even though these societies score relatively low in terms of emancipative values as conceptualized by Ronald Inglehart and Christian Welzel (2005). If these four countries are removed from the analysis, the association becomes significantly stronger ($r = .58$, $p < .001$, $N = 39$). Hence our results point to a robust association between journalists' political trust and emancipative value change for most of the countries. The emancipation of a society from authority does not lead to a decline in confidence in political institutions among journalists. To the contrary, journalists tend to be more trusting of politics when they work in societies that place greater emphasis on emancipative values. However, one will have to take into account that the prevalence of emancipative values is itself strongly correlated with democratic performance (Welzel 2013).

The results presented in table 9.2 also indicate that journalists' trust in political institutions is associated with other aspects of journalistic culture. On the country level, we found a significant correlation between aggregates of journalists' political trust and the levels of political influence journalists reported. For influence from political actors, the distribution of countries is similar to the one reported in figure 9.3. Journalists' political trust tends to be high in liberal democracies in which news workers experience relatively little influence from political actors. Examples of such countries are Belgium, Germany, Sweden, and Switzerland. However, some of the highest levels of political trust are reported by journalists from countries where these journalists report relatively strong political pressures, such as Bhutan and Oman.

Further, table 9.2 shows that journalistic roles play into the way news workers conceive of political institutions. Journalists tend to have greater trust in politics in journalistic cultures that value a collaborative role more highly. Media professionals in these countries may be more willing to accept the political status quo, or even see themselves as partners of the government, on the assumption that they have shared interests with those in power (Catterberg and Moreno 2006; also see chapter 7). At the same time journalists are less confident in their political institutions in professional cultures that place greater emphasis on an interventionist role. In these societies, news workers may have become aware of social grievances and have chosen an interventionist role aiming to challenge the status quo and to promote change.

Figure 9.4 is instructive in this regard. The interventionist role of journalists is more pronounced in socioeconomically less developed countries and in countries that are undergoing disruptive changes (see chapter 7; also Stępińska and Ossowski 2012). The cluster of countries with the lowest level of political trust and a relatively high emphasis on the interventionist role comprises those East European countries that have experienced profound political, economic, and cultural transformation, and which continue to do so. Examples are Albania, Bulgaria, Hungary, Kosovo, Moldova, Romania, and Serbia. In close proximity to this group is another cluster of countries where journalists tend to have slightly more political trust but a similar preference for an interventionist role. These are societies that experienced economic or political instability in recent years. For instance, Greece, Portugal, and Spain—countries belonging to the third wave of democratization

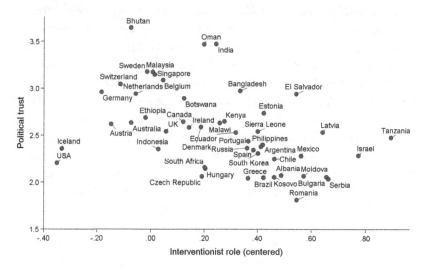

Figure 9.4 Journalists' political trust and relevance of interventionist role

Source: WJS; N = 50.

Note: Mean scores for interventionist role centered.

in the mid-1970s—have recently faced a severe economic crisis. Other societies that belong to this group have gone through political discontinuities, such as Argentina, Chile, Mexico, and Russia. Here low levels of trust among journalists in these interventionist professional cultures likely emanate from political and economic volatility resulting in high levels of uncertainty and, consequently, distrust. Earlier findings from Gabriel Catterberg and Alejandro Moreno (2005) speak to the significance of disruption in the formation and maintenance of trust: the higher the level of political radicalism, the lower the political trust in a society.

Figure 9.5 visualizes the association between journalists' trust in politics and the prevalence of a collaborative role in a country's journalistic culture. A collaborative role calls on journalists to act as partners of the government and to support it in its efforts to bring about development and social well-being. As we argued in chapter 7, this role may be rooted in a condition of fierce press restrictions, or in a cultural context that prioritizes social harmony. Singapore, Malaysia, Oman, Bhutan, and India form one cluster. In these countries, journalists' relatively high levels of political trust

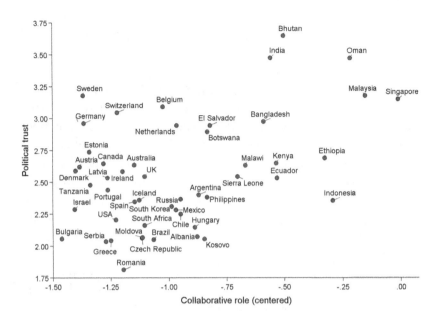

Figure 9.5 Journalists' political trust and relevance of collaborative role

Source: WJS; N = 50.

Note: Mean scores for collaborative role centered.

coincide with a considerable willingness on their part to embrace a collaborative role. Singapore is a good example to illustrate this point. Journalists operate in a climate of "calibrated coercion," or soft media control, and in a culture that emphasizes social harmony and respect for authority (George 2007; Xu 2005).

Another group of countries, including many transitional societies spanning the space between Bulgaria to the left and Kosovo and the Philippines to the right of the figure, comprise journalistic cultures where journalists have relatively little confidence in political institutions and are generally reluctant to see themselves as partners of the government. A third cluster, finally, mostly consists of Western countries (in the space to the upper left of figure 9.5, between Sweden, the Netherlands, and the United Kingdom), where journalists have stronger faith in politics and show little inclination to follow a collaborative approach to journalism.

Political Trust Among Journalists and the General Public

Having examined the cross-national differences in journalists' political trust, we now turn to comparing journalists' and the general public's attitudes toward political institutions. The focus of this analysis is whether journalists have more or less trust in political institutions than do citizens. Recent studies have shown that the relationship between politicians and journalists, once symbiotic, is now characterized by mutual mistrust (Brants et al. 2010; Van Aelst et al. 2008). Arguably this political skepticism makes its way into the news, thus producing negative coverage of politics, which in turn may affect public trust in representative institutions. Hence we compared journalists' confidence in politics with results from representative population surveys. Here we draw on data from the sixth (2010–2014) wave of the World Values Survey (WVS), in which the question of trust is the same as the one we used. The comparison is limited to a narrower range of twenty countries that were included in both the most recent WVS and WJS waves. Since the WVS used a slightly different scale, we transformed the answers in both the WVS and the WJS to a range from 0 to 1.

Figure 9.6 shows that there is a strong linear relationship between journalists' trust and trust among the public. The diagonal line in the chart represents a correlation of 1.0, which means that journalists' political trust would perfectly match public trust if all countries' averages fall onto this line. In other words, in countries closer to the line there is stronger agreement between journalists and audiences with regard to confidence in public institutions than in societies farther removed from the line.

The results show that there are no significant differences between journalists' and the general public's levels of political trust in Argentina, Brazil, Chile, Ecuador, Estonia, Mexico, and Spain. In Sweden, differences are statistically significant but negligible. In the remaining societies, journalists have either significantly more (countries above the diagonal line) or significantly less (countries below the diagonal) confidence in their political institutions than does the general public.[9] These differences are particularly pronounced for the Philippines and South Africa.

The general pattern of the relationship between journalists' trust and public trust in political institutions, established in a previous study (Hanitzsch and Berganza 2014), is also found in this study, with India and the United States being the exceptions. In most Western countries, either

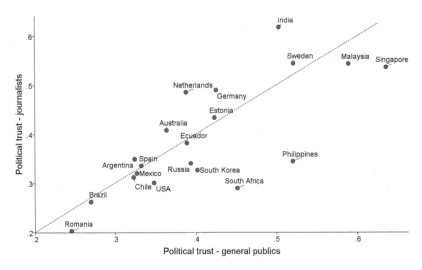

Figure 9.6 Political trust among journalists and among the general public

Source: WVS (countries with data collected after 2010), WJS; N = 20.

journalists have more faith in political institutions than do the general populations or differences are negligible. In these societies, journalists tend to be well-educated (see chapter 4), and studies have shown that education can positively influence institutional trust among citizens (Gronke and Cook 2007; Hudson 2006). Besides being well-educated, journalists deal with the important news of the day as part of their job; hence they may have more firsthand experience and more sophisticated views of politics. Judgments of the wider public, on the other hand, strongly depend on media content that has become more negative over time in most Western democracies as journalists increasingly cater to news values related to drama, sensation, and conflict in political discourse (Patterson 1994; Lengauer, Esser, and Berganza 2012). In other words, journalists tend to have much more direct interactions with political institutions; hence their trust levels are more likely to be affected by personal experience than those of the general public.

The picture is different for the group of countries belonging to the Global South. If there are substantive differences in levels of trust, it is typically journalists who are more skeptical of political institutions than is the general public. Journalists have privileged access to information about political processes owing to the nature of their work. They are usually the first to become aware of political deficiencies and misconduct. Much of this first-hand information, however, might not be exposed to the public because of restrictions on press freedom, threats to journalists' safety, and intersecting interests of political, economic, and media elites. Furthermore, in a climate of deceptive and restrictive information policies of governments and state authorities in several countries, journalists likely become subject to political pressure and intimidation, which may well affect their attitudes toward political actors.

As noted earlier, journalists in India and the United States stand in notable contrast to the general pattern. The situation in India, on the one hand, is difficult to explain; we could only speculate in the absence of relevant literature. In the United States, on the other hand, such a trend had already been established more than twenty years ago, when the Times Mirror Center (1995) discovered that American citizens were considerably more cynical about their political institutions than journalists. In the first WJS, however, U.S. journalists were found to be just as skeptical as citizens in the country (Hanitzsch and Berganza 2014). According to our recent survey, the situation seems to have changed again. Now the United States is the only Western country where journalists have significantly less trust in politics than does the general population. This is yet another indication of the unique, if not exceptional, status of American journalism even within the Western world.

Conclusions

In this chapter we investigated how journalists from around the world view public institutions of various kinds. Our results indicate that journalists' trust varies depending on the national context and the type of public institution. Across the globe, journalists have greater confidence in regulative institutions (the judiciary, military, and police) than in representative ones (parliament, government, political parties, and politicians in general). Journalists' trust in political parties and politicians, in particular, is almost universally low, mirroring a trend of growing distrust in political institutions charted for most parts of the Western world (Mair 2006; Moy, Pfau, and Kahlor 1999; Torcal and Montero 2006). That being said, our data also illustrate that, despite this high level of skepticism, journalists carefully distinguish between institutions. Overall, these results are consistent with findings from the first wave of the Worlds of Journalism Study (Hanitzsch and Berganza 2014). Further, in most countries for which comparable data were available, journalists' trust in political institutions strongly correlates with corresponding perceptions among the larger public. Where significant differences exist, we observed a split between Western and non-Western countries. In these cases, journalists' trust tends to be higher than that of the general populations in liberal democracies, while there is an opposite trend for most non-Western countries. This empirical pattern, too, is consistent with previous analyses of this type (Hanitzsch and Berganza 2014).

Viewing journalists' trust in institutions from a comparative point of view, we found three patterns. First, journalists in countries that belong to democratic-corporatist media systems (Hallin and Mancini 2004) have relatively high levels of institutional confidence (e.g., Belgium, Germany, the Netherlands, Sweden, and Switzerland). These societies, which have long democratic traditions, are governed by strong public institutions. Journalism is characterized by a high degree of media freedom, institutionalized professional self-regulation, and a strong public service ethos.

However, while democratic corporatism may be conducive to the formation of trust among journalists, it is not a precondition. In our study, high levels of trust were also reported by journalists from countries that do not meet these conditions, such as Malaysia, Oman, and Singapore. In these societies, journalists operate under substantive restrictions on their political and editorial freedoms. Unlike their colleagues in many other countries, journalists in these countries are willing to accept giving a certain amount of support to the ruling elites, either because authorities leave them little choice or because they willingly adopt the general goals and aspirations of the government.

At the same time, we found the lowest confidence in public institutions among journalists working in countries that have experienced significant political, economic, and cultural instability and transformation. This group of countries includes many postcommunist societies in Europe and younger democracies in South America. Despite the existence of established democratic structures and constitutionally guaranteed freedoms, journalists in these countries tend to be highly skeptical of their public institutions as actual institutional performance does not meet the people's expectations of quality in democracy and governance; expectations that may have risen as part of the modernization process. Journalists here adhere to an interventionist role aimed at changing social realities.

It is this complex relationship among journalistic roles, democratic performance, and political trust that we think should be the subject of further research, preferably by utilizing a longitudinal perspective. Further research should also look into the *consequences* of journalists' political trust. Observation studies could show how journalists with different levels of political trust interact with politicians. Content analysis could reveal the political and media-related conditions in which low levels of trust translate into overtly negative coverage about politics.

A major conclusion from this comparative analysis is that—in line with institutional theories explaining differences in public trust—journalists' institutional trust is indeed related to contextual factors, notably democratic performance and quality of governance as well as the prevalence of interventionist and collaborative journalistic roles, but these associations often exhibit a nonlinear pattern. These findings complicate developmental views that suggest a linear transformation of journalistic culture toward some kind of "optimum" stage. As we will argue in the concluding chapter of this book, each journalistic culture needs to find its own response to the problems posed by the political, economic, and sociocultural contexts within which it exists.

Notes

1. Reporters Without Borders, Serbia, https://rsf.org/en/serbia.
2. "Sejdinović: Sve što se lose moglo desiti novinarstvu, desilo se u Srbiji," *Cenzolovka*, 2017, https://www.cenzolovka.rs/scena/sejdinovic-sve-sto-se-lose-moglo-desiti-novinarstvu-desilo-se-u-srbiji/.
3. The question was optional; information is reported for fifty out of the sixty-seven countries: Albania, Argentina, Australia, Austria, Bangladesh, Belgium, Bhutan, Botswana, Brazil, Bulgaria, Canada, Chile, Czech Republic, Denmark, Ecuador, El Salvador, Estonia, Ethiopia, Germany, Greece, Hungary, Iceland, India, Indonesia, Ireland, Israel, Kenya, Kosovo, Latvia, Malawi, Malaysia, Mexico, Moldova, Netherlands, Oman, Philippines, Portugal, Romania, Russia, Serbia, Sierra Leone, Singapore, South Africa, South Korea, Spain, Sweden, Switzerland, Tanzania, the United Kingdom, and the United States.
4. Transparency International, Corruption Perceptions Index, 2015, https://www.transparency.org/cpi2015.
5. World Values Survey, 2014, Online Data Analysis, http://www.worldvaluessurvey.org/WVSOnline.jsp.

6. Maja Krek, "Šta znači 'prosečna zarada' ako je većina nema?," *Peščanik*, April 1, 2018, http://pescanik.net/sta-znaci-prosecna-zarada-ako-je-vecina-nema/.

7. "Gradani Srbije ne veruju institucijama," EurActiv.rs, February 1, 2015, http://www.euractiv.rs/pregovori-sa-eu/8212-graani-srbije-ne-veruju-institucijama-.

8. Measured by the World Values Survey/European Values Study question, "Generally speaking, would you say that most people can be trusted or that you need to be very careful in dealing with people?"

9. T-tests for differences between citizens' and journalists' political trust: Australia: $t = -4.72$, $df = 2,054$, $p < .001$; Germany: $t = -7.43$, $df = 2,754$, $p < .001$; India: $t = -9.15$, $df = 5,911$, $p < .001$; Malaysia: $t = 3.18$, $df = 1,588$, $p < .01$; Netherlands: $t = -9.84$, $df = 2,322$, $p < .001$; Philippines: $t = 13.38$, $df = 1,524$, $p < .001$; Romania: $t = 3.01$, $df = 1,803$, $p < .01$; Russia: $t = 3.89$, $df = 2,813$, $p < .001$; Singapore: $t = 4.12$, $df = 1,615$, $p < .001$; South Africa: $t = 10.92$, $df = 3,821$, $p < .001$; South Korea: $t = 5.86$, $df = 1,533$, $p < .001$; Sweden: $t = -2.47$, $df = 1,779$, $p < .05$; United States: $t = 4.56$, $df = 2,597$, $p < .001$. Differences in other countries were not significant.

10

TRANSFORMATIONS

Journalists' Reflections on Changes in News Work

Folker Hanusch, Edson C. Tandoc, Jr., Dimitra Dimitrakopoulou,
Nurhaya Muchtar, Kevin Rafter, Mireya Márquez Ramírez,
Verica Rupar, and Vittoria Sacco

In 2016 an online job portal in the United States ranked being a newspaper reporter as the worst job, citing shrinking job opportunities and meager salaries (Hare 2016); being a broadcaster was ranked only somewhat higher—as the third-worst job. These were "noble careers," it acknowledged, but the portal also suggested that "those embarking on these positions should understand the dangers, as well as the surprisingly low pay for each" (CareerCast.com 2016). Those already in the profession in the United States seem to have similarly dismal views; their levels of job satisfaction have decreased over time, as assessed by surveys since 1971 (Willnat and Weaver 2014), because traditional journalism has gone through enormous upheaval, particularly in recent years. Concerns about journalism's sustainability as an industry have risen in the past several years owing to the impact of digitization and the related lack of a profitable business model. Today the profession is witnessing increasing workloads and new responsibilities for journalists as news organizations go digital-first, prioritizing their online platforms to accommodate news audiences migrating to online. While the U.S. news industry appears to be particularly hard hit by digitization, news media in many other countries have not escaped its impact (see, e.g., Levy and Nielsen 2010; Tong and Lo 2017).

Scholarship on change has significantly increased in the past decade, triggered by the call to examine the impact of technology on social life. The field of journalism studies is no exception. The digitization of news has triggered massive shifts in how journalism is produced, distributed, and consumed (Hermida 2012). Technological change apart, broad economic, societal, and cultural shifts have also contributed to developments such as cutbacks in editorial resources, increases in journalists' workloads, loss of jobs, larger focus on profit making, stronger pressure from advertising demands, greater importance of audience measures, sensationalism, and shrinking editorial independence. These developments over the past decade or two have led, both in the academic literature and in journalistic narratives, to the emergence of a "crisis in journalism" frame (Franklin 2012, 665).

A close look at the scholarship on journalism reveals that these developments have been viewed predominantly in the context of the United States and other Western nations. Thus our knowledge about transformations in journalism is influenced to a large degree by the Western experience (Mitchelstein and Boczkowski 2009). Scholars have called for studies that have greater regional diversity. Such studies would help broaden our understanding of change because political transitions and upheavals that have swept through countries across the globe have transformed both media systems and the practice of journalism almost everywhere (Gross 2004). Further, such studies would fill the current lacuna in the vast literature on transformations in journalistic work, a literature wherein journalists and their practices "have not often been the main objects of study" (Dickinson, Matthews, and Saltzis 2013, 5). The Worlds of Journalism Study does precisely this. It seeks to understand change from within, by studying transformations as perceived by journalists themselves, rather than at the institutional level, because journalists experience many of these changes themselves as they engage in day-to-day journalistic activities. Further, changes at the institutional and organizational level, such as the restructuring of newsrooms, as well as the demand for new skills and for establishing stronger relationships with audiences, have direct consequences for journalism's professional identity, values, and norms (Fenton 2010).

Hence from the vantage point of journalism as a discursive institution, one that defines its conditions and conventions in negotiation with societal structures that enable or restrain it (see chapter 2), this chapter attempts to study change in journalists' own terms, through their own perceptions. More specifically, we investigate how change is unfolding across different journalistic cultures and in journalists' day-to-day work. As we show in this chapter, journalists around the world generally perceive significant increases in the influence of technology, audiences, and commercial pressures. They perceive the importance of using search engines and technical skills, as well as their working hours, to have increased, but their time for research has decreased. It appears that the more highly developed in terms of information communication technologies a given country is, the more likely it is that journalists in that country perceive a stronger influence of technological aspects in their work over the past five years. At the same time, in countries with a traditionally strong newspaper market, journalists do not report audience influences to have increased as strongly as elsewhere. Further, in media markets that are still expanding or which have not encountered drastic declines, journalists tend to be more positive about their work and place stronger emphasis on increases in professionalization. Given this, we find that the narrative about journalism in crisis is particularly dominant in the West but less so in other parts of the world, pointing to the importance of comparative research on transformations in journalism for a better global understanding.

Studying Change in Journalism

In their attempt to comprehend the complexity of the world, scholars in all disciplinary fields have to contend with the concept of change because change is inherent in all societal institutions. As a concept, change is related to such other concepts as development, evolution, innovation, revolution, and transition (Stickland 1998). As "structural transformation" (Ryder 1965, 843), change refers to a departure from the status quo. Departures that have long-term effects on a particular field in terms of structures and processes need scholarly attention in particular. The magnitude of these effects depends in part on how agents within the field perceive and internalize particular changes. The literature on change focuses on radical institutional reconfigurations caused by external shocks. It pays little attention to the shifts from internal developments that often unfold incrementally (Mahoney and Thelen 2010). But these internal changes, operating as they do, almost invisibly within the field, are also influential and need attention.

The global economic recession of the recent past severely affected media organizations around the world (Paulussen 2012). In an institution where precariousness of employment is becoming common, such employment conditions are further aggravated by organizational changes in a media market pressured to reduce costs and increase profits (Altmeppen 2008). Additionally, digital technologies have enabled the emergence of a plurality of news providers that threatens major media companies' delivery monopolies. These developments have affected journalists in two major areas: in their practices and ideologies as well as in their relationships with their audiences (Hermans, Vergeer, and d'Haenens 2009; Mitchelstein and Boczkowski 2009; Singer 2011).

Journalists are working in a complex time trying to formulate and understand what it means to be a professional in an online and social media–enabled age (Sacco and Bossio 2014). Digital technologies have facilitated the daily work of journalists, but they have also made these routines more complex. Journalists are now expected to be capable of producing multiple types of content for very different platforms using several tools in newsrooms that count smaller workforces owing to budget cuts. Proficiency in computer and technological skills has become indispensable to successfully managing the different tasks expected of a journalist (Singer 2011). Studies have focused on new ways in which journalists have to search for news content, to present it in innovative ways, and to distribute it instantly (e.g., Hirst and Treadwell 2011; Phillips 2012). These new routines sometimes contradict existing norms. For example, journalists now struggle to reconcile their role as marketers on social media with their normative belief in and practice of their autonomy (Tandoc and Vos 2016).

The use of search engines in doing journalistic fact finding has also become commonplace, yet this creates dilemmas for journalists because search engines are also susceptible to manipulation (Machill and Beiler 2009) and have consequences for journalistic decisions (Dick 2011). Thus while digital technologies have not changed the need for good reporting (Baker 2004), they have placed additional pressures on journalists. Journalists also find themselves shouldered with additional responsibilities, such as reporting via social media (Hanusch 2013). These new tasks increase the amount of time needed to complete their work; today younger journalists report higher rates of burnout than their older colleagues (Reinardy 2011). New responsibilities in the newsroom also require new skill sets, which poses enormous challenges to journalism education around the world (Deuze 2006b).

Changes in technology have led to developments that in turn have affected the relationship between journalists and their audiences. These developments include the rise of crowdsourcing (Akagi and Linning 2013; Poell and Borra 2012), audiences' ability to distribute news content (Hermida 2012; Thorson 2008), and the increased significance of audience preferences in the production and delivery of news content (Tandoc 2014; Lee and Tandoc 2017). New technologies allow audiences to get involved in the entire cycle of news creation from newsgathering to selecting, editing, producing, and delivering news content (Borger et al. 2013). Blogging and social media have created a space where professional journalists and citizens can have a conversation (Reese et al. 2007). A majority of studies have focused on the relationship between journalists and user-generated content (UGC) in the news production cycle (e.g., Thurman 2008; Boczkowski 2004). Some of these have explored the ways in which UGC affects journalistic norms of impartiality, detachment, and balanced coverage (e.g., Hermida, Lewis, and Zamith 2012). Others have focused on matters such as whether UGC leads to publication of manipulated or unverified information, lack of original investigation, and poor information quality and have in fact found otherwise (e.g., Quandt and Singer 2009).

While measuring perceived changes in journalism is important, it is not easy to do. When we ask journalists about their own perceptions of changes, we run the risk of confounding retrospective assessments of change with respondents' current circumstances (Pudney 2011). The gold standard is to conduct longitudinal or panel studies to assess changes in journalists' perceptions over time. Surveys of journalists also suffer from a gap between perception and practice, as recent studies on journalistic role enactment have shown (e.g., Tandoc, Hellmueller, and Vos 2013). Further, journalists may reflect on changes in the journalistic community more generally rather than on changes in their own work. Hence it is important to consider journalists' assessment of the amount of change in a way similar to the understanding we bring to their role perceptions: that these reflect a discourse about the changes that journalists in a particular community experience. Still, journalists' change perceptions provide important insights into trends in journalistic transformations not only within particular national boundaries but also in a comparative context across the globe.

Our analysis of perceived changes in journalism is based on a subsample of 19,069 journalists interviewed for the WJS (69 percent of the global sample) for two reasons: in some countries (Denmark, Qatar, and Sudan) the change questions were not asked, and only those journalists who had worked in journalism for a minimum of five years were asked to respond to these questions, based on the reasoning that five years of experience gave them sufficient expertise to make an informed assessment. We used two questions to assess change perceptions. The first was: "The importance of some influences on journalism may have changed over time. Please tell me to what extent these influences have become stronger or weaker during the past five years in your country." Response options ranged from 5 ("influences strengthened a lot") to 1 ("influences weakened a lot"), with 3 meaning no change at all. The second question was: "Journalism is in a state of change. Please tell me whether you think there has been an increase or a decrease in the importance of the following aspects of work in your country." Again, a 5-point scale provided response options ranging from 5 ("importance increased a lot") to 1 ("importance decreased a lot"), with 3 meaning no change.

Changes in Work Influences

Chapter 2 conceptualized journalism as a field of forces in which institutional actors find themselves in constant struggle (Bourdieu 1998). At the macro level journalism finds itself confronted with pressures from other fields, notably the economic and political fields (Bourdieu 2005). At the micro level agents within journalism participate in a struggle to either transform or preserve the field (Benson and Neveu 2005). What is at stake at both levels is journalism's autonomy. Journalism, similar to other fields of practice, is dominated by two forms of power, economic capital and cultural capital. Economic capital refers to assets that can be directly converted into money, such as advertising; cultural capital refers to resources that distinguish journalism from other fields, such as expertise, knowledge, and educational credentials (Benson and Neveu 2005). Journalism's cultural capital helps preserve its autonomy, while its economic capital makes it susceptible to external influences, such as economic pressures (Bourdieu 2005). This relative influence of cultural versus economic capital is subject to constant discursive negotiation within the newsroom and in the institution of journalism as a whole.

The various factors that were assessed for change can be conceptually grouped into influences related to journalism's economic and cultural

Table 10.1 Perceived changes in influences on journalism across countries

	N	Mean[a]	F[b]	Eta²
Social media	18,331	4.44	46.04	.137
User-generated content, such as blogs	18,143	4.06	28.32	.090
Competition	18,276	4.00	27.75	.088
Audience feedback	18,158	3.91	29.01	.092
Profit making pressures	17,930	3.89	37.37	.116
Audience involvement in news production	18,045	3.84	25.95	.083
Advertising considerations	17,877	3.79	25.82	.084
Pressure toward sensational news	18,035	3.69	33.30	.105
Audience research	17,634	3.64	26.57	.087
Public relations	17,956	3.60	33.79	.106
Western ways of practicing journalism	4,450	3.47	22.50	.105
Journalism education	17,535	3.38	56.28	.169
Ethical standards	18,143	3.07	73.36	.204

[a] Weighted.
[b] df = 63, except for "Western ways of practicing journalism" (df = 23); all p < .001.

capital. In general, journalists around the world see influences related to economic capital, such as audiences and competition, as having become stronger, while those related to cultural capital, particularly journalism education and even ethical standards, have remained relatively stable (see table 10.1).

Globally, the strongest perception of change was in the influence of social media. This seems to be almost universal, with national differences accounting for 14 percent of the variance in journalists' responses. The influence of UGC came next, marked by even more agreement across countries, with national differences accounting for only 9 percent of variance. Social media and UGCs are platforms for audiences' participation in news construction (Loosen and Schmidt 2012); thus it is not surprising that the influence of audience feedback and involvement in news production were also perceived to have become significantly stronger over the past five years, ranking fourth and sixth, respectively. In essence, journalists around the world recognize the increasing influence of the audience on journalism, facilitated now, it appears, by participatory technologies.

Our respondents also perceived increasing impact from economic factors such as competition and profit-making pressures, which ranked third and fifth. To a lesser extent, the influence of external factors, particularly advertising considerations and public relations, was also perceived to have strengthened in the past five years. National variations were not large, accounting for between 8 percent and 12 percent of the variance for these factors. It is clear, then, that journalists around the world perceived that the influence of economic aspects had increased; as a result, they likely recognize that these factors have become increasingly central to their work.

The influence of journalism education was perceived to have increased only slightly. However, in the case of the influence of ethical standards, despite this period when trust in journalism seems to be shaky, marked by accusations of media bias across different media systems and the migration of audiences to other—albeit more questionable—information sources (Hanitzsch, Van Dalen, and Steindl 2018), journalists did not see any increase. National differences, however, accounted for 20 percent of the variance, indicating a considerable range of opinions in this regard across countries (see fig. 10.1).

Social media and UGC appear to be key influences on journalists across the globe, and this was predominantly the case in countries that are highly developed in the use of information communication technologies (ICTs). We found significant correlations between the 2015 ICT Development Index (IDI), published by the United Nations International Telecommunication Union (ITU 2015), and a perceived growth in the influence of social media and of UGC (see table 10.2). The IDI measures three main indicators—ICT access, use, and skills—that together make up a composite index that provides a snapshot of ICT development across the globe. Hence our results indicate that the more technologically developed countries are, the more likely are journalists there to perceive social media and UGC as having become increasingly growing influences on journalism.

Recent journalism scholarship is replete with studies of the impact of these technologies on journalism in the West (see, e.g., Bossio 2017; Hedman and Djerf-Pierre 2013; Naab and Sehl 2017), and it does appear that technologies are foremost on journalists' mind in countries in Western Europe and North America. One typical example is Australia, which reports some of the highest increases in these influences. Recent studies have noted

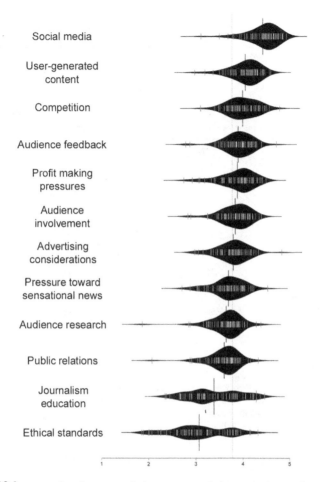

Figure 10.1 Journalists' perceived changes in influences on journalism across countries (distribution of mean scores)

Source: WJS; N = 64 (for Western ways of practicing journalism: N = 24).

Note: Scale: 5 = "strengthened a lot" . . . 1 = "weakened a lot."

how digital influences have contributed to a significant transformation of journalism culture in Australia, with increased job precariousness, significant declines in circulation and profits for legacy media, the emergence of a number of digital-only media, and high social media use among journalists (Hanusch 2017; Hanusch and Bruns 2017; Zion et al. 2016).

Table 10.2 Correlates of perceived changes in influences on journalism

	Journalism education	Ethical standards	Competition	Advertising considerations	Profit-making pressures
Press freedom (FH)[a]	−.330**	−.387**	.167	.014	.296*
Press freedom (RSF)[b]	−.146	−.220	.150	−.007	.216
ICT development[c]	−.597***	−.497***	−.161	−.035	.256
Print advertising[d]	.327*	.322*	−.054	−.212	−.297*
Internet advertising[e]	−.379**	−.175	−.094	.059	.232
Democracy[f]	−.317*	−.376**	.123	−.032	.283*
Rule of law[g]	−.358**	−.348**	.007	−.013	.233
Economic growth[h]	.379**	.433***	.064	−.086	−.208
Human development[i]	−.575***	−.502***	−.196	−.069	.205
Emancipative values[j]	−.235	−.223	.037	−.086	.240

Notes: Pearson's correlation coefficient. ***p < .001; **p < .01; *p < .05. N = 64 (countries) unless otherwise indicated.
[a] Freedom House; Freedom of the Press Index; scale reversed.
[b] Reporters Without Borders; World Press Freedom Index; scale reversed.
[c] United Nations International Telecommunication Union; N = 57.
[d] WARC, in percent of all advertising spending; N = 53.
[e] WARC, in percent of all advertising spending; N = 48.
[f] Economist Intelligence Unit; EIU Democracy Index; N = 63.
[g] World Bank; percentile rank.
[h] World Bank; growth of real GDP; N = 63; current US$.
[i] UNDP; Human Development Index; N = 63.
[j] Scores calculated based on WVS/EVS data; N = 56.
[k] All N = 24, except for [c] N = 21, [d] N = 17, [e] N = 14, [j] N = 18.

In contrast, journalists in many African countries and in South Asia, which score comparatively low on the IDI, did not indicate as large an increase in the influence of these technologies as their Western counterparts. This is not to say that technologies like social media are irrelevant in these countries. In Egypt, for example, even though journalists ranked the rise in influence of social media lower than did journalists in a vast majority of countries, the national average rating was 3.98 on our 5-point scale (see table A.6 in the appendix). This still represents a considerable increase, and

Public relations	Audience research	User-generated contents, such as blogs	Social media	Audience involvement in news production	Audience feedback	Pressure toward sensational news	Western ways of practicing journalism[k]
.048	.254*	.416***	.447***	.089	−.050	.106	.061
.042	.155	.330**	.390***	−.041	−.105	.101	.355
.088	.257	.339**	.307*	.171	−.032	.233	−.341
−.144	−.344*	−.319*	−.365**	−.340*	−.375**	−.074	.311
−.031	.031	.303*	.237	.028	−.136	.002	−.663**
.058	.274*	.440***	.453***	.116	−.013	.043	−.073
.012	.165	.197	.166	−.093	−.223	.012	−.249
−.128	.182	−.237	−.251*	−.134	−.071	−.304*	.250
.026	.176	.296*	.246	.106	−.090	.099	−.486*
.163	.284*	.415***	.377**	.109	−.029	.104	−.009

the role that social media have played in the country in recent years is well documented (see, e.g., Hamdy and Gomaa 2012; Tufekci and Wilson 2012).

Digital technologies have also played an important role in reshaping the relationship between journalists and their audiences (Loosen and Schmidt 2012), and our results demonstrate the increasing influence of audience feedback and audience research perceived by journalists. As noted earlier, there was little variance by country, and it is therefore difficult to identify any significant relationships with specific factors at the societal level.

However, some trends do emerge across countries. Our results suggest that influences from audience feedback are related to the dominance of print journalism in a particular country. The relative strength of print journalism is indicated in the percentage of advertising that is spent on newspapers in a given country (according to the WARC Adspend Database, 2015). This advertising spending is significantly correlated with audience feedback, audience research, and audience involvement in news production (table 10.2). Hence the stronger a country's newspaper market, the less likely it is that journalists in that country view audience feedback and research as increasingly important influences on their work. A number of studies have repeatedly pointed to resistance among print journalists to accept audience feedback and research (Anderson 2011; MacGregor 2007; Singer 2004). We find a small increase in perceived influence from audience feedback, research, and involvement in countries such as Austria, Germany, Japan, and Switzerland, all of which have maintained a relatively strong print journalism sector (Newman et al. 2017). At the other end of the spectrum, journalists in countries like Argentina, Brazil, and Mexico—all of which have historically strong broadcasting markets (Newman et al. 2017)—were more likely to have perceived influences from audience feedback and research to have become stronger.

Across the globe, journalists also perceived economic factors as increasingly influential. As noted earlier, there was very little cross-national variance in the perception of how the influence of competition, profit-making pressures, advertising considerations, and public relations on journalism have changed. At the national level these were all highly correlated with each other, with $r > .55$ in all cases. The strongest correlation was for advertising considerations and profit-making pressures ($r = .80$, $p < .001$, $N = 64$), indicating that the more journalists in a country perceived that the influence of profit-making pressures had increased, the more likely they were to also perceive increases in influence from advertising.

The countries in which journalists reported the largest increases in pressure from competition are located across the world. Among these, Austria, Finland, Germany, and Switzerland are beginning to experience important transformations and market pressures in their traditional print markets. Switzerland and Austria, for example, are seeing a slow decline in print circulation, the emergence of digital competitors, and government initiatives to maintain or enhance diversity in their media markets that have historically been considerably concentrated (Dal Zotto, Sacco, and Schenker 2017; Trappel 2017). These factors possibly led journalists in these countries to perceive more acutely the increase in competition pressures than did journalists in the United Kingdom, for example, which has always had one of the most competitive environments for journalism (Davis 2014), and from which vantage point the change may not have appeared as drastic.

From the Global South, Kenyan and South African journalists also reported increasing influence from competition, in fact more strongly than did their counterparts in many other countries. Both countries have indeed experienced increased competition in their media markets in recent years (Ireri et al. 2018; Lohner, Neverla, and Banjac 2017). Another case in point is New Zealand, where journalists scored the influence of all commercial factors—increased competition, profit-making pressures, advertising considerations, and public relations—high. News media in New Zealand have experienced significant transformations, through organizational restructuring, shrinking revenues, stronger competition, and a decline in offline advertising revenue coupled with slow growth in digital advertising income (Hollings, Hanusch, and Balasubramanian 2016).

We found considerable association between perceptions of influence from commercial pressures and from the pressure to produce sensational news. In particular, the influence of pressure to produce sensational news was significantly correlated with that of profit-making pressures ($r = .73$, $p < .001$, $N = 64$), a finding consistent with research that suggests sensationalism is driven by profit orientation (Skovsgaard 2014). We also found that the more journalists in a country perceived the influence of competition to have increased, the more likely they were to perceive increasing influence from the pressure to produce sensational news ($r = .37, p < .01, N = 64$). Studies have found that more competitive media systems lead to a higher prevalence of sensationalized news content (Arbaoui, De Swert, and Van der Brug 2016). Several southeastern European countries, such as Croatia, Serbia, Hungary, Albania, and Kosovo, were among the countries in which journalists perceived a particularly high increase in the influence of pressure to produce sensational news. Media in these and other postcommunist countries have been undergoing enormous transformations since the late twentieth century (Gross and Jakubowicz 2013), including in particular witnessing the arrival of pluralistic media markets marked by strong competition and increased sensational content (Pjesivac, Spasovska, and Imre 2016).

The largest, and most substantial, variations in perceptions were found for the influence of journalism education and of ethical standards (table 10.1).

Both of these were strongly correlated at the national level (r = .77, p < .001, N = 64), indicating that in countries where journalists perceived an increase in the influence of journalism education, they also perceived an increase in the influence of ethical standards. We found a relatively even split in the number of countries where journalists thought the influence of both had increased and those where journalists thought it had decreased. Among those where journalists saw an increase, we find countries of the Global South, predominantly South Asia, sub-Saharan Africa, and parts of Latin America. Indeed, we found significant correlations between the level of human development and perceived increases in the influence of journalism education and ethical standards (see table 10.2). Thus the less developed countries are, the more likely journalists are to perceive an increase in these influences. This may be explained by the fact that formalized journalism education has only recently become a concern in these countries, as they set about further professionalizing their journalistic workforce, particularly in terms of developing their own, de-Westernized approaches to such education (Skjerdal 2012; Ullah 2014). Bhutan is a particularly interesting case in this regard. The country became a democracy only in 2008, and this development led to the adoption of a free media system (Josephi 2017). Hence journalism in Bhutan underwent a fundamental transition from being state-controlled to being free, bringing with it a renewed focus on journalism training. In our study, Bhutanese journalists saw journalism education as the one influence that had increased the most, more so than commercial and technological influences.

Where the influence was perceive to have decreased, we found predominantly Western, developed media markets in Europe and North America, but also countries like Russia and Israel. In Russia, for example, this may be explained by the fact that tertiary journalism education is experiencing an important era of transition, with tension between unprecedented media reforms in the digital age and educational reforms (Lukina and Vartanova 2017). This situation is also found in many Western countries, which have for a long time experienced such tensions between industry demands for hands-on, practical skills and university educational priorities (Obijiofor and Hanusch 2011).

Journalists' perception of changes in the influence of ethical standards is similar to, and goes hand-in-hand with, their perceptions about changes in the influence of journalism education. It is also negatively related to the perceived change in the influence of profit-making pressures ($r = -.41$, $p < .001$, $N = 64$) and of pressure to produce sensational news ($r = -.30$, $p < .05$, $N = 64$), suggesting that increasing influence of such pressures is related to the decreasing influence of ethical standards. It is striking that in countries where journalists support collaborative and accommodative roles (see chapter 7), they are also more likely to perceive an increase in the influence of ethical standards (collaborative role: $r = .59$, $p < .001$; accommodative role: $r = .55$, $p < .001$, $N = 64$). Alternatively, it can be said that journalists in countries that reject the collaborative and accommodative roles—which can be found mostly in the West (chapter 7)—are most likely to perceive a decline in the influence of ethical standards. These findings suggest important connections among perceptions about roles, about commercial influences on journalism, and about the influence of ethical standards in journalism. Our finding is consistent with the broader critical position in the West that laments an increase in profit motives, a reduction in autonomy, and a lowering of ethical standards in journalism (McManus 1997).

The exportation of Western journalistic values and practices to the Global South has been a topic of discussion in journalism scholarship for some time (Boyd-Barrett 2014). Journalists in twenty-four non-Western countries indicated how much the influence of Western ways of practicing journalism had changed. While in general this influence had not become stronger to the same degree as technological, audience, or commercial influences had, journalists still reported a significant increase. We found the largest increases in influence in Kenya, the United Arab Emirates, Sierra Leone, and Malawi, while Singapore and Russia actually perceived a decrease. The latter findings may arguably be related to these being more mature media markets, which are more assertive of having developed their own journalistic values and practices. Singapore, for example, has a long history of developing its own brand of development journalism juxtaposed to Western traditions (Xu 2005), while in Russia what Western journalism represents is seen as potentially undermining the cultural code of the field (Lowrey and Erzikova 2013). We found that perceptions of an increase in the influence of Western ways of practicing journalism are related to a similar perception about the influence of journalism education ($r = .77$, $p < .001$, $N = 24$). In many African countries in particular, journalism education is still largely imported through Western textbooks and curricula. There is a heightened awareness of this problem, as displayed through regular calls for a de-Westernization and Africanization of journalism on the continent (Banda et al. 2007; Dube 2016).

Changes in Aspects of Work

We also asked journalists to indicate their perceptions about changes (increases or decreases) in their respective countries in certain often researched and discussed aspects of their work such as technical skills, time, freedom, education, and credibility. Our results indicate that, much like for influences, technological aspects appear to have changed the most (table 10.3).

The use of search engines and technical skills were ranked first and second, while interaction with audiences—arguably the result of technological innovations—was ranked fourth overall; the relatively small amount of variance in these variables indicates considerable agreement across countries (see fig. 10.2). Journalists perceived substantial increases in the

Table 10.3 Perceived changes in aspects of journalistic work across countries

	N	Mean[a]	F[b]	Eta^2
Use of search engines	18,292	4.45	50.91	.150
Technical skills	18,236	4.13	35.10	.108
Average working hours of journalists	18,006	3.86	25.96	.084
Interactions of journalists with their audiences	18,051	3.69	23.57	.076
Having a university degree	17,823	3.51	59.09	.173
Having a degree in journalism or a related field	17,804	3.40	60.93	.178
Relevance of journalism for society	18,128	3.40	62.04	.178
Journalists' freedom to make editorial decisions	17,894	3.07	57.13	.168
Credibility of journalism	18,139	2.94	98.70	.256
Time available for researching stories	18,141	2.54	99.14	.257

[a] Weighted.
[b] df = 63; all p < .001.

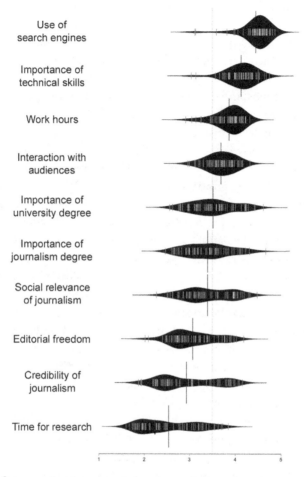

Figure 10.2 Journalists' perceived changes in aspects of work across countries (distribution of mean scores)

Source: WJS; N = 64.

Note: Scale: 5 = "increased a lot" ... 1 = "decreased a lot."

number of hours they worked, relatively uniformly across countries, and a decrease in the time they had available for researching stories, with considerable national differences as indicated by the relatively large variances (roughly 26 percent). Journalists also reported a slight decrease in journalism's credibility, but here, too, national differences accounted for 26 percent of the variance. They reported increases in the importance of having a university degree as well as in having a degree in journalism or a related field. Journalists also perceived a slight increase in journalism's relevance for society, but their perception of their freedom to make editorial decisions remained more or less at the same level. All these aspects of journalists' work exhibited substantial variance—around 17 to 18 percent—pointing to a diversity of perceptions across countries.

As for the importance of technical skills and the use of search engines, it was predominantly journalists in Western countries who reported the largest increases (much like they indicated the increasing influence of technology earlier). These countries have high press freedom, and thus it was not surprising that we found significant correlations between these perceptions and the level of press freedom as measured by Freedom House (see table 10.4). Among the nations scoring in the top twenty, we found Anglophone countries (Australia, Ireland, New Zealand, South Africa, the United Kingdom, and the United States) but also countries from southern Europe and Latin America (Argentina, Brazil, Cyprus, Greece, Italy, Mexico, and Spain; see table A.7 in the appendix). This finding appears in line with a study of Spanish and UK journalists, in which José Alberto García Avilés et al. (2004) found that journalists saw a need to develop technical skills. In contrast, technological aspects are less of a concern in countries that have a less free media system and that may be less advanced technologically. China, which has a highly controlled media system but is technologically very advanced, presents an anomaly: its journalists rank toward the bottom in terms of their perception of increases in the importance of technical skills and in the use of search engines. Broadly, the strong political influences on their work (see chapter 5; see also Tong 2017) as well as tight censorship of search engines in China may be the explanation (Tang and Sampson 2012; Xu 2015). Further, China's complex system of personal networks—known as *guanxi*—and its impact on journalistic work (Xu 2016) may make personal connections comparatively more important when researching stories.

Scholars have for some time documented the negative impact that technological innovations have on the time journalists have for completing core tasks like researching stories (Underwood, Anthony, and Stamm 1994). We found that in countries where journalists perceived an increased importance of technical skills, they also noted an increase in work hours ($r = .47$, $p < .001$, $N = 64$) and a decrease in time available for research ($r = -.36$, $p < .01$, $N = 64$). A similar relationship was found for the use of search

Table 10.4 Correlates of perceived changes in aspects of journalistic work

	Journalists' freedom to make editorial decisions	Average working hours of journalists	Time available for researching stories	Interactions of journalists with their audiences	Technical skills	Use of search engines	Having a university degree	Having a degree in journalism or related field	Credibility of journalism	Relevance of journalism for society
Press freedom (FH)[a]	−.411***	.282*	−.726***	.033	.355**	.453**	−.320*	−.311*	−.514***	−.414***
Press freedom (RSF)[b]	−.285*	.283*	−.607***	.124	.390***	.495***	−.155	−.146	−.389**	−.298*
ICT development[c]	−.634***	.031	−.708***	−.161	.244	.213	−.499**	−.522***	−.647***	−.651***
Print advertising[d]	.294*	−.150	.359**	.098	−.026	−.333*	.309*	.324*	.367**	.308*
Internet advertising[e]	−.471***	−.194	−.428**	−.200	−.038	−.223	−.348*	−.310*	−.459***	−.428**
Democracy[f]	−.439***	.277*	−.722***	−.051	.320*	.484***	−.236	−.235	−.510***	−.408***
Rule of law[g]	−.389**	.161	−.590***	−.186	.093	.083	−.341**	−.353*	−.473***	−.470**
Growth of real GDP[h]	.364**	−.089	.444***	.057	−.102	−.275*	.432***	.411***	.395***	.422***
Human development[i]	−.602***	.045	−.678***	−.251*	.143	.220	−.492***	−.515***	−.604***	−.619***
Emancipative values[j]	−.440***	.116	−.677***	.091	.262	.250	−.136	−.133	−.521***	−.453***

Notes: Pearson's correlation coefficient. ***p < .001; **p < .01; *p < .05. N = 64 (countries) unless otherwise indicated.

[a] Freedom House; scale reversed.

[b] Reporters Without Borders; scale reversed.

[c] United Nations International Telecommunication Union; N = 57.

[d] WARC, in percent of all advertising spending; N = 53.

[e] WARC, in percent of all advertising spending; N = 48.

[f] Economist Intelligence Unit; N = 63.

[g] World Bank; percentile rank.

[h] World Bank; Atlas method; N = 63; current US$.

[i] UNDP; N = 63.

[j] Scores calculated based on WVS/EVS data; N = 56.

engines (work hours: r = .51, p < .001; time available: r = -.52, p < .001, N = 64). On a broader plane, the Global ICT Development Index was also negatively correlated with time available for research (see table 10.4). The more technologically advanced a country is, the more likely are its journalists to perceive that they have less time for researching stories, suggesting possibly that these technologies are introducing new routines and taking journalists away from their core tasks. The largest decreases in research time were perceived by journalists from technologically advanced countries in Western Europe. Growing time pressures have been documented for some time by UK journalists, for example, who report they are increasingly fulfilling administrative functions (Witschge and Nygren 2009). Similar examples can be found across Europe and in the United States, with news organizations aiming to produce more with less, and journalists increasingly expected not only to produce content but to also moderate and curate online (Bakker 2012), and to promote their stories and interact with audiences on social media (Tandoc and Vos 2016).

While our results support the narrative that journalism is experiencing a crisis in the West (Franklin 2012), as well as in a number of transitional countries, we also found that nearly one in three countries actually reported a slight increase in time available to research stories. As noted earlier, these countries included Middle Eastern, African, and South Asian nations that are still on the other side of the digital divide. Further, news media in the industrialized and technologized countries of the Global North have experienced relatively good work conditions but have in recent years also seen significant downturns in their industry. In contrast, journalism and the news media are still expanding, or at least not contracting to a similar degree, in many countries of the Global South. One good example in this regard is Bangladesh, which has experienced exponential growth in its media sector since the turn of the century, spurred on by deregulation of the media market but also through growth of the country's middle class, increased literacy, higher purchasing power, and consumer demand for pluralistic media (Ullah 2016). India, which in recent times has undergone an "explosion" in its media scene in terms of numbers, is another example (Jain 2015). Despite this dynamic and pluralistic Indian media landscape, structural developments like commercialism, rising levels of concentration and cross-media ownership are also beginning to affect journalism on the subcontinent (Chadha 2017). This may explain why journalists in India reported little change in the time they have available for research.

The crisis narrative is also evident when we examine journalists' perceptions of their freedom to make editorial decisions. Here we found that perceptions of increases or decreases in editorial freedom are strongly correlated with perceptions of the time journalists have available for research ($r = .82$, $p < .001$, $N = 64$). This suggests that in countries where journalists felt they had less time for core tasks, they also felt they had less autonomy. Further, in countries where journalists perceived decreasing editorial freedom, they also believed that journalistic credibility and the relevance of journalism for society were decreasing (credibility: $r = .90$, $p < .001$; relevance: $r = .85$, $p < .001$, $N = 64$). At the societal level, perceptions of increases in editorial freedom are also related to press freedom, human development, and emancipative values (see table. 10.4), indicating the importance of journalism's opportunity structures. These results shed further light on the earlier findings that journalists in countries with high press freedom, high human development, and a stronger appreciation for emancipative values enjoy greater editorial autonomy (see chapter 6). While this editorial autonomy was not correlated with journalists' perception of increases or decreases in editorial freedom, it would appear that in societies that provide for larger amounts of freedom, journalists more acutely see these as under threat.

Hence we found very similar national trends across journalists' perceptions of changes in editorial autonomy, in the credibility of journalism, as well as in journalism's relevance for society. Largely, journalists in countries with saturated media markets that have experienced substantial pressures in recent years were quite pessimistic about these aspects and adhered to the well-documented crisis narrative that has been the subject of so much recent journalism scholarship. An additional factor for this pessimism may be that public trust in the news media is typically declining in these countries (Hanitzsch, Van Dalen, and Steindl 2018). Faced with a skeptical public, journalists themselves may adopt a more negative view of the news media. On the other hand, we found a significant number of countries where journalists appear to be comparatively more positive about these aspects of their work. These media systems tend to be still expanding, or at least they are not under as much pressure as elsewhere.

In line with this expansion, we can also interpret our findings in relation to perceived increases in the importance of university education generally, and journalism education more specifically. Here we found strong correlations between the perceived changes in the influence of journalism education and the importance of having both a university degree ($r = .76$, $p < .001$, $N = 64$) and a degree in journalism or a related field ($r = .81$, $p < .001$, $N = 64$). While globally journalists typically saw such degrees as playing a more important role, this was particularly pronounced in countries that had placed an increasing focus on the tertiary education of journalists, such as in Africa and parts of Latin America. Tertiary journalism education has a longer tradition in many Western countries and is thus well established there, while in many countries of the Global South, this educational trend has emerged only more recently (Skjerdal 2012). For example, Ethiopia has invested considerable effort into formalizing educational programs for journalism (Skjerdal and Ngugi 2007), and we found that Ethiopian journalists perceived a strong increase in the importance of journalism education. Similarly, formalized journalism education in Malawi—where journalists also reported an increase in its importance—emerged only in the mid-1990s, and news media still have some way to go along the path of professionalization (Manda 2015).

Conclusions

This chapter explored the degree to which journalists around the world perceived changes in their profession, in terms of both changing influences and changing aspects of work. Predominantly, our results paint a picture of the growing significance of technological and commercial pressures, a trend that has been well documented in journalism scholarship over recent years (see, e.g., Altmeppen 2008; Boczkowski 2004; Bruns 2008; Lowrey and Anderson 2005; Paulussen 2012; Robinson 2007). This transformation appears to be a global phenomenon, but, as we have noted throughout, there are important differences based on journalism's opportunity structures. First, a society's level of ICT development is related to journalists' perceptions of changes in the role technology plays in their work. Second, in countries with strong newspaper markets—as indicated through advertising spending in newspapers—journalists perceive a less pronounced increase in audience influences compared with elsewhere. Third, in media systems that are still expanding—or which have not experienced the drastic decline as elsewhere—journalists tend to be more positive about their conditions of work and feel that increases in pressures from technology and commercial aspects are not as strong as elsewhere. In these countries there is instead slightly greater emphasis on processes of professionalization, indicated through perceptions about journalism education and ethical standards.

Journalists' perceptions of how different aspects of and influences on their work are changing are relevant, because such perceptions can affect how they do their work. Therefore future studies should examine how perceptions of change are related to how journalists carry out their work, such as when it comes to choosing what to report about. How journalists perceive and experience change can also affect them psychologically, and scholars should, for example, examine how journalists' perceptions of the various transformations in their day-to-day routines affect levels of job satisfaction and feelings of burnout.

In terms of limitations, we need to acknowledge the possible impact of the period—2012 to 2016—when data were gathered for the WJS. During this period many journalists were affected not only by the aforementioned technological changes but also, like workers in other professions, by the global economic crisis, which no doubt affected many countries in our sample. In this regard, employment-related pressures, including increased work hours, would not be exclusive to journalists. For example, the ongoing process of precarization is not limited to the journalism profession; rather, it is occurring in a large number of professions (Elefante and Deuze 2012) and appears to be strongly pronounced in the Western media systems in our study. The economic crisis may well be another external factor influencing how journalists rate the relevance and credibility of their profession. For example, in several European countries, the external economic environment that necessitated bailouts by the International Monetary Fund and European governments may have dampened journalists' perceptions of their work even if nothing much had changed in journalism per se.

Most significantly, while our findings largely confirm the crisis narratives established in the literature, the crisis appears to be particularly pertinent to Western, developed countries; many other journalistic cultures are perhaps not (yet) quite as severely affected. Thus, as journalism scholars, it is important that we differentiate our assessments of the state of journalism across the globe and take account of the specific political, economic, social, cultural, and technological contexts of particular countries and regions.

11

MODELING JOURNALISTIC CULTURES
A Global Approach

Folker Hanusch and Thomas Hanitzsch

In this book we set out to challenge assumptions of a universal understanding of journalism by charting a "world of journalism" populated with a rich panoply of journalistic cultures. These cultures, we argued, not only operate in varied societal contexts but are also subject to change on multiple levels. Each journalistic culture is traversing its own path, as it has found its own answers to the question of how to cope with contextual forces, such as differing levels of press freedom, democracy, or socioeconomic development. The rich empirical evidence presented in this book is consistent with this argument.

This chapter aims to draw together the various aspects of journalistic cultures we have examined in this book. We establish some key universals, as well as particularities, of journalists' discourses about their work. We chart the contours of a global professional ideology (Deuze 2005), contributing to scholarship that tries to ascertain foundational aspects that journalists adhere to around the world. We also pay particular attention to those aspects of journalism about which journalists disagree the most to identify the various individualities in these cultures. This focus on differences enables us to propose four models of journalistic culture, allowing us to contribute to the growing comparative literature on media systems. As will become apparent, our results confirm many established truths while also challenging existing work spanning the field.

In chapter 2 we outlined our conceptual roadmap for studying journalistic cultures comparatively. At the core of this framework are the three intrinsic and two extrinsic dimensions of journalistic culture as well as the relevant national opportunity structures that shape the form of journalism in a given country. Among the intrinsic dimensions of journalistic culture, which are articulations of journalism's relationship with society, we designated journalistic roles, journalistic ethics, and journalists' trust in public institutions. Journalistic roles are generalized and aggregate expectations, which journalists believe are deemed desirable in society (normative roles), and which incorporate the professional values and beliefs individual journalists embrace as a result of their professional socialization (cognitive roles). Journalistic ethics refer to journalists' news gathering and reporting decision making in situations in which their actions can have potentially harmful consequences for individual persons, groups of individuals, or society as a whole. Here we distinguished between journalists' general ethical orientations (subjective dispositions informing journalists' moral reasoning as applied in the profession) and their views on specific reporting practices marked as controversial in professional discourse. Journalists' trust is the willingness of journalists to be vulnerable to the performance of public institutions based on the anticipation that these institutions will meet the citizens' expectations.

The two extrinsic dimensions of journalistic culture, relating to subjective experiences of and reflections on external constraints, encompass journalists' perceived influences and editorial autonomy. Perceived influences refer to journalists' subjective perceptions of the various forces that shape the process of news production. Editorial autonomy is the latitude journalists have in selecting stories and deciding which aspects of stories to stress.

The notion of opportunity structure references the set of external contexts within which journalists may act individually or as part of an occupational group to construct and articulate a subjective sense of professional identity, desirable editorial practice, confidence in public institutions, editorial autonomy, and the influences they confront. The opportunity structures assessed in this book broadly fall into three general domains that we further elaborate on later in this chapter; these domains are politics and governance, socioeconomic development, and cultural value systems. In this way our contribution differs from existing models, which operate mainly on the structural level alone (Brüggemann et al. 2014; Christians et al. 2009; Hallin and Mancini 2004, 2017; Voltmer 2012); we focus instead on discursively constituted journalistic cultures and assess them against structural contexts.

In this chapter we structure our analysis along the intrinsic and extrinsic dimensions to identify broad similarities and differences in journalistic cultures across the globe as well as to pinpoint underlying geographic patterns. We also use these dimensions to test the key differences we uncover against the broader contexts of journalistic culture, namely, politics and governance, socioeconomic development, and cultural value systems. This comparative analysis, we argue, yields a structure consisting of four models of journalistic culture: monitorial, advocative, developmental, and collaborative.

Similarities in Journalistic Cultures

An important advantage of comparative research is that it enables us to question long-held assumptions about the nature of journalism by avoiding an ethnocentric view based on the experience of one nation only (Blumler, McLeod, and Rosengren 1992; Kohn 1989). The past couple of decades have seen an enormous increase in the number of studies that explore journalism through a comparative lens (Hanusch and Vos 2019). While this is a welcome and necessary development for a more comprehensive understanding of global news work, it may also be said that these studies have often, by necessity, through their comparative designs, emphasized more strongly differences rather than similarities among their samples (Blumler, McLeod, and Rosengren 1992). In the face of this, some researchers have increasingly argued for a more transnational understanding of journalism, calling for a focus on the similarities that exist across the globe regarding journalistic practices and ethics (Berglez 2008; Hellmueller 2017; Ward 2010).

To avoid overstating the differences in journalistic cultures we found in our sample of sixty-seven countries, we first engage areas of broad agreement. We begin by reporting on the extrinsic dimensions. For influences—the way in which journalists discursively articulate the importance of a range of influences on their work—we found some agreement on several individual influences as well as on the general hierarchy of influences. Predominantly, journalists around the world rank those aspects of their work that they experience more directly as more influential. In particular these include information access and time to research stories, that is, what we designate in this book as procedural influences, as well as organizational influences. On the other hand, colleagues in their own and other organizations and friends and family, that is, personal networks' influence, were more often than not ranked relatively low in influence. Political and economic influences were also rated as having a small influence, possibly a counterintuitive finding probably explained by the fact that for many journalists at the reporter level, these influences are often experienced only indirectly. We did, however, find substantial differences for other sources of influence, as well as for the second extrinsic dimension of journalistic culture, autonomy, detailed later in this chapter. Still, we want to point out that in most countries journalists reported relatively high autonomy in their work, despite frequent claims in the literature that journalistic freedom is deteriorating (Bagdikian 1983; Glasser and Gunther 2005; McManus 2009). Yet in a different analysis, that of perceived changes in journalistic work, we found that journalists in saturated, highly developed media systems at times reported considerable decreases in editorial freedom.

Here are our findings for the intrinsic dimensions. Among normative roles, journalism's political obligations are a dominant concern for journalists across the globe. The classic concepts about roles that permeate journalism textbooks—informer, reporter, watchdog, investigator, monitor, educator—were present in journalists' appraisal of the dominant roles of the news media. For journalists' cognitive roles, we found similar hierarchies, with journalists the world over proclaiming to want to monitor the powerful. Journalists have generally supported this role more strongly than alternative concepts, such as roles calling on journalists to act as supporters of ruling powers.

For ethical norms, journalists in all sixty-seven countries were most likely to support an absolutist approach, a belief that journalists should always adhere to codes of professional ethics, regardless of the situation and context. Journalists were somewhat divided in their approval of certain controversial practices of reporting, such as the use of classified documents without authorization. Here it was journalists of the Global North, mainly from established and wealthy democracies with high levels of press and political freedoms, who most agreed that these practices were justifiable. In the case of journalists' trust, we found that, across the board, journalists tended to have low trust in political institutions, a finding in line with existing scholarship (Hanitzsch and Berganza 2014). Journalists have exceptionally little confidence in politicians and political parties, which is a strikingly consistent pattern in all countries studied. Typically, regulative institutions—especially the judiciary—ranked considerably higher in trust.

As journalism has experienced considerable transformation in the past decade, we had also asked our respondents to reflect on how they had experienced changes in their work over the past five years. Here, too, we found considerable similarities across some aspects. For example, journalists in almost all countries cited the phenomenal rise of social media across the globe as the one influence on their work that had undergone the most significant change. Across most investigated societies, we found considerable agreement among journalists with regard to the growing influence of social media, and to a slightly lower extent user-generated content. Similarly, concerning changes in journalistic work (not changes in perceived influences on work), technological skills and the use of online search engines were cited across the globe as the most prominent changes.

Overall, then, it would seem that, despite ongoing changes and transformations in journalism, what are often referred to as key elements of journalistic ideology (Deuze 2005; Kovach and Rosenstiel 2001) remain intact. News workers claim they have considerable autonomy in their day-to-day work, they primarily position journalism's contribution to society within the realm of politics (though they have relatively little confidence in political institutions), and they conceive of their roles in terms of journalism's contribution to the political process, even though what this contribution actually entails differs across countries.

Differences in Journalistic Cultures

As demonstrated above, discursive negotiation in the context of a diversity of opportunity structures in nations across the world can result in similarities regarding key elements of the institution and practice of journalism. One of the consequences of major interest to our study, however, is the variety of journalistic cultures it spawns. Journalists' beliefs about their role in society and about the influences they perceived on their work were marked by large differences. While journalists around the world considered the monitorial function important, they disagreed considerably about the importance of the interventionist role (actively contributing to social reform) and the collaborative role (supporting political authorities). For influences, political and economic pressures accounted for the largest percentage of cross-national variation in line with the literature that cites these as significant limiters of journalistic work. Ethical belief systems, notably with regard to the use of confidential documents without authorization, also varied substantially. The evidence on changes in journalism points to an acutely noted crisis in journalistic standards and credibility—in some countries more so than in others. In the various chapters of this book, these differences received considerable in-depth analyses in and of themselves, but more critical also within the context of a range of factors stemming from the opportunity structures of journalism. Here we try to summarize these analyses to identify broader global patterns.

One of the key patterns seems to be the distinction along major political and socioeconomic factors, that is, democratic performance, human development, and the presence of emancipative values in society. We found differences along the classic distinction between Western nations, with their highly developed, relatively free media systems, on the one hand, and the "rest" of the world, on the other. Overall, our analysis found strong evidence to support existing scholarship in identifying political context as a major source of cross-national variation in journalistic cultures (Gurevitch and Blumler 2004; Hallin and Mancini 2004; Weaver 1998a).

Journalists in non-Western, less democratic, and socioeconomically less developed countries tended to perceive political and economic influences as stronger than did their counterparts in other regions of the globe. Journalists in many of these countries also tended to be comparatively more supportive of a collaborative approach to journalism, and those in developing countries marked by internal conflict leaned toward favoring an interventionist approach. Countries in the Middle East and North Africa were more likely to align with subjectivism, while those in the Global South valued situationist and exceptionist approaches to ethical issues. Journalists in countries experiencing political instability, income inequality, and profound political, economic, and societal transformations reported the lowest levels of political trust. In contexts where journalists supported interventionist roles, they tended to be less trusting of public institutions, while journalists in countries supportive of a collaborative role exhibited higher levels of trust.

On the contrary, in countries that are typically lumped together as "the West," journalists felt they had a more substantial amount of editorial freedom in their work and were less affected by political and organizational influences; further, these journalists were considerably more supportive of a monitorial role. In developed and politically stable countries, journalism's accommodative role, which is about accommodating the public's communicative needs, was also, by and large, supported slightly more strongly. At the same time, there was little support for the collaborative role in these countries. With the notable exception of the United States, journalists in countries with higher levels of political and press freedom appeared to be more trusting of political institutions. Further, journalists in the West strongly emphasized the importance of adhering to professional codes of ethics and were most likely to justify controversial news-gathering practices such as the use of confidential business or government documents without authorization. Moreover, these journalists tended to feel technology-related influences more acutely and seemed to emphasize more generally a crisis narrative about journalism that was not quite as evident in non-Western contexts.

Still, a distinction between merely Western and non-Western contexts would be too simplistic, as our results suggest a range of nuanced geographic and other patterns. In Western European countries with a strong tradition of public service media, journalists typically perceived weak influences from the political, economic, and organizational domains when compared with other Western countries. At the same time, these journalists also exhibited medium to high levels of trust in political institutions. In contrast, journalists in Eastern European countries showed higher levels of perceived political, economic, and organizational influences and lower levels of political trust. These journalists were also more likely to support the interventionist role, with a combination of the monitorial role, while journalists in Western Europe tended to be more supportive of the monitorial and also the accommodative roles. Notable exceptions in Eastern Europe were Hungary and Russia, two countries increasingly heading toward a new kind of authoritarianism. Here journalists were much less supportive of the monitorial role.

The Scandinavian countries showed some similarities as a group, particularly regarding influences. Journalists here considered economic aspects as comparatively less influential, pointing to low levels of economic pressure as a distinctive feature of Nordic journalism. There were also some similarities between Scandinavia and the nearby Baltic countries of Estonia and Latvia in terms of their perceptions of influences as well as their degree of editorial autonomy.

We found similarities in sub-Saharan Africa in that journalists perceived political and economic influences as quite pronounced, reported only weak support for journalism's monitorial role, and showed antisubjectivist ethical ideals. In the Gulf states, journalists reported strong political and economic influences in their work, as well as low levels of editorial autonomy. The monitorial role was also not supported strongly; instead, journalists saw the collaborative role as relatively important. In terms of journalism ethics, they exhibited strong support for subjectivism and were less likely than journalists in other regions to justify controversial news-gathering processes, in particular, the use of confidential business or government documents without authorization.

Across Southeast Asia, we found relatively high regard among journalists for the collaborative role, but in other parts of Asia the picture was quite different. Japan and Hong Kong, for example, represent regionally distinct journalistic cultures, especially in terms of perceived influences. Japan in particular was considerably different; here journalists reported very low political influences. In terms of role perceptions, Japan and Hong Kong, as well as South Korea, were the only Asian countries in which the monitorial role was appreciated to a reasonably high extent.

Other trends in our results highlight the risk of considering regionalism as the sole criterion for distinguishing among journalistic cultures. In some cases, postcolonial and language ties matter across vast distances. For example, Australian and New Zealand journalists were much more similar to their Western European and North American counterparts than to those in Asia, a finding well supported in journalism scholarship (Jones and Pusey 2010). The same was true for Latin American journalists, on one hand, and their Spanish and Portuguese colleagues, on the other, a finding also supported by other research (Hallin and Papathanassopoulos 2002). Journalists in Spain and Portugal, but also Greece—all countries belonging to Daniel Hallin and Paolo Mancini's (2004) Polarized Pluralist Model—had the highest degree of appreciation for the interventionist role compared to their colleagues in other Western societies. This made them similar to their counterparts in Latin America, who also placed a strong emphasis on the interventionist role.

Finally, one country that stood out in some of the regional analyses was the United States. Journalists' responses there demonstrated that American journalistic culture is somewhat particular when compared to other Western countries. For example, U.S. journalists exhibited exceptionally low political trust and were somewhat different from other Western societies in their strong support for both the monitorial and accommodative roles of journalism in society. While these journalists perceived their editorial freedom to be very high, they also reported strong levels of organizational influences—arguably due to the more pronounced free market model of U.S. media (Hallin and Mancini 2004). Extreme ideological polarization, as well as a growing sense of antielitism and public discontent with politics, may also account for some of these results, especially the exceptionally low confidence of U.S. journalists in their political institutions (Hanitzsch, Van Dalen, and Steindl 2018). These findings demonstrate that, rather than necessarily being seen as a typical example of Western journalistic culture, the United States should be considered more as an exceptional case within the broader context of Western nations. This finding has significant implications for the U.S.-centric nature of many studies of journalism, as discussed in chapter 1.

Journalistic Cultures Across Media Systems

Having established that journalists all over the world have certain values and views in common but also differ on some important aspects, we now turn to the question: What does this all mean? Most important, as we have argued from the outset of this book, the rich variety of findings and insights into journalistic cultures across the world demonstrate that while there are some universals, there are also quite different forms of journalism, pressures, understandings, and contextual environments. In this way we hope to have clearly demonstrated the value of comparative inquiry in providing a more nuanced and comprehensive understanding of journalistic culture. A logical next step from this natural insight is to develop a typology of journalistic cultures, each of which may be more or less likely to exist in certain contextual environments.

The idea of building such models has a long tradition in communication research, dating back to Fred Siebert, Theodore Peterson, and Wilbur Schramm's famous *Four Theories of the Press* (1956), which, despite its limitations, became a cornerstone for comparative research on journalism and the news media for some decades. The typology was developed during a particular time in history when communication research was dominated by U.S.-based studies that compared the United States to the rest of the world and which was infused with modernization theory values, typifying the West as modern and non-Western countries as being held back by tradition (Hanitzsch 2009). Yet its simplified approach to classifying the range of complex media systems around the world into four models appealed to countless students and faculty, making it an enormous success and thus very influential in the field (Merrill 2002).

The four theories—authoritarian, libertarian, social responsibility, and Soviet communist—were based on contextual aspects such as the nature of man, the nature of society and the state, the relation of man to the state, and the nature of knowledge and truth. The authoritarian theory posited that the press was a servant of the state, merely there to act as a mouthpiece for those in power, while the libertarian theory posited that the press instead acted as a check on government, fulfilling a watchdog role in a free society. In the social responsibility theory, the press was considered free, as in the libertarian model, but had obligations and responsibilities to society, while in the Soviet communist theory—an offshoot of the authoritarian theory— the press was a servant not of the state but of the Communist Party (Siebert, Peterson, and Schramm 1956). Over time the theories have been widely criticized and are typically considered ideologically biased, too simplistic, outdated, and overtaken by political events, as well as not even truly comparative (Hallin and Mancini 2004; Nerone 1995; Nordenstreng 2006). Still, the field of comparative journalism studies continues to take some inspiration from the book's original aims, as well as some of its analytical categories, in particular, the relationship between the media and the state.

Perhaps most important, Siebert, Peterson, and Schramm's work spawned a range of different conceptualizations of press systems in an attempt to better reflect the changing geopolitical realities of the late twentieth and early twenty-first centuries. Such works include William Hachten's (1981) classification of authoritarian, Western, communist, revolutionary, and developmental press or media concepts. Robert Picard (1985) later expanded this approach to include a democratic socialist model (mostly representing the Scandinavian countries). Denis McQuail (1994) added a democratic participant model (mostly representing European countries). Others proposed Western, communist and Third World models (Martin and Chaudhary 1983), or—in a more economics-focused approach—market, communitarian, and advancing models (Altschull 1995).

Other scholars have used a wider perspective to propose a variety of conceptualizations about the role of journalism and news media in society (Nordenstreng 1997). More recently, Clifford Christians et al. (2009) proposed a new and updated approach to normative models of the media, a classification that has had a substantial impact in the field. The model proposes four normative roles for journalism in democratic societies that are located on a matrix along the key factors of institutional power (ranging from weak to strong) and degree of media dependency or autonomy. The four roles are: the monitorial role in which journalism is largely viewed as a provider of information (high in media autonomy and with strong institutional power); the radical role that provides a challenge to authority and voices support for reform (high in media autonomy and with low institutional power); the facilitative role that reports information but also aims to strengthen civil society (high in media dependency and with low institutional power); and the collaborative role, with the purpose of being supportive of those in power, and aiming to advance mutual interests (high in media dependency and with strong institutional power).

Convincing as these conceptualizations are, they all suffer from one key shortcoming: the focus has typically been on theories of journalism and the media, with—at least until relatively recently—little empirical validation of the extent to which these approaches are present in individual media systems. One highly influential attempt to address the shortage of evidence-based conceptualizations and analysis of individual countries has been Hallin and Mancini's (2004) seminal classification of media systems in Western Europe and North America. Based on an examination of available structural data and a historicized analysis of national developments in the media, these scholars assessed four key contextual factors: development of media markets, political parallelism, the development of journalistic professionalism, and the degree and nature of state intervention in eighteen Western democracies. As a result, Hallin and Mancini proposed three models: the Liberal or North Atlantic Model, with its main feature being the influence of market forces and the predominance of commercial media; the Democratic Corporatist or Northern European Model marked by a mutually beneficial relationship that exists between commercial media and media that are tied to social and political groups; and the Polarized Pluralist or Mediterranean Model, which is a mix of weaker commercial media and a more active relationship between journalism and party politics as well as the state.

Hallin and Mancini's work has been highly influential in political communication and journalism research, spawning a number of follow-on studies that have attempted to validate their proposed models or at least used them as starting points (e.g., Albaek et al. 2014; Benson et al. 2012; Brüggemann et al. 2014; Esser et al. 2012; also see the overview by Hallin and Mancini 2017), as well as attempts to expand the classification to countries beyond those of the West (see, e.g., Castro Herrero et al. 2017; Hallin and Mancini 2012a; Voltmer 2013). At the same time, Hallin and Mancini's (2004) classification has had its critics, who have, for example, questioned the benefit of the classification for comparative analysis, the identification of individual cases within the classification, as well as its application beyond the West (Hardy 2012; Norris 2009). Hallin and Mancini (2012b) have themselves addressed these critiques and offered food for thought for future studies. Hence we will restrict ourselves here to mentioning this development rather than providing an in-depth critique. Our aim, instead, has been to provide some background to the ways in which scholars have classified models of journalism and news media over the past sixty or so years, as these studies have broadly inspired some of our analytical categories, enabling us to build on them and broaden our understanding of the diverse range of journalistic cultures globally.

Four Models of Journalistic Culture

Our conceptual framework, outlined in chapter 2, provides a starting point for us to outline what we believe our empirical results on journalistic culture suggest, as articulated by the more than 27,500 journalists who were interviewed across sixty-seven countries for this study. From the outset, however, we want to clarify that while this is an ambitious undertaking, we are well aware that any classification we suggest is limited by the variables we have employed. As argued throughout this book, owing to the natural limitations of survey data (including questionnaire length), our study can provide only one part of the bigger picture, even though we believe it is an important one and central to an understanding of the concept of journalistic culture as we have proposed it. Still, we did not study actual practices on the ground. Hence we offer our models as one way of thinking about different kinds of journalistic culture, which future studies may want to explore further and in greater depth.

With these disclaimers, we now turn to our qualitative assessment of models of journalistic culture. We propose four models of journalistic culture, which can be described as monitorial, advocative, developmental, and collaborative. Table 11.1 summarizes these models in terms of the underlying features that define each one (i.e., the internal and external dimensions of journalistic culture) and places them vis-à-vis the specific opportunity structures within which these models tend to exist. Here we need to point out that the various variables, although treated as analytically distinct in table 11.1, interact in much more complex ways, as we have outlined throughout the discussions in this book.

In our description of the models below, we also mention countries that best reflect the characteristics of the model. As others have argued before us (see, e.g., Hallin and Mancini 2004; Nordenstreng 1997), it is sometimes difficult to definitively place countries within models, and obviously national opportunity structures can be more heterogeneous within themselves than abstractions on the national level may suggest. Thus, by necessity, ours is a sweeping assessment, and we are acutely aware that some countries that are grouped within the same models differ substantially in terms of aspects of their journalistic cultures or of their opportunity structures. However, after an in-depth examination of our results, we believe this categorization presents a relatively parsimonious solution that can help us to think about global journalistic cultures. We now turn to describe each of these models.

Monitorial journalistic cultures are rather typical for countries that are highly developed economically and with long traditions of a free media. Included here are North America, Australia and New Zealand, all Western European countries in our study, several Eastern European countries, such as the Czech Republic and Estonia, as well as Japan and Hong Kong. The latter two bear many similarities to the West in terms of their media markets, which led us to include them here. Therefore the monitorial model encapsulates what is typically referred to as the Western, liberal approach

Table 11.1 Four models of journalistic cultures

	Monitorial	Advocative	Developmental	Collaborative
Intrinsic Dimensions				
Journalistic roles	Monitorial and accommodative	Strongly interventionist; some monitorial	Interventionist; somewhat collaborative	Strongly collaborative
Journalism ethics	Strongly absolutist	Absolutist and situationist	Absolutist and situationist	Subjectivist
Political trust	Medium-high	Low	Medium	High
Extrinsic Dimensions				
Perceived influences	Low political and economic influences	Medium political, high organizational influences	Medium political, high organizational influences	High political influences
Editorial autonomy	High	Medium-high	Medium	Low
Opportunity Structures				
Media system	Strong press freedom; private media and public service broadcasting	Medium press freedom; private media, public service broadcasting, and some state-run	Medium-low press freedom; private and state-run media	Low press freedom; private and state-run media
Political system	Liberal democracy	Transitional	Transitional	Authoritarian
Rule of law	High	Medium (uneven)	Medium-low	High
Transparency	High	Medium	Low	Medium-high
Economic development	Very high	Medium	Low	High
Human development	Very high	Medium-high	Low	High
Emancipative values	High	Medium-high	Low	Low

to journalism. In these societies the idea of journalism's institutional independence from other powers is a defining element of democracy. Editorial autonomy is typically protected through formal regulatory design, ethical norms, and sometimes labor contract clauses. In these countries it is considered a fundamental value to ensure that individuals and institutions that are supposed to serve the public remain transparent and are held accountable (Nerone 2013). Our results show that journalists in countries that belong to the monitorial model tend to have more freedom to select story ideas and angles, as they work in societies that grant them greater political liberties. Largely, journalists in these countries perceive relatively low levels of political and economic influences on their work and consequently report high levels of autonomy. Structurally, these countries exhibit high levels of press freedom and have a long tradition of a strong mass circulation press, though this is not the case everywhere (for example, southern European nations) (see Hallin and Mancini 2004).

The monitorial role of journalism is what unites journalists in all these countries, though they differ to quite an extent in how they perceive the importance of the accommodative role. Journalists in Denmark, Portugal, and Spain, for example, consider the latter role much less important than do their colleagues in Austria, Germany, and Iceland. Overall, the monitorial role is at the very heart of the news media's legitimacy in most liberal democracies, grounded in a liberal pluralist understanding that sees journalism as essential to the creation and maintenance of participatory democracy (Gans 1998).

As regards their ethical orientations, the monitorial model of journalistic culture tends to align with moral absolutism, with journalists considering it important to always follow professional codes of conduct. In countries where journalists enjoy considerable stability and certainty with regard to media freedom and press laws, they can safely rely on established codes of conduct with few exceptions. As chapter 8 has demonstrated, the relative emphasis on absolutism (or adherence to professional codes of conduct) correlates strongly with high levels of press freedom, with functional democracy, and to a lesser extent with a tendency to avoid uncertainty in society. These are prevalent societal features in the Global North where the history of journalistic professionalism is the longest (e.g., Waisbord 2013b; Slattery 2014). In these contexts, journalists are also more likely to justify investigative reporting practices, such as using confidential documents without authorization, as there is a strong normative push toward a monitorial approach of positioning journalism as a robust force to hold authorities and politicians to account.

This assessment may explain why journalists in countries included in the monitorial model do not have particularly high levels of trust in public institutions (though trust ranges from very low in the United States to considerably higher in Central Europe). Maintaining a certain distance to bearers of political power and authority is at the heart of monitorial journalism. In most societies that belong to the monitorial model, citizens not only have become more skeptical of social institutional arrangements including governments, big corporations, and the news media but also have developed higher aspirations in terms of the social liberties they are entitled to have (Norris 1999; Welzel 2013). As we argued in chapter 7, journalistic culture is likely to emphasize a monitorial role more vigorously in countries where the public has more appreciation for emancipative values and where the authority of social institutions is less taken for granted. We have related this finding to long-term cultural drift, or emancipative value change, which emphasizes the importance of individual autonomy, self-expression, and free choice (Inglehart and Welzel 2005).

A number of caveats need to be placed on our discussion of the monitorial model. For one, the model includes a larger number of countries than in each of the other three models, which should not be taken to mean that the monitorial model is the dominant one globally speaking. Instead, it reflects the composition of our country sample, which, despite all efforts to yield adequate global coverage of journalistic cultures, still considerably overrepresents developed liberal democracies. Furthermore, the monitorial model is far less monolithic than the discussion above may suggest. There are considerable differences between regions and countries subsumed under this model. Anglo-Saxon countries, for instance, stand out for their higher levels of editorial autonomy and a stronger appreciation of the accommodative role. Throughout this book we have also stressed the fact that according to our results, the United States may not be the best representative of a "Western" understanding of journalism, which may also be true for its position within the monitorial model. Further, journalists in the southern European countries included in the Worlds of Journalism Study (Greece, Portugal, and Spain) have—different from most other societies in the model—a relatively strong preference for an interventionist role. This, we argued, is likely related to recent developments, notably a severe economic crisis, as well as the specific histories of these three southern European countries, which shook off their authoritarian heritage only in the 1970s.

The second model, *advocative journalistic cultures*, encompasses a group of countries primarily located in Eastern Europe and Latin America. Advocative journalistic cultures are first and foremost characterized by a strong interventionist ethos in terms of their role perceptions. They differ, however, in terms of the extent to which they pursue monitorial aims, with journalists in Croatia, for example, being strongly monitorial, while their counterparts in many Latin American countries display much less interest in the monitorial role. This finding is in line with existing scholarship that has described several Latin American societies as "captured-liberal" media systems (Guerrero and Márquez 2014a).

A strong emphasis on advocacy is a defining element of journalism in Latin America, most postcommunist societies in Eastern Europe, and the countries that resulted from the violent breakup of former Yugoslavia. In journalistic culture in Latin America, the advocative model resonates with a journalistic heritage that champions journalism as advocacy and active interpretation of political reality (Waisbord 2000). Despite a notable move toward more independent and objective news, journalism in Latin America has historically been rooted in a tradition of ideological attachment and overt opinionated coverage. Latin American societies have also gone through disruptive changes, an experience journalists in these countries have in common with their colleagues in Eastern Europe. Throughout that region, societies have experienced profound political, economic, and cultural transformations. At the same time, the democratization process has rendered the political climate more susceptible for journalists from this part of Europe to play a more proactive role in political discourse.

Similar to their colleagues in developmental journalistic cultures, which we outline below, journalists in the advocative model can also be described as a mix of absolutists and situationists with regard to their ethical orientations. While these journalists show a relatively strong commitment to professional codes of ethical conduct, they still need to exercise a certain degree of flexibility in the application of professional norms—especially when the legal framework (e.g., with regard to journalists' safety and impunity) is still weak and efforts to politically influence media coverage may put journalists' careers at risk. Nonetheless, journalists reported a lower level of political influence and a higher level of editorial autonomy than their colleagues in the following two models, despite the strong organizational influence they experience in the newsroom. However, the relatively high levels of reported editorial freedoms in many of these countries are often contradicted by considerable restrictions on journalism: most are considered only partly free in the Freedom House Press Freedom rankings.

Another defining characteristic of the advocative model is the considerably low trust journalists have in public and political institutions. This is particularly true for Eastern Europe. Journalists in Albania, the Czech Republic, Hungary, Kosovo, Moldova, Romania, and Serbia have exceptionally little confidence in politics. What these young democracies have in common is a certain level of political discontinuity resulting from their transition to democracy, which in many cases has left representative institutions in a state of fragility (Catterberg and Moreno 2006). The precarious state of institutions is evidenced, among others explanations, by the fact that corruption is widespread in these countries, while at the same time, journalists—and their fellow citizens—may have developed high expectations of institutional performance as a result of the democratization process.

This analysis clearly indicates that the advocative model is rather typical of transitional democracies, in which transition extends into public discourse. In such a climate of ideological contestation, journalists tend to involve themselves in political struggles rather than act as disinterested bystanders. In this sense, advocative journalistic cultures can best be described through the framework of hybridization (Mancini 2015; Mellado et al. 2017). In several countries, as is the case for Latin America, hybridization likely resulted from colonial history and the adoption of Western ways of practicing journalism, which were adjusted to the political and sociocultural realities in the region. In Eastern Europe this process may be driven primarily by what one could call a "pan-Europeanization" of journalism, in which journalistic cultures have adapted to Western European standards, which were brought to these countries through journalism training and textbooks, as well as through European trade associations, international media corporations, and foreign capital and media ownership.

Developmental journalistic cultures share a number of traits with the advocative model but also with the collaborative model, which is discussed later in this chapter. Countries in parts of Asia, such as Bangladesh, Bhutan, India, and Indonesia, as well as most societies in sub-Saharan Africa, including Ethiopia, Kenya, Malawi, Sierra Leone, Sudan, and Tanzania, belong in this model. Politically, these countries are typically classified as flawed democracies or hybrid regimes, which continue to have relatively low levels of press freedom (for details, see table A.8 in the appendix). Economically, these countries are very much developing, ranking lower in terms of socioeconomic development (with the significant exception of India) in comparison to other countries covered by this study. They are characterized by large socioeconomic inequalities and high levels of corruption.

A defining element of the developmental model is the strong presence of an interventionist approach to journalistic culture, often combined with a stronger emphasis on a collaborative role than is the case for advocative journalistic cultures. In this model, journalists are keenest to advocate for social change, set the political agenda, and support national development. Journalists here are more willing to act as "agents of change" in societies facing problems of low human and economic development, as well as strong legal and institutional uncertainty. Furthermore, in societies that are less effective in fighting corruption, journalists are more eager to embrace the developmental model. Not coincidentally, then, we see many similarities to the models that scholars previously proposed in terms of a developmental function of journalism (Hachten 1981; Kunczik 1988) and to the concept of development journalism, particularly in terms of the articulation of journalistic roles (Ogan 1982).

That being said, there is no single, unitary mode of journalism aspiring to contribute to national development (Edeani 1993; Kalyango, Jr., et al. 2017; Romano 2005). Our analysis of journalistic roles in chapter 7, in particular, has clearly pointed to the coexistence of multiple paradigms under the larger conceptual umbrella of a developmental journalistic culture. The most purely interventionist approach, for instance, calls on journalists to drive social reform and defend certain social, cultural, or national values. Journalists acting as agents of empowerment assume a strong responsibility toward the citizenry and help audience members not only to be well informed but also to be meaningfully educated, motivated, inspired, and moved into action (Edeani 1993; Kalyango, Jr., et al. 2017). When an interventionist approach blends with an emphasis on collaborative roles, on the other hand, journalists tend to see themselves as partners of political and state authorities working together toward the goal of bringing about socioeconomic development (De Beer et al. 2016; Ogan 1982).

In terms of journalism ethics, developmental journalistic cultures embrace a mix of absolutism and situationism, similar to many countries in the advocative model. In developing societies, journalists often face significant regulatory and legal uncertainty. In these countries, they need a more flexible ethical tool kit, one that allows them to exercise greater care and base their decisions in the situational context. At the same time, these journalists reported higher amounts of political influences and less editorial autonomy than their counterparts in the former two models did.

Finally, journalists in countries that belong to the developmental model of journalistic culture tend to have somewhat higher trust in regulative and representative institutions than their colleagues in the advocative model. Bangladesh, Bhutan, and India were among the countries where journalists had the strongest faith in public and political authorities. Interestingly, for several countries—among those for which data were available—we noted that journalists' confidence in political institutions was considerably lower than were the trust levels of the corresponding general populations. In this regard, the Philippines was an extreme case. Here and in many other countries in this model, journalists have privileged access to information about political processes because of the nature of their work. They are usually the first to become aware of political scandals and governmental misconduct. However, because journalists operate in an environment of restrictions on press freedom and many of them work in state-run media organizations, much of this firsthand information might not be exposed to the public.

Collaborative journalistic cultures, finally, are found in Middle Eastern countries such as Oman, Qatar, and the United Arab Emirates, as well as in China and the Southeast Asian nations of Malaysia, Singapore, and Thailand. A main characteristic of these societies is an opportunity structure that is strongly shaped by state authorities. Authoritarian governments in these countries grant citizens limited political liberties, and journalists here experience very low levels of press freedom (for details, see table A.8). Consequently, our findings show that journalists in this model, many of whom work for state-run media organizations, report strong political influence and low levels of editorial freedoms. At the same time, these journalists do not always face open censorship in the way journalists in China do. There seems to be an increasing tendency among state authorities in some contexts to replace open press restrictions by softer means of coercion, such as providing economic disincentives for nonco-operation with the state. Singapore is a prime example in this respect. The government has achieved effective media control by way of creative legislation and by exercising subtle political judgment to maintain a press system that balances government interests, the profit motives of publishers, the professional needs of journalists, and the public's demand for information (George 2007). Our use of the term collaborative is thus quite similar to Christians et al.'s (2009) discussion rather than a normative framing of the term as positive, which may exist in the West, such as when journalists collaborate with each other. Rather, as Christians and colleagues argue, "a collaborative role for the media implies a partnership, a relationship between the media and the state built on mutual trust and a shared commitment to mutually agreeable means and ends" (198).

In countries that are part of the collaborative model, journalists tend to subscribe to journalistic roles that call on journalists to actively support government policies and portray political leaders in a positive light. In many of these societies, journalism is seen as serving the state's development agenda. The "official" role of news media and of journalists is to help forge public consensus for governments in pursuit of economic growth and social development. Journalists are assumed to have responsibilities for publicly shared development goals, such as socioeconomic well-being and national unity. This rationale is particularly interesting if one considers the fact that many of the countries in the collaborative model, such as Singapore and Qatar, are economically quite well developed, since they have in recent decades achieved significant amounts of wealth and a growing middle class. Furthermore, in many countries in Southeast Asia, including Malaysia and Singapore, the collaborative model resonates with the idea of journalism being driven by "Asian values," which stresses government-media partnerships to "promote the larger good of social harmony and stability together with economic growth and development" (Wong 2004, 37). Hence the acceptance of the practice of collaboration is not always based on coercion, but also at times on broader cultural values that resonate with demands for social harmony and respect for authority.

At the same time, journalists in the societies subsumed in the collaborative model reported a relatively high amount of trust in representative and regulative institutions. Oman, Singapore, and Malaysia were among the countries where journalists had extraordinarily strong confidence in political institutions. In part, the high political trust of journalists may represent an opportunist attitude. At the same time, however, most of the countries in this model have made enormous economic progress, from which middle-class journalists may have particularly benefited. Hence journalists may be considerably satisfied with institutional performance in these countries despite the fact that they face significant restrictions on their work.

Concerning journalism ethics, our findings show that collaborative journalistic cultures most strongly lean toward a subjectivist orientation. Despite authoritarian tendencies, the political and legal environments in these cultures tend to be relatively stable and predictable. Journalists nonetheless need to apply subjective judgment to strike a workable balance between journalistic imperatives, on the one hand, and political and organizational restrictions, on the other. Furthermore, journalists in countries belonging to the collaborative model are least likely to justify specific investigative and controversial reporting practices. This is particularly true for the use of confidential documents without authorization. Clearly this characteristic of the collaborative model can be attributed to a politically restrictive climate in which journalists who make unauthorized use of official information will almost certainly face punishment.

As we have reiterated above, the four models outlined in this chapter are ideal types. In reality, a country may fit a given model more or less perfectly; other countries may straddle different models. Furthermore, boundaries between models may, in reality, be fluid and porous. Despite these limitations, we think the models are a useful tool to map the global diversity of journalistic cultures systematically. Furthermore, the four models are quite consistent with the classification proposed by Christians et al. (2009), who distinguished between a monitorial model (journalism as a provider of information), radical model (journalism challenging authority and voicing support for reform), facilitative model (strengthening civil society), and collaborative model (supporting those in power and aiming to advance mutual interests).

Having discussed the four models of journalistic cultures as we see them emerge from our empirical data from surveys with more than 27,500 journalists in sixty-seven countries, it is important to place our overall study in context. We therefore highlight below the study's limitations as well as its significant contributions to journalism scholarship.

A Final Note on the Study's Limitations and Contribution

While the WJS has been described as a "comparative leap forward" (Blumler 2017, 682) in journalism studies, we do not claim to have found answers to all questions that concern the topic. In fact, as we have highlighted in this book, the study needs to be viewed in the context of some important limitations. Owing to its focus on discursively constituted journalistic cultures, it has relied solely on surveys of journalists. Hence we have dealt with journalists' professional orientations, which may not always fully correspond to their practice, a limitation discussed in chapter 2. It is impossible to say to what extent the journalists surveyed for this book may be able to enact these orientations in their practice, and we are therefore unable to comment on the extent to which the journalistic cultures identified here are constituted in actual journalistic practices around the world. Further, we employed a comparatively traditional definition of who counts as a journalist, which means that our results apply predominantly to traditional, mainstream journalism, with most journalists in some kind of employment situation in journalism. Scholars have increasingly challenged such traditional definitions, pointing to the range of new kinds of journalistic actors who have emerged in the digital age (Deuze and Witschge 2018).

Our questionnaire was developed in 2010 and 2011 and captured what we considered relevant aspects of journalism at the time, particularly in relation to journalistic transformations. As a result, the study was unable to capture the many developments in news media across the globe that occurred rapidly in subsequent years. Back in 2010, social media was still somewhat in its infancy, and in many countries traditional business models were still slightly more stable than they are today. The complexities of organizing a study across sixty-seven diverse national contexts, with their own respective challenges for data gathering, also resulted in considerable variability in terms of sampling approaches and the way field research was conducted. These limitations resulted in some less desirable variation in the quality of some national datasets as outlined in chapter 3, even though a range of safeguards were implemented that enable us to place a large amount of trust in the overall quality of our dataset. Still, the experience from this wave of the WJS, as well as recent events in the journalistic profession and its opportunity structures across the globe, are key insights that will help us to develop the next wave of the study, which is in its planning phase.

Despite these apparent shortcomings, we believe the WJS will be viewed as having made a major contribution to journalism scholarship on theoretical, methodological, and substantive levels. We have applied a new theoretical lens to the (comparative) study of journalism by conceptualizing journalism as a social institution that is discursively (re)created, (re)interpreted, appropriated, and contested. We argue that this approach has proven immensely productive in the context of this study. Its application allowed us to establish a link between methodological individualism, on the one hand, and studies of larger—social and cultural—institutional structures, on the other. It enabled us to analyze journalistic culture through the professional characteristics, views, and perceptions of individual journalists.

On the methodological level, the WJS constitutes the largest comparative endeavor in the field of journalism and media research. In this way, the collaborative approach of the Worlds of Journalism Study has, in our view, become a role model for comparative research in the field. We genuinely believe that collaborative research is going to play a central role in the future development of journalism studies. Collaboration allows us to pool intellectual expertise and share scarce research resources. In an era of networked science, collaborative research may even become the norm rather than the exception. The "lone scholar" may no longer be the standard model of research in the social sciences and humanities. In fact, we believe that collaboration is key to the production of scientific knowledge and the development of scholarly careers.

While sheer size alone does not always equate to quality, we are particularly pleased that we were able to include a considerable number of countries that are rarely studied in journalism scholarship, particularly those from sub-Saharan Africa, but also many others from the Global South. This allows comparative journalism studies as a field to reach a new level; one which allows for a significantly broader and culturally more sensitive understanding of journalistic cultures around the world.

This improved understanding of the various kinds of journalistic cultures across the globe, we argue, allows us to recalibrate journalism scholarship's compass. It challenges the dominant view of journalism in the literature, which is heavily informed by Western models and research, by pointing to alternative ideologies of journalism, which may be just as legitimate as traditional Western approaches to news making. While some argue that journalism is an Anglo-American invention (Chalaby 1996), and we can certainly see the diffusion of Western ideas of journalism across the globe to some extent, our study also highlights that different countries and regions have developed their own particular models of journalistic cultures to respond to their own unique sets of opportunity structures. Our approach, therefore, also calls normative expectations and ideals into question when they are applied by Western scholars to non-Western countries. The "world of journalism" is indeed populated by a rich, complex, and fascinating combination of approaches to what journalism is, and what it ought to be.

APPENDIX 1

ADDITIONAL TABLES

Table A.1 Political, economic, and organizational influences

	Politicians		Government officials		Pressure groups		Business representatives		Profit expectations	
	Mean	(SD)	Mean	(SD)	Mean	(SD)	Mean	(SD)	Mean	(SD)
Albania	1.95	(1.17)	2.13	(1.20)	1.56	(0.78)	1.87	(1.05)	2.42	(1.36)
Argentina	2.43	(1.10)	2.45	(1.10)	2.11	(1.02)	2.08	(0.99)	2.46	(1.26)
Australia	2.27	(1.04)	2.30	(1.04)	2.12	(0.92)	2.29	(0.97)	2.13	(1.21)
Austria	1.55	(0.75)	1.37	(0.65)	1.76	(0.76)	1.65	(0.79)	2.10	(1.07)
Bangladesh	2.27	(1.35)	2.07	(1.30)	2.23	(1.35)	2.06	(1.29)	2.30	(1.27)
Belgium	1.72	(0.97)	1.47	(0.76)	1.82	(0.99)	1.70	(1.02)	1.82	(1.13)
Bhutan	3.24	(1.19)	3.49	(1.24)	3.09	(1.15)	2.89	(1.10)	3.18	(1.24)
Botswana	2.91	(1.44)	3.20	(1.44)	2.43	(1.25)	2.72	(1.36)	2.62	(1.38)
Brazil	2.18	(1.15)	2.06	(1.08)	1.99	(1.04)	2.14	(1.09)	2.68	(1.28)
Canada	1.65	(0.96)	1.75	(1.03)	1.54	(0.81)	1.64	(0.86)	1.54	(0.90)
Chile	2.12	(1.19)	2.14	(1.20)	2.17	(1.26)	2.26	(1.25)	2.66	(1.37)
China	3.22	(1.06)	3.34	(0.98)	2.51	(0.87)	2.54	(0.89)	3.04	(0.98)
Colombia	2.48	(1.33)	2.52	(1.34)	2.58	(1.40)	2.66	(1.34)	2.95	(1.43)
Croatia	2.20	(1.33)	2.11	(1.31)	2.03	(1.30)	2.24	(1.34)	2.69	(1.47)
Cyprus	1.81	(0.92)	1.75	(0.87)	1.68	(0.81)	1.63	(0.86)	2.75	(1.53)
Czech Republic	1.86	(1.08)	1.57	(0.89)	1.47	(0.78)	1.65	(0.95)	2.16	(1.17)
Denmark	2.05	(1.07)	1.88	(0.98)	2.10	(1.05)	1.85	(1.01)	2.24	(1.27)
Ecuador	2.86	(1.31)	2.98	(1.29)	2.73	(1.33)	2.59	(1.31)	2.95	(1.28)
Egypt	2.79	(1.27)	2.70	(1.26)	2.64	(1.33)	2.45	(1.43)	3.07	(1.23)
El Salvador	2.88	(1.32)	2.90	(1.33)	2.64	(1.25)	2.79	(1.31)	3.16	(1.34)
Estonia	1.64	(0.85)	1.78	(0.93)	1.80	(0.98)	1.67	(0.89)	2.20	(1.29)
Ethiopia	3.35	(1.42)	3.63	(1.40)	2.85	(1.39)	2.75	(1.34)	2.80	(1.30)
Finland	1.96	(1.00)	2.24	(1.10)	1.88	(0.91)	1.82	(0.85)	2.04	(1.06)
France	1.54	(0.68)	1.48	(0.64)	1.43	(0.61)	1.42	(0.75)	1.96	(0.97)
Germany	1.41	(0.70)	1.24	(0.58)	1.86	(0.93)	1.78	(0.94)	2.43	(1.27)
Greece	1.91	(1.12)	1.90	(1.14)	1.89	(1.08)	1.93	(1.15)	2.31	(1.20)
Hong Kong	2.26	(0.96)	2.32	(1.01)	2.22	(0.92)	2.20	(0.93)	2.24	(1.10)
Hungary	2.04	(1.16)	2.01	(1.10)	1.90	(1.09)	1.95	(1.06)	3.01	(1.21)

Economic influences				Organizational influences							
Advertising considerations		Audience research and data		Managers of news organization		Higher editors		Owners of news organization		Editorial policy	
Mean	(SD)	Mean	(SD)	Mean	(SD)	Mean	(SD)	Mean	(SD)	Mean	(SD)
2.54	(1.28)	3.33	(1.15)	3.01	(1.17)	3.22	(0.99)	2.97	(1.32)	3.39	(1.06)
2.44	(1.15)	2.62	(1.19)	3.36	(1.14)	3.50	(0.96)	3.34	(1.24)	3.61	(1.05)
2.10	(1.12)	3.19	(1.17)	2.64	(1.24)	3.73	(0.90)	2.04	(1.17)	3.79	(1.08)
1.97	(1.02)	2.58	(1.05)	2.18	(0.97)	2.92	(0.94)	2.04	(0.97)	3.09	(1.02)
2.85	(1.19)	3.44	(1.20)	3.20	(1.27)	3.43	(1.19)	3.16	(1.40)	3.82	(1.29)
1.73	(1.00)	2.65	(1.11)	2.33	(1.14)	3.24	(1.05)	1.91	(1.13)	3.45	(1.02)
3.20	(1.21)	3.19	(1.30)	3.59	(1.19)	3.92	(1.06)	3.35	(1.27)	3.58	(1.13)
2.59	(1.37)	3.71	(1.23)	3.75	(1.28)	3.92	(1.10)	3.47	(1.50)	4.42	(0.91)
2.59	(1.25)	3.13	(1.20)	3.35	(1.06)	3.46	(0.89)	3.34	(1.23)	3.65	(0.98)
1.47	(0.77)	2.68	(1.18)	2.66	(1.18)	3.35	(0.99)	1.77	(0.99)	3.19	(1.42)
2.58	(1.34)	2.89	(1.33)	3.37	(1.26)	3.79	(1.03)	3.16	(1.35)	3.72	(1.10)
3.06	(0.97)	3.19	(0.93)	3.70	(0.89)	3.67	(0.83)	3.18	(1.04)	3.64	(0.89)
3.08	(1.45)	3.25	(1.35)	3.61	(1.35)	3.78	(1.19)	3.61	(1.35)	3.80	(1.23)
2.62	(1.44)	2.92	(1.20)	2.78	(1.36)	3.14	(1.19)	2.82	(1.44)	3.43	(1.22)
2.73	(1.43)	2.24	(1.18)	4.01	(1.02)	3.92	(0.98)	3.93	(1.19)	3.74	(1.02)
2.30	(1.23)	3.04	(1.15)	3.04	(1.22)	3.60	(1.06)	2.61	(1.28)	3.43	(1.07)
1.66	(1.00)	2.66	(1.09)	2.74	(1.18)	3.47	(1.03)	2.03	(1.21)	3.63	(1.07)
2.74	(1.32)	3.34	(1.19)	3.56	(1.08)	3.63	(1.02)	3.55	(1.21)	3.67	(1.14)
3.07	(1.24)	3.63	(1.06)	3.45	(1.05)	3.49	(1.03)	3.39	(1.29)	3.92	(1.07)
3.11	(1.32)	3.21	(1.28)	3.94	(1.12)	4.06	(0.96)	3.99	(1.23)	3.98	(1.06)
2.14	(1.21)	3.21	(1.09)	2.72	(1.16)	3.27	(0.99)	2.17	(1.24)	3.31	(1.15)
2.68	(1.33)	3.14	(1.24)	3.76	(1.24)	3.84	(1.14)	3.71	(1.34)	3.97	(1.22)
1.58	(0.77)	3.02	(0.87)	2.05	(0.96)	3.43	(0.83)	1.83	(0.97)	3.78	(0.93)
1.85	(0.85)	2.65	(1.06)	2.31	(1.04)	2.89	(0.96)	2.01	(1.05)	3.23	(1.04)
2.35	(1.26)	2.89	(1.09)	2.49	(1.17)	3.27	(0.97)	2.14	(1.21)	3.34	(1.13)
2.65	(1.22)	2.89	(1.23)	3.32	(1.26)	3.17	(1.21)	3.12	(1.35)	3.08	(1.22)
2.29	(1.05)	2.44	(1.03)	3.37	(1.06)	3.50	(0.98)	3.00	(1.16)	3.35	(1.00)
2.94	(1.13)	3.39	(1.10)	3.40	(1.19)	3.67	(1.08)	3.20	(1.26)	3.45	(1.16)

(continued)

Table A.1 Political, economic, and organizational influences (*continued*)

	Political influences									
	Politicians		Government officials		Pressure groups		Business representatives		Profit expectations	
	Mean	(SD)	Mean	(SD)	Mean	(SD)	Mean	(SD)	Mean	(SD)
Iceland	1.60	(0.85)	1.61	(0.84)	1.62	(0.77)	1.62	(0.86)	1.75	(1.03)
India	2.61	(1.25)	2.80	(1.25)	2.35	(1.20)	2.37	(1.25)	3.08	(1.30)
Indonesia	2.28	(1.06)	2.43	(1.11)	2.28	(1.04)	2.18	(1.02)	2.68	(1.17)
Ireland	2.18	(1.11)	2.16	(1.07)	2.13	(1.04)	2.11	(0.99)	1.98	(1.06)
Israel	1.72	(1.03)	1.81	(1.11)	1.70	(0.97)	1.59	(0.93)	1.88	(1.25)
Italy	1.69	(0.95)	1.51	(0.83)	1.71	(0.98)	1.61	(0.86)	2.17	(1.15)
Japan			1.92	(0.87)	1.82	(0.76)			2.32	(0.99)
Kenya	2.48	(1.13)	2.91	(1.16)	2.38	(1.10)	2.67	(1.19)	3.38	(1.18)
Kosovo	2.19	(1.30)	2.33	(1.30)	2.10	(1.19)	1.99	(1.17)	1.92	(1.12)
Latvia	1.38	(0.71)	1.40	(0.74)	1.37	(0.66)	1.50	(0.77)	2.14	(1.19)
Malawi	2.82	(1.34)	3.16	(1.29)	2.57	(1.21)	2.94	(1.25)	3.04	(1.32)
Malaysia	3.34	(1.00)	3.54	(0.98)	3.20	(0.94)	3.10	(1.02)	3.30	(1.02)
Mexico	2.52	(1.28)	2.51	(1.28)	2.68	(1.14)	2.38	(1.17)	2.90	(1.36)
Moldova	1.82	(1.02)	1.92	(1.04)	1.77	(1.03)	1.78	(0.98)	2.84	(1.29)
Netherlands	1.78	(0.95)	1.74	(0.94)	2.04	(0.94)	1.98	(1.03)	2.23	(1.17)
New Zealand	1.96	(1.05)	2.08	(1.09)	1.93	(0.94)	2.09	(1.05)	2.21	(1.22)
Norway	1.93	(0.85)	1.84	(0.82)	1.82	(0.74)	1.66	(0.72)	1.96	(1.06)
Oman	3.12	(1.22)	3.48	(1.18)	2.84	(1.06)	2.70	(1.19)	3.00	(1.09)
Philippines	2.38	(1.07)	2.57	(1.09)	2.23	(0.96)	2.37	(1.02)	2.65	(1.10)
Portugal	1.60	(0.89)	1.54	(0.84)	1.61	(0.88)	1.62	(0.90)	2.36	(1.11)
Qatar	2.68	(1.36)	2.65	(1.42)	2.56	(1.38)	2.74	(1.34)	3.08	(1.31)
Romania	1.80	(1.09)	1.88	(1.10)	1.78	(1.07)	1.75	(0.99)	2.82	(1.28)
Russia	2.24	(1.16)	2.34	(1.17)	2.22	(1.00)	2.19	(1.04)	2.55	(1.32)
Serbia	2.27	(1.23)	2.27	(1.23)	1.88	(1.11)	2.07	(1.11)	2.84	(1.27)
Sierra Leone	2.52	(1.30)	2.74	(1.35)	2.89	(1.25)	2.75	(1.26)	2.99	(1.27)
Singapore	2.93	(1.13)	2.99	(1.09)	2.97	(1.14)	2.81	(1.05)	2.80	(1.20)
South Africa	2.28	(1.23)	2.37	(1.23)	2.28	(1.08)	2.63	(1.20)	2.59	(1.26)
South Korea	2.66	(1.06)	2.68	(1.03)	2.60	(1.02)	2.75	(1.02)	3.04	(1.13)

| Economic influences | | | | Organizational influences | | | | | |
| Advertising considerations | | Audience research and data | | Managers of news organization | | Higher editors | | Owners of news organization | | Editorial policy | |
Mean	(SD)	Mean	(SD)	Mean	(SD)	Mean	(SD)	Mean	(SD)	Mean	(SD)
1.47	(0.81)	2.07	(1.07)	1.74	(0.95)	3.25	(1.06)	1.54	(0.91)	3.32	(1.10)
3.21	(1.26)	3.86	(1.05)	3.28	(1.30)	3.65	(1.20)	3.50	(1.38)	4.08	(1.00)
2.67	(1.14)	3.61	(0.93)	3.23	(1.06)	3.35	(0.96)	3.24	(1.13)	3.60	(0.97)
2.07	(1.09)	2.89	(1.12)	2.22	(1.08)	3.56	(0.95)	2.26	(1.15)	3.61	(1.06)
2.40	(1.37)	2.81	(1.26)	2.86	(1.40)	3.42	(1.20)	2.41	(1.48)	3.17	(1.33)
2.08	(1.14)	2.74	(1.20)	2.25	(1.18)	2.80	(1.13)	2.34	(1.21)	3.20	(1.10)
2.49	(1.03)	3.00	(0.90)	3.48	(0.96)	3.43	(0.90)	2.87	(1.19)	3.35	(0.92)
3.46	(1.06)	3.82	(1.04)	3.79	(1.10)	3.94	(0.90)	3.65	(1.26)	4.20	(1.02)
2.41	(1.26)	3.23	(1.35)	2.91	(1.25)	3.09	(1.25)	2.84	(1.29)	3.35	(1.23)
2.31	(1.20)	2.91	(1.18)	2.54	(1.13)	3.26	(0.97)	2.12	(1.18)	3.33	(1.11)
3.32	(1.13)	3.89	(1.08)	3.93	(1.09)	4.07	(0.99)	3.90	(1.23)	4.28	(0.96)
3.25	(0.98)	3.60	(0.91)	3.54	(0.93)	3.64	(0.87)	3.58	(1.02)	3.84	(0.89)
2.64	(1.32)	3.18	(1.23)	3.70	(1.25)	3.73	(1.12)	3.72	(1.30)	3.95	(1.02)
2.58	(1.30)	3.26	(1.22)	2.87	(1.21)	3.35	(1.06)	2.76	(1.30)	3.58	(1.15)
2.31	(1.14)	2.71	(1.04)	2.46	(1.03)	3.19	(0.95)	2.17	(1.07)	3.31	(0.95)
2.15	(1.14)	3.08	(1.17)	2.81	(1.17)	3.43	(1.02)	2.21	(1.24)	3.54	(1.00)
1.56	(0.88)	2.37	(1.04)	1.81	(0.82)	3.28	(0.76)	1.60	(0.82)	3.52	(0.80)
3.33	(1.04)	3.44	(1.01)	3.27	(1.10)	3.44	(1.16)	3.72	(1.06)	3.76	(0.95)
2.71	(1.08)	3.59	(1.00)	3.49	(0.96)	3.64	(0.89)	3.26	(1.13)	4.03	(0.84)
2.09	(1.04)	2.63	(1.12)	2.70	(1.11)	3.41	(0.94)	2.45	(1.13)	3.81	(0.94)
3.12	(1.32)	2.80	(1.31)	2.63	(1.30)	2.71	(1.25)	2.49	(1.33)	3.38	(1.31)
2.51	(1.23)	3.25	(1.16)	2.79	(1.24)	3.19	(1.14)	2.60	(1.27)	3.48	(1.18)
2.40	(1.30)	3.07	(1.17)	3.69	(1.03)	3.59	(1.06)	3.52	(1.24)	3.31	(1.26)
2.75	(1.17)	3.21	(1.20)	3.20	(1.14)	3.42	(1.00)	3.11	(1.22)	3.68	(1.09)
3.40	(1.15)	3.73	(1.12)	3.85	(1.08)	4.02	(1.10)	3.85	(1.21)	4.29	(1.00)
2.83	(1.12)	3.16	(0.99)	2.88	(1.18)	3.05	(1.23)	2.86	(1.30)	3.06	(1.31)
2.53	(1.21)	3.55	(1.07)	3.40	(1.10)	3.85	(0.92)	2.89	(1.30)	4.08	(0.96)
3.14	(1.10)	3.60	(0.84)	3.42	(1.02)	3.94	(0.71)	3.22	(1.16)	3.63	(0.87)

(*continued*)

Table A.1 Political, economic, and organizational influences (*continued*)

| | Political influences | | | | | | | | |
| | Politicians | | Government officials | | Pressure groups | | Business representatives | | Profit expectations | |
	Mean	(SD)	Mean	(SD)	Mean	(SD)	Mean	(SD)	Mean	(SD)
Spain	2.42	(1.21)	1.90	(1.02)	2.22	(1.13)	2.37	(1.16)	2.84	(1.21)
Sudan	3.16	(1.59)	3.22	(1.60)	3.13	(1.64)	3.12	(1.69)	3.39	(1.32)
Sweden	1.73	(0.79)	1.42	(0.66)	1.76	(0.71)	1.78	(0.72)	2.37	(1.30)
Switzerland	1.87	(0.82)	1.75	(0.76)	2.00	(0.81)	1.89	(0.78)	2.12	(0.99)
Tanzania	2.62	(1.07)	3.09	(0.78)	2.40	(0.98)	2.09	(0.77)	2.50	(1.06)
Thailand	3.75	(1.01)	3.75	(0.90)	3.67	(0.98)	3.73	(1.00)	3.79	(0.83)
Turkey	3.18	(1.35)	3.26	(1.35)	3.02	(1.27)	2.55	(1.26)	2.31	(1.22)
United Arab Emirates	2.56	(1.45)	2.56	(1.51)	2.70	(1.49)	3.04	(1.41)	3.24	(1.35)
United Kingdom	1.94	(0.95)	1.92	(0.92)	2.00	(0.92)	2.32	(1.12)	2.43	(1.11)
United States	1.95	(1.01)	2.14	(1.07)	1.65	(0.81)	1.99	(0.93)	1.86	(0.98)

Scale: 5 = "extremely influential" . . . 1 = "not influential."

Economic influences				Organizational influences							
Advertising considerations		Audience research and data		Managers of news organization		Higher editors		Owners of news organization		Editorial policy	
Mean	(SD)	Mean	(SD)	Mean	(SD)	Mean	(SD)	Mean	(SD)	Mean	(SD)
2.93	(1.30)	2.83	(1.17)	3.19	(1.33)	3.75	(0.96)	3.10	(1.45)	3.54	(1.11)
3.68	(1.18)	3.95	(1.09)	3.49	(1.09)	3.74	(1.02)	3.44	(1.23)	4.20	(0.95)
1.84	(0.98)	2.58	(1.00)	2.68	(1.09)	3.49	(0.84)	2.12	(1.12)	3.32	(0.94)
1.97	(0.96)	2.45	(0.97)	2.22	(0.97)	2.93	(0.90)	1.86	(0.93)	3.02	(0.99)
2.57	(1.12)	1.56	(0.63)	4.19	(0.71)	3.74	(0.77)	4.19	(0.71)	4.09	(0.69)
3.81	(0.91)	3.70	(0.80)	3.92	(0.81)	3.91	(0.83)	3.99	(0.84)	4.04	(0.74)
2.38	(1.21)	2.57	(1.18)	2.91	(1.22)	2.62	(1.17)	2.89	(1.34)	3.30	(1.23)
2.90	(1.35)	3.11	(1.35)	3.01	(1.42)	2.99	(1.34)	3.29	(1.41)	2.67	(1.41)
2.35	(1.09)	3.26	(1.08)	2.93	(1.12)	3.44	(0.96)	2.51	(1.21)	3.77	(0.96)
1.72	(0.90)	3.10	(1.09)	3.44	(1.20)	3.72	1.05)	2.64	(1.33)	3.74	(1.23)

Table A.2 Procedural and personal networks influences

	Procedural influences							
	Information access		Journalism ethics		Media laws and regulation		Availability of news-gathering resources	
	Mean	(SD)	Mean	(SD)	Mean	(SD)	Mean	(SD)
Albania	3.95	(0.81)	4.23	(0.73)	3.83	(0.97)	3.52	(1.11)
Argentina	3.89	(0.90)	4.19	(0.89)	2.92	(1.14)	3.32	(1.17)
Australia	3.94	(0.81)	4.34	(0.68)	4.08	(0.95)	3.96	(0.85)
Austria	3.42	(1.09)	3.87	(0.93)	2.77	(1.12)	3.53	(1.00)
Bangladesh	3.47	(1.29)	4.31	(1.05)	3.90	(1.24)	3.33	(1.16)
Belgium	3.64	(0.96)	4.03	(0.97)	3.16	(1.19)	3.32	(1.00)
Bhutan	4.20	(0.89)	3.49	(1.51)	3.67	(1.25)	3.36	(1.33)
Botswana	4.46	(0.85)	4.61	(0.74)	4.40	(0.91)	4.27	(0.94)
Brazil	3.90	(0.93)	4.15	(1.05)	3.10	(1.09)	3.54	(1.08)
Canada	3.68	(1.02)	4.53	(0.72)	3.68	(1.22)	3.71	(0.95)
Chile	3.72	(1.23)	4.33	(0.92)	2.90	(1.24)	3.36	(1.28)
China	3.60	(0.81)	3.88	(0.91)	3.57	(0.86)	3.54	(0.88)
Colombia	3.81	(1.23)	4.19	(1.11)	3.64	(1.20)	2.66	(1.45)
Croatia	3.98	(0.91)	4.28	(0.97)	3.59	(1.08)	3.71	(1.07)
Cyprus	4.02	(0.94)	4.07	(1.10)	3.41	(1.27)	3.54	(1.20)
Czech Republic	4.38	(0.83)	4.42	(0.83)	3.95	(1.12)	3.91	(0.99)
Denmark	2.96	(1.16)	3.95	(0.98)	2.76	(1.19)	3.60	(1.05)
Ecuador	4.07	(0.96)	4.47	(0.82)	3.81	(0.98)	3.26	(1.29)
Egypt	3.61	(1.50)	4.47	(0.90)	3.44	(1.38)	4.21	(0.89)
El Salvador	4.01	(0.97)	4.36	(0.87)	3.41	(1.13)	3.58	(1.21)
Estonia	4.11	(0.95)	4.28	(0.88)	2.94	(1.25)	3.84	(0.99)
Ethiopia	3.93	(1.06)	3.62	(1.29)	3.80	(1.15)	3.65	(1.06)
Finland	3.08	(1.22)	4.34	(0.73)	3.99	(0.99)	3.87	(0.90)
France	3.54	(1.03)	4.21	(0.89)	3.16	(1.13)	3.27	(1.02)
Germany	3.75	(0.98)	4.05	(0.91)	2.96	(1.20)	3.55	(0.97)
Greece	3.95	(0.99)	4.15	(0.97)	3.45	(1.12)	3.50	(1.10)
Hong Kong	3.13	(0.95)	3.53	(1.05)	3.00	(0.92)	3.10	(1.10)

| Time limits | | Personal networks influences | | | | | | |
| | | Friends, acquaintances, and family | | Colleagues in other media | | Peers on the staff | |
Mean	(SD)	Mean	(SD)	Mean	(SD)	Mean	(SD)
3.80	(0.96)	2.28	(1.14)	2.08	(0.99)	2.54	(0.98)
3.57	(1.02)	2.58	(1.06)	2.74	(0.93)	3.02	(0.99)
4.03	(0.80)	2.07	(0.98)	2.37	(1.06)	2.98	(0.97)
3.70	(0.99)	2.09	(0.86)	2.06	(0.79)	2.64	(0.84)
3.28	(1.12)	2.00	(1.34)	2.15	(1.29)	2.58	(1.17)
3.56	(1.02)	2.15	(0.99)	2.35	(0.98)	2.94	(0.97)
3.35	(1.52)	3.58	(1.46)	3.62	(1.22)	3.69	(1.10)
4.13	(0.96)	2.14	(1.29)	2.66	(1.25)	2.78	(1.16)
3.86	(1.05)	2.42	(1.03)	2.64	(0.99)	2.97	(0.90)
3.78	(0.93)	1.91	(0.93)	2.22	(1.00)	2.83	(1.00)
3.79	(1.11)	2.19	(1.18)	2.35	(1.14)	2.97	(1.18)
3.35	(0.86)	2.51	(0.97)	2.66	(0.86)	2.93	(0.84)
3.63	(1.21)	2.32	(1.27)	2.52	(1.29)	2.97	(1.28)
3.84	(1.09)	2.77	(1.30)	2.67	(1.18)	2.64	(1.23)
4.05	(0.92)	1.38	(0.83)	1.84	(0.97)	2.50	(1.20)
3.80	(1.02)	2.87	(1.33)	2.43	(1.00)	3.37	(1.01)
3.87	(1.05)	1.89	(0.91)	1.93	(0.92)	3.24	(1.06)
3.50	(1.13)	2.68	(1.30)	2.74	(1.24)	2.98	(1.18)
4.04	(0.99)	2.46	(1.34)	2.61	(1.23)	2.95	(1.08)
3.65	(1.15)	2.32	(1.26)	2.47	(1.16)	2.95	(1.16)
3.69	(1.09)	2.38	(1.07)	2.21	(0.98)	3.19	(0.94)
3.78	(1.10)	2.42	(1.22)	2.27	(1.20)	2.97	(1.13)
3.86	(0.85)	2.46	(0.94)	2.28	(0.83)	2.90	(0.89)
3.80	(1.06)	2.29	(0.98)	2.42	(0.94)	2.83	(0.88)
3.68	(0.99)	2.01	(0.91)	2.20	(0.94)	3.03	(0.94)
3.72	(1.07)	2.02	(1.10)	2.10	(1.04)	2.64	(1.23)
3.42	(0.98)	2.32	(0.95)	2.54	(0.93)	2.80	(0.91)

(continued)

Table A.2 Procedural and personal networks influences (*continued*)

	Information access		Journalism ethics		Media laws and regulation		Availability of news-gathering resources	
							Procedural influences	
	Mean	(SD)	Mean	(SD)	Mean	(SD)	Mean	(SD)
Hungary	3.84	(0.99)	4.02	(0.97)	3.49	(1.11)	3.58	(0.98)
Iceland	4.15	(0.84)	3.82	(1.08)	3.03	(1.19)	3.88	(0.98)
India	4.02	(0.99)	4.23	(1.00)	3.97	(1.05)	3.94	(1.06)
Indonesia	3.73	(0.77)	4.08	(0.93)	3.83	(0.87)	3.68	(0.93)
Ireland	3.88	(0.83)	4.16	(0.86)	3.74	(1.00)	3.84	(0.91)
Israel	3.70	(1.13)	4.43	(0.85)	3.19	(1.40)	3.43	(1.18)
Italy	3.61	(0.98)	4.19	(0.94)	3.01	(1.07)	3.11	(1.27)
Japan	3.31	(0.91)	3.77	(0.87)	3.02	(0.96)	3.13	(0.84)
Kenya	4.20	(0.84)	4.13	(1.00)	4.22	(0.84)	4.07	(0.90)
Kosovo	3.77	(1.11)	4.40	(0.96)	4.04	(1.01)	2.86	(1.27)
Latvia	3.81	(1.03)	3.63	(1.23)	2.96	(1.29)	3.54	(1.04)
Malawi	4.20	(0.84)	4.50	(0.80)	4.35	(0.80)	4.23	(0.87)
Malaysia	3.95	(0.81)	3.97	(0.95)	3.91	(0.81)	3.76	(0.88)
Mexico	3.97	(0.99)	4.54	(0.76)	3.41	(1.19)	3.12	(1.28)
Moldova	4.20	(0.95)	4.17	(0.94)	3.75	(1.14)	3.62	(1.05)
Netherlands	2.69	(1.03)	3.31	(1.06)	2.40	(0.98)	3.40	(0.94)
New Zealand	3.83	(0.92)	4.17	(0.86)	3.79	(1.05)	3.71	(0.96)
Norway	3.67	(0.78)	3.92	(0.78)	3.63	(0.90)	2.87	(0.97)
Oman	3.75	(0.99)	3.54	(1.21)	3.84	(0.94)	3.98	(1.00)
Philippines	4.13	(0.77)	4.47	(0.66)	3.84	(0.90)	4.06	(0.80)
Portugal	4.10	(0.92)	4.60	(0.71)	2.78	(1.15)	3.73	(0.97)
Qatar	3.08	(1.38)	2.87	(1.36)	3.08	(1.39)	3.35	(1.30)
Romania	4.33	(0.89)	4.25	(0.95)	3.91	(1.08)	3.83	(1.04)
Russia	3.64	(1.00)	3.17	(1.27)	3.36	(1.09)	2.99	(1.30)
Serbia	3.76	(1.13)	4.39	(0.93)	3.65	(1.11)	3.47	(1.13)
Sierra Leone	4.23	(0.89)	4.44	(0.93)	4.22	(0.95)	4.14	(0.97)
Singapore	3.15	(1.22)	3.39	(1.39)	3.28	(1.28)	2.99	(1.15)

| Time limits | | Personal networks influences | | | | | |
| | | Friends, acquaintances, and family | | Colleagues in other media | | Peers on the staff | |
Mean	(SD)	Mean	(SD)	Mean	(SD)	Mean	(SD)
3.82	(0.97)	2.84	(1.17)	2.59	(1.08)	3.30	(0.95)
3.95	(0.93)	2.64	(1.04)	2.07	(0.93)	3.24	(0.97)
4.21	(0.96)	2.33	(1.33)	2.54	(1.26)	2.93	(1.27)
3.42	(0.86)	2.74	(1.03)	2.76	(1.03)	2.93	(1.04)
3.96	(0.91)	2.20	(0.97)	2.49	(0.92)	2.97	(0.93)
3.67	(1.19)	2.14	(1.17)	2.34	(1.11)	3.02	(1.16)
3.63	(1.08)	2.03	(1.00)	2.16	(0.91)	2.35	(0.98)
3.75	(0.86)	2.45	(0.99)	2.54	(0.94)	3.05	(0.83)
3.90	(1.05)	2.73	(1.27)	3.14	(1.09)	3.08	(1.04)
3.66	(1.15)	2.18	(1.27)	2.08	(1.09)	2.63	(1.25)
3.56	(1.07)	2.23	(1.05)	2.14	(1.01)	3.07	(1.02)
4.08	(0.94)	2.87	(1.33)	3.25	(1.24)	3.29	(1.14)
3.78	(0.90)	3.10	(1.19)	3.23	(1.04)	3.16	(0.93)
3.56	(1.16)	2.19	(1.19)	2.38	(1.14)	2.72	(1.20)
3.65	(1.08)	2.35	(1.19)	2.42	(1.01)	2.79	(1.07)
3.53	(0.93)	2.21	(0.93)	2.39	(0.90)	2.97	(0.85)
3.87	(0.90)	2.43	(1.01)	2.48	(0.97)	2.95	(1.01)
3.55	(0.87)	2.20	(0.76)	2.16	(0.73)	3.17	(0.69)
2.96	(1.45)	2.67	(1.21)	2.71	(1.19)	3.30	(1.14)
3.91	(0.94)	2.28	(0.96)	2.53	(0.91)	2.83	(0.89)
3.98	(0.96)	2.25	(1.10)	2.33	(1.05)	3.01	(0.93)
3.19	(1.43)	2.90	(1.43)	3.11	(1.33)	2.51	(1.29)
3.87	(1.02)	2.45	(1.26)	2.52	(1.13)	2.97	(1.05)
2.99	(1.24)	2.50	(1.21)	2.26	(1.01)	2.93	(1.17)
3.56	(1.10)	2.41	(1.20)	2.44	(1.07)	3.11	(1.03)
4.10	(0.94)	2.23	(1.26)	3.20	(1.28)	3.14	(1.20)
3.14	(1.30)	2.81	(1.17)	2.86	(1.10)	2.95	(1.01)

(*continued*)

Table A.2 Procedural and personal networks influences (*continued*)

	Procedural influences							
	Information access		Journalism ethics		Media laws and regulation		Availability of news-gathering resources	
	Mean	(SD)	Mean	(SD)	Mean	(SD)	Mean	(SD)
South Africa	4.10	(1.02)	4.57	(0.68)	4.02	(1.01)	4.12	(0.87)
South Korea	3.97	(0.69)	3.81	(0.80)	3.33	(0.85)	3.96	(0.76)
Spain	4.03	(0.89)	4.39	(0.79)	2.93	(1.17)	3.60	(1.13)
Sudan	4.05	(1.38)	4.66	(0.73)	3.97	(1.35)	4.33	(0.92)
Sweden	3.64	(0.84)	3.78	(0.84)	3.03	(0.98)	3.55	(1.00)
Switzerland	3.49	(0.97)	3.68	(0.92)	2.73	(1.01)	3.47	(0.96)
Tanzania	4.07	(0.76)	3.81	(0.94)	4.12	(0.80)	4.19	(0.70)
Thailand	4.01	(0.72)	4.15	(0.79)	3.99	(0.76)	3.86	(0.76)
Turkey	3.56	(1.09)	3.46	(1.28)	3.86	(1.01)	2.85	(1.17)
United Arab Emirates	2.87	(1.51)	2.88	(1.59)	3.10	(1.55)	2.98	(1.34)
United Kingdom	3.77	(0.99)	4.10	(0.91)	3.75	(1.10)	3.64	(0.99)
United States	4.01	(0.87)	4.59	(0.79)	4.01	(1.11)	3.85	(0.92)

Scale: 5 = "extremely influential" . . . 1 = "not influential."

Time limits		Friends, acquaintances, and family		Colleagues in other media		Peers on the staff	
			Personal networks influences				
Mean	(SD)	Mean	(SD)	Mean	(SD)	Mean	(SD)
4.12	(0.92)	2.23	(1.11)	2.68	(1.12)	3.05	(1.03)
3.78	(0.81)	2.89	(0.95)	3.01	(0.87)	3.37	(0.75)
3.94	(1.01)	2.08	(1.09)	2.13	(0.97)	3.06	(0.98)
4.35	(0.96)	2.34	(1.61)	3.04	(1.49)	3.42	(1.11)
3.50	(0.99)	2.19	(0.77)	2.24	(0.77)	2.86	(0.82)
3.55	(0.99)	2.30	(0.87)	2.17	(0.74)	2.82	(0.84)
3.17	(0.95)	2.25	(0.71)	1.93	(0.73)	2.35	(0.64)
3.80	(0.72)	3.82	(1.02)	3.79	(0.95)	3.71	(0.85)
3.32	(1.23)	2.44	(0.99)	2.19	(0.91)	2.44	(1.08)
3.35	(1.43)	2.62	(1.35)	3.10	(1.40)	3.16	(1.28)
3.80	(0.92)	2.27	(1.01)	2.60	(0.98)	3.13	(0.96)
3.82	(0.97)	2.21	(1.06)	2.64	(1.02)	3.25	(1.01)

Table A.3 Monitorial, collaborative, and interventionist roles

| | Monitorial role | | | | | | | |
| | Provide political information | | Monitor and scrutinize politics | | Monitor and scrutinize business | | Motivate people to participate in politics | |
	Mean	(SD)	Mean	(SD)	Mean	(SD)	Mean	(SD)
Albania	3.33	(1.31)	3.02	(1.19)	2.74	(1.13)	2.14	(1.12)
Argentina	3.76	(1.16)	3.96	(0.96)	3.69	(1.13)	3.28	(1.26)
Australia	3.59	(1.26)	3.56	(1.38)	3.43	(1.22)	2.45	(1.20)
Austria	3.67	(1.26)	3.18	(1.38)	3.03	(1.36)	3.32	(1.26)
Bangladesh	3.74	(1.16)	3.84	(1.02)	3.52	(1.20)	3.09	(1.36)
Belgium	3.43	(1.30)	3.38	(1.28)	3.25	(1.25)	2.52	(1.24)
Bhutan	4.10	(1.06)	3.87	(0.99)	3.78	(1.00)	3.78	(1.16)
Botswana	4.24	(1.10)	4.13	(1.06)	4.17	(1.04)	3.81	(1.29)
Brazil	3.70	(1.19)	3.56	(1.11)	3.10	(1.18)	3.19	(1.30)
Bulgaria	3.79	(1.30)	3.63	(1.17)	3.47	(1.23)	2.97	(1.35)
Canada	3.90	(1.27)	3.85	(1.32)	3.72	(1.29)	2.93	(1.33)
Chile	3.68	(1.40)	3.87	(1.27)	3.72	(1.30)	2.92	(1.40)
China	3.35	(1.02)	3.14	(1.11)	3.19	(1.03)	3.05	(1.09)
Colombia	4.05	(1.15)	4.19	(1.06)	3.86	(1.23)	3.66	(1.29)
Croatia	4.27	(0.91)	4.51	(0.79)	4.50	(0.77)	4.00	(1.03)
Cyprus	3.11	(1.47)	3.67	(1.36)	3.43	(1.32)	2.69	(1.15)
Czech Republic	3.17	(1.32)	3.44	(1.25)	3.14	(1.21)	2.32	(1.23)
Denmark	4.42	(0.77)	4.18	(0.89)	4.03	(0.87)	2.94	(1.12)
Ecuador	3.82	(1.21)	4.01	(1.07)	3.50	(1.15)	3.67	(1.28)
Egypt	4.27	(0.91)	4.05	(1.00)	3.56	(1.13)	4.21	(0.92)
El Salvador	4.06	(1.08)	4.28	(0.91)	3.78	(1.10)	3.58	(1.31)
Estonia	3.29	(1.25)	3.43	(1.23)	3.36	(1.21)	2.93	(1.21)
Ethiopia	4.03	(1.11)	3.25	(1.34)	3.53	(1.25)	3.85	(1.15)
Finland	3.61	(1.25)	3.73	(1.30)	3.55	(1.24)	2.57	(1.15)
France	3.88	(1.17)	3.64	(0.92)	3.41	(1.02)	3.06	(1.32)
Germany	3.36	(1.45)	2.79	(1.46)	2.80	(1.39)	3.10	(1.42)

| Collaborative role | | | | Interventionist role | | | | | | | |
| Support government policy | | Convey a positive image of political leaders | | Advocate for social change | | Influence public opinion | | Support national development | | Set the political agenda | |
Mean	(SD)	Mean	(SD)	Mean	(SD)	Mean	(SD)	Mean	(SD)	Mean	(SD)
2.06	(1.07)	2.21	(1.25)	3.88	(1.02)	4.02	(1.00)	3.85	(1.13)	2.28	(1.20)
2.51	(1.18)	1.94	(1.05)	3.83	(1.19)	3.46	(1.13)	3.35	(1.30)	3.38	(1.12)
1.55	(0.77)	1.59	(0.87)	3.03	(1.23)	2.63	(1.15)	2.62	(1.27)	2.31	(1.20)
1.34	(0.65)	1.27	(0.58)	2.96	(1.17)	2.59	(1.06)	2.33	(1.08)	2.22	(1.01)
2.76	(1.30)	2.94	(1.37)	4.16	(1.11)	3.69	(1.25)	4.19	(1.08)	3.04	(1.28)
1.49	(0.74)	1.50	(0.75)	2.59	(1.15)	2.48	(1.06)	2.38	(1.14)	2.76	(1.17)
2.96	(1.31)	2.91	(1.40)	3.44	(1.29)	3.35	(1.05)	3.21	(1.48)	3.40	(1.16)
3.21	(1.34)	2.40	(1.40)	4.08	(1.16)	3.36	(1.38)	4.54	(0.86)	3.07	(1.37)
2.03	(1.04)	1.63	(0.98)	3.84	(1.19)	3.22	(1.17)	3.56	(1.20)	2.65	(1.10)
1.60	(0.91)	1.47	(0.79)	4.00	(1.17)	3.72	(1.10)	4.23	(1.00)	2.70	(1.19)
1.24	(0.56)	1.26	(0.57)	2.91	(1.32)	2.81	(1.20)	2.30	(1.23)	2.51	(1.25)
2.57	(1.33)	2.01	(1.17)	3.80	(1.27)	3.93	(1.17)	3.70	(1.28)	3.36	(1.43)
3.54	(1.00)	3.40	(1.16)	3.32	(1.04)	3.58	(0.94)	3.90	(0.93)	2.77	(1.14)
3.03	(1.27)	2.40	(1.32)	4.40	(0.94)	4.08	(1.05)	4.14	(1.10)	3.82	(1.20)
1.88	(1.21)	1.85	(1.23)	4.08	(1.03)	3.90	(0.99)	4.01	(1.11)	3.47	(1.19)
1.94	(1.11)	2.17	(1.45)	4.14	(0.91)	3.29	(1.24)	4.26	(1.05)	2.76	(1.33)
1.35	(0.71)	1.51	(0.90)	2.71	(1.28)	2.63	(1.20)	2.65	(1.25)	2.91	(1.15)
1.11	(0.37)	1.23	(0.50)	2.69	(1.18)	2.65	(1.15)	2.75	(1.14)	2.93	(1.07)
3.20	(1.31)	2.84	(1.38)	4.04	(1.10)	3.66	(1.21)	4.16	(1.04)	3.57	(1.25)
2.61	(1.30)	2.60	(1.27)	4.17	(0.97)	4.19	(0.95)	4.04	(1.10)	3.60	(1.10)
3.04	(1.28)	2.44	(1.32)	4.26	(0.97)	4.06	(1.06)	4.24	(1.00)	3.91	(1.09)
1.77	(0.90)	1.55	(0.78)	3.53	(1.06)	3.60	(1.02)	3.42	(1.26)	3.15	(1.23)
3.51	(1.31)	3.30	(1.37)	4.13	(0.98)	3.17	(1.44)	4.38	(0.95)	3.15	(1.33)
1.20	(0.45)	1.25	(0.55)	2.98	(1.04)	3.12	(0.98)	2.94	(1.02)	2.37	(1.07)
1.26	(0.63)	1.21	(0.52)	2.51	(1.22)	2.27	(1.11)	2.43	(1.25)	2.44	(1.05)
1.27	(0.58)	1.25	(0.57)	2.77	(1.21)	2.68	(1.12)	2.14	(1.14)	2.10	(1.06)

(*continued*)

Table A.3 Monitorial, collaborative, and interventionist roles (*continued*)

	Monitorial role							
	Provide political information		Monitor and scrutinize politics		Monitor and scrutinize business		Motivate people to participate in politics	
	Mean	(SD)	Mean	(SD)	Mean	(SD)	Mean	(SD)
Greece	3.98	(1.14)	3.82	(1.25)	3.61	(1.25)	3.14	(1.34)
Hong Kong	3.44	(1.03)	4.09	(0.91)	4.04	(0.90)	2.98	(1.09)
Hungary	3.24	(1.45)	3.12	(1.45)	3.03	(1.35)	2.85	(1.42)
Iceland	3.12	(1.45)	3.20	(1.25)	3.24	(1.35)	1.99	(1.20)
India	3.77	(1.19)	3.78	(1.11)	3.43	(1.19)	3.42	(1.35)
Indonesia	3.81	(0.80)	3.60	(0.91)	3.40	(0.89)	3.59	(0.96)
Ireland	3.42	(1.28)	3.66	(1.26)	3.44	(1.25)	2.49	(1.25)
Israel	3.73	(1.39)	3.66	(1.44)	3.47	(1.45)	2.74	(1.48)
Italy	3.15	(1.33)	3.28	(1.23)	3.29	(1.20)	2.72	(1.33)
Japan	4.27	(0.81)	4.47	(0.69)	3.82	(0.86)	3.47	(1.09)
Kenya	3.73	(1.19)	3.52	(1.25)	3.47	(1.22)	3.39	(1.26)
Kosovo	3.46	(1.36)	3.75	(1.19)	3.36	(1.23)	2.88	(1.45)
Latvia	3.46	(1.33)	3.37	(1.34)	2.95	(1.30)	3.29	(1.32)
Malawi	4.29	(1.05)	4.13	(1.04)	4.10	(0.94)	4.02	(1.12)
Malaysia	3.75	(0.97)	3.55	(0.93)	3.46	(0.91)	3.17	(1.08)
Mexico	4.37	(0.88)	4.33	(0.90)	3.72	(1.11)	3.71	(1.22)
Moldova	3.59	(1.36)	3.52	(1.33)	3.04	(1.26)	2.97	(1.45)
Netherlands	2.82	(1.22)	2.72	(1.32)	2.86	(1.24)	2.61	(1.09)
New Zealand	3.54	(1.29)	3.69	(1.30)	3.60	(1.26)	2.72	(1.34)
Norway	3.10	(1.29)	2.96	(1.27)	2.86	(1.25)	2.77	(1.24)
Oman	3.59	(0.93)	3.30	(0.88)	3.43	(1.17)	3.16	(1.20)
Philippines	4.17	(0.91)	4.18	(0.88)	3.99	(0.94)	3.84	(1.09)
Portugal	3.71	(1.21)	4.14	(1.03)	4.06	(1.04)	2.91	(1.26)
Qatar	2.78	(1.40)	2.58	(1.35)	2.61	(1.34)	2.78	(1.41)
Romania	3.42	(1.38)	3.40	(1.36)	3.10	(1.31)	2.78	(1.39)
Russia	3.18	(1.27)	2.96	(1.09)	2.83	(1.11)	3.10	(1.16)

Collaborative role				Interventionist role							
Support government policy		Convey a positive image of political leaders		Advocate for social change		Influence public opinion		Support national development		Set the political agenda	
Mean	(SD)	Mean	(SD)	Mean	(SD)	Mean	(SD)	Mean	(SD)	Mean	(SD)
1.43	(0.79)	1.68	(1.03)	3.91	(1.15)	2.87	(1.26)	3.52	(1.31)	2.39	(1.17)
1.90	(1.00)	1.75	(1.01)	3.17	(1.04)	3.24	(0.94)	2.31	(1.08)	2.99	(1.00)
2.20	(1.31)	2.08	(1.27)	3.45	(1.15)	3.35	(1.24)	3.49	(1.25)	2.61	(1.29)
1.08	(0.33)	1.12	(0.38)	2.13	(1.16)	1.69	(0.92)	2.43	(1.34)	1.39	(0.78)
3.01	(1.28)	2.82	(1.38)	4.03	(1.10)	3.67	(1.25)	4.22	(1.06)	2.94	(1.35)
3.26	(0.75)	3.15	(1.06)	4.03	(0.78)	3.30	(1.13)	3.96	(0.82)	2.84	(1.11)
1.38	(0.67)	1.49	(0.79)	3.08	(1.22)	2.80	(1.15)	2.69	(1.20)	2.53	(1.16)
1.62	(1.03)	1.70	(1.07)	4.27	(1.11)	4.24	(1.04)	3.50	(1.46)	3.34	(1.49)
1.32	(0.65)	1.37	(0.77)	3.28	(1.30)	2.52	(1.23)	1.32	(0.67)	2.54	(1.20)
1.69	(0.72)	1.60	(0.70)	3.06	(1.01)	3.33	(1.06)	3.42	(1.05)	3.73	(0.88)
3.25	(1.17)	2.65	(1.37)	4.08	(1.11)	3.81	(1.13)	3.79	(1.24)	3.30	(1.32)
2.20	(1.17)	2.71	(1.32)	4.05	(1.23)	4.04	(1.19)	4.01	(1.10)	2.92	(1.40)
1.80	(0.95)	1.45	(0.87)	3.88	(0.96)	3.77	(0.94)	3.77	(1.16)	2.68	(1.28)
3.50	(1.28)	2.95	(1.49)	4.30	(0.91)	4.07	(1.10)	4.37	(0.93)	3.78	(1.23)
3.47	(1.07)	3.25	(1.15)	3.67	(0.95)	3.57	(1.00)	3.84	(0.97)	2.99	(1.04)
3.07	(1.21)	2.31	(1.19)	4.50	(0.84)	4.21	(1.05)	4.29	(0.96)	3.90	(1.08)
2.10	(1.04)	1.68	(0.94)	4.04	(1.10)	3.49	(1.23)	3.89	(1.28)	2.86	(1.28)
1.62	(0.72)	1.54	(0.64)	2.66	(1.08)	2.70	(1.09)	2.16	(1.00)	2.41	(1.10)
1.37	(0.70)	1.46	(0.80)	3.07	(1.25)	2.80	(1.22)	2.63	(1.23)	2.42	(1.18)
1.31	(0.53)	1.56	(0.78)	2.96	(1.14)	2.81	(1.12)	2.63	(1.16)	2.95	(1.20)
3.32	(1.23)	3.35	(0.96)	4.03	(1.01)	3.75	(1.09)	4.04	(1.14)	3.19	(1.08)
2.84	(1.07)	2.37	(1.12)	4.30	(0.84)	3.80	(0.96)	4.01	(0.97)	3.29	(1.10)
1.37	(0.72)	1.64	(0.94)	3.35	(1.19)	2.82	(1.15)	3.52	(1.21)	2.86	(1.11)
3.35	(1.29)	3.34	(1.28)	3.64	(1.19)	3.66	(1.24)	3.58	(1.19)	2.93	(1.37)
1.96	(0.97)	1.63	(0.93)	4.08	(1.10)	3.30	(1.26)	4.01	(1.17)	2.75	(1.34)
2.03	(1.06)	2.01	(1.05)	3.87	(1.05)	3.42	(1.11)	3.59	(1.21)	2.43	(1.14)

Table A.3 Monitorial, collaborative, and interventionist roles (*continued*)

	Monitorial role							
	Provide political information		Monitor and scrutinize politics		Monitor and scrutinize business		Motivate people to participate in politics	
	Mean	(SD)	Mean	(SD)	Mean	(SD)	Mean	(SD)
Serbia	3.79	(1.30)	3.93	(1.20)	3.87	(1.20)	3.06	(1.33)
Sierra Leone	4.14	(1.04)	4.17	(1.05)	3.50	(1.13)	3.59	(1.28)
Singapore	3.20	(1.26)	3.30	(1.29)	3.13	(1.19)	3.06	(1.26)
South Africa	3.63	(1.35)	3.62	(1.40)	3.63	(1.28)	2.68	(1.36)
South Korea	3.68	(0.98)	4.34	(0.78)	4.37	(0.74)	3.54	(0.97)
Spain	3.97	(1.09)	4.17	(1.04)	4.14	(1.08)	3.71	(1.04)
Sudan	4.49	(0.91)	4.39	(0.97)	4.37	(1.00)	4.07	(1.26)
Sweden	4.23	(0.93)	4.35	(0.93)	4.20	(0.95)	2.92	(1.20)
Switzerland	3.79	(1.16)	3.25	(1.20)	3.07	(1.17)	3.24	(1.15)
Tanzania	4.30	(0.62)	4.28	(0.62)	2.72	(0.64)	4.11	(0.72)
Thailand	3.96	(0.84)	4.05	(0.82)	3.90	(0.78)	3.89	(0.84)
Turkey	3.96	(1.09)	4.14	(0.92)	3.61	(1.09)	2.91	(1.32)
United Arab Emirates	3.42	(1.45)	3.37	(1.36)	2.87	(1.36)	2.97	(1.46)
United Kingdom	2.83	(1.45)	3.26	(1.48)	3.61	(1.30)	2.20	(1.26)
United States	4.41	(0.85)	4.33	(0.94)	3.89	(0.97)	3.29	(1.23)

Scale: 5 = "extremely important" . . . 1 = "not important."

Collaborative role				Interventionist role							
Support government policy		Convey a positive image of political leaders		Advocate for social change		Influence public opinion		Support national development		Set the political agenda	
Mean	(SD)	Mean	(SD)	Mean	(SD)	Mean	(SD)	Mean	(SD)	Mean	(SD)
1.91	(1.09)	2.00	(1.22)	4.13	(1.08)	4.10	(1.04)	4.18	(1.16)	3.14	(1.41)
3.25	(1.22)	2.77	(1.38)	4.52	(0.76)	3.87	(1.13)	4.56	(0.77)	3.49	(1.22)
3.14	(1.16)	3.08	(1.38)	3.17	(1.20)	3.13	(1.07)	3.20	(1.11)	3.09	(1.42)
1.95	(1.07)	1.77	(1.11)	3.62	(1.19)	3.27	(1.23)	3.46	(1.25)	2.24	(1.24)
2.15	(0.85)	1.99	(0.85)	3.70	(0.92)	3.02	(0.92)	3.39	(0.99)	3.75	(0.89)
2.15	(1.05)	1.85	(0.92)	3.90	(1.04)	3.50	(1.09)	3.60	(1.17)	3.13	(1.13)
2.92	(1.54)	2.83	(1.55)	4.72	(0.65)	4.64	(0.72)	4.79	(0.61)	3.58	(1.41)
1.03	(0.20)	1.37	(0.70)	2.98	(1.24)	2.62	(1.20)	2.10	(1.17)	2.50	(1.14)
1.50	(0.71)	1.29	(0.54)	2.60	(1.16)	2.52	(1.06)	2.26	(1.05)	2.59	(1.07)
1.99	(0.67)	2.21	(0.59)	4.37	(0.61)	4.28	(0.71)	4.44	(0.60)	4.26	(0.63)
3.63	(0.84)	3.68	(0.98)	4.02	(0.76)	3.74	(0.77)	4.12	(0.76)	3.78	(0.74)
1.85	(1.07)	2.09	(1.20)	4.19	(0.94)	4.07	(1.12)	3.41	(1.44)	3.74	(1.15)
4.24	(1.03)	4.14	(1.08)	3.23	(1.47)	3.85	(1.23)	4.08	(1.11)	2.63	(1.45)
1.37	(0.66)	1.43	(0.74)	2.77	(1.29)	2.72	(1.16)	2.44	(1.21)	2.29	(1.17)
1.49	(0.88)	1.51	(0.92)	2.72	(1.32)	2.40	(1.22)	2.33	(1.19)	2.09	(1.11)

Table A.4 Accommodative and other roles

	Accommodative role						Other roles									
	Provide entertainment and relaxation		Provide news that attracts largest audience		Provide advice, orientation, and direction for daily life		Be a detached observer		Report things as they are		Provide analysis of current affairs		Be an adversary of the government		Let people express their views	
	Mean	(SD)	Mean	(SD)	Mean	(SD)	Mean	(SD)	Mean	(SD)	Mean	(SD)	Mean	(SD)	Mean	(SD)
Albania	3.24	(1.19)	4.14	(0.89)	3.50	(1.07)	4.31	(0.80)	4.57	(0.57)	3.94	(0.72)	3.67	(1.19)	4.06	(0.83)
Argentina	2.83	(1.24)	3.16	(1.23)	2.91	(1.22)	3.42	(1.16)	4.48	(0.75)	4.08	(0.87)	1.98	(1.17)	3.96	(1.06)
Australia	3.52	(1.18)	3.70	(1.12)	3.02	(1.17)	4.07	(0.99)	4.62	(0.65)	3.47	(1.26)	1.96	(1.11)	3.94	(1.02)
Austria	3.37	(1.11)	3.73	(1.03)	3.70	(1.06)	4.41	(0.81)	4.63	(0.61)	4.44	(0.79)	2.46	(1.24)	3.42	(1.11)
Bangladesh	3.16	(1.23)	4.16	(1.03)	3.45	(1.16)	3.31	(1.40)	4.13	(1.09)	4.14	(0.89)	2.54	(1.52)	4.21	(0.98)
Belgium	2.78	(1.19)	2.90	(1.22)	2.96	(1.11)	4.34	(0.85)	4.59	(0.63)	3.85	(0.95)	1.45	(0.74)	3.52	(1.10)
Bhutan	3.30	(1.32)	3.66	(1.42)	3.77	(1.22)	3.93	(1.16)	4.16	(1.18)	4.04	(1.10)	3.04	(1.35)	4.23	(0.89)
Botswana	3.73	(1.25)	4.04	(1.20)	3.95	(1.19)	3.86	(1.34)	4.80	(0.51)	4.55	(0.73)	2.62	(1.45)	4.51	(0.86)
Brazil	2.69	(1.25)	3.36	(1.22)	3.09	(1.20)	4.13	(1.02)	4.57	(0.75)	3.85	(0.99)	1.77	(0.99)	4.08	(1.08)
Bulgaria	3.09	(1.33)	3.51	(1.20)	3.43	(1.58)	3.96	(1.26)	4.85	(0.41)	4.40	(0.83)	3.01	(1.29)	4.46	(0.88)
Canada	2.54	(1.21)	2.78	(1.15)	2.62	(1.22)	4.12	(1.02)	4.82	(0.49)	4.10	(0.94)	2.04	(1.22)	3.88	(1.17)

Chile	3.30	(1.39)	3.59	(1.35)	3.44	(1.31)	3.52	(1.32)	4.51	(0.90)	4.40	(0.97)	2.05	(1.22)	3.96	(1.26)
China	3.17	(1.05)	3.70	(0.95)	3.77	(0.84)	3.70	(0.93)	4.10	(0.75)	3.84	(0.88)	2.44	(1.32)	3.66	(1.00)
Colombia	3.91	(1.08)	3.86	(1.19)	3.59	(1.29)	3.19	(1.33)	4.66	(0.74)	4.56	(0.77)	2.47	(1.29)	4.26	(1.03)
Croatia	2.57	(1.29)	3.02	(1.28)	3.40	(1.12)	4.39	(0.94)	4.75	(0.55)	4.48	(0.72)	2.34	(1.31)	4.42	(0.78)
Cyprus	2.19	(1.25)	2.71	(1.26)	2.63	(1.59)	4.21	(0.99)	4.84	(0.44)	4.68	(0.57)	2.65	(1.40)	3.88	(0.98)
Czech Republic	2.96	(1.12)	3.09	(1.24)	2.93	(1.28)	4.53	(0.77)	4.91	(0.38)	3.84	(0.97)	1.54	(0.85)	3.83	(1.16)
Denmark	2.29	(0.92)	2.20	(0.90)	2.92	(1.01)	3.80	(1.09)	4.51	(0.69)	3.99	(0.89)	3.25	(1.22)	3.48	(1.01)
Ecuador	2.87	(1.46)	3.87	(1.20)	3.92	(1.08)	3.19	(1.39)	4.48	(0.91)	4.35	(0.84)	2.23	(1.42)	4.24	(0.98)
Egypt	3.11	(1.24)	3.84	(1.14)	3.90	(0.96)	4.65	(0.67)	4.36	(0.80)	4.17	(0.86)	3.57	(1.14)	4.29	(0.89)
El Salvador	3.10	(1.43)	3.75	(1.21)	3.62	(1.19)	3.33	(1.33)	4.60	(0.72)	3.81	(1.20)	2.20	(1.28)	4.30	(0.83)
Estonia	3.22	(1.25)	4.23	(0.91)	3.55	(1.14)	4.45	(0.69)	4.70	(0.59)	4.06	(0.90)	2.45	(1.15)	4.06	(0.97)
Ethiopia	3.98	(1.03)	4.25	(1.02)	4.23	(1.03)	3.51	(1.36)	3.84	(1.28)	4.25	(0.90)	2.27	(1.36)	4.14	(1.09)
Finland	2.99	(1.07)	3.34	(1.01)	3.22	(1.02)	4.51	(0.73)	4.55	(0.72)	4.30	(0.79)	2.08	(1.09)	3.84	(1.01)
France	2.26	(1.06)	2.67	(1.15)	2.96	(1.06)	4.19	(0.94)	4.73	(0.52)	4.09	(0.84)	1.35	(0.64)	4.02	(0.98)
Germany	3.51	(1.09)	4.00	(0.95)	3.82	(1.06)	4.27	(0.95)	4.59	(0.73)	4.31	(0.96)	2.27	(1.30)	3.27	(1.24)
Greece	2.57	(1.36)	2.77	(1.32)	3.28	(1.26)	3.92	(1.12)	4.75	(0.53)	4.17	(0.95)	2.24	(1.31)	4.41	(0.93)
Hong Kong	2.46	(1.02)	3.14	(0.95)	3.26	(0.88)	3.57	(0.82)	3.99	(0.75)	3.80	(0.91)	2.34	(1.10)	3.82	(1.01)
Hungary	3.79	(1.18)	3.74	(1.18)	3.58	(1.14)	4.38	(0.74)	4.50	(0.75)	4.10	(0.99)	2.42	(1.35)	3.59	(1.15)
Iceland	3.22	(1.11)	3.17	(1.10)	2.65	(1.20)	4.09	(0.98)	4.76	(0.59)	4.47	(0.84)	1.78	(1.02)	3.80	(1.14)

(continued)

Table A.4 Accommodative and other roles (*continued*)

	Accommodative role					Other roles		
	Provide entertainment and relaxation	Provide news that attracts largest audience	Provide advice, orientation, and direction for daily life	Be a detached observer	Report things as they are	Provide analysis of current affairs	Be an adversary of the government	Let people express their views
	Mean (SD)	Mean (SD)	Mean (SD)	Mean (SD)	Mean (SD)	Mean (SD)	Mean (SD)	Mean (SD)
India	3.43 (1.21)	3.94 (1.11)	3.63 (1.24)	4.04 (1.19)	4.43 (0.81)	4.31 (0.81)	2.94 (1.34)	4.28 (0.96)
Indonesia	3.59 (0.82)	3.96 (0.73)	3.48 (0.91)	3.70 (1.05)	4.51 (0.68)	3.93 (0.88)	2.67 (0.94)	4.12 (0.66)
Ireland	3.10 (1.16)	3.37 (1.10)	2.76 (1.17)	4.05 (0.94)	4.63 (0.66)	3.71 (1.13)	2.31 (1.20)	3.70 (1.12)
Israel	2.83 (1.44)	3.57 (1.35)	3.63 (1.29)	3.36 (1.42)	4.64 (0.74)	4.16 (1.11)	3.22 (1.41)	3.90 (1.26)
Italy	2.65 (1.20)	3.09 (1.26)	2.73 (1.25)	4.47 (0.81)	4.60 (0.71)	4.13 (0.89)	1.52 (0.88)	3.82 (1.17)
Japan	3.01 (0.93)	3.26 (1.00)	3.25 (0.98)	3.37 (0.94)	3.81 (0.95)	4.22 (0.73)	2.24 (0.98)	2.83 (1.04)
Kenya	3.48 (1.23)	3.78 (1.30)	3.83 (1.06)	3.57 (1.20)	4.46 (0.75)	4.08 (1.00)	2.76 (1.44)	4.23 (0.89)
Kosovo	3.26 (1.33)	3.80 (1.18)	3.76 (1.16)	4.67 (0.68)	4.83 (0.47)	4.50 (0.74)	4.09 (1.08)	4.15 (1.14)
Latvia	2.85 (1.29)	3.53 (1.16)	3.10 (1.23)	4.63 (0.58)	4.75 (0.47)	4.19 (0.95)	1.84 (1.00)	4.03 (1.08)
Malawi	3.89 (1.15)	4.28 (1.00)	3.95 (1.10)	3.97 (1.27)	4.74 (0.65)	4.51 (0.71)	2.98 (1.58)	4.54 (0.72)
Malaysia	3.47 (1.00)	3.88 (0.93)	3.74 (0.88)	3.89 (0.89)	4.13 (0.83)	3.93 (0.83)	3.27 (1.14)	3.95 (0.88)
Mexico	3.29 (1.25)	4.09 (1.14)	3.71 (1.19)	3.47 (1.29)	4.69 (0.65)	4.35 (0.90)	2.40 (1.26)	4.50 (0.81)

Moldova	3.02	(1.37)	3.77	(1.21)	3.04	(1.27)	4.30	(0.86)	4.79	(0.47)	4.19	(0.90)	2.72	(1.41)	4.00	(1.11)
Netherlands	3.34	(1.12)	2.85	(1.15)	3.91	(0.95)	3.76	(0.98)	4.52	(0.68)	3.81	(1.05)	3.26	(1.25)	3.63	(1.03)
New Zealand	3.12	(1.15)	3.27	(1.19)	2.70	(1.24)	3.95	(0.99)	4.57	(0.64)	3.83	(1.02)	2.08	(1.15)	3.96	(0.98)
Norway	2.87	(1.19)	2.96	(1.07)	2.69	(1.10)	3.64	(1.03)	4.26	(0.90)	3.30	(1.15)	2.56	(1.18)	3.66	(1.13)
Oman	3.58	(1.02)	3.93	(1.11)	3.76	(0.95)	4.23	(0.83)	3.75	(1.22)	3.90	(1.04)	2.54	(1.23)	3.67	(1.11)
Philippines	2.91	(1.10)	3.49	(1.07)	3.38	(1.07)	3.88	(0.86)	4.49	(0.60)	4.15	(0.85)	2.77	(1.13)	4.22	(0.81)
Portugal	2.44	(1.14)	2.77	(1.12)	2.98	(1.16)	4.42	(0.89)	4.71	(0.63)	4.22	(0.81)			4.01	(1.01)
Qatar	3.33	(1.27)	3.38	(1.23)	3.23	(1.27)	3.48	(1.22)	3.51	(1.23)	3.19	(1.23)	1.96	(1.29)	2.90	(1.40)
Romania	3.32	(1.29)	3.81	(1.18)	3.22	(1.24)	4.45	(0.85)	4.80	(0.55)	4.23	(1.01)	2.20	(1.25)	4.06	(1.09)
Russia	2.74	(1.20)	3.94	(1.05)	3.84	(1.16)	3.81	(0.94)	4.22	(0.82)	3.83	(1.01)	2.34	(1.19)	3.73	(1.13)
Serbia	3.09	(1.30)	3.47	(1.28)	3.69	(1.18)	3.79	(1.26)	4.79	(0.54)	4.53	(0.79)	2.89	(1.36)	4.27	(0.98)
Sierra Leone	3.60	(1.22)	4.01	(1.29)	4.07	(0.88)	3.89	(1.15)	4.59	(0.67)	4.43	(0.76)	2.64	(1.35)	4.58	(0.65)
Singapore	3.06	(0.99)	3.16	(1.23)	3.05	(1.10)	3.16	(1.34)	3.21	(1.66)	3.14	(1.32)	2.92	(1.53)	3.35	(1.24)
South Africa	3.27	(1.27)	3.68	(1.19)	3.49	(1.24)	3.78	(1.24)	4.62	(0.73)	3.97	(1.22)	2.05	(1.21)	4.28	(0.91)
South Korea	2.17	(0.87)	2.91	(0.97)	3.11	(0.95)	3.80	(0.76)	4.55	(0.66)	4.33	(0.69)	2.71	(0.95)	3.65	(0.96)
Spain	3.13	(1.15)	2.95	(1.20)	3.12	(1.12)	3.92	(1.00)	4.79	(0.55)	4.38	(0.76)	2.45	(1.20)	4.46	(0.76)
Sudan	3.71	(1.36)	4.52	(0.82)	4.51	(0.86)	4.72	(0.62)	4.56	(0.76)	4.56	(0.76)	3.12	(1.62)	4.59	(0.88)
Sweden	2.54	(0.98)	2.00	(0.91)	3.23	(0.96)	4.41	(0.76)	4.59	(0.58)	4.05	(0.92)	2.78	(1.39)	4.41	(0.75)

(continued)

Table A.4 Accommodative and other roles (*continued*)

	Accommodative role						Other roles									
	Provide entertainment and relaxation		Provide news that attracts largest audience		Provide advice, orientation, and direction for daily life		Be a detached observer		Report things as they are		Provide analysis of current affairs		Be an adversary of the government		Let people express their views	
	Mean	(SD)	Mean	(SD)	Mean	(SD)	Mean	(SD)	Mean	(SD)	Mean	(SD)	Mean	(SD)	Mean	(SD)
Switzerland	3.13	(1.04)	3.34	(1.04)	3.20	(1.03)	4.26	(0.84)	4.53	(0.64)	4.21	(0.81)	2.56	(1.21)	3.54	(1.06)
Tanzania	2.87	(0.75)	4.58	(0.54)	2.96	(0.72)	3.14	(0.71)	4.25	(0.66)	2.63	(0.73)	1.98	(0.67)	4.39	(0.62)
Thailand	3.76	(0.92)	4.02	(0.78)	3.92	(0.77)	4.26	(0.84)	4.37	(0.69)	4.23	(0.71)	3.74	(1.01)	4.25	(0.83)
Turkey	2.68	(1.30)	3.65	(1.33)	3.02	(1.25)	4.66	(0.80)	4.79	(0.57)	4.31	(0.83)	3.00	(1.47)	4.30	(1.05)
United Arab Emirates	3.48	(1.22)	4.11	(1.07)	3.92	(1.12)	3.45	(1.28)	4.04	(1.05)	3.82	(1.14)	1.73	(1.28)	3.76	(1.19)
United Kingdom	3.36	(1.28)	3.30	(1.16)	2.57	(1.29)	4.11	(0.89)	4.59	(0.63)	3.81	(1.14)	1.93	(1.09)	3.43	(1.23)
United States	2.87	(1.09)	3.52	(1.13)	2.84	(1.10)	4.09	(0.94)	4.82	(0.48)	3.79	(1.00)	2.30	(1.28)	4.21	(1.03)

Scale: 5 = "extremely important" . . . 1 = "not important."

Table A.5 Trust in public institutions

	Parliament		Government		Political parties		Politicians in general		Judiciary/the courts		Police		Military		Political trust (index)	
	Mean	SD	Mean	SD	Mean	(SD)	Mean	SD	Mean	SD	Mean	SD	Mean	SD	Mean	SD
Albania	2.32	(0.93)	2.25	(0.99)	1.65	(0.73)	1.64	(0.72)	1.90	(0.90)	2.57	(0.83)	2.33	(1.03)	2.07	(0.74)
Argentina	1.62	(0.51)	2.64	(0.97)	2.39	(0.79)	2.35	(0.76)	2.51	(0.80)	1.96	(0.81)	1.92	(0.80)	2.40	(0.73)
Australia	2.87	(0.73)	2.71	(0.72)	2.33	(0.71)	2.46	(0.71)	3.81	(0.63)	3.39	(0.80)	3.29	(0.82)	2.63	(0.61)
Austria	2.97	(0.84)	2.63	(0.81)	2.27	(0.74)	2.41	(0.71)	3.24	(0.86)	3.04	(0.88)	2.63	(0.93)	2.62	(0.70)
Bangladesh	3.57	(1.19)	3.01	(1.08)	2.30	(1.01)	2.17	(1.09)	3.34	(1.24)	2.08	(1.09)	3.18	(1.19)	2.97	(0.99)
Belgium	3.34	(0.69)	3.25	(0.71)	2.68	(0.74)	2.74	(0.71)	3.27	(0.80)	3.16	(0.76)	2.95	(0.89)	3.09	(0.61)
Bhutan	3.78	(1.01)	3.77	(0.88)	3.39	(1.01)	3.32	(1.08)	3.21	(1.12)	3.12	(1.20)	3.10	(1.18)	3.65	(0.90)
Botswana	3.33	(1.16)	2.92	(1.15)	2.43	(1.00)	2.14	(1.00)	3.27	(1.06)	3.27	(1.02)	3.10	(1.13)	2.90	(0.94)
Brazil	1.98	(0.78)	2.37	(0.83)	1.80	(0.73)	1.89	(0.72)	2.61	(0.84)	2.17	(0.86)	2.20	(0.89)	2.05	(0.65)
Bulgaria	2.14	(0.84)	2.17	(0.85)	1.85	(0.74)	1.82	(0.75)	2.02	(0.85)	2.18	(0.83)	2.35	(0.85)	2.06	(0.72)
Canada	2.93	(0.80)	2.69	(0.83)	2.29	(0.78)	2.47	(0.78)	3.73	(0.77)	2.94	(0.89)	2.91	(0.91)	2.65	(0.70)
Chile	2.31	(0.94)	2.54	(0.97)	1.89	(0.87)	1.96	(0.86)	2.57	(0.99)	2.91	(1.03)	2.48	(1.10)	2.25	(0.82)
Czech Republic	2.24	(0.84)	2.17	(0.87)	1.78	(0.66)	1.88	(0.68)	3.15	(0.90)	3.12	(0.81)	3.19	(0.94)	2.06	(0.69)
Denmark	2.96	(0.81)	2.55	(0.77)	2.26	(0.74)	2.42	(0.73)	3.63	(0.76)	3.10	(0.82)	2.58	(0.83)	2.59	(0.65)
Ecuador	2.57	(1.17)	2.82	(1.17)	2.21	(0.99)	2.18	(0.97)	2.61	(1.03)	2.83	(1.03)	3.00	(1.04)	2.53	(1.00)

(continued)

Table A.5 Trust in public institutions (*continued*)

	Parliament		Government		Political parties		Politicians in general		Judiciary/the courts		Police		Military		Political trust (index)	
	Mean	SD	Mean	SD	Mean	(SD)	Mean	SD	Mean	SD	Mean	SD	Mean	SD	Mean	SD
El Salvador	2.99	(1.10)	3.02	(0.98)	2.84	(1.17)	2.86	(1.12)	2.99	(1.05)	3.01	(0.93)	2.99	(1.00)	2.94	(0.98)
Estonia	3.03	(0.88)	2.98	(0.90)	2.20	(0.83)	2.41	(0.82)	3.80	(0.79)	3.81	(0.74)	3.83	(0.82)	2.74	(0.74)
Ethiopia	2.99	(1.37)	2.85	(1.35)	2.23	(1.02)	2.28	(1.01)	2.95	(1.22)	2.92	(1.16)	3.36	(1.24)	2.69	(1.06)
Germany	3.26	(0.84)	3.06	(0.84)	2.56	(0.78)	2.63	(0.73)	3.60	(0.81)	3.54	(0.78)	2.84	(0.93)	2.96	(0.70)
Greece	2.21	(0.84)	2.17	(0.87)	1.74	(0.70)	1.76	(0.67)	2.53	(0.82)	2.31	(0.90)	2.46	(1.02)	2.04	(0.69)
Hungary	2.29	(1.14)	2.07	(1.16)	2.04	(1.03)	2.06	(1.04)	2.73	(1.10)	2.68	(1.08)	2.91	(1.13)	2.15	(1.02)
Iceland	2.43	(0.80)	2.45	(0.86)	2.17	(0.65)	2.33	(0.62)	3.31	(0.88)	3.79	(0.84)			2.36	(0.67)
India	4.07	(1.10)	3.75	(1.19)	2.60	(1.15)	2.40	(1.16)	3.87	(1.09)	3.14	(1.16)	3.92	(1.12)	3.47	(1.00)
Indonesia	2.30	(0.73)	2.71	(0.70)	2.06	(0.73)	2.15	(0.67)	2.49	(0.70)	2.35	(0.75)	2.62	(0.77)	2.35	(0.62)
Ireland	2.79	(0.72)	2.55	(0.71)	2.40	(0.69)	2.53	(0.69)	3.31	(0.81)	2.86	(0.81)	3.22	(0.78)	2.58	(0.63)
Israel	2.58	(1.01)	2.27	(1.00)	2.01	(0.89)	1.90	(0.85)	3.48	(1.06)	2.66	(0.99)	3.40	(1.15)	2.29	(0.84)
Kenya	2.77	(0.95)	2.88	(0.90)	2.29	(0.93)	2.14	(1.00)	3.16	(0.90)	2.46	(0.98)	2.68	(1.01)	2.65	(0.79)
Kosovo	2.39	(1.07)	1.97	(0.94)	1.73	(0.85)	1.76	(0.86)	2.21	(1.02)	3.09	(1.06)	3.41	(1.20)	2.05	(0.89)
Latvia	2.64	(0.74)	2.85	(0.69)	2.12	(0.76)	2.26	(0.71)	2.64	(0.89)	3.09	(0.80)	3.58	(0.81)	2.53	(0.62)
Malawi	3.22	(1.07)	2.59	(1.07)	2.09	(0.86)	1.98	(0.97)	3.43	(1.07)	2.67	(1.05)	3.35	(1.10)	2.63	(0.82)
Malaysia	3.42	(0.96)	3.24	(0.95)	2.88	(0.85)	2.82	(0.92)	3.47	(0.94)	3.24	(0.99)	3.41	(0.96)	3.18	(0.82)

Mexico	2.56 (1.03)	2.45 (1.01)	1.83 (0.84)	1.93 (0.86)	2.23 (1.00)	1.93 (0.94)	2.85 (1.15)	2.28 (0.83)
Moldova	2.13 (0.86)	2.20 (0.86)	1.87 (0.81)	1.84 (0.73)	2.43 (1.01)	2.43 (0.99)	2.93 (1.08)	2.07 (0.76)
Netherlands	3.10 (0.75)	3.04 (0.81)	2.68 (0.77)	2.71 (0.74)	3.49 (0.84)	3.30 (0.81)	3.18 (0.83)	2.94 (0.70)
Oman	3.46 (1.13)	3.48 (1.18)		2.84 (1.06)	2.69 (1.19)	3.03 (1.19)	3.55 (1.02)	3.47 (0.90)
Philippines	2.40 (0.72)	2.64 (0.76)	2.10 (0.70)	2.10 (0.73)	2.94 (0.71)	2.55 (0.73)	2.67 (0.75)	2.38 (0.59)
Portugal	2.85 (0.91)	2.30 (0.91)	2.16 (0.85)	2.20 (0.81)	2.80 (0.92)	3.19 (0.90)	3.17 (0.89)	2.44 (0.78)
Romania	1.91 (0.90)	1.94 (0.87)	1.57 (0.76)	1.60 (0.74)	2.78 (0.97)	2.55 (0.93)	3.01 (1.06)	1.81 (0.75)
Russia	2.31 (0.95)	2.58 (1.03)	2.21 (0.97)	2.24 (0.91)	2.47 (0.97)	2.47 (0.91)	2.62 (0.99)	2.36 (0.83)
Serbia	2.26 (0.95)	2.17 (0.92)	1.69 (0.83)	1.65 (0.81)	2.08 (0.93)	2.40 (1.00)	2.69 (1.09)	2.04 (0.81)
Sierra Leone	2.71 (1.01)	2.69 (0.98)	2.20 (1.01)	2.01 (1.01)	2.35 (1.13)	2.25 (1.03)	3.53 (1.07)	2.54 (0.83)
Singapore	3.16 (1.16)	3.16 (0.98)	3.15 (0.69)	3.06 (0.74)	3.22 (1.27)	3.24 (1.15)	3.10 (1.05)	3.15 (0.79)
South Africa	2.50 (0.95)	2.06 (0.87)	1.93 (0.73)	1.82 (0.76)	3.30 (0.95)	2.22 (0.91)	2.28 (0.96)	2.16 (0.73)
South Korea	2.34 (0.68)	2.45 (0.72)	2.14 (0.62)	2.17 (0.67)	2.74 (0.76)	2.54 (0.72)	2.19 (0.74)	2.31 (0.58)
Spain	2.81 (1.01)	2.24 (0.97)	1.98 (0.80)	2.11 (0.80)	2.96 (0.94)	3.31 (1.02)	3.03 (1.17)	2.35 (0.76)
Sweden	3.49 (0.67)	3.09 (0.80)	2.97 (0.66)	3.03 (0.61)	3.53 (0.67)	3.11 (0.75)	2.82 (0.80)	3.18 (0.60)
Switzerland	3.22 (0.73)	3.38 (0.73)	2.55 (0.68)	2.64 (0.66)	3.57 (0.75)	3.39 (0.78)	2.72 (0.95)	3.04 (0.60)
Tanzania	2.21 (0.83)	2.48 (0.86)	2.74 (1.02)	3.50 (0.95)	3.11 (0.96)	1.51 (0.66)	1.60 (0.67)	2.48 (0.83)
United Kingdom	2.79 (0.78)	2.51 (0.83)	2.33 (0.71)	2.39 (0.69)	3.35 (0.78)	3.04 (0.80)	3.10 (0.84)	2.54 (0.68)
United States	2.27 (0.79)	2.52 (0.88)	1.82 (0.76)	2.16 (0.74)	3.27 (0.77)	3.19 (0.82)	3.26 (0.89)	2.20 (0.66)

Scale: 5 = "complete trust" . . . 1 = "no trust at all."

Table A.6 Perceived changes in influences

	Journalism education		Ethical standards		Competition		Advertising considerations		Profit-making pressures		Public relations		Audience research	
	Mean	(SD)	Mean	(SD)	Mean	(SD)	Mean	(SD)	Mean	(SD)	Mean	(SD)	Mean	(SD)
Albania	3.30	(1.12)	3.24	(1.03)	4.09	(0.97)	4.22	(0.97)	4.19	(0.91)	3.65	(1.03)	3.26	(1.02)
Argentina	3.46	(1.32)	2.78	(1.29)	3.72	(1.10)	3.52	(1.16)	3.60	(1.10)	3.64	(0.9)	3.57	(0.96)
Australia	3.06	(1.02)	2.74	(0.87)	3.75	(0.99)	3.69	(0.82)	4.10	(0.79)	3.73	(0.83)	3.89	(0.78)
Austria	3.65	(1.05)	2.90	(0.98)	4.43	(0.68)	3.97	(0.79)	4.16	(0.78)	3.78	(0.78)	3.74	(0.80)
Bangladesh	4.17	(1.05)	3.33	(1.27)	4.29	(0.92)	3.85	(1.12)	3.55	(1.13)	3.48	(1.08)	3.67	(1.11)
Belgium	3.41	(0.96)	3.03	(0.88)	4.05	(0.84)	3.52	(0.97)	3.70	(0.97)	3.26	(0.91)	3.70	(0.83)
Bhutan	4.29	(0.91)	4.14	(0.74)	4.18	(0.83)	3.94	(1.07)	3.92	(1.05)	3.78	(0.99)	3.80	(1.00)
Botswana	4.23	(1.04)	3.87	(1.05)	4.34	(0.87)	3.72	(1.02)	3.75	(1.20)	3.74	(1.08)	3.45	(1.14)
Brazil	3.13	(1.16)	3.07	(1.11)	3.85	(1.05)	3.72	(0.88)	4.05	(0.85)	3.44	(0.82)	4.04	(0.83)
Bulgaria	2.45	(1.22)	2.38	(1.30)	3.78	(1.27)	3.81	(1.22)	4.04	(1.06)	3.93	(0.93)	3.79	(1.02)
Canada	3.19	(0.97)	2.90	(0.93)	3.69	(1.21)	3.77	(0.94)	4.00	(0.89)	3.49	(0.90)	3.93	(0.81)
Chile	2.77	(1.29)	2.92	(1.28)	3.52	(1.12)	3.00	(1.22)	3.07	(1.23)	3.07	(1.25)	3.23	(1.20)
China	3.16	(1.16)	3.23	(1.10)	3.91	(0.95)	3.79	(0.93)	3.94	(0.92)	3.67	(0.79)	3.61	(0.86)
Colombia	3.19	(1.36)	2.85	(1.37)	3.41	(1.15)	3.55	(1.21)	3.41	(1.29)	3.76	(1.1)	3.68	(1.18)
Croatia	2.68	(1.09)	2.01	(0.93)	4.00	(0.99)	3.61	(1.32)	4.39	(0.76)	3.76	(0.92)	3.22	(1.04)

Cyprus	3.79 (1.38)	1.85 (1.06)	4.80 (0.54)	4.84 (0.48)	4.31 (0.86)	4.16 (0.85)	4.39 (0.71)
Czech Republic	2.90 (0.90)	2.71 (0.90)	3.86 (0.89)	3.90 (0.96)	3.91 (0.86)	3.79 (0.88)	3.54 (0.82)
Ecuador	4.37 (0.93)	4.32 (0.94)	3.95 (1.03)	3.32 (1.10)	3.33 (1.21)	3.76 (1.12)	3.78 (1.18)
Egypt	3.64 (1.12)	3.62 (1.10)	3.77 (1.06)	3.56 (1.15)	3.57 (1.10)	3.40 (1.03)	3.28 (1.07)
El Salvador	3.87 (1.25)	3.72 (1.31)	4.00 (1.06)	3.47 (1.15)	3.58 (1.10)	3.61 (1.00)	3.63 (1.11)
Estonia	2.67 (0.91)	3.24 (0.95)	3.94 (0.85)	3.78 (0.95)	3.93 (0.92)	3.60 (0.82)	3.48 (0.76)
Ethiopia	4.06 (1.04)	3.25 (1.21)	3.84 (1.04)	3.70 (1.06)	3.83 (1.15)	3.75 (0.98)	3.27 (1.15)
Finland	3.34 (0.88)	3.02 (0.87)	4.47 (0.72)	3.76 (0.83)	4.42 (0.66)	3.39 (0.76)	3.68 (0.73)
France	3.72 (1.08)	2.86 (1.10)	4.19 (0.95)	3.87 (0.89)	4.07 (0.88)	3.65 (0.89)	4.29 (0.76)
Germany	3.04 (1.04)	2.59 (0.91)	4.35 (0.72)	3.82 (0.89)	3.98 (0.89)	3.68 (0.84)	3.70 (0.90)
Greece	3.17 (1.41)	2.07 (1.18)	4.10 (1.14)	3.96 (1.35)	4.31 (0.94)	3.82 (1.05)	3.54 (1.01)
Hong Kong	3.17 (0.91)	2.68 (1.01)	3.66 (0.94)	3.37 (0.78)	3.39 (0.82)	3.28 (0.75)	3.40 (0.66)
Hungary	3.07 (1.22)	2.61 (1.28)	4.28 (0.93)	4.18 (0.80)	4.43 (0.70)	3.75 (0.84)	3.74 (0.99)
Iceland	3.82 (0.77)	3.50 (0.71)	3.82 (0.90)	3.46 (0.75)	3.59 (0.68)	3.50 (0.73)	3.54 (0.79)
India	4.05 (1.18)	3.28 (1.29)	4.57 (0.71)	4.17 (0.97)	4.04 (1.08)	3.90 (1.04)	3.94 (1.03)
Indonesia	4.00 (0.82)	3.73 (0.91)	4.34 (0.66)	3.98 (0.77)	3.97 (0.79)	3.57 (0.80)	3.83 (0.72)
Ireland	3.12 (1.22)	2.97 (1.12)	4.04 (0.91)	3.72 (0.87)	3.89 (0.87)	3.49 (0.90)	3.69 (0.86)
Israel	2.37 (1.42)	1.88 (1.15)	4.38 (1.10)	4.33 (1.03)	4.50 (0.84)	4.33 (0.92)	3.91 (1.10)
Italy	2.70 (1.31)	2.25 (1.11)	3.88 (1.07)	3.88 (0.93)	4.08 (0.91)	3.67 (0.92)	3.99 (0.87)

(continued)

Table A.6 Perceived changes in influences (*continued*)

	Journalism education		Ethical standards		Competition		Advertising considerations		Profit-making pressures		Public relations		Audience research	
	Mean	(SD)	Mean	(SD)	Mean	(SD)	Mean	(SD)	Mean	(SD)	Mean	(SD)	Mean	(SD)
Japan	3.18	(0.91)	3.66	(1.04)	3.61	(0.87)	3.56	(0.82)	3.74	(0.77)	3.48	(0.66)	3.72	(0.74)
Kenya	4.21	(1.04)	3.79	(1.18)	4.52	(0.74)	4.25	(0.88)	4.22	(1.01)	3.76	(1.12)	4.03	(0.93)
Kosovo	3.55	(1.22)	3.09	(1.22)	3.79	(0.95)	3.70	(1.08)	3.76	(1.06)	3.21	(1.09)	2.85	(1.04)
Latvia	3.04	(1.05)	3.02	(1.03)	4.02	(0.94)	4.04	(0.82)	4.14	(0.79)	3.88	(0.77)	3.75	(0.9)
Malawi	4.29	(0.85)	3.84	(1.09)	4.48	(0.69)	4.11	(0.78)	4.00	(0.89)	3.84	(0.86)	3.58	(0.92)
Malaysia	3.88	(1.02)	3.67	(1.02)	4.18	(0.76)	3.92	(0.82)	3.80	(0.89)	3.78	(0.73)	3.89	(0.74)
Mexico	3.84	(1.29)	3.57	(1.26)	4.04	(1.00)	3.55	(1.08)	3.56	(1.08)	3.68	(0.93)	3.65	(1.08)
Moldova	3.76	(1.2)	3.78	(1.29)	3.94	(1.10)	3.79	(1.11)	3.84	(1.19)	3.47	(1.16)	3.80	(1.17)
Netherlands	2.67	(0.92)	2.61	(0.88)	3.89	(0.77)	3.93	(0.73)	3.99	(0.72)	3.67	(0.75)	3.53	(0.72)
New Zealand	2.91	(1.17)	2.46	(0.95)	3.90	(1.12)	4.08	(0.79)	4.36	(0.71)	3.95	(0.83)	4.10	(0.80)
Norway	3.47	(0.82)	3.31	(0.91)	4.10	(0.78)	3.78	(0.80)	4.19	(0.79)	3.84	(0.76)	3.87	(0.67)
Oman	3.80	(1.00)	3.85	(0.99)	3.49	(1.21)	3.33	(1.25)	3.09	(1.14)	3.09	(1.14)	3.16	(1.06)
Philippines	3.19	(1.13)	3.04	(1.14)	4.18	(0.84)	3.94	(0.87)	3.97	(0.85)	3.59	(0.88)	3.92	(0.91)
Portugal	3.85	(1.02)	2.76	(1.09)	4.19	(0.83)	3.91	(0.88)	4.04	(0.81)	3.72	(0.86)	3.82	(0.82)
Romania	3.71	(1.33)	3.78	(1.25)	3.78	(1.09)	3.43	(1.33)	3.19	(1.44)	3.04	(1.25)	3.68	(1.19)

Russia	2.35	(1.14)	2.59	(1.24)	3.68	(1.16)	4.01	(0.93)	3.96	(0.99)	3.54	(1.01)	3.56	(1.04)
Serbia	2.65	(1.30)	2.20	(1.19)	3.81	(1.13)	4.13	(0.98)	4.24	(0.87)	3.83	(0.90)	3.65	(0.96)
Sierra Leone	4.47	(0.88)	4.16	(1.01)	4.37	(0.78)	3.88	(0.94)	3.61	(1.17)	3.87	(1.12)	3.82	(1.03)
Singapore	3.07	(1.11)	3.12	(1.05)	3.11	(1.31)	3.05	(1.15)	2.93	(1.19)	2.91	(0.95)	2.88	(1.02)
South Africa	3.26	(1.15)	3.11	(1.23)	4.13	(0.91)	3.84	(0.95)	4.32	(0.87)	3.56	(1.02)	3.87	(0.94)
South Korea	2.86	(1.02)	2.75	(1.17)	4.34	(0.83)	4.06	(0.81)	4.21	(0.82)	3.43	(0.79)	3.31	(0.76)
Spain	2.75	(1.14)	2.26	(0.99)	3.69	(1.02)	3.54	(1.24)	3.72	(1.12)	3.34	(0.92)	3.87	(0.89)
Sweden	3.16	(0.90)	2.83	(0.80)	4.06	(0.86)	3.72	(0.82)	4.06	(0.86)	3.61	(0.75)	3.77	(0.77)
Switzerland	3.58	(0.97)	2.79	(0.90)	4.24	(0.77)	3.91	(0.74)	4.05	(0.75)	3.93	(0.79)	3.73	(0.76)
Tanzania	3.37	(0.93)	3.00	(0.82)	3.49	(1.13)	2.97	(0.91)	2.75	(1.00)	2.07	(1.10)	1.87	(0.91)
Thailand	3.82	(0.79)	3.95	(0.84)	4.31	(0.63)	4.18	(0.71)	4.05	(0.67)	3.90	(0.77)	3.81	(0.75)
Turkey	2.66	(1.09)	2.00	(1.11)	3.61	(1.33)	4.28	(0.93)	4.23	(0.95)	3.44	(1.20)	3.54	(1.29)
United Arab Emirates	4.24	(0.95)	3.89	(1.17)	4.26	(0.85)	4.16	(0.88)	4.02	(1.02)	4.12	(0.91)	3.73	(1.06)
United Kingdom	3.04	(1.17)	3.25	(1.14)	3.91	(0.96)	3.85	(0.87)	4.09	(0.80)	3.73	(0.87)	3.90	(0.87)
United States	2.87	(0.93)	2.68	(0.90)	3.93	(1.02)	3.15	(0.93)	3.72	(1.01)	2.87	(0.91)	3.34	(0.97)

(continued)

Table A.6 Perceived changes in influences (*continued*)

	User-generated contents, such as blogs		Social media		Audience involvement in news production		Audience feedback		Pressure toward sensational news		Western ways of practicing journalism	
	Mean	(SD)	Mean	(SD)	Mean	(SD)	Mean	(SD)	Mean	(SD)	Mean	(SD)
Albania	4.38	(0.89)	4.60	(0.66)	3.73	(1.00)	3.62	(0.95)	4.04	(0.90)		
Argentina	4.31	(0.88)	4.63	(0.67)	4.12	(0.84)	4.13	(0.86)	3.80	(1.11)	3.64	(0.98)
Australia	4.58	(0.70)	4.86	(0.39)	4.14	(0.8)	4.19	(0.74)	3.61	(0.77)		
Austria	4.27	(0.74)	4.67	(0.54)	3.80	(0.81)	3.86	(0.80)	3.70	(0.81)		
Bangladesh	3.51	(1.27)	3.94	(1.18)	3.76	(1.05)	3.84	(1.02)	3.03	(1.30)	3.14	(1.18)
Belgium	4.04	(0.91)	4.58	(0.71)	3.65	(0.81)	3.61	(0.80)	3.60	(0.93)		
Bhutan	3.63	(1.06)	3.69	(1.16)	3.49	(1.24)	3.78	(1.26)	3.65	(1.21)	3.60	(1.22)
Botswana	3.59	(1.20)	4.21	(1.07)	3.47	(1.10)	3.77	(1.06)	3.45	(1.20)	3.67	(1.18)
Brazil	4.48	(0.69)	4.75	(0.54)	4.40	(0.71)	4.41	(0.67)	3.82	(0.95)	3.58	(0.81)
Bulgaria	4.27	(0.85)	4.71	(0.57)	4.21	(0.82)	4.14	(0.85)	3.96	(1.02)		
Canada	4.11	(0.86)	4.78	(0.49)	3.76	(0.85)	3.92	(0.83)	3.52	(0.89)		
Chile	3.75	(1.16)	4.27	(0.93)	3.69	(1.11)	3.86	(1.01)	3.03	(1.40)	3.26	(1.07)
China	4.20	(0.86)	4.30	(0.84)	4.14	(0.79)	4.01	(0.88)	3.54	(1.00)		
Colombia	4.03	(1.07)	4.44	(0.82)	4.00	(1.04)	3.95	(1.04)	3.60	(1.31)		

Croatia	4.02	(0.80)	3.82	(1.06)	3.63	(0.95)	3.55	(1.00)	4.53	(0.71)		
Cyprus	4.32	(0.73)	4.95	(0.25)	4.35	(0.77)	4.73	(0.54)	3.94	(0.96)		
Czech Republic	4.14	(0.87)	4.67	(0.63)	3.63	(0.90)	3.57	(0.84)	3.83	(0.85)		
Ecuador	4.00	(1.03)	4.43	(0.85)	4.10	(0.91)	4.20	(0.83)	3.06	(1.36)	3.54	(1.07)
Egypt	3.37	(1.04)	3.98	(0.90)	3.70	(1.06)	3.91	(0.92)	3.85	(1.02)		
El Salvador	4.28	(0.93)	4.63	(0.77)	4.22	(0.89)	4.29	(0.82)	3.63	(1.27)	3.64	(0.96)
Estonia	4.29	(0.83)	4.53	(0.67)	3.92	(0.79)	3.78	(0.78)	3.71	(0.92)		
Ethiopia	3.74	(1.17)	4.10	(1.02)	3.47	(1.21)	3.53	(1.13)	3.37	(1.20)	3.50	(1.20)
Finland	4.44	(0.65)	4.72	(0.52)	4.00	(0.68)	3.49	(0.77)	3.89	(0.82)		
France	4.17	(0.75)	4.60	(0.69)	3.98	(0.85)	3.87	(0.80)	4.12	(0.86)		
Germany	4.22	(0.80)	4.63	(0.61)	3.61	(0.88)	3.80	(0.87)	3.67	(0.87)		
Greece	4.45	(0.78)	4.77	(0.56)	4.02	(0.98)	4.11	(0.96)	3.66	(1.12)		
Hong Kong	3.82	(0.83)	4.09	(0.76)	3.84	(0.85)	3.74	(0.87)	3.50	(0.84)		
Hungary	4.32	(0.79)	4.66	(0.65)	4.10	(0.86)	4.01	(0.89)	4.21	(0.84)		
Iceland	4.10	(0.74)	4.47	(0.61)	3.45	(0.69)	3.67	(0.75)	3.23	(0.59)		
India	4.10	(0.98)	4.28	(0.95)	3.92	(0.92)	4.04	(0.93)	3.80	(1.12)	3.58	(1.15)
Indonesia	4.23	(0.67)	4.45	(0.62)	4.16	(0.67)	4.16	(0.66)	3.68	(0.93)	3.72	(0.79)
Ireland	4.25	(0.86)	4.74	(0.50)	3.87	(0.80)	3.87	(0.82)	3.67	(0.86)		
Israel	4.60	(0.74)	4.86	(0.48)	4.27	(0.99)	4.23	(1.02)	4.18	(0.97)		

(continued)

Table A.6 Perceived changes in influences (*continued*)

	User-generated contents, such as blogs		Social media		Audience involvement in news production		Audience feedback		Pressure toward sensational news		Western ways of practicing journalism	
	Mean	(SD)	Mean	(SD)	Mean	(SD)	Mean	(SD)	Mean	(SD)	Mean	(SD)
Italy	4.33	(0.82)	4.68	(0.62)	3.84	(0.91)	3.87	(0.91)	4.02	(0.88)		
Japan	4.02	(0.74)	4.23	(0.71)	3.64	(0.71)	3.69	(0.69)	3.36	(0.74)	3.01	(0.59)
Kenya	4.19	(1.04)	4.51	(0.86)	4.03	(0.89)	4.31	(0.76)	3.99	(1.02)	3.96	(1.05)
Kosovo	3.86	(1.19)	4.37	(0.91)	3.25	(1.05)	3.43	(0.99)	4.04	(0.92)		
Latvia	4.05	(0.91)	4.50	(0.78)	3.92	(0.93)	3.74	(0.99)	3.97	(0.93)		
Malawi	4.03	(1.03)	4.44	(0.84)	3.60	(0.99)	4.06	(0.97)	3.57	(1.16)	3.81	(1.14)
Malaysia	4.08	(0.82)	4.22	(0.77)	3.84	(0.78)	3.99	(0.77)	3.86	(0.84)	3.61	(0.86)
Mexico	4.12	(0.94)	4.55	(0.76)	4.11	(0.86)	4.28	(0.79)	3.50	(1.23)		
Moldova	3.57	(1.07)	3.79	(1.10)	3.55	(1.17)	3.98	(0.90)	3.69	(1.34)	3.48	(1.15)
Netherlands	4.17	(0.64)	4.50	(0.62)	3.88	(0.73)	3.87	(0.71)	3.75	(0.80)		
New Zealand	4.43	(0.69)	4.81	(0.45)	4.10	(0.74)	4.12	(0.78)	4.17	(0.81)		
Norway	4.20	(0.71)	4.53	(0.60)	3.86	(0.67)	3.87	(0.67)	3.77	(0.86)		
Oman	3.20	(1.05)	3.51	(1.00)	3.26	(1.00)	3.40	(1.03)	3.57	(1.01)		
Philippines	3.99	(0.93)	4.49	(0.73)	4.16	(0.83)	4.26	(0.80)	3.71	(0.99)		

Portugal	3.98 (0.86)	4.45 (0.68)	3.70 (0.83)	3.88 (0.82)	3.47 (1.03)	
Romania	3.69 (1.16)	4.05 (1.05)	3.55 (1.24)	4.00 (1.07)	3.18 (1.41)	
Russia	3.96 (0.99)	4.20 (0.94)	3.98 (0.97)	4.00 (0.93)	3.74 (1.00)	2.72 (1.14)
Serbia	3.87 (0.97)	4.32 (0.86)	3.63 (0.97)	3.70 (0.96)	4.24 (0.99)	
Sierra Leone	3.85 (1.14)	4.43 (0.91)	4.02 (0.95)	4.27 (0.76)	4.00 (0.93)	3.82 (1.01)
Singapore	2.98 (1.40)	3.12 (1.64)	2.90 (1.24)	2.88 (1.16)	2.88 (1.04)	2.91 (0.83)
South Africa	4.40 (0.71)	4.85 (0.38)	4.21 (0.73)	4.16 (0.85)	4.01 (0.89)	3.49 (0.97)
South Korea	3.77 (0.85)	4.18 (0.77)	3.98 (0.72)	3.95 (0.76)	3.27 (0.93)	3.15 (0.90)
Spain	4.32 (0.82)	4.68 (0.60)	3.88 (0.93)	4.02 (0.81)	3.90 (0.98)	
Sweden	4.28 (0.70)	4.56 (0.59)	3.98 (0.73)	3.83 (0.72)	3.76 (0.78)	
Switzerland	4.15 (0.73)	4.56 (0.58)	3.85 (0.76)	3.71 (0.78)	3.87 (0.77)	
Tanzania	3.82 (0.81)	4.41 (0.49)	2.83 (1.02)	2.79 (1.17)	2.70 (1.07)	3.52 (0.91)
Thailand	3.98 (0.74)	4.62 (0.58)	4.05 (0.72)	4.21 (0.69)	3.99 (0.67)	
Turkey	4.19 (0.89)	4.87 (0.34)	3.89 (0.95)	4.02 (0.89)	3.66 (1.13)	3.00 (1.06)
UAE	4.13 (0.83)	4.50 (0.78)	4.06 (0.91)	4.18 (0.84)	4.03 (0.98)	3.90 (1.04)
UK	4.45 (0.73)	4.78 (0.47)	3.94 (0.84)	4.02 (0.77)	3.60 (0.97)	
USA	3.80 (1.12)	4.47 (0.86)	3.61 (0.94)	3.80 (0.82)	3.08 (1.10)	

Scale: 5 = "strengthened a lot" . . . 1 = "weakened a lot."

Table A.7 Perceived changes in aspects of work

	Journalists' freedom to make editorial decisions		Average working hours of journalists		Time available for research-ing stories		Interactions of journalists with their audiences	
	Mean	(SD)	Mean	(SD)	Mean	(SD)	Mean	(SD)
Albania	3.23	(0.98)	3.25	(0.94)	3.26	(0.99)	3.64	(0.86)
Argentina	2.73	(1.16)	4.03	(0.91)	2.13	(1.08)	4.09	(0.90)
Australia	2.98	(0.75)	4.01	(0.75)	1.98	(0.91)	3.87	(0.99)
Austria	2.73	(0.79)	3.98	(0.91)	1.81	(0.83)	3.81	(0.89)
Bangladesh	3.77	(1.13)	4.00	(0.92)	3.63	(1.17)	3.77	(1.00)
Belgium	2.76	(0.79)	3.87	(0.88)	2.04	(0.93)	3.67	(0.86)
Bhutan	3.90	(0.79)	4.08	(0.75)	3.54	(0.73)	3.50	(0.93)
Botswana	3.54	(1.31)	4.11	(0.89)	3.21	(1.11)	3.58	(1.14)
Brazil	2.91	(0.95)	3.93	(0.88)	1.96	(0.87)	3.94	(1.02)
Bulgaria	3.04	(1.13)	4.12	(0.82)	2.27	(1.05)	3.99	(1.06)
Canada	2.86	(0.82)	4.00	(0.76)	2.00	(0.91)	4.13	(0.83)
Chile	2.93	(1.06)	3.91	(1.06)	2.32	(1.05)	3.44	(1.24)
China	2.88	(1.06)	3.14	(1.32)	3.05	(1.17)	2.97	(1.28)
Colombia	3.21	(1.26)	3.25	(1.33)	2.76	(1.33)	3.48	(1.21)
Croatia	2.49	(1.01)	4.16	(0.88)	1.84	(0.90)	3.13	(1.25)
Cyprus	3.77	(0.99)	4.02	(0.83)	2.48	(0.99)	4.16	(0.61)
Czech Republic	3.10	(0.73)	4.04	(0.80)	2.35	(0.78)	3.69	(0.87)
Ecuador	3.13	(1.37)	3.68	(1.01)	3.21	(1.19)	3.76	(0.97)
Egypt	3.82	(0.97)	3.47	(0.97)	3.70	(0.88)	3.91	(0.86)
El Salvador	3.41	(0.93)	4.10	(0.86)	2.89	(1.21)	4.13	(0.98)
Estonia	3.14	(0.82)	3.76	(0.91)	2.46	(1.07)	3.40	(0.91)
Ethiopia	3.39	(1.14)	3.67	(0.98)	3.09	(1.20)	3.48	(1.16)
Finland	2.66	(0.80)	3.73	(0.76)	2.03	(0.85)	3.92	(0.89)
France	2.48	(0.98)	3.76	(1.26)	1.60	(0.94)	3.93	(0.91)
Germany	2.71	(0.81)	3.99	(0.77)	2.03	(0.89)	3.72	(0.93)
Greece	2.51	(1.28)	4.22	(1.19)	1.95	(1.13)	3.00	(1.31)
Hong Kong	2.75	(0.84)	3.85	(0.89)	2.79	(1.00)	3.63	(0.84)

Technical skills		Use of search engines		Having a university degree		Having a degree in journalism or a related field		Credibility of journalism		Relevance of journalism for society	
Mean	(SD)	Mean	(SD)	Mean	(SD)	Mean	(SD)	Mean	(SD)	Mean	(SD)
4.02	(0.79)	4.75	(0.54)	2.97	(0.99)	3.00	(1.01)	3.06	(1.02)	3.62	(1.01)
4.13	(0.99)	4.77	(0.55)	3.68	(1.01)	3.55	(1.04)	2.41	(1.18)	3.30	(1.16)
4.28	(0.80)	4.70	(0.53)	3.66	(0.94)	3.44	(0.94)	2.51	(0.74)	3.36	(0.91)
4.35	(0.70)	4.64	(0.61)	3.20	(0.90)	3.19	(0.87)	2.30	(0.79)	2.77	(0.91)
4.45	(0.74)	4.50	(0.70)	4.24	(0.85)	4.10	(0.91)	3.65	(1.23)	4.29	(0.93)
4.12	(0.83)	4.47	(0.72)	3.16	(0.97)	3.18	(0.91)	2.47	(0.90)	3.11	(0.91)
3.86	(0.86)	3.82	(1.00)	3.70	(1.13)	3.57	(1.02)	3.49	(1.21)	3.58	(1.16)
3.88	(1.01)	4.17	(1.05)	4.41	(0.76)	4.31	(0.87)	3.92	(1.05)	4.32	(0.83)
4.00	(1.01)	4.68	(0.53)	3.11	(1.10)	2.94	(1.09)	2.63	(1.16)	3.21	(1.10)
4.51	(0.68)	4.63	(0.63)	3.46	(1.17)	2.77	(1.06)	2.28	(1.23)	2.57	(1.27)
4.36	(0.75)	4.55	(0.66)	3.47	(0.91)	3.26	(0.94)	2.53	(0.91)	3.49	(1.05)
3.66	(1.15)	4.43	(0.80)	3.58	(1.20)	3.48	(1.25)	3.07	(1.20)	3.28	(1.19)
3.04	(1.43)	3.14	(1.63)	3.00	(1.04)	2.92	(1.08)	3.04	(1.08)	3.33	(1.14)
4.29	(1.00)	4.49	(0.79)	4.13	(1.15)	3.97	(1.27)	3.68	(1.30)	3.97	(1.16)
4.14	(1.05)	4.43	(0.81)	2.85	(1.11)	2.64	(1.01)	1.94	(0.98)	2.86	(1.16)
3.88	(0.88)	4.75	(0.57)	3.78	(1.05)	3.75	(1.15)	3.99	(1.07)	3.99	(0.84)
4.28	(0.68)	4.53	(0.60)	2.79	(0.70)	2.61	(0.82)	2.60	(0.85)	3.14	(0.89)
4.17	(0.86)	4.55	(0.73)	4.61	(0.65)	4.66	(0.65)	3.85	(1.25)	3.98	(1.06)
4.08	(0.79)	3.99	(0.88)	3.42	(1.09)	3.38	(1.08)	4.09	(0.98)	4.06	(0.90)
4.18	(1.05)	4.66	(0.55)	4.28	(0.85)	4.30	(0.87)	3.64	(1.21)	4.11	(0.95)
4.33	(0.69)	4.41	(0.65)	2.96	(0.89)	2.67	(0.84)	2.78	(0.88)	3.26	(0.95)
3.85	(1.09)	4.33	(0.93)	4.24	(0.94)	4.06	(0.98)	2.98	(1.27)	3.46	(1.28)
4.47	(0.60)	4.53	(0.65)	3.14	(0.89)	3.00	(0.80)	2.53	(0.81)	3.12	(0.85)
4.36	(0.66)	4.60	(0.60)	3.50	(0.94)	3.68	(0.97)	1.92	(0.97)	2.51	(1.18)
4.45	(0.64)	4.60	(0.65)	3.35	(0.98)	2.99	(0.89)	2.37	(0.88)	2.96	(0.99)
4.64	(0.67)	4.87	(0.40)	3.73	(1.10)	3.57	(1.12)	2.25	(1.39)	2.87	(1.36)
3.56	(0.92)	4.39	(0.88)	3.33	(0.83)	3.10	(0.80)	2.71	(1.00)	3.62	(0.93)

(continued)

Table A.7 Perceived changes in aspects of work (*continued*)

	Journalists' freedom to make editorial decisions		Average working hours of journalists		Time available for research-ing stories		Interactions of journalists with their audiences	
	Mean	(SD)	Mean	(SD)	Mean	(SD)	Mean	(SD)
Hungary	2.89	(1.16)	4.18	(0.83)	2.51	(1.07)	3.42	(0.92)
Iceland	3.38	(0.79)	3.60	(0.85)	2.26	(0.93)	3.38	(0.89)
India	3.32	(1.20)	4.15	(0.99)	2.94	(1.19)	3.58	(1.15)
Indonesia	3.98	(0.88)	3.95	(0.76)	3.13	(1.07)	3.88	(0.77)
Ireland	2.74	(0.87)	4.32	(0.70)	1.74	(0.72)	3.48	(1.18)
Israel	2.72	(1.26)	4.22	(1.08)	1.67	(0.98)	3.93	(1.25)
Italy	2.09	(0.87)	3.90	(1.09)	1.85	(0.77)	3.44	(1.31)
Japan	2.83	(0.72)	3.70	(0.97)	2.35	(0.86)	3.23	(0.80)
Kenya	3.88	(1.10)	3.83	(0.98)	3.37	(1.06)	4.07	(0.91)
Kosovo	3.23	(1.12)	2.92	(1.32)	2.95	(1.21)	3.30	(1.03)
Latvia	3.33	(0.91)	3.56	(0.82)	2.50	(1.06)	3.57	(0.88)
Malawi	4.19	(0.83)	3.98	(0.83)	3.21	(1.07)	3.97	(0.94)
Malaysia	3.64	(0.84)	3.77	(0.85)	3.43	(0.93)	3.73	(0.91)
Mexico	3.44	(1.15)	4.14	(0.97)	3.20	(1.23)	3.90	(0.98)
Moldova	3.24	(1.27)	4.13	(1.01)	2.65	(1.19)	3.77	(1.06)
Netherlands	2.62	(0.74)	3.65	(0.83)	1.96	(0.65)	3.71	(0.84)
New Zealand	2.69	(1.00)	4.04	(0.76)	1.75	(0.81)	3.57	(1.17)
Norway	2.79	(0.79)	3.51	(0.82)	1.97	(0.79)	3.56	(0.95)
Oman	3.92	(0.89)	3.87	(0.75)	3.85	(0.91)	3.93	(0.83)
Philippines	3.39	(0.98)	4.00	(0.86)	2.94	(1.11)	4.07	(0.89)
Portugal	2.78	(1.00)	4.15	(0.81)	1.86	(0.95)	3.71	(0.91)
Romania	2.91	(1.23)	4.22	(0.97)	2.27	(1.09)	3.61	(1.20)
Russia	2.49	(0.99)	3.45	(0.96)	2.43	(0.97)	3.60	(1.06)
Serbia	2.55	(1.14)	3.91	(0.94)	2.33	(1.04)	3.21	(1.14)
Sierra Leone	3.77	(1.11)	3.94	(0.96)	3.56	(1.16)	4.32	(0.80)
Singapore	2.96	(0.83)	3.05	(1.28)	3.29	(0.95)	3.12	(1.16)
South Africa	3.10	(1.03)	4.02	(0.95)	2.31	(1.28)	4.16	(1.01)

Technical skills		Use of search engines		Having a university degree		Having a degree in journalism or a related field		Credibility of journalism		Relevance of journalism for society	
Mean	(SD)	Mean	(SD)	Mean	(SD)	Mean	(SD)	Mean	(SD)	Mean	(SD)
4.20	(0.82)	4.42	(0.81)	2.99	(1.07)	3.19	(1.10)	2.52	(1.16)	2.77	(1.12)
4.23	(0.68)	4.54	(0.55)	3.92	(0.76)	3.59	(0.71)	3.07	(0.96)	3.62	(0.87)
4.28	(0.92)	4.53	(0.76)	3.96	(1.09)	3.93	(1.12)	3.46	(1.28)	3.96	(1.06)
3.99	(0.83)	4.39	(0.62)	4.01	(0.78)	3.83	(0.83)	3.87	(0.89)	3.97	(0.75)
4.68	(0.54)	4.76	(0.49)	3.70	(0.92)	3.63	(0.90)	2.55	(0.93)	3.19	(1.10)
4.75	(0.58)	4.81	(0.48)	2.63	(1.32)	2.66	(1.23)	2.19	(1.14)	3.15	(1.37)
3.79	(1.33)	4.67	(0.61)	3.16	(1.14)	3.11	(1.12)	1.88	(0.90)	2.27	(1.10)
3.75	(0.98)	4.32	(0.76)	2.80	(0.66)	2.83	(0.71)	2.50	(0.99)	3.04	(0.89)
4.23	(0.88)	4.48	(0.70)	4.21	(0.95)	4.11	(1.01)	3.89	(1.11)	4.15	(1.03)
3.76	(0.84)	4.43	(0.69)	3.11	(1.17)	3.07	(1.27)	3.54	(1.02)	3.80	(1.02)
4.37	(0.68)	4.41	(0.69)	2.80	(0.94)	2.72	(0.91)	3.06	(1.14)	3.20	(1.03)
4.05	(0.82)	4.53	(0.80)	4.23	(0.93)	4.23	(0.95)	3.97	(1.03)	4.19	(0.81)
3.88	(0.79)	4.28	(0.77)	3.83	(0.95)	3.81	(0.95)	3.81	(1.01)	4.00	(0.96)
4.32	(0.83)	4.68	(0.64)	4.22	(1.01)	3.85	(1.10)	3.62	(1.24)	3.83	(1.06)
4.09	(1.13)	4.54	(0.75)	3.48	(1.18)	3.45	(1.21)	3.04	(1.44)	3.58	(1.22)
3.98	(0.75)	4.30	(0.61)	3.17	(0.84)	2.92	(0.82)	2.48	(0.74)	3.01	(0.81)
4.01	(1.05)	4.64	(0.53)	3.64	(0.86)	3.64	(0.86)	2.25	(0.90)	2.93	(1.12)
4.37	(0.67)	4.44	(0.63)	3.65	(0.80)	3.60	(0.81)	2.73	(0.85)	3.10	(0.85)
3.85	(0.99)	3.59	(1.18)	3.95	(0.77)	3.78	(1.01)	4.16	(0.89)	4.04	(0.85)
4.22	(0.91)	4.58	(0.65)	3.72	(0.95)	3.48	(1.04)	3.37	(1.16)	3.84	(1.06)
4.02	(0.93)	4.60	(0.59)	3.59	(0.92)	3.45	(0.94)	2.71	(1.04)	3.24	(1.07)
4.02	(1.11)	4.59	(0.73)	3.24	(1.31)	2.98	(1.27)	2.42	(1.21)	3.02	(1.26)
4.14	(0.87)	4.38	(0.75)	2.56	(1.13)	2.47	(1.11)	2.45	(1.11)	2.94	(1.10)
4.18	(1.04)	4.62	(0.71)	2.76	(1.23)	2.68	(1.18)	2.20	(1.23)	2.63	(1.29)
4.25	(0.84)	3.97	(1.03)	4.21	(0.97)	4.31	(0.85)	4.07	(1.08)	4.48	(0.80)
3.14	(1.32)	3.12	(1.59)	3.21	(1.16)	3.11	(0.96)	3.45	(0.99)	3.32	(1.14)
4.22	(1.03)	4.77	(0.55)	3.45	(1.10)	3.45	(1.08)	2.80	(1.26)	3.78	(1.15)

(continued)

Table A.7 Perceived changes in aspects of work (*continued*)

	Journalists' freedom to make editorial decisions		Average working hours of journalists		Time available for research-ing stories		Interactions of journalists with their audiences	
	Mean	(SD)	Mean	(SD)	Mean	(SD)	Mean	(SD)
South Korea	2.84	(1.09)	3.87	(0.93)	2.49	(0.97)	3.45	(1.00)
Spain	2.40	(0.94)	4.23	(0.93)	1.78	(0.82)	3.88	(0.90)
Sweden	2.60	(0.75)	3.67	(0.78)	1.89	(0.75)	3.52	(0.95)
Switzerland	2.69	(0.77)	3.90	(0.79)	1.97	(0.88)	3.70	(0.92)
Tanzania	2.84	(0.86)	3.47	(1.21)	2.85	(1.00)	3.74	(0.89)
Thailand	4.03	(0.70)	3.89	(0.71)	3.73	(0.80)	3.94	(0.70)
Turkey	2.02	(0.99)	3.94	(0.94)	2.11	(0.86)	3.30	(1.20)
United Arab Emirates	3.71	(0.90)	3.85	(0.93)	3.30	(1.03)	4.05	(0.95)
United Kingdom	2.74	(0.93)	4.18	(0.77)	1.81	(0.74)	3.64	(1.19)
United States	3.14	(0.77)	4.03	(0.87)	2.13	(0.89)	3.85	(0.98)

Scale: 5 = "increased a lot" . . . 1 = "decreased a lot."

Technical skills		Use of search engines		Having a university degree		Having a degree in journalism or a related field		Credibility of journalism		Relevance of journalism for society	
Mean	(SD)	Mean	(SD)	Mean	(SD)	Mean	(SD)	Mean	(SD)	Mean	(SD)
3.88	(0.86)	4.37	(0.64)	2.98	(0.89)	2.75	(0.92)	2.38	(1.10)	2.63	(1.07)
4.24	(0.77)	4.64	(0.60)	3.38	(1.06)	3.14	(1.06)	2.28	(0.98)	2.99	(1.05)
4.38	(0.67)	4.47	(0.64)	3.24	(0.83)	3.36	(0.93)	2.60	(0.84)	3.00	(0.94)
4.23	(0.71)	4.52	(0.65)	3.37	(0.88)	3.43	(0.79)	2.24	(0.80)	2.74	(0.88)
3.72	(0.72)	4.06	(0.64)	3.40	(0.65)	3.25	(0.69)	3.20	(0.90)	3.62	(0.65)
3.99	(0.81)	4.49	(0.58)	3.66	(0.69)	3.57	(0.79)	3.79	(0.88)	3.96	(0.85)
4.50	(0.82)	4.43	(0.92)	3.58	(1.12)	3.49	(1.01)	1.94	(1.12)	2.53	(1.01)
4.50	(0.61)	4.58	(0.51)	4.43	(0.87)	4.15	(0.88)	3.89	(1.05)	3.95	(1.23)
4.09	(1.04)	4.69	(0.53)	3.42	(1.01)	3.18	(1.01)	2.29	(0.89)	3.23	(1.01)
4.53	(0.66)	4.69	(0.60)	3.41	(0.98)	3.08	(0.93)	2.56	(0.91)	3.49	(1.11)

Table A.8 Contextual information

	Reference year[a]	Press freedom[b]		Democracy[c]		Rule of law[d]
		index	classific.	(index)	classification	
Albania	2012	49	Partly free	5.67	Hybrid Regime	40.9
Argentina	2014	51	Partly free	6.84	Flawed Democracy	18.3
Australia	2012	21	Free	9.22	Full Democracy	96.2
Austria	2015	23	Free	8.54	Full Democracy	96.2
Bangladesh	2013	54	Partly free	5.86	Hybrid Regime	26.0
Belgium	2013	11	Free	8.05	Full Democracy	88.9
Bhutan	2013	59	Partly free	4.82	Hybrid Regime	67.8
Botswana	2014	44	Partly free	7.87	Flawed Democracy	74.0
Brazil	2015	46	Partly free	6.96	Flawed Democracy	55.3
Bulgaria	2016	40	Partly free	7.14	Flawed Democracy	52.9
Canada	2015	18	Free	9.08	Full Democracy	94.7
Chile	2014	31	Partly free	7.80	Flawed Democracy	88.0
China	2015	87	Not free	3.14	Authoritarian	42.8
Colombia	2013	54	Partly free	6.55	Flawed Democracy	42.3
Croatia	2013	40	Partly free	6.93	Flawed Democracy	65.9
Cyprus	2014	25	Free	7.40	Flawed Democracy	82.2
Czech Republic	2013	20	Free	8.06	Full Democracy	84.6
Denmark	2015	12	Free	9.11	Full Democracy	99.5
Ecuador	2015	66	Not free	5.87	Hybrid Regime	13.5
Egypt	2012	62	Not free	4.56	Hybrid Regime	31.3
El Salvador	2015	39	Partly free	6.64	Flawed Democracy	35.6
Estonia	2013	16	Free	7.61	Flawed Democracy	86.5
Ethiopia	2014	83	Not free	3.72	Authoritarian	38.9
Finland	2013	11	Free	9.03	Full Democracy	100.0
France	2015	28	Free	7.92	Flawed Democracy	88.5
Germany	2015	20	Free	8.64	Full Democracy	93.3
Greece	2015	48	Partly free	7.45	Flawed Democracy	67.3
Hong Kong	2012	35	Partly free	6.42	Flawed Democracy	93.8
Hungary	2014	37	Partly free	6.90	Flawed Democracy	70.7

Economic development			Human development[h]		Emancipative values[i]
GNI[e]	classific.[f]	Transparency[g]	index	classification	
4360	Transition	33	.729	High	.39
13480	Developing	34	.836	Very high	.52
59810	Developed	85	.932	Very high	.59
49600	Developed	76	.885	Very high	.52
1010	Developing	27	.567	Medium	.33
47240	Developed	75	.888	Very high	.49
2340	Developing	63	.595	Medium	
7240	Developing	63	.698	Medium	
11790	Developing	38	.755	High	.47
7480	Developing	41	.782	High	.46
51630	Developed	83	.913	Very high	.59
14910	Developing	73	.832	Very high	.51
7400	Developing	37	.727	High	.39
7770	Developing	36	.720	High	.42
13460	Developed	48	.817	Very high	.40
26370	Developed	63	.850	Very high	.44
19170	Developed	48	.868	Very high	.49
61330	Developed	91	.923	Very high	.63
6090	Developing	32	.732	High	.41
2850	Developing	32	.688	Medium	.30
3920	Developing	39	.666	Medium	
18390	Developed	68	.859	Very high	.48
550	Developing	33	.442	Low	.47
49050	Developed	89	.882	Very high	.62
42950	Developed	70	.888	Very high	.58
47590	Developed	81	.916	Very high	.60
22810	Developed	46	.865	Very high	.46
36320	Developing	77	.906	Very high	.48
13340	Developed	54	.828	Very high	.50

(continued)

Table A.8 Contextual information (*continued*)

	Reference year[a]	Press freedom[b]		Democracy[c]		Rule of law[d]
		index	classific.	(index)	classification	
Iceland	2012	14	Free	9.65	Full Democracy	90.9
India	2014	40	Partly free	7.92	Flawed Democracy	54.3
Indonesia	2015	49	Partly free	7.03	Flawed Democracy	41.8
Ireland	2014	16	Free	8.72	Full Democracy	92.8
Israel	2014	30	Free	7.63	Flawed Democracy	83.2
Italy	2015	31	Partly free	7.98	Flawed Democracy	66.8
Japan	2013	25	Free	8.08	Full Democracy	89.4
Kenya	2014	57	Partly free	5.13	Hybrid Regime	37.5
Kosovo	2015	49	Partly free			37.0
Latvia	2014	28	Free	7.48	Flawed Democracy	77.9
Malawi	2014	49	Partly free	5.66	Hybrid Regime	45.7
Malaysia	2014	65	Not free	6.49	Flawed Democracy	75.0
Mexico	2014	63	Not free	6.68	Flawed Democracy	38.0
Moldova	2013	53	Partly free	6.32	Flawed Democracy	46.6
Netherlands	2014	11	Free	8.92	Full Democracy	97.1
New Zealand	2015	20	Free	9.26	Full Democracy	98.6
Norway	2013	10	Free	9.93	Full Democracy	99.0
Oman	2015	71	Not free	3.04	Authoritarian	73.1
Philippines	2015	44	Partly free	6.84	Flawed Democracy	43.3
Portugal	2014	18	Free	7.79	Flawed Democracy	84.1
Qatar	2013	67	Not free	3.18	Authoritarian	81.3
Romania	2014	42	Partly free	6.68	Flawed Democracy	63.5
Russia	2015	83	Not free	3.31	Authoritarian	26.4
Serbia	2014	40	Partly free	6.71	Flawed Democracy	50.5
Sierra Leone	2015	53	Partly free	4.55	Hybrid Regime	17.8
Singapore	2014	67	Not free	6.03	Flawed Democracy	95.2
South Africa	2014	37	Partly free	7.82	Full Democracy	63.9
South Korea	2014	32	Partly free	8.06	Full Democracy	80.8
Spain	2014	28	Free	8.05	Full Democracy	79.8

Economic development		Transparency[g]	Human development[h]		Emancipative values[i]
GNI[e]	classific.[f]		index	classification	
40530	Developed	82	.897	Very high	.61
1570	Developing	38	.609	Medium	.34
3630	Developing	36	.684	Medium	.34
46520	Developed	74	.916	Very high	.45
35320	Developing	60	.894	Very high	.51
34580	Developed	44	.873	Very high	.50
46330	Developed	74	.888	Very high	.51
1290	Developing	25	.548	Low	
		33			.38
15250	Developed	55	.819	Very high	.45
250	Developing	33	.449	Low	
11120	Developing	52	.779	High	.36
9870	Developing	35	.756	High	.46
2470	Transition	35	.690	Medium	.41
51860	Developed	83	.922	Very high	.61
41070	Developed	88	.913	Very high	.58
104010	Developed	86	.942	Very high	.72
16870	Developing	45	.793	High	
3500	Developing	35	.668	Medium	.40
21360	Developed	63	.830	Very high	.42
89210	Developing	68	.849	Very high	.27
9520	Developed	43	.793	High	.42
13220	Transition	29	.798	High	.40
5820	Transition	41	.771	High	.47
700	Developing	29	.413	Low	
55150	Developing	84	.912	Very high	.43
6800	Developing	44	.666	Medium	.46
27090	Developing	55	.898	Very high	.44
29390	Developed	60	.876	Very high	.56

(*continued*)

Table A.8 Contextual information (*continued*)

	Reference year[a]	Press freedom[b] index	Press freedom[b] classific.	Democracy[c] (index)	Democracy[c] classification	Rule of law[d]
Sudan	2014	81	Not free	2.54	Authoritarian	9.6
Sweden	2013	10	Free	9.73	Full Democracy	97.6
Switzerland	2014	13	Free	9.09	Full Democracy	98.1
Tanzania	2014	54	Partly free	5.77	Hybrid Regime	39.4
Thailand	2014	75	Not free	5.39	Hybrid Regime	51.4
Turkey	2014	65	Not free	5.12	Hybrid Regime	59.6
UAE	2014	76	Not free	2.64	Authoritarian	76.4
UK	2015	25	Free	8.31	Full Democracy	94.2
USA	2013	22	Free	8.11	Full Democracy	89.9

[a] Year for which data obtained (matched with time of data collection for WJS).
[b] Freedom House; Freedom of the Press Index and classification.
[c] Economist Intelligence Unit; EIU Democracy Index and classification.
[d] World Bank; percentile rank.
[e] World Bank; GNI per capita, Atlas method, current US$.
[f] UN DESA; classification of economies (Developed = Developed economy, Transition = Economy in transition, Developing = Developing economy).
[g] Transparency International; Corruption Perceptions Index.
[h] UNDP; Human Development Index and classification.
[i] Scores calculated based on WVS/EVS data.

| Economic development | | | Human development[h] | | Emancipative values[i] |
GNI[e]	classific.[f]	Transparency[g]	index	classification	
1710	Developing	11	.479	Low	
61340	Developed	89	.905	Very high	.72
84720	Developed	86	.930	Very high	.65
920	Developing	31	.521	Low	.36
5780	Developing	38	.726	High	.37
10830	Developing	45	.761	High	.33
44600	Developing	70	.835	Very high	
43390	Developed	81	.907	Very high	.58
53720	Developed	73	.913	Very high	.54

APPENDIX 2

QUESTIONNAIRE

Worlds of Journalism Study—Master questionnaire, 2012–16

(Version 2.5.1 consolidated)

NOTE: *Questions printed in italics were optional.*

C1   Which of the following categories best describes your current position in your newsroom? (Read list.)

1	Editor in chief
2	Managing editor
3	Desk head or assignment editor
4	Department head
5	Senior editor
6	Producer
7	Reporter
8	News writer
9	Trainee
10	Other, please specify:
777	Don't know
999	Refused

C2   Which of the following categories best describes your current employment: full-time, part-time, freelancer, or other?

1	Full-time employment
2	Part-time employment
3	Freelancer GO TO C3
4	Other, please specify (Record verbatim.)
777	Don't know
999	Refused

ask only If C2 <> 3:

O1 *Do you have a permanent position, or do you work on a temporary contract?*
    1   Permanent
    2   Temporary
    777   Don't know
    999   Refused

C3   For how many newsrooms do you work at present? Different news outlets produced by the same newsroom count as one. (Record verbatim.)
    777   Don't know
    999   Refused

O2 *For how many news outlets do you work? (Record verbatim.)*
    777   Don't know
    999   Refused

C4   Besides working as a journalist, do you engage in any other paid activities?
    1   Yes
    2   No
    777   Don't know
    999   Refused

C5   Do you belong to any organizations or associations that are primarily for people in journalism or the communications field?
    1   Yes
    2   No
    777   Don't know
    999   Refused

C6   Do you usually work on or supervise a specific beat or subject area (such as politics, economy or sports), or do you usually work on or supervise various types of stories?
    1   Work on a specific beat
    2   Work on various topic and subjects GO TO O3/C8
    777   Don't know
    999   Refused

ask only If C6 = 1:

C7   Which beat or area do you primarily supervise or work on? (Do not read categories!)
    1   News/current affairs
    2   Politics

3   Foreign politics
4   Domestic politics
5   Economy
6   Crime & law
7   Culture
8   Sports
9   Health
10   Entertainment
11   Other, please specify (Record verbatim.)
777 Don't know
999 Refused

O3 *On average, how many news items do you produce and/or edit in a usual week?*

   777   *Don't know*
   999   *Refused*

C8 Please tell me, in your own words, what <u>should be</u> the three most important roles of journalists in [add country]? (Record verbatim.)

   777 Don't know
   999 Refused

C9 Thinking of your work overall, how much freedom do you personally have in selecting news stories you work on? 5 means complete freedom, 4 means a great deal of freedom, 3 means some freedom, 2 means little freedom, and 1 means no freedom at all.

   5   complete freedom
   4   a great deal of freedom
   3   some freedom
   2   little freedom
   1   no freedom at all
   777 Don't know
   999 Refused

C10 How much freedom do you personally have in deciding which aspects of a story should be emphasized? Again, 5 means complete freedom, 4 means a great deal of freedom, 3 means some freedom, 2 means little freedom, and 1 means no freedom at all.

   5   complete freedom
   4   a great deal of freedom
   3   some freedom
   2   little freedom
   1   no freedom at all

777   Don't know
999   Refused

C11 How often do you participate in editorial and newsroom coordination, such as attending editorial meetings or assigning reporters? 5 means always, 4 means very often, 3 means sometimes, 2 means rarely, and 1 means almost never.

    5   always
    4   very often
    3   sometimes
    2   rarely
    1   almost never
  777   Don't know
  999   Refused

C12 Please tell me how important each of these things is in your work. 5 means you find them extremely important, 4 means very important, 3 means somewhat important, 2 means little importance, and 1 means unimportant.

    5   extremely important
    4   very important
    3   somewhat important
    2   little important
    1   unimportant
  777   Don't know
  999   Refused
    A   Be a detached observer.
    B   Report things as they are.
    C   Provide analysis of current affairs.
    D   Monitor and scrutinize political leaders.
    E   Monitor and scrutinize business.
    F   Set the political agenda.
    G   Influence public opinion.
    H   Advocate for social change.
    J   Be an adversary of the government.
    K   Support national development.
    L   Convey a positive image of political leadership.
    M   Support government policy.
    O   Provide entertainment and relaxation.
    P   Provide the kind of news that attracts the largest audience.
    R   Provide advice, orientation and direction for daily life.
    S   Provide information people need to make political decisions.
    T   Motivate people to participate in political activity.
    U   Let people express their views.

W   *Educate the audience.*
X   *Tell stories about the world.*
Z   *Promote tolerance and cultural diversity.*

C13   The following statements describe different approaches to journalism. For each of them, please tell me how strongly you agree or disagree. 5 means you strongly agree, 4 means somewhat agree, 3 means undecided, 2 means somewhat disagree, and 1 means strongly disagree.

5   strongly agree
4   somewhat agree
3   undecided
2   somewhat disagree
1   strongly disagree
777   Don't know
999   Refused
A   Journalists should always adhere to codes of professional ethics, regardless of situation and context.
B   What is ethical in journalism depends on the specific situation.
C   What is ethical in journalism is a matter of personal judgment.
D   It is acceptable to set aside moral standards if extraordinary circumstances require it.

C14   Given an important story, which of the following, if any, do you think may be justified on occasion and which would you not approve of under any circumstances? 1 means it is always justified, 2 means it is justified on occasion, and 3 means you would not approve under any circumstances.

1   always justified
2   justified on occasion
3   not approve under any circumstances
777   Don't know
999   Refused
A   Paying people for confidential information
B   Using confidential business or government documents without authorization
C   Claiming to be somebody else
D   Exerting pressure on unwilling informants to get a story
E   Making use of personal documents such as letters and pictures without permission
F   Getting employed in a firm or organization to gain inside information
G   Using hidden microphones or cameras
H   Using re-creations or dramatizations of news by actors
J   Publishing stories with unverified content

K	Accepting money from sources
L	*Altering or fabricating quotes from sources*
M	*Altering photographs*

C15 Here is a list of potential sources of influence. Please tell me how much influence each of the following has on your work. 5 means it is extremely influential, 4 means very influential, 3 means somewhat influential, 2 means little influential, and 1 means not influential. If a source is not relevant to your work, please choose 8.

5	extremely influential
4	very influential
3	somewhat influential
2	little influential
1	not influential
8	not relevant to respondent's work
777	Don't know
999	Refused
A	Your personal values and beliefs
B	Your peers on the staff
C	Your editorial supervisors and higher editors
D	The managers of your news organization
E	The owners of your news organization
F	Editorial policy
G	Advertising considerations
H	Profit expectations
J	Audience research and data
K	Availability of news-gathering resources
L	Time limits
M	Journalism ethics
N	*Religious considerations*

C16 Here is another list. Again, please tell me on a scale of 5 to 1 how influential each of the following is in your work.

5	extremely influential
4	very influential
3	somewhat influential
2	little influential
1	not influential
777	Don't know
999	Refused
A	Your friends, acquaintances and family
B	Colleagues in other media
C	Feedback from the audience

D	Competing news organizations
E	Media laws and regulation
F	Information access
G	Censorship
H	Government officials
J	Politicians
K	Pressure groups
L	Business people
M	Public relations
N	Relationships with news sources
O	*The military, police and state security*

C17 How many years have you been working in journalism? (Record verbatim.)
IF < 5 years GO TO O4/C20

777	Don't know GO TO O4/C20
999	Refused GO TO O4/C20

ask only If C17 ≥ 5:

C18 The importance of some influences on journalism may have changed over time. Please tell me to what extent these influences have become stronger or weaker during the past five years in [add country]. 5 means they have strengthened a lot, 4 means they have somewhat strengthened, 3 means they did not change, 2 means they have somewhat weakened, and 1 means they have weakened a lot.

5	strengthened a lot
4	somewhat strengthened
3	did not change
2	somewhat weakened
1	weakened a lot
777	Don't know
999	Refused
A	Journalism education
B	Ethical standards
C	Competition
D	Advertising considerations
E	Profit making pressures
F	Public relations
G	Audience research
H	User-generated contents, such as blogs
J	Social media, such as [add 1 or 2 examples]
K	Audience involvement in news production

L   Audience feedback
M   Pressure toward sensational news
O   *Western ways of practicing journalism*

ask only If C17 ≥ 5:

C19 Journalism is in a state of change. Please tell me whether you think there has been an increase or a decrease in the importance of following aspects of work in [add country]. 5 means they have increased a lot, 4 means they have somewhat increased, 3 means there has been no change, 2 means they have somewhat decreased, and 1 means they have decreased a lot.

5	increased a lot
4	somewhat increased
3	did not change
2	somewhat decreased
1	decreased a lot
777	Don't know
999	Refused
A	Journalists' freedom to make editorial decisions
B	Average working hours of journalists
C	Time available for researching stories
D	Interactions of journalists with their audiences
E	The importance of technical skills
F	The use of search engines
G	The importance of having a university degree
H	The importance of having a degree in journalism or a related field
J	The credibility of journalism
K	The relevance of journalism for society

O4 Please tell me on a scale of 5 to 1 how much you personally trust each of the following institutions. 5 means you have complete trust, 4 means you have a great deal of trust, 3 means have you some trust, 2 means you have little trust, and 1 means you have no trust at all.

5	complete trust
4	a great deal of trust
3	some trust
2	little trust
1	no trust at all
777	Don't know
999	Refused
A	The parliament [add name]
B	The government [add name]
C	Political parties

D   Politicians in general
E   The judiciary/the courts
F   The police
G   The military
H   Trade unions
J   Religious leaders
K   The news media

O5   Generally speaking, would you say that most people can be trusted, or that you cannot be too careful in dealing with people?
    1   most people can be trusted
    2   one cannot be too careful
    777   Don't know
    999   Refused

O6   Do you think that most people would try to take advantage of you if they got the chance, or would they try to be fair?
    1   most people would try to take advantage of me
    2   they would try to be fair
    777   Don't know
    999   Refused

C20 What is the highest grade of school or level of education you have completed?
(Read list.)
    1   Not completed high school GO TO O7/C22
    2   Completed high school GO TO O7/C22
    3   College/Bachelor's degree or equivalent
    4   Master's degree or equivalent
    5   Doctorate
    6   Undertook some university studies, but no degree
    777   Don't know
    999   Refused

ask only If C20 > 2:

C21 During your studies, did you specialize in journalism or another communication field?
    1   Yes, specialized in journalism
    2   Yes, specialized in other communication field
    3   Yes, specialized both in journalism and another communication field
    4   No, did not specialize in these fields

777   Don't know
999   Refused

ask only If C20 > 2 AND C6 = 1:

O7   During your studies, did you specialize in a field that relates to your area of coverage?
    1   Yes, did specialize
    2   No, did not specialize
    777   Don't know
    999   Refused

C22 What is your gender?
    1   Female
    2   Male
    777   Don't know
    999   Refused

C23 In what year were you born? (Record verbatim.)
    777   Don't know
    999   Refused

O8   In political matters, people talk of "the left," "the right," and the "center." On a scale where 0 is left, 10 is right, and 5 is center, where would you place yourself? (Record verbatim.)
    777   Don't know
    999   Refused

O9   What is your ethnic group?
[Add a list of common ethnic groups in your country.]
    20   Other, please specify (Record verbatim.)
    777   Don't know
    999   Refused

O10 How important is religion or religious belief to you? 5 means you find it extremely important, 4 means very important, 3 means somewhat important, 2 means it is of little importance, and 1 means unimportant.
    5   extremely important
    4   very important
    3   somewhat important
    2   little important
    1   unimportant
    777   Don't know
    999   Refused

O11 Do you consider yourself as affiliated with any particular religion or religious denomination? If yes, which one? (Do not read the list!)
- 1 No religion or denomination
- 2 Buddhist
- 3 Christian: Protestant/Lutheran
- 4 Christian: Orthodox
- 5 Christian: Roman Catholic
- 6 Hindu
- 7 Jewish
- 8 Muslim
- 9 Other, please specify (Record verbatim.)
- 777 Don't know
- 999 Refused

O12 In which of the following categories does your monthly salary fall, after taxes?
[Add a list of 10 income brackets according to instructions.]
- 777 Don't know
- 999 Refused

TECHNICAL QUESTIONS (to be filled upon completion of the interview)

T1 Interview code (Record verbatim.)

T2 Interview date (ddmmjj) (Record verbatim.)

T3 Interviewer code (Record verbatim.)

T4 Interview mode
- 1 Telephone
- 2 Face to face
- 3 Mail or E-mail
- 4 Online

T5 Rank of respondent
- 1 Senior/executive manager with strategic authority
- 2 "Junior" manager with operational authority
- 3 Rank-and-file journalist with limited authority

T6 Name of medium (Record verbatim.)

T7 Type of medium
- 1 Daily newspaper
- 2 Weekly newspaper
- 3 Magazine

    4   Television
    5   Radio
    6   News agency
    7   Online outlet (stand-alone)
    8   Online outlet (of offline outlet)

T8 Reach of medium
    1   Local
    2   Regional
    3   National
    4   Transnational

T9 Ownership of medium
    1   Purely private ownership
    2   Purely public ownership
    3   Purely state ownership
    4   Mixed ownership but mostly private
    5   Mixed ownership but mostly public
    6   Mixed ownership but mostly state-owned
  777   No information

T10 Notes (Record verbatim.)

APPENDIX 3

INSTITUTIONS FUNDING THE STUDY

Austrian Science Fund
Charles University, Czech Republic
Cyprus University of Technology
Donald W. Reynolds Journalism Institute, USA
Estonian Ministry of Education and Research
Friedrich Ebert Foundation, Germany
Fundação Carlos Chagas Filho de Amparo à Pesquisa do Estado do Rio de Janeiro, Brazil
Fundação para a Ciência e a Tecnologia, Portugal
German Research Foundation
Helsingin Sanomat Foundation, Finland
Icelandic Student Innovation Fund
KEA svf, Akureyri, Iceland
LMU Munich, Germany
Massey University, New Zealand
Ministry of Education, Science and Culture, Iceland
Nihon University, Japan
Ohio University, USA
Qatar University
Research Foundation—Flanders (FWO), Belgium
Ryerson Journalism Research Centre, Canada
The Second Authority for Television and Radio, Israel
Social Sciences and Humanities Research Council of Canada
South African National Research Foundation
State University of Rio de Janeiro, Brazil

Stellenbosch University, South Africa
Swiss National Science Foundation
Universidad del Norte, Colombia
Universidad Nacional de la Matanza, Argentina
University of Agder, Norway
University of Bergen, Norway
University of Miami, USA
University of Pennsylvania, USA
University of the Sunshine Coast, Australia
University of Tartu, Estonia
University of Tirana, Albania
Windesheim University of Applied Sciences, The Netherlands
Zayed University, UAE

REFERENCES

Aguilar, Filomeno V., Meynardo P. Mendoza, and Anne Lan K. Candelaria. 2014. "Keeping the State at Bay: The Killing of Journalists in the Philippines, 1998–2012." *Critical Asian Studies* 46, no. 1:649–77. https://doi.org/10.1080/14672715.2014.960719.

Ahva, Laura, Arjen van Dalen, Jan Fredrik Hovden, Guðbjörg Hildur Kolbeins, Monica Löfgren Nilsson, Morten Skovsgaard, and Jari Väliverronen. 2017. "A Welfare State of Mind?: Nordic Journalists' Conception of Their Role and Autonomy in International Context." *Journalism Studies* 18, no. 5:595–613. https://doi.org/10.1080/1461670X.2016.1249005.

Akagi, Katie, and Stephanie Linning. 2013. "Crowdsourcing Done Right." *Columbia Journalism Review*, April 29, 2013. http://www.cjr.org/between_the_spreadsheets/crowdsourcing_done_right.php.

Albaek, Erik, Arjen Van Dalen, Nael Jebril, and Claes H. de Vreese. 2014. *Political Journalism in Comparative Perspective*. Cambridge: Cambridge University Press.

Aldridge, Meryl, and Julia Evetts. 2003. "Rethinking the Concept of Professionalism: The Case of Journalism." *British Journal of Sociology* 54, no. 4:547–64. https://doi.org/10.1111/j.1468-4446.2003.00547.

Alexander, Amy C., Ronald Inglehart, and Christian Welzel. 2012. "Measuring Effective Democracy: A Defense." *International Political Science Review* 33, no. 1:41–62. https://doi.org/10.1177/0192512111414682.

Alexander, Anne, and Miriyam Aouragh. 2014. "Egypt's Unfinished Revolution: The Role of the Media Revisited." *International Journal of Communication* 8:890–915.

Alexander, Jeffrey C., Elizabeth Butler Breese, and María Luengo, eds. 2016. *The Crisis of Journalism Reconsidered: Democratic Culture, Professional Codes, Digital Future*. Cambridge: Cambridge University Press.

Allan, Stuart, Gill Branston, and Cynthia Carter, eds. 2002. *News, Gender and Power.* London: Routledge.

Altheide, David L. 1976. *Creating Reality: How TV News Distorts Events.* Beverly Hills: Sage.

Altmeppen, Klaus-Dieter. 2008. "The Structure of News Production: The Organizational Approach to Journalism Research." In *Global Journalism Research: Theories, Methods, Findings, Future,* edited by Martin Löffelholz and David H. Weaver, 52–64. Malden, Mass.: Blackwell.

Altschull, J. Herbert. 1995. *Agents of Power: The Media and Public Policy.* White Plains, N.Y.: Longman.

Anderson, Chris W. 2011. "Between Creative and Quantified Audiences: Web Metrics and Changing Patterns of Newswork in Local US Newsrooms." *Journalism* 12, no. 5:550–66. https://doi.org/10.1177/1464884911402451.

——. 2013. *Rebuilding the News: Metropolitan Journalism in the Digital Age.* Philadelphia: Temple University Press.

Andresen, Kenneth, Abit Hoxha, and Jonila Godole. 2017. "New Roles for Media in the Western Balkans: A Study of Transitional Journalism." *Journalism Studies* 18, no. 5:614–28. https://doi.org/10.1080/1461670X.2016.1268928.

Arbaoui, Bouchra, Knut De Swert, and Wouter van der Brug. 2016. "Sensationalism in News Coverage: A Comparative Study in 14 Television Systems." *Communication Research* (August). https://doi.org/10.1177/0093650216663364.

Arroyave, Jesus, and Marta Barrios. 2012. "Journalists in Colombia." In *The Global Journalist in the 21st Century,* edited by David Weaver and Lars Willnat, 400–412. New York: Routledge.

Artemas, Katie, Tim P. Vos, and Margaret Duffy. 2018. "Journalism Hits a Wall: Rhetorical Construction of Newspapers' Editorial and Advertising Relationship." *Journalism Studies* 19, no. 7: 1004–20. https://doi.org/10.1080/1461670X.2016.1249006.

Bagdikian, Ben. 1983. *The Media Monopoly.* Boston: Beacon.

Bagozzi. Richard P. 1994. "Structural Equation Models in Marketing Research: Basic Principles." In *Principles of Marketing Research,* edited by Richard Bagozzi, 317–85. Oxford: Blackwell.

Baker, C. Edwin. 2004. *Media, Market and Democracy.* Cambridge: Cambridge University Press.

Bakker, Piet. 2012. "Aggregation, Content Farms and Huffinization: The Rise of Low-Pay and No-Pay Journalism." *Journalism Practice* 6, no. 5–6:627–37. https://doi.org/10.1080/17512786.2012.667266.

Banda, Fackson. 2008. "Negotiating Journalism Ethics in Zambia: Towards a 'Glocal' Ethics." In *Media Ethics: Beyond Borders,* edited by Stephen J. A. Ward and Herman Wasserman, 157–71. Johannesburg, South Africa: Heinemann.

——. 2013. "Introduction." In *Model Curricula for Journalism Education,* edited by UNESCO, 7–21. Paris: UNESCO.

Banda, Fackson, Catherine M. Beukes-Amiss, Tanja Bosch, Winston Mano, Polly McLean, and Lynette Steenveld. 2007. "Contextualising Journalism Education and

Training in Southern Africa." *Ecquid Novi* 28, no. 1–2:156–75. https://doi.org/10.1080/02560054.2007.9653364.

Barrios, Marta Milena, and Jesús Arroyave. 2007. "Perfil Sociológico de la Profesión del Periodista en Colombia: Diálogo Íntimo con el ser Humano Detrás de las Noticias." *Diálogos de la Comunicación* 75:1–26.

Bartholomé, Guus, Sophie Lecheler, and Clas de Vreese. 2015. "Manufacturing Conflict? How Journalists Intervene in the Conflict Frame Building Process." *International Journal of Press/Politics* 20, no. 4:438–57. https://doi.org/10.1177/1940161215595514.

Bartsch, Anne, and Frank M. Schneider. 2014. "Entertainment and Politics Revisited: How Non-Escapist Forms of Entertainment Can Stimulate Political Interest and Information Seeking." *Journal of Communication* 64, no. 3:369–96. https://doi.org/10.1111/jcom.12095.

Beam, Randal A. 1990. "Journalism Professionalism as an Organizational-Level Concept." *Journalism Monographs* 121:1–43.

Beam, Randal A., David H. Weaver, and Bonnie J. Brownlee. 2009. "Changes in Professionalism of U.S. Journalists in the Turbulent Twenty-First Century." *Journalism & Mass Communication Quarterly* 86, no. 2:277–98. https://doi.org/10.1177/107769900908600202.

Becker, Lee Bernard, Tudor Vlad, and Holly Anne Simpson. 2014. "2013 Annual Survey of Journalism Mass Communication Enrollments." *Journalism & Mass Communication Educator* 69, no. 4:349–65. https://doi.org/10.1177/1077695814555432.

Bennett, W. Lance. 2016. *News: The Politics of Illusion*. Chicago. University of Chicago Press.

Benson, Rodney, Mark Blach-Ørsten, Matthew Powers, Ida Willig, and Sandra Vera Zambrano. 2012. "Media Systems Online and Off: Comparing the Form of News in the United States, Denmark, and France." *Journal of Communication* 62, no. 1:21–38. http://dx.doi.org/10.1111/j.1460-2466.2011.01625.x.

Benson, Rodney, and Erik Neveu. 2005. "Introduction: Field Theory as a Work in Progress." In *Bourdieu and the Journalistic Field*, edited by Rodney Benson and Erik Neveu, 1–28. Malden, Mass.: Polity Press.

Berganza, Rosa, Beatriz Herrero-Jiménez, and Carlos Arcila-Calderón. 2016. "Perceived Influences and Trust in Political Institutions of Public vs Private Television Journalists in Spain." *Communication & Society* 29, no. 4:185–201. https://doi.org/10.15581/003.29.4.185–201.

Berger, Guy, and Joe Foote. 2017. "Taking Stock of Contemporary Journalism Education: The End of the Classroom as We Know It." In *Global Journalism Education in the 21st Century: Challenges & Innovations*, edited by Robyn Goodman and Elanie Steyn, 245–65. Austin: Knight Center for Journalism in the Americas, University of Texas at Austin.

Berglez, Peter. 2008. "What Is Global Journalism? Theoretical and Empirical Conceptualisations." *Journalism Studies* 9, no. 6:845–58. https://doi.org/10.1080/14616700802337727.

Berkowitz, Dan. 2000. "Doing Double Duty: Paradigm Repair and the Princess Diana What-a-Story." *Journalism* 1, no. 2:125–43. https://doi.org/10.1177/146488490000 100203.

Bernhard, Michael, Christopher Reenock, and Timothy Nordstrom. 2003. "Economic Performance and Survival in New Democracies: Is There a Honeymoon Effect?" *Comparative Political Studies* 36, no. 4:404–31. https://doi.org/10.1177/001041400 3251175.

Berrigan, Frances J. 1979. *Community Communications: The Role of Community Media in Development*. Reports and Papers on Mass Communication No. 90. New York: UNIPUB.

Bieber, Florian. 2003. "The Serbian Opposition and Civil Society: Roots of the Delayed Transition in Serbia." *International Journal of Politics, Culture and Society* 17, no. 1:73–90. https://www.jstor.org/stable/20020198.

Bittner, Andreas. 2011. *Managing Change: Innovation and Trade Unionism in the News Industry*. Brussels: European Federation of Journalists.

Blofield, Merike, ed. 2011. *The Great Gap: Inequality and the Politics of Redistribution in Latin America*. University Park: Pennsylvania State University Press.

Blumler, Jay G. 2017. "Epilogue for a Comparative Leap Forward." *Journalism Studies* 18, no. 5:682–90. https://doi.org/10.1080/1461670X.2017.1294392.

Blumler, Jay G., Jack M. McLeod, and Karl Erik Rosengren. 1992. "An Introduction to Comparative Communication Research." In *Comparatively Speaking: Communication and Culture Across Space and Time*, edited by Jay G. Blumler, Jack M. McLeod, and Karl Erik Rosengren, 3–18. Newbury Park, Calif.: Sage.

Boczkowski, Pablo J. 2004. *Digitizing the News: Innovation in Online Newspapers*. Cambridge, Mass.: MIT Press.

Boczkowski, Pablo J., and Charles W. Anderson, eds. 2017. *Remaking the News: Essays on the Future of Journalism Scholarship in the Digital Age*. Cambridge, Mass.: MIT Press.

Bonfadelli, Heinz, Guido Keel, Mirko Marr, and Vinzenz Wyss. 2012. "Journalists in Switzerland." In *The Global Journalist in the 21st Century*, edited by David H. Weaver and Lars Willnat, 320–30. New York: Routledge.

Bonin, Geneviève, Filip Dingerkus, Annik Dubied, Stefan Mertens, Heather Rollwagen, Vittoria Sacco, Ivor Shapiro, Olivier Standaert, and Vinzenz Wyss. 2017. "Quelle différence? Language, Culture and Nationality as Influences on Francophone Journalists' Identity." *Journalism Studies* 18, no. 5: 536–54. https://doi.org/10.1080/1461 670X.2016.1272065.

Borden, Sandra L. 2010. "The Moral Justification for Journalism." In *Journalism Ethics: A Philosophical Approach*, edited by Christopher Meyers, 53–68. Oxford: Oxford University Press.

Borg, Ingwer, and Patrick Groenen. 1997. *Modern Multidimensional Scaling: Theory and Applications*. New York: Springer.

Borger, Merel, Anita van Hoof, Irene Costera Meijer, and José Sanders. 2013. "Constructing Participatory Journalism as a Scholarly Object." *Digital Journalism* 1, no. 1:117–34. https://doi.org/10.1080/21670811.2012.740267.

Bossio, Diana. 2017. *Journalism and Social Media: Practitioners, Organisations and Institutions.* Basingstoke, U.K.: Palgrave Macmillan.

Bourdieu, Pierre. 1998. *On Television.* New York: New Press.

——. 2005. "The Political Field, the Social Science Field, and the Journalistic Field." In *Bourdieu and the Journalistic Field,* edited by Rodney Benson and Erik Neveu, 29–47. Cambridge: Polity Press.

Bourdieu, Pierre, and Loïc J. Wacquant. 1992. *An Invitation to Reflexive Sociology.* Cambridge: Polity Press.

Boyd-Barrett, Oliver. 2014. *Media Imperialism.* London: Sage.

Boyle, Gregory J. 1991. "Does Item Homogeneity Indicate Internal Consistency of Item Redundancy in Psychometric Scales?" *Personality and Individual Differences* 12, no. 3:291–94. https://doi.org/10.1016/0191-8869(91)90115-R.

Boynton, Robert S. 2008. "Checkbook Journalism Revisited: Sometimes We Owe Our Sources Everything." *Columbia Journalism Review* 46, no. 5:12–15.

Brambila, Julieta, and Sallie Hughes. 2019. "Violence Against Journalists." In *The International Encyclopedia of Journalism Studies,* edited by Tim P. Vos and Folker Hanusch. Hoboken, N.J.: Wiley.

Brants, Kees, Claes de Vreese, Judith Möller, and Philip van Praag. 2010. "The Real Spiral of Cynicism? Symbiosis and Mistrust Between Politicians and Journalists." *International Journal of Press/Politics* 15, no. 1:25–40. https://doi.org/10.1177/1940161209351005.

Braun, Paul. 1988. "Deception in Journalism." *Journal of Mass Media Ethics* 3, no. 1:77–83. https://doi.org/10.1080/08900528809358312.

Bravata, Denah M., Kaveh G. Shojania, Ingram Olkin, and Adi Raveh. 2008. "CoPlot: A Tool for Visualizing Multivariate Data in Medicine." *Statistics in Medicine* 27, no. 12:2234–47. https://doi.org/10.1002/sim.3078.

Breed, Warren. 1955. "Social Control in the Newsroom: A Functional Analysis." *Social Forces* 33, no. 4:326–35.

Brennen, Bonnie S. 2000. "What the Hacks Say: The Ideological Prism of US Journalism Texts." *Journalism* 1, no. 1:106–13. https://doi.org/10.1177/146488490000100112.

Brevini, Benedetta, Arne Hintz, and Patrick McCurdy, eds. 2013. *Beyond WikiLeaks. Implications for the Future of Communications, Journalism and Society.* New York: Palgrave Macmillian.

Brüggemann, Michael, Sven Engesser, Florin Büchel, Edda Humprecht, and Laia Castro. 2014. "Hallin and Mancini Revisited: Four Empirical Types of Western Media Systems." *Journal of Communication* 64, no. 6:1037–65. http://dx.doi.org/10.1111/jcom.12127.

Bruns, Axel. 2008. "The Active Audience: Transforming Journalism from Gatekeeping to Gatewatching." In *Making Online News: The Ethnography of New Media Production,* edited by Chris A. Paterson and David Domingo, 171–84. New York: Peter Lang.

Byerly, Carolyn, ed. 2013. *The Palgrave International Handbook of Women and Journalism.* Basingstoke, U.K.: Palgrave.

Cappella, Joseph N., and Kathleen H. Jamieson. 1997. *Spiral of Cynicism: The Press and the Public Good.* New York: Oxford University Press.

CareerCast.com. 2016. "The Worst Jobs of 2016." *Career Cast.* Accessed February 26, 2018. http://www.careercast.com/jobs-rated/worst-jobs-2016.

Carlson, Matt. 2016. "Metajournalistic Discourse and the Meanings of Journalism: Definitional Control, Boundary Work, and Legitimation." *Communication Theory* 26, no. 4:349–68. https://doi.org/10.1111/comt.12088.

——. 2017. *Journalistic Authority: Legitimating News in the Digital Era.* New York: Columbia University Press.

Carlson, Matt, and Seth C. Lewis, eds. 2015. *Boundaries of Journalism: Professionalism, Practices and Participation.* New York: Routledge.

Castro Herrero, Laia, Edda Humprecht, Sven Engesser, Michael Brüggemann, and Florin Büchel. 2017. "Rethinking Hallin and Mancini Beyond the West: An Analysis of Media Systems in Central and Eastern Europe." *International Journal of Communication* 11:27. http://ijoc.org/index.php/ijoc/article/view/6035.

Catterberg, Gabriel, and Alejandro Moreno. 2006. "The Individual Basis of Political Trust: Trends in New and Established Democracies." *International Journal of Public Opinion Research* 18, no. 1:31–48. https://doi.org/10.1093/ijpor/edh081.

Chadha, Kalyani. 2017. "The Indian News Media Industry: Structural Trends and Journalistic Implications." *Global Media and Communication* 13, no. 2:139–56. https://doi.org/10.1177/1742766517704674.

Chalaby, Jean K. 1996. "Journalism as an Anglo-American Invention: A Comparison of the Development of French and Anglo-American Journalism, 1830s–1920s." *European Journal of Communication* 11, no. 3:303–26. https://doi.org/10.1177/0267323119 6011003002.

——. 2011. "The Making of an Entertainment Revolution: How the TV Format Trade Became a Global Industry." *European Journal of Communication* 26, no. 4:293–309. http://doi.org/10.1177/0267323111423414.

Chan, Joseph M., Francis L. F. Lee, and Clement Y. K. So. 2012. "Journalists in Hong Kong." In *The Global Journalist in the 21st Century,* edited by David H. Weaver and Lars Willnat, 22–35. New York: Routledge.

Chan Joseph M., Zhongdan Pan, and Francis L. F. Lee. 2004. "Professional Aspirations and Job Satisfaction: Chinese Journalists at a Time of Change in the Media." *Journalism & Mass Communication Quarterly* 81, no. 2:254–73. https://doi.org/10.1177/107769900408100203.

Chan, M. Joseph, and Clement Y. K. So. 2005. "The Surrogate Democracy Function of the Media: Citizens' and Journalists' Evaluations of Media Performance in Hong Kong." In *Journalism and Democracy in Asia,* edited by Angela Romano and Michael Bromley, 66–80. New York: Routledge.

Chang, Tsan-Kua, Pat Pat Berg, Anthony Ying-Him Fung, Kent D. Kedl, Catherine A. Luther, and Janet Szuba. 2001. "Comparing Nations in Mass Communication Research, 1970–97: A Critical Assessment of How We Know What We Know."

International Communication Gazette 63, no. 5:415–34. https://doi.org/10.1177/0016
549201063005004.

Charlebois, Justin. 2015. "Interpretative Repertoire." In *The International Encyclopedia of Language and Social Interaction*, edited by Karen Tracy, 1–5. Hoboken, N.J.: Wiley. doi:10.1002/9781118611463/wbielsi017.

Cheung, Meily M. F., and Tin Chi Wong. 2016. "News Information Censorship and Changing Gatekeeping Roles: Non-Routine News Coverage and News Routines in the Context of Police Digital Communications in Hong Kong." *Journalism & Mass Communication Quarterly* 93, no. 4:1091–1114. https://doi.org/10.1177/107769901 6628818.

Christians, Clifford G. 2014. "Review of International Media Ethics." *Comunicação e Sociedade* 25:34–48. http://dx.doi.org/10.17231/comsoc.25(2014).1855.

Christians, Clifford G., John P. Ferré, and P. Mark Fackler. 1993. *Good News: Social Ethics and the Press*. Oxford: Oxford University Press.

Christians, Clifford G., Theodore L. Glasser, Denis McQuail, Kaarle Nordenstreng, and Robert A. White. 2009. *Normative Theories of the Media: Journalism in Democratic Societies*. Urbana: University of Illinois Press.

Christians, Clifford G., Shakuntala Rao, Stephen J. A. Ward, and Herman Wasserman. 2008. "Toward a Global Media Ethics: Theoretical Perspectives." *Ecquid Novi* 29, no. 2:135–72. https://doi.org/10.1080/02560054.2008.9653382.

Christians, Clifford G., Kim B. Rotzoll, and Mark Fackler. 1991. *Media Ethics: Cases and Moral Reasoning*. White Plains, N.Y.: Longman.

Coddington, Mark. 2015. "The Wall Becomes a Curtain: Revisiting Journalism's News-Business Boundary." In *Boundaries of Journalism: Professionalism, Practices and Participation*, edited by Matt Carlson and Seth C. Lewis, 67–82. New York: Routledge.

Cohen, Akiba A. 2013. "Where in the World Is the Global Village?" In *Foreign News on Television: Where in the World Is the Global Village?*, edited by Akiba A. Cohen, 319–30. New York: Peter Lang.

Cohen Bernhard C. 1963. *The Press and Foreign Policy*. Princeton, N.J.: Princeton University Press.

Coleman, Renita, and Lee Wilkins. 2002. "Searching for the Ethical Journalist: An Exploratory Study of the Moral Development of News Workers." *Journal of Mass Media Ethics* 17, no. 3:209–25. https://doi.org/10.1207/S15327728JMME1703_03.

Coltman, Tim, Timothy M. Divenney, David F. Midgley, and Sunil Venaik. 2008. "Formative Versus Reflective Measurement Models." *Journal of Business Research* 61, no. 12:1250–62. https://doi.org/10.1016/j.jbusres.2008.01.013.

Cook, Timothy E. 1998. *Governing with the News: The News Media as a Political Institution*. Chicago: University of Chicago Press.

Cornia, Alessio. 2014. "Will Italian Political Journalism Ever Change?" In *Political Journalism in Transition: Western Europe in a Comparative Perspective*, edited by Raymond Kuhn and Rasmus Kleis Nielsen, 47–73. London: I. B. Tauris.

Coronel, Sheila. 2003. *The Role of the Media in Deepening Democracy.* United Nations Public Administration Network. http://unpan1.un.org/intradoc/groups/public/documents/un/unpan010194.pdf

Craft, Stephanie, and Wayne Wanta. 2004. "Women in the Newsroom: Influences of Female Editors and Reporters on the News Agenda." *Journalism & Mass Communication Quarterly* 81, no. 1:124–38. https://doi.org/10.1177/107769900408100109.

Curran, James. 2011. "Questioning a New Orthodoxy." In *Communication and Society: Media and Democracy,* edited by James Curran, 28–46. London: Routledge.

Dal Zotto, Ciniza, Vittoria Sacco, and Yoann Schenker. 2017. "Market Structure and Innovation Policies in Switzerland." In *Innovation Policies in the European News Media Industry: A Comparative Study,* edited by Hans van Kranenburg, 205–18. Cham, Switzerland: Springer.

Davis, Aeron. 2014. "The Impact of Market Forces, New Technologies, and Political PR on UK Journalism." In *Political Journalism in Transition: Western Europe in a Comparative Perspective,* edited by Raymond Kuhn and Rasmus Kleis Nielsen, 111–28. London: I. B. Tauris.

De Beer, Arnold S., ed. 2009. *Global Journalism—Topical Issues and Media Systems.* Boston: Pearson.

——. 2010a. "Looking for Journalism Education Scholarship in Some Unusual Places: The Case of Africa." *Communicatio: South African Journal for Communication Theory and Research* 36, no. 2:213–26. https://doi.org/10.1080/02500167.2010.485367.

——. 2010b. "News from and in the 'Dark Continent': Afro-pessimism, News Flows, Global Journalism and Media Regimes." *Journalism Studies* 11, no. 4:596–609. https://doi.org/10.1080/14616701003638509.

De Beer, Arnold S., Vanessa Malila, Sean Beckett, and Herman Wasserman. 2016. "Binary Opposites—Can South African Journalists Be Both Watchdogs and Developmental Journalists?" *Journal of African Media Studies* 8, no. 1:35–53. https://doi.org/10.1386/jams.8.1.35_1.

De Bruin, Marianne. 2000. "Gender, Organizational and Professional Identities in Journalism." *Journalism* 1, no. 2:217–38. https://doi.org/10.1177/146488490000100205.

De Bruin, Marianne, and Karen Ross. 2004. *Gender and Newsroom Cultures: Identities at Work.* Cresskill, N.J.: Hampton Press.

De Burgh, Hugo. 2000. "The Emergence of Investigative Journalism." In *Investigative Journalism: Context and Practice,* edited by Hugo de Burgh, 32–51. London: Routledge.

De Cock, Rozane, and Hedwig de Smaele. 2016. "Freelancing in Flemish News Media and Entrepreneurial Skills as Pivotal Elements in Job Satisfaction." *Journalism Practice* 10, no. 2:251–65. https://doi.org/10.1080/17512786.2015.1123106.

Deuze, Mark. 2005. "What Is Journalism? Professional Identity and Ideology of Journalists Reconsidered." *Journalism* 6, no. 4:442–64. https://doi.org/10.1177/1464884905056815.

——. 2006a. "Ethnic Media, Community Media and Participatory Culture." *Journalism* 7, no. 3:262–80. https://doi.org/10.1177/1464884906065512.

——. 2006b. "Global Journalism Education: A Conceptual Approach." *Journalism Studies* 7, no. 1:19–34. https://doi.org/10.1080/14616700500450293.

Deuze, Mark, and Tamara Witschge. 2018. "Beyond Journalism: Theorizing the Transformation of Journalism." *Journalism* 19, no. 2:165–81. https://doi.org/10.1177/146 4884916688550.

Deuze, Mark, and Daphna Yeshua. 2001. "Online Journalists Face New Ethical Dilemmas: Lessons from the Netherlands." *Journal of Mass Media Ethics* 16, no. 4:273–92. https://doi.org/10.1207/S15327728JMME1604_03.

Dexter, Lewis Anthony, and David Manning White. 1964. *People, Society, and Mass Communications*. New York: Free Press.

Dick, Murray. 2011. "Search Engine Optimisation in UK News Production." *Journalism Practice* 5, no. 4:462–77. https://doi.org/10.1080/17512786.2010.551020.

Dickinson, Roger, Julia Matthews, and Kostas Saltzis. 2013. "Studying Journalists in Changing Times: Understanding News Work as Socially Situated Practice." *International Communication Gazette* 75, no. 1:3–18. https://doi.org/10.1177/174804 8512461759.

Donsbach, Wolfgang. 2012. "Journalists' Role Perception." *International Encyclopedia of Communication*. Accessed February 15, 2018. https://doi.org/10.1002/9781405 186407.wbiecj010.pub2.

Downie, Leonard, and Michael Schudson. 2009. "The Reconstruction of American Journalism." *Columbia Journalism Review* 6 (November/December): 1–100. http://archives.cjr.org/reconstruction/the_reconstruction_of_american.php.

Dube, Bevelyn. 2016. "Rethinking Journalism Education in African Journalism Institutions: Perspectives of Southern African Journalism Scholars on the Africanisation of Journalism Curricula." *AFFRIKA Journal of Politics, Economics and Society* 6, no. 1:13–45.

Durazo Herrmann, Julián. 2012. "Neo-Patrimonialism and Subnational Authoritarianism in Mexico: The Case of Oaxaca." *Journal of Politics in Latin America* 2, no. 2:85–112.

Easton, David. 1965. *A System Analysis of Political Life*. New York: Wiley.

Economist Intelligence Unit. 2016. *Democracy Index 2015: Democracy in an Age of Anxiety*. London: EIU.

Edeani, David O. 1993. "Role of Development Journalism in Nigeria's Development." *Gazette* 52, no. 2:123–43. https://doi.org/10.1177/001654929305200204.

Eide, Martin, and Graham Knight. 1999. "Public/Private Service: Service Journalism and the Problems of Everyday Life." *European Journal of Communication* 14, no. 4:525–47. https://doi.org/10.1177/0267323199014004004.

Elefante, Phoebe Harris, and Mark Deuze. 2012. "Media Work, Career Management, and Professional Identity: Living Labour Precarity." *Northern Lights: Film & Media Studies Yearbook* 10, no. 1:9–24. https://doi.org/10.1386/nl.10.1.9_1.

El Issawi, Fatima, and Bart Cammaerts. 2015. "Shifting Journalistic Roles in Democratic Transitions: Lessons from Egypt." *Journalism* 17, no. 5:549–66. https://doi.org/10.1177 /1464884915576732.

Elliott, Deni. 1988. "All Is Not Relative: Essential Shared Values and the Press." *Journal of Mass Media Ethics* 3, no. 1:28–32. https://doi.org/10.1080/08900528809358306.

——. 1989. "Journalistic Deception." In *Ethical Issues in the Professions*, edited by Peter Y. Windt, Peter C. Appleby, Margaret Pabst Battin, Leslie P. Francis, and B. M. Landesman, 144–46. Englewood Cliffs, N.J.: Prentice Hall.

Elliott, Deni, and Culver, Charles. 1992. "Defining and Analyzing Journalistic Deception." *Journal of Mass Media Ethics* 7, no. 2:69–84. https://doi.org/10.1207/ s15327728jmme0702_1.

Esser, Frank, and Thomas Hanitzsch. 2012. "On the Why and How of Comparative Inquiry in Communication Studies." In *The Handbook of Comparative Communication Research*, edited by Frank Esser and Thomas Hanitzsch, 3–47. New York: Routledge.

Esser, Frank, Claes H. de Vreese, Jesper Strömbäck, Peter van Aelst, Toril Aalberg, James Stanyer, Günther Lengauer et al. 2012. "Political Information Opportunities in Europe: A Longitudinal and Comparative Study of Thirteen Television Systems." *International Journal of Press/Politics* 17, no. 3:247–74. https://doi.org/10.1177 /1940161212442956.

Ettema, James S., and D. Charles Whitney, eds. 1994. *Audience-Making. How the Media Create the Audience.* London: Sage.

Ettema, James S., D. Charles Whitney, and Daniel B. Wackman. 1987. "Professional Mass Communicators." In *Handbook of Communication Science*, edited by Charles R. Berger and Steven H. Chaffee, 747–80. Beverley Hills, Calif.: Sage.

Falk, Armin, and Michael Kosfeld. 2006. "The Hidden Costs of Control." *American Economic Review* 96, no. 5:1611–30. https://doi.org/10.1257/aer.96.5.1611.

Feldstein, Mark. 2006. "A Muckraking Model: Investigative Reporting Cycles in American History." *International Journal of Press/Politics* 11, no. 2:105–20. https://doi.org /10.1177/1081180X06286780.

Fengler, Susanne, Tobias Eberwein, Salvador Alsius, Olivier Baisnée, Klaus Bichler, Boguslawa Dobek-Ostrowska, Huub Evers, Michal Glowacki, et al. 2015. "How Effective Is Media Self-Regulation? Results from a Comparative Survey of European Journalists." *European Journal of Communication* 30, no. 3:249–66. https://doi.org /10.1177/0267323114561009.

Fenton, Natalie. 2010. "Drowning or Waving? New Media, Journalism and Democracy." In *New Media, Old News*, edited by Natalie Fenton, 3–16. London: Sage.

Fischer, Ronald. 2004. "Standardization to Account for Cross-Cultural Response Bias: A Classification of Score Adjustment Procedures and Review of Research in JCCP." *Journal of Cross-Cultural Psychology* 35, no. 3:263–82. https://doi.org/10.1177/0022 022104264122.

Fishman, Mark. 1980. *Manufacturing the News.* Austin: University of Texas Press.

Flanagan, Owen, Hagop Sarkissian, and David Wong. 2008. "Naturalizing Ethics." *Moral Psychology* 1:1–26.

Flegel, Ruth, and Steven H. Chaffee. 1971. "Influences of Editors, Readers, and Personal Influences on Reporters." *Journalism Quarterly* 48, no. 4:645–651. https://doi.org/10 .1177/107769907104800404.

Flew, Terry, and Adam Swift. 2013. "Regulating Rournalists? The Finkelstein Review, the Convergence Review and News Media Regulation in Australia." *Journal of Applied Journalism & Media Studies* 2, no. 1:181–99. https://doi.org/10.1386/ajms.2.1.181_1.

Forsyth, Donelson R. 1980. "A Taxonomy of Ethical Ideologies." *Journal of Personality and Social Psychology* 39, no. 1:175–84. http://dx.doi.org/10.1037/0022-3514.39.1.175.

——. 1981. "Moral Judgment: The Influence of Ethical Ideology." *Personality and Social Psychology Bultetin* 7, no. 2:218–23. https://doi.org/10.1177/014616728172006.

Forsyth, Donelson R., and Judith L. Nye. 1990. "Personal Moral Philosophies and Moral Choice." *Journal of Research in Personality* 24, no. 4:398–414. https://doi.org/10.1016 /0092-6566(90)90030-A.

Forsyth, Donelson R., Ernest H. O'Boyle, and Michael A. McDaniel. 2008. "East Meets West: A Meta-Analytic Investigation of Cultural Variations in Idealism and Relativism." *Journal of Business Ethics* 83, no. 4:813–33. https://doi.org/10.1007/s10551-008 -9667-6.

Foucault, Michel. 1980. *Power/Knowledge*. Brighton, U.K.: Harvester.

Franklin, Bob. 2012. "The Future of Journalism: Developments and Debates." *Journalism Studies* 13, no. 5–6:663–81. https://doi.org/10.1080/1461670X.2012.712301.

Franks, Suzanne. 2013. *Women and Journalism*. London: I. B. Tauris.

Freedom House. 2015. *Discarding Democracy: Return to the Iron Fist—Freedom in the World 2015*. New York: Freedom House.

Friedman, Thomas L. 2005. "Listen to Your Heart. Commencement Address to Williams College." Accessed February 26, 2018. http://www.humanity.org/voices/commencements/tom-friedman-williams-college-speech-2005.

Frisch, Nicholas, Valerie Belair-Gagnon, and Colin Agur. 2017. "Media Capture with Chinese Characteristics: Changing Patterns in Hong Kong's News Media System." *Journalism* (2017): 1–17. https://doi.org/10.1177/1464884917724632.

Fröhlich, Romy, and Christina Holtz-Bacha, eds. 2003. *Journalism Education in Europe and North America. An International Comparison*. Cresskill, N.J.: Hampton Press.

Gamson, William, and David Meyer. 1996. "Framing Political Opportunity." In *Comparative Perspectives on Social Movements: Political Opportunities, Mobilizing Structures, and Cultural Framings*, edited by Dough McAdam, John McCarthy, and Mayer Zald, 275–90. Cambridge: Cambridge University Press.

Gans, Herbert J. 1979. *Deciding What's News: A Study of CBS Evening News, NBC Nightly News, Newsweek, and Time*. New York: Pantheon Books.

Gans, Herbert J. 1998. "What Can Journalists Actually Do for American Democracy?" *Harvard International Journal of Press/Politics* 3, no. 4:6–12. https://doi.org/10.1177 /1081180X98003004003.

Garcés Prettel, Miguel E., and Jesús Arroyave Cabrera. 2017. "Autonomía Profesional y Riesgos de Seguridad de los Periodistas en Colombia." *Perfiles Latinoamericanos* 25, no. 49:1–19. http://dx.doi.org/10.18504/pl2549-002-2017.

García Avilés, José Alberto, Bienvenido León, Karen Sanders, and Jackie Harrison. 2004. "Journalists at Digital Television Newsrooms in Britain and Spain: Workflow and Multi-Skilling in a Competitive Environment." *Journalism Studies* 5, no. 1:87–100. https://doi.org/10.1080/1461670032000174765.

Geddes, Barbara. 2003. "How the Cases You Choose Affect the Answers You Get: Selection Bias in Comparative Politics." In *Paradigms and Sand Castles: Theory Building and Research Design in Comparative Politics*, edited by Barbara Geddes, 89–129. Ann Arbor: University of Michigan Press.

George, Cherian. 2007. "Consolidating Authoritarian Rule: Calibrated Coercion in Singapore." *Pacific Review* 20, no. 2:127–45. https://doi.org/10.1080/0951274070130 6782.

George, Cherian. 2013. "Diversity Around a Democratic Core: The Universal and the Particular in Journalism." *Journalism* 14, no. 4:490–503. https://doi.org/10.1177 /1464884912464169.

Geringer de Oedenberg, Lidia. 2013. "A View from the European Parliament: The World's Youngest Democracy." https://lidiageringer.wordpress.com/2013/06/28/the -worlds-youngest-democracy.

Gerring, John. 1999. "What Makes a Concept Good? A Criterial Framework for Understanding Concept Formation in the Social Sciences." *Polity* 31, no. 3:357–93. https: //doi.org/10.2307/3235246.

Gibson, Edward L. 2012. *Boundary Control: Subnational Authoritarianism in Federal Democracies*. New York: Cambridge University Press.

Giddens, Anthony. 1984. *The Constitution of Society*. Cambridge: Polity Press.

Gieryn, Thomas F. 1983. "Boundary-Work and the Demarcation of Science from Non-Science: Strains and Interests in Professional Ideologies of Scientists." *American Sociological Review* 48, no. 6:781–95. http://www.jstor.org/stable/2095325.

Glasser, Theodore L., and Marc Gunther. 2005. "The Legacy of Autonomy in American Journalism." In *Institutions of Democracy: The Press*, edited by Geneva Overholser and Kathleen H. Jamieson, 384–99. New York: Oxford University Press.

Global Gender Gap Report. 2016. *Insight Report*. Geneva: World Economic Forum.

Global Media Monitoring Project (GMMP). 2015. *Who Makes the News?* London: WACC.

Golding, Peter. 1977. "Media Professionalism in the Third World: The Transfer of an Ideology." In *Mass Communication and Society*, edited by James Curran, Michael Gurevitch, and Janet Woollacott, 291–308. London: Arnold.

Gollmitzer, Mirjam. 2014. "Precariously Employed Watchdogs?" *Journalism Practice* 8, no. 6:826–41. https://doi.org/10.1080/17512786.2014.882061.

González de Bustamante, Celeste, and Jeannine E. Relly. 2015. "Professionalism Under Threat of Violence: Journalism, Reflexivity and the Potential for Collective

Professional Autonomy in Northern Mexico." *Journalism Studies* 17, no. 6:684–702. https://doi.org/10.1080/1461670X.2015.1006903.

Goodman, Robyn, and Elanie Steyn, eds. 2017. *Global Journalism Education in the 21st Century: Challenges & Innovations*. Austin: Knight Center for Journalism in the Americas, University of Texas at Austin.

Gravengaard, Gitte, and Lene Rimestad. 2014. "Socializing Journalist Trainees in the Newsroom: On How to Capture the Intangible Parts of the Process." *Nordicom Review* 35 (August): 81–95.

Gronke, Paul, and Timothy E. Cook. 2007. "Disdaining the Media: The American Public's Changing Attitudes Toward the News." *Political Communication* 24, no. 3:259–81. https://doi.org/10.1080/10584600701471591.

Gross, Peter. 2004. "Between Reality and Dream: Eastern European Media Transition, Transformation, Consolidation, and Integration." *East European Politics & Societies* 18, no. 1:110–31. https://doi.org/10.1177/0888325403259919.

Gross, Peter, and Karol Jakubowicz, eds. 2013. *Media Transformations in the Post-Communist World: Eastern Europe's Tortured Path to Change*. Lanham, Md.: Lexington Books.

Grosskopf, Anke. 2008. "Explaining the Democratic Trust Conundrum. The Source of Institutional Trust in the Reunited Germany." *International Social Science Review* 83, no. 1–2:3–26. https://www.jstor.org/stable/41889.

Grüne, Anne, and Dirk-Claas Ulrich. 2012. "Editorial: (De)-Westernizing Media and Journalism Studies: Demarcating, Transcending and Subverting Borders." *Global Media Journal: German Edition* 2, no. 2:1–10. URN:nbn:de:gbv:547-201200201.

Guerrero, Manuel A., and Mireya Márquez-Ramírez. 2014a. "The 'Captured-Liberal'-Model: Media Systems, Journalism and Communication Policies in Latin America." *International Journal of Hispanic Media* 7:1–12.

——, eds. 2014b. *Media Systems and Communication Policies in Latin America*. New York: Palgrave Macmillan.

Guðmundsson, Birgir, and Sigurður Kristinsson. 2017. "Journalistic Professionalism in Iceland: A Framework for Analysis and an Assessment." *Journalism* (2017): 1–20. http://dx.doi.org/10.1177/1464884917695416.

Gurevitch, Michael, and Jay G. Blumler. 1990. "Comparative Research: The Extending Frontier." In *New Directions in Political Communication: A Resource Book*, edited by David L. Swanson and Dan Nimmo, 305–25. Newbury Park, Calif.: Sage.

——. 2004. "State of the Art of Comparative Political Communication Research: Poised for Maturity?" In *Comparing Political Communication: Theories, Cases, and Challenges*, edited by Frank Esser and Barbara Pfetsch, 325–43. New York: Cambridge University Press.

Haagerup, Ulrik. 2014. *Constructive News: Why Negativity Destroys the Media and Democracy—and How to Improve Journalism of Tomorrow*. Copenhagen: InnoVatio.

Hachten, William A. 1981. *The World News Prism: Changing Media, Clashing Ideologies*. Ames: Iowa State University Press.

Hall, Peter A., and Rosemary C. R. Taylor. 1996. "Political Science and the Three New Institutionalisms." *Political Studies* 44, no. 5:936–57. https://doi.org/10.1111/j.1467-9248.1996.tb00343.x.

Hall, Stuart. 1992. "The West and the Rest: Discourse and Power." In *Formations of Modernity*, edited by Stuart Hall and Bram Gieben, 275–331. Cambridge: Polity Press.

——. 1997. "The Work of Representation." In *Representation: Cultural Representations and Signifying Practices*, edited by Stuart Hall, 13–74. Sage: London.

Hallin, Daniel C. 2000. "Media, Political Power, and Democratization in Mexico." In *De-Westernizing Media Studies*, edited by James Curran and Myung-Jin Park, 97–110. London: Routledge.

Hallin, Daniel C., and Paolo Mancini. 2004. *Comparing Media Systems: Three Models of Media and Politics*. New York: Cambridge University Press.

——, eds. 2012a. *Comparing Media Systems Beyond the Western World*. Cambridge: Cambridge University Press.

——. 2012b. "Comparing Media Systems: A Response to Critics." In *Handbook of Comparative Communication Research*, edited by Frank Esser and Thomas Hanitzsch, 207–20. London: Routledge.

——. 2017. "Ten Years After Comparing Media Systems: What Have We Learned?" *Political Communication* 34, no. 2:155–171. https://doi.org/10.1080/10584609.2016.1233158

Hallin, Daniel C., and Stylianos Papathanassopoulos. 2002. "Political Clientelism and the Media: Southern Europe and Latin America in Comparative Perspective." *Media, Culture & Society* 24, no. 2:175–195. https://doi.org/10.1177/016344370202400202.

Halloran, James D. 1998. "Social Science, Communication Research and the Third World." *Media Development* 45, no. 2:43–46. www.infoamerica.org/documentos_pdf/halloran_1.pdf.

Hamada, Basyouni I. 2008. "Satellite Television and Public Sphere in Egypt: Is There a Link?" *Global Media Journal* 7. Accessed February 19, 2018. http://www.globalmediajournal.com/open-access/satellite-television-and-public-sphere-in-egypt-is-there-a-link.php?aid=35196.

Hamdy, Naila, and Ehab H. Gomaa. 2012. "Framing the Egyptian Uprising in Arabic Language Newspapers and Social Media." *Journal of Communication* 62, no. 2:195–211. https://doi.org/10.1111/j.1460-2466.2012.01637.x.

Hanitzsch, Thomas. 2006. "Selling the Autonomy of Journalism: The Malpractice of Corruption Among Indonesian Journalists." In *Issues and Challenges in Asian Journalism*, edited by Hao Xiaoming and Sunanda K. Datta-Ray, 169–88. Singapore: Marshall Cavendish Academic.

——. 2007. "Deconstructing Journalism Culture: Towards a Universal Theory." *Communication Theory* 17, no. 4:367–85. https://doi.org/10.1111/j.1468-2885.2007.00303.x.

——. 2008. "Comparing Journalism Across Cultural Boundaries: State of the Art, Strategies, Problems and Solutions." In *Global Journalism Research: Theories, Methods, Findings, Future*, edited by Martin Löffelholz and Daniel Weaver, 93–105. Oxford: Blackwell.

——. 2009. "Comparative Journalism Studies." In *Handbook of Journalism Studies*, edited by Karin Wahl-Jorgensen and Thomas Hanitzsch, 413–27. New York: Routledge.

——. 2011. "Populist Disseminators, Detached Watchdogs, Critical Change Agents and Opportunist Facilitators: Professional Milieus, the Journalistic Field and Autonomy in 18 Countries." *International Communication Gazette* 73, no.6:477–94. https://doi.org/10.1177/1748048511412279.

——. 2013. "Comparative Journalism Research: Mapping a Growing Field." *Australian Journalism Review* 35, no. 2:9–19. https://search.informit.com.au/documentSumm ary;dn=843479898465412;res=IELAPA.

Hanitzsch, Thomas, and Rosa Berganza. 2012. "Explaining Journalists' Trust in Public Institutions Across 20 Countries: Media Freedom, Corruption and Ownership Matter Most." *Journal of Communication* 62, no. 5:794–814. https://doi.org/10.1111/j .1460-2466.2012.01663.x.

——. 2014. "Political Trust Among Journalists. Comparative Evidence from 21 Countries." In *Comparing Political Communication Across Time and Space*, edited by María J. Canei and Katrin Voltmer, 153–74. Basingstoke, U.K.: Palgrave McMillan.

Hanitzsch, Thomas, and Wolfgang Donsbach. 2012. "Comparing Journalism Cultures." In *The Handbook of Comparative Communication Research*, edited by Frank Esser and Thomas Hanitzsch, 262–75. New York: Routledge.

Hanitzsch, Thomas, and Folker Hanusch. 2012. "Does Gender Determine Journalists' Professional Views? A Re-Assessment Based on Cross-National Evidence." *European Journal of Communication* 27, no. 3:257–77. https://doi.org/10.1177/0267323112454804.

Hanitzsch, Thomas, and Claudia Mellado. 2011. "What Shapes the News Around the World? How Journalists in Eighteen Countries Perceive Influences on Their Work." *International Journal of Press/Politics* 16, no. 3:404–26. https://doi.org/10.1177 /1940161211407334.

Hanitzsch, Thomas, and Tim P. Vos. 2017. "Journalistic Roles and the Struggle Over Institutional Identity: The Discursive Constitution of Journalism." *Communication Theory* 27, no. 2:115–35. https://doi.org/10.1111/comt.12112.

——. 2018. "Journalism Beyond Democracy: A New Look into Journalistic Roles in Political and Everyday Life." *Journalism* 19, no. 2:146–64. https://doi.org/10.1177 /1464884916673386.

Hanitzsch, Thomas, Maria Anikina, Rosa Berganza, Incilay Cangoz, Mihai Coman, Basyouni Hamada, Folker Hanusch, et al. 2010. "Modeling Perceived Influences on Journalism: Evidence from a Cross-National Survey of Journalists." *Journalism & Mass Communication Quarterly* 87, no. 1:7–24. https://doi.org/10.1177/10776990 1008700101.

Hanitzsch, Thomas, Folker Hanusch, and Corinna Lauerer. 2016. "Setting the Agenda, Influencing Public Opinion, and Advocating for Social Change: Determinants of Journalistic Interventionism in 21 Countries." *Journalism Studies* 17, no. 1:1–20. https://doi.org/10.1080/1461670X.2014.959815.

Hanitzsch, Thomas, Folker Hanusch, Claudia Mellado, María Anikina, Rosa Berganza, Incilay Cangoz, Mihai Coman, et al. 2011. "Mapping Journalism Cultures Across Nations: A Comparative Study of 18 Countries." *Journalism Studies* 12, no. 3:273–93. https://doi.org/10.1080/1461670X.2010.512502.

Hanitzsch, Thomas, Josef Seethaler, Elizabeth A. Skewes, María Anikina, Rosa Berganza, Incilay Cangoz, Mihai Coman, et al. 2012. "Worlds of Journalism: Journalistic Cultures, Professional Autonomy, and Perceived Influences Across 18 Nations." In *The Global Journalist in the 21st Century*, edited by David H. Weaver and Lars Willnat, 473–94. New York: Routledge.

Hanitzsch, Thomas, Arjen Van Dalen, and Nina Steindl. 2018. "Caught in the Nexus: A Comparative and Longitudinal Analysis of Public Trust in the Press." *International Journal of Press/Politics* 23, no. 1:3–23. https://doi.org/10.1177/1940161217740695.

Hantrais, Linda. 1999. "Cross Contextualization in Cross-National Comparative Research." *International Journal of Social Research Methodology* 2, no. 2:93–108. https://doi.org/10.1080/136455799295078.

Hantrais, Linda, and Steen Mangen. 2007. *Cross-National Research: Methodology and Practice*. London: Routledge.

Hanusch, Folker. 2013. "Journalists in Times of Change: Evidence from a New Survey of Australia's Journalistic Workforce." *Australian Journalism Review* 35, no. 11:29–42.

——. 2017. "Web Analytics and the Functional Differentiation of Journalism Cultures: Individual, Organizational and Platform-Specific Influences on Newswork." *Information, Communication & Society* 20, no. 10:1571–86. https://doi.org/10.1080/1369118X.2016.1241294.

Hanusch, Folker, and Axel Bruns. 2017. "Journalistic Branding on Twitter: A Representative Study of Australian Journalists' Profile Descriptions." *Digital Journalism* 5, no. 1:26–43. https://doi.org/10.1080/21670811.2016.1152161.

Hanusch, Folker, and Thomas Hanitzsch. 2013. "Mediating Orientation and Self-Expression in the World of Consumption: Australian and German Lifestyle Journalists' Professional Views." *Media, Culture & Society* 35, no. 8:943–59. https://doi.org/10.1177/0163443713501931.

——. 2017. "Introduction: Comparing Journalistic Cultures Across Nations." *Journalism Studies* 18, no. 5:525–35. https://doi.org/10.1080/1461670X.2017.1280229.

Hanusch, Folker, Thomas Hanitzsch, and Corinna Lauerer. 2017. "'How Much Love Are You Going to Give this Brand?' Lifestyle Journalists on Commercial Influences in Their Work." *Journalism* 18, no. 2:141–58. https://doi.org/10.1177/1464884915608818.

Hanusch, Folker, and Charu Uppal. 2015. "Combining Detached Watchdog Journalism with Development Ideals: An Exploration of Fijian Journalism Culture." *International Communication Gazette* 77, no. 6:557–76. https://doi.org/10.1177/1748048515597873.

Hanusch, Folker, and Tim P. Vos. 2019. "Charting the Development of a Field: A Systematic Review of Comparative Studies of Journalism." *International Communication Gazette*. https://doi.org/10.1177/1748048518822606.

Hardy, Jonathan. 2008. *Western Media Systems*. New York: Routledge.

——. 2012. "Comparing Media Systems." In *The Handbook of Comparative Communication Research*, edited by Frank Esser and Thomas Hanitzsch, 185–206. New York: Routledge.

Hare, Kristen. 2016. "Newspaper Reporter Is the 'Worst Job,' Study Says. Do You Agree?" *Poynter*. April 13, 2016. https://www.poynter.org/news/newspaper-reporter-worst-job-study-says-do-you-agree.

Harlow, Summer, and Ramón Salaverría. 2016. "Regenerating Journalism: Exploring the "Alternativeness" and "Digital-Ness" of Online-Native Media in Latin America." *Digital Journalism* 4, no. 8:1–19. https://doi.org/10.1080/21670811.2015.1135752.

Harrison, Jackie. 2000. *Terrestrial TV News in Britain: The Culture of Production*. Manchester, U.K.: Manchester University Press.

Harro-Loit, Halliki. 2015. "Journalists' Views About Accountability to Different Societal Groups." *Journal of Media Ethics* 1, no. 1:31–43.

Hartley, John. 2000. "Communicative Democracy in a Redactional Society: The Future of Journalism Studies." *Journalism* 1, no. 1:39–48. https://doi.org/10.1177/146488490000100107.

Hartsock, John. 2015. "Journalism and the Aesthetics of Experience: Svetlana Alexievich." *Literary Journalism Studies* 7, no. 2:36–49.

Haruna, Mahama. 2009. "Role of Journalism in the Development of Ghana." *Modern Ghana*, March 22. https://www.modernghana.com/news/207542/1/role-of-journalism-in-the-development-of-ghana.html.

Hedman, Ulrika, and Monika Djerf-Pierre. 2013. "The Social Journalist: Embracing the Social Media Life or Creating a New Digital Divide?" *Digital Journalism* 1, no. 3:368–85. https://doi.org/10.1080/21670811.2013.776804.

Hellmueller, Lea. 2017. "Gatekeeping Beyond Geographical Borders: Developing an Analytical Model of Transnational Journalism Cultures." *International Communication Gazette* 79, no. 1:3-25. https://doi.org/10.1177/1748048516656304.

Hermans, Lisbeth, Maurice Vergeer, and Leen d'Haenens. 2009. "Internet in the Daily Life of Journalists: Explaining the Use of the Internet by Work-Related Characteristics and Professional Opinions." *Journal of Computer Mediated Communication* 15, no. 1:138–57. https://doi.org/10.1111/j.1083-6101.2009.01497.x.

Hermida, Alfred. 2012. "Social Journalism: Exploring How Social Media Is Shaping Journalism." In *The Handbook of Global Online Journalism*, edited by Eugenia Siapera and Andreas Veglis, 309–28. Malden, Mass.: Wiley-Blackwell.

Hermida, Alfred, Seth Lewis, and Rodrigo Zamith. 2012. "Sourcing the Arab Spring: A Case Study of Andy Carvin's Sources During the Tunisian and Egyptian Revolutions." *Journal of Computer-Mediated Communication* 19, no. 3:479–99. https://doi.org/10.1111/jcc4.12074.

Herscovitz, Heloiza G. 2004. Brazilian Journalists' Perceptions of Media Roles, Ethics and Foreign Influences on Brazilian Journalism. *Journalism Studies* 5, no. 1:71–86. https://doi.org/10.1080/1461670032000174756.

Heuvel, Jon Vanden, and Everette E. Dennis. 1993. *The Unfolding Lotus: East Asia's Changing Media*. New York: Freedom Forum Media Studies Center, Columbia University.

Hirst, Martin, and Greg Treadwell. 2011. "Blogs Bother Me. Social Media, Journalism Students and the Curriculum." *Journalism Practice* 5, no. 4:446–61. https://doi.org /10.1080/17512786.2011.555367.

Hofstede, Geert. 1980. *Culture's Consequences: International Differences in Work-Related Values*. Thousand Oaks, Calif.: Sage.

——. 1998. "A Case for Comparing Apples with Oranges: International Differences." In *Values and Attitudes Across Nations and Time*, edited by Masamichi Sasaki, 16–31. Leiden: Brill.

——. 2001. *Culture's Consequences: Comparing Values, Behaviors, Institutions and Organizations Across Nations*. Thousand Oaks, Calif.: Sage Publications.

Hollings, James, Thomas Hanitzsch, and Ravi Balasubramanian. 2017. "Risky Choices? Modelling Journalists' Perceptions of Aggressive Newsgathering Practices." *Journalism Studies*, 1–18. https://doi.org/10.1080/1461670X.2017.1353431.

Hollings, James, Folker Hanusch, Ravi Balasubramanian, and Geoff Lealand. 2016. "Causes for Concern: The State of New Zealand Journalism in 2015." *Pacific Journalism Review: Te Koakoa* 22, no. 2:122–38. https://doi.org/10.24135/pjr.v22i2.29.

Hovden, Jan Fredrik. 2016. "Journalism Re-Examined: Changing Journalistic Professionalism?" In *Journalism Re-Examined: Digital Challenges and Professional Orientations (Lessons from Northern Europe)*, edited by Martin Eide, Helle Sjøvaag, and Leif Ove Larsen. Chicago: University of Chicago Press.

Hovden, Jan Fredrik, Gunnar Nygren, and Henrika Zilliacus-Tikkanaen, eds. 2016. *Becoming a Journalist. Journalism Education in the NordicCcountries*. Göteborg: Nordicom.

Hudson, John. 2006. "Institutional Trust and Subjective Well-Being Across the EU." *Kyklos* 59, no. 1:43–62. https://doi.org/10.1111/j.1467-6435.2006.00319.x.

Hughes, Sallie. 2006. *Newsrooms in Conflict: Journalism and the Democratization of Mexico*. Pittsburgh: University of Pittsburgh Press.

Hughes, Sallie, and Chappell H. Lawson. 2004. "Propaganda and Crony Capitalism: Partisan Bias in Mexican Television News." *Latin American Research Review* 39, no. 3:81–105. https://doi.org/10.1353/lar.2004.0050.

Hughes, Sallie, and Mireya Márquez-Ramírez. 2017. "How Unsafe Contexts and Overlapping Risks Influence Journalism Practice: Evidence from a Survey of Mexican Journalists." In *The Assault on Journalism. Building Knowledge to Protect Freedom of Expression*, edited by Ulla Carlsson and Reeta Pöyhtäri, 303–18. Göteborg: Nordicom.

——. 2018. "Local-Level Authoritarianism, Democratic Normative Aspirations, and Antipress Harassment: Predictors of Threats to Journalists in Mexico." *International Journal of Press/Politics*, 23 no. 4:539–60.

Hughes, Sallie, and Paola Prado. 2011. "Media Diversity and Social Inequality in Latin America." In *The Great Gap: Inequality and the Politics of Redistribution in Latin America*, edited by Merike Blofield, 109–46. University Park: Pennsylvania State University Press.

Hughes, Sallie, Miguel Garcés, Mireya Márquez-Ramírez, M., and Jesús Arroyave. 2017. "Rethinking Professional Autonomy: Autonomy to Develop and to Publish News in Mexico and Colombia." *Journalism* 18, no. 8:956–76. https://doi.org/10.1177/146 4884916659409

Hughes, Sallie, Claudia Mellado, Jesus Arroyave, Jose L. Benitez, Arnold de Beer, Miguel Garcés, Katharina Lang, and Mireya Márquez-Ramírez. 2017. "Expanding Influences Research to Insecure Democracies: How Violence, Public Insecurity, Economic Inequality and Uneven Democratic Performance Shape Journalists' Perceived Work Environments." *Journalism Studies* 18, no. 5:645–65.

Huszka, Béata. 2017. "Human Rights on the Losing End of EU Enlargement: The Case of Serbia." *JCMS: Journal of Common Market Studies* 56, no. 2:352–67. https://doi.org /10.1111/jcms.12604.

Inglehart, Ronald. 1977. *The Silent Revolution: Changing Values and Political Styles Among Western Public*. Princeton, N.J.: Princeton University Press.

——. 1997. *Modernization and Postmodernization: Cultural, Economic and Political Change in 43 Societies*. Princeton, N.J.: Princeton University Press.

——. 1999. "Trust, Well-Being and Democracy." In *Democracy and Trust*, edited by Mark Warren, 88–120. Cambridge, Mass.: Cambridge University Press.

——. 2006. "Mapping Global Values." *Comparative Sociology* 5, no. 2:115–36. https:// doi.org/10.1163/156913306778667401.

Inglehart, Ronald, and Christian Welzel. 2005. *Modernization, Cultural Change and Democracy*. Cambridge: Cambridge University Press.

International Federation of Journalists (IFJ). 2016. *World Day for Decent Work*. 06.10.2016. Accessed February 26, 2018. http://www.ifj.org/nc/news-single-view /backpid/51/article/world-day-for-decent-work-secure-collective-bargaining-for -all-journalists-says-the-ifj/.

International Labour Organization (ILO). 2017. "ILO Labour Force Estimates and Projections: 1990–2030 (2017 Edition)." Accessed January 9, 2018. http://www.ilo.org /ilostat.

International Telecommunication Union (ITU). 2015. *Measuring the Information Society Report 2015: Executive Summary*. Geneva: International Telecommunication Union.

Ireri, Kioko, Eannes Ongus, Edna Laboso, Kangai Mwiti, and Jared Onsongo. 2018. "First Level Agenda Setting: A Study of Press vs. Public Opinion in Kenya." *African Journalism Studies* 38, no. 3–4:1–24. https://doi.org/10.1080/23743670.2017 .1364654.

Jain, Savyasaachi. 2015. "India: Multiple Media Explosions." In *Mapping BRICS Media*, edited by Kaarle Nordenstreng and Daya Kishan Thussu, 145–64. London, Routledge.

Janowitz, Morris. 1975. "Professional Models in Journalism: The Gatekeeper and the Advocate." *Journalism Quarterly* 52, no. 4:618–26. https://doi.org/10.1177/107769907505200402.

Jarvis, Cheryl Burke, Scott B. MacKenzie, and Philip M. Podsakoff. 2003. "A Critical Review of Construct Indicators and Measurement Model Misspecification in Marketing and Consumer Research." *Journal of Consumer Research* 30, no. 2:199–218. https://doi.org/10.1086/376806.

Jones, Paul K., and Michael Pusey. 2010. "Political Communication and 'Media System': The Australian Canary." *Media, Culture & Society* 32, no. 3:451–71. https://doi.org/10.1177/0163443709361172.

Josephi, Beate. 2005. "Journalism in the Global Age: Between Normative and Empirical." *Gazette* 67, no. 6:575–90. https://doi.org/10.1177/0016549205057564.

——. 2009. "Journalists: International Profiles." In *Global Journalism: Topical Issues and Media Systems*, edited by Arnold S. de Beer and John Calhoun Merrill, 143–52. Boston: Pearson.

——, ed. 2010. *Journalism Education in Countries with Limited Media Freedom*. New York: Peter Lang.

——. 2013. "How Much Democracy Does Journalism Need?" *Journalism* 14, no. 4:474–89. https://doi.org/10.1177/1464884912464172.

——. 2017. "Journalists for a Young Democracy." *Journalism Studies* 18, no. 4:495–510. https://doi.org/10.1080/1461670X.2015.1065199.

Josephi, Beate, and Ian Richards. 2010. "The Australian Journalist in the 21st Century." In *The Global Journalist in the 21st Century*, edited by David H. Weaver and Lars Willnat, 115–25. New York: Routledge.

Juntunen, Laura. 2010. "Explaining the Need for Speed: Speed and Competition as Challenges to Journalism Ethics." In *The Rise of 24-hour News Television: Global Perspectives*, edited by Stephen Cushion and Justin Lewis, 167–80. New York: Peter Lang.

Kalyango, Yusuf, Jr., Folker Hanusch, Jyotika Ramaprasad, Terje Skjerdal, Mohd Safar Hasim, Nurhaya Muchtar, Mohammad Sahid Ullah, Levi Zeleza Manda, and Sarah Bomkapre Kamara. 2017. "Journalists' Development Journalism Role Perceptions: Select Countries in Southeast Asia, South Asia, and Sub-Saharan Africa." *Journalism Studies* 18, no. 5:576–94. http://dx.doi.org/10.1080/1461670X.2016.1254060.

Kang, Jay Caspian. 2013. "Should Reddit Be Blamed for the Spreading of a Smear?" *New York Times Magazine*, July 25. http://www.nytimes.com/2013/07/28/magazine/should-reddit-be-blamed-for-the-spreading-of-a-smear.html?pagewanted=all&_r=0.

Keeble, Richard. 2005. "Journalism Ethics: Towards an Orwellian Critique?" In *Journalism: Critical Issues*, edited by Stuart Allan, 54–66. Maidenhead, U.K.: Open University Press.

Kepplinger, Hans M., Hans-Bernd Brosius, and Joachim F. Staab. 1991. "Instrumental Actualization: A Theory of Mediated Conflicts." *European Journal of Communication* 6, no. 3:263–90. https://doi.org/10.1177/0267323191006003002.

Kharel, P. 1996. "Asian Values in Journalism: Do They Exist?" In *Asian Values in Journalism*, edited by Murray Masterton, 30–34. Singapore: AMIC.

Kian, Edward M., and Marie Hardin. 2009. "Framing of Sport Coverage Based on the Sex of Sports Writers: Female Journalists Counter the Traditional Gendering of Media Coverage." *International Journal of Sport Communication* 2, no. 2:185–204. https://doi.org/10.1123/ijsc.2.2.185.

Kim, Kyung-Hee. 2006. "Obstacles to the Success of Female Journalists in Korea." *Media, Culture & Society* 28, no. 1:123–41. https://doi.org/10.1177/0163443706059578.

Kim, Tae Guk. 1976. "Formal Journalism Education Not Widely Accepted in Japan." *Journalism Educator* 31, no. 3:45–47. https://doi.org/10.1177/107769587603100314.

Klaidman Stephen, and Tom L. Beauchamp. 1987. *The Virtuous Journalist*. New York: Oxford University Press.

Klasen, Stephan. 2006. "UNDP's Gender-Related Measures: Some Conceptual Problems and Possible Solutions." *Journal of Human Development* 7, no. 2:243–74. https://doi.org/10.1080/14649880600768595.

Knack, Stephen, and Philip Keefer. 1997. "Does Social Capital Have a Payoff? A Cross-Country Investigation." *Quarterly Journal of Economics* 112, no. 4:1251–88. https://doi.org/10.1162/003355300555475.

Köcher, Renate. 1986. "Bloodhounds or Missionaries: Role Definitions of German and British Journalists." *European Journal of Communication* 1, no. 1:43–64. https://doi.org/10.1080/14649880600768595.

Kohlberg, Lawrence, and Richard H. Hersh. 1977. "Moral Development: A Review of the Theory." *Theory Into Practice* 16, no. 2:53–59. https://doi.org/10.1080/00405847709542675.

Kohn, Melvin L. 1989. "Cross-National Research as an Analytic Strategy." In *Cross-National Research in Sociology*, edited by Melvin L. Kohn, 77–102. Newbury Park, Calif.: Sage.

Koljonen, Kari. 2013. "The Shift from High to Liquid Ideals: Making Sense of Journalism and Its Change Through a Multidimensional Model." *Nordicom Review* 34, special issue: 141–54.

Kotzian, Peter. 2011. "Public Support for Liberal Democracy." *International Political Science Review* 3, no. 1:23–41. https://doi.org/10.1177/0192512110375938.

Kovach, Bill, and Tom Rosenstiel. 2001. *The Elements of Journalism*. London: Atlantic Books.

Kraidy, Marwan. M. 2002. "Hybridity in Cultural Globalization." *Communication Theory* 12, no. 3:316–39. https://doi.org/10.1111/j.1468-2885.2002.tb00272.x/

Krastev, Ivan. 2011. "Paradoxes of the New Autoritarianism." *Journal of Democracy* 22, no. 2:5–16. https://doi.org/10.1353/jod.2011.0027.

Kunczik, Michael. 1988. *Concepts of Journalism North and South*. Bonn: Concepts of Journalism North and South.

Kunioka, Todd, and Gary M. Woller. 1999. "In (a) Democracy We Trust: Social and Economic Determinants of Support for Democratic Procedures in Central and Eastern

Europe." *Journal of Socio-Economics* 28, no. 5:577–96. https://doi.org/10.1016/S1053 -5357(99)00035-9.

Láb, Filip, and Alice Němcová Tejkalová. 2016. "Czech Journalists: Little Guidance on Ethical Issues." Paper presented at the 2016 IAMCR Conference, Leicester, U.K.

Ladd, Jonathan M. 2012. *Why Americans Hate the Media and How It Matters.* Princeton, N.J.: Princeton University Press.

Lambeth, Edmund B. 1992. *Committed Journalism: An Ethic for the Profession.* Bloomington: Indiana University Press.

Lasorsa, Dominic L., Seth C. Lewis, and Avery E. Holton. 2011. "Normalizing Twitter: Journalism Practice in an Emerging Communication Space." *Journalism Studies* 13, no. 1:19–36. https://doi.org/10.1080/1461670x.2011.571825.

Lauk, Epp. 2008. "How Will It All Unfold? Media Systems and Journalism Cultures in Post-Communist Countries." In *Finding the Right Place on the Map: Central and Eastern European Media Change in a Global Perspective,* edited by Karol Jakubowicz and Miklós Sükösd, 193–212. Bristol, U.K.: IntellectBooks.

Lauk, Epp, and Halliki Harro-Loit. 2016. "Journalistic Autonomy as a Professional Value and Element of Journalism Culture: The European Perspective." *International Journal of Communication* 11, 1956–1974.

Lee, Chin-Chuan. 2001. "Servants of the State or the Market? Media and Journalists in China." In *Media Occupations and Professions: A Reader,* edited by Jeremy Tunstall, 240–52. New York: Oxford University Press.

Lee, Eun-Ju, and Edson Tandoc. 2017. "When News Meets the Audience: How Audience Feedback Online Affects News Production and Consumption." *Human Communication Research* 43, no. 4:436–49. https://doi.org/10.1111/hcre.12123.

Lee, Seow Ting. 2004. "Lying to Tell the Truth: Journalists and the Social Context of Deception." *Mass Communication and Society* 7, no. 1:97–120. https://doi.org/10.1207 /s15327825mcs0701_7.

——. 2005. "Predicting Tolerance of Journalistic Deception." *Journal of Mass Media Ethics* 20, no. 1:22–42. https://doi.org/10.1207/s15327728jmme2001_3.

Lengauer, Günther, Frank Esser, and Rosa Berganza. 2012. "Negativity in Political News: A Review of Concepts, Operationalizations and Key Findings." *Journalism* 13, no. 2:179–202. https://doi.org/10.1177/1464884911427800.

Levy, David A. L., and Rasmus Kleis Nielsen. 2010. *The Changing Business of Journalism and Its Implications for Democracy.* Oxford: Reuters Institute for the Study of Journalism, University of Oxford.

Lewis, Seth C. 2012. "The Tension Between Professional Control and Open Participation: Journalism and Its Boundaries." *Information, Communication & Society* 15, no. 6:836–66. https://doi.org/10.1080/1369118X.2012.674150.

Li, Shuang. 2012. "A New Generation of Lifestyle Magazine Journalism in China: The Professional Approach." *Journalism Practice* 6, no. 1:122–37. https://doi.org/10.1080 /17512786.2011.622901.

Livingstone, Sonia. 2003. "On the Challenges of Cross-national Comparative Media Research." *European Journal of Communication* 18, no. 4:477–500. https://doi.org/10.1177/0267323103184003.

Livingstone, Sonia. 2012. "Challenges to Comparative Research in a Globalizing Media Landscape." In *Handbook of Comparative Communication Research*, edited by Frank Esser and Thomas Hanitzsch, 415–29. New York: Routledge.

Lobo, Paula, Maria J. Silveirinha, Marisa Torres da Silva, and Filipa Subtil. 2017. "'In Journalism, We Are All Men.' Material Voices in the Production of Gender Meanings." *Journalism Practice* 18, 9:1148–66. https://doi.org/10.1080/1461670X.2015.1111161.

Lodamo, Berhanu, and Terje S. Skjerdal. 2009. "Freebies and Brown Envelopes in Ethiopian Journalism." *Ecquid Novi: African Journalism Studies* 30, no. 2:134–54. https://doi.org/10.1080/02560054.2009.9653399.

Lodola, Germán, and Mitchell A. Seligson. 2012. *The Political Culture of Democracy in Argentina and in the Americas, 2012: Towards Equality of Opportunity*. Buenos Aires: Universidad Torcuato Di Tella.

Lohner, Judith, Irene Neverla, and Sandra Banjac. 2017. "Structural Working Conditions of Journalism in Egypt, Kenya, Serbia and South Africa: Empirical Findings from Interviews with Journalists Reporting on Democratisation Conflicts." Working Paper. MeCoDEM.

Loo, Eric. 1996. "Value Formation in Journalism Education in Asia." In *Asian Values in Journalism*, edited by Murray Masterton, 114–23. Singapore: AMIC.

Loosen, Wiebke, and Jan-Hindrik Schmidt. 2012. "(Re-)Discovering the Audience: The Relationship Between Journalism and Audience in Networked Digital Media." *Information, Communication & Society* 15, no. 6:867–87. https://doi.org/10.1080/1369118X.2012.665467.

Lopes, Helena, Sérgio Lagoa, and Teresa Calapez. 2014. "Work Autonomy, Work Pressure, and Job Satisfaction: An Analysis of European Union Countries." *Economic and Labour Relations Review* 25, no. 2:306–26. https://doi.org/10.1177/1035304614533868.

Lowrey, Wilson, and Elina Erzikova. 2013. "One Profession, Multiple Identities: Russian Regional Reporters' Perceptions of the Professional Community." *Mass Communication & Society* 16, no. 5:639–60. https://doi.org/10.1080/15205436.2013.770031.

Lowrey, Wilson, and William Anderson. 2005. "The Journalist Behind the Curtain: Participatory Functions on the Internet and Their Impact on Perceptions of the Work of Journalism." *Journal of Computer-Mediated Communication* 10, no. 3. https://doi.org/10.1111/j.1083-6101.2005.tb00261.x.

Lucht, Tracy. 2016. "Job Satisfaction and Gender. Qualitative Differences at Iowa Newspapers." *Journalism Practice* 10, no. 3:405–23. https://doi.org/10.1080/17512786.2015.1025416.

Lühiste, Kadri. 2006. "Explaining Trust in Political Institutions: Some Illustrations from the Baltic States." *Communist and Post-Communist Studies* 39, no. 4:475–96. https://doi.org/10.1016/j.postcomstud.2006.09.001.

Luhmann, Niklas. 1979. *Trust and Power.* Chichester, U.K.: Wiley.

Lukina, Maria, and Elena Vartanova. 2017. "Journalism Education in Russia: How the Academy and the Media Collide, Cooperate, and Coexist." In *Global Journalism Education*, edited by Robyn S. Goodman and Elanie Steyn, 155–74. Austin: Knight Center for Journalism in the Americas, University of Texas at Austin.

Luljak, Tom. 2000. "The Routine Nature of Journalistic Deception." In *Holding the Media Accountable: Citizens, Ethics, and the Law,* edited by David Pritchard, 11–26. Bloomington: Indiana University Press.

Lynch, Jake, and Annabel McGoldrick. 2005. *Peace Journalism.* Stroud: Hawthorn Press.

MacGregor, Phil. 2007. "Tracking the Online Audience: Metric Data Start a Subtle Revolution." *Journalism Studies* 8, no. 2:280–98. https://doi.org/10.1080/14616700601148879.

Machill, Marcel, and Markus Beiler. 2009. "The Importance of the Internet for Journalistic Research: A Multi-Method Study of the Research Performed by Journalists Working for Daily Newspapers, Radio, Television and Online." *Journalism Studies* 10, no. 2:178–203. https://doi.org/10.1080/14616700802337768.

Mahoney, James, and Kathleen Thelen. 2010. *Explaining Institutional Change: Ambiguity, Agency, and Power.* Cambridge: Cambridge University Press.

Mair, Peter. 2006. *Polity Scepticism, Party Failings, and the Challenge to European Democracy.* Wassenaar, Netherlands: NIAS.

Mancini, Paolo. 1993. "Between Trust and Suspicion: How Political Journalists Solve the Dilemma." *European Journal of Communication* 8, no. 1:33–51. https://doi.org/10.1177/0267323193008001002.

——. 2013. "What Scholars Can Learn from the Crisis of Journalism." *International Journal of Communication* 7:127–36.

——. 2015. "The News Media Between Volatility and Hybridization." In *Media and Politics in New Democracies: Europe in a Comparative Perspective*, edited by Jan Zielonka, 28–34. Oxford: Oxford University Press.

Manda, Levi Zeleza. 2015. "Factors Affecting the Quality of Malawian Journalism." *African Journalism Studies* 36, no. 1:156–62. https://doi.org/10.1080/23743670.2015.1008184.

Mann, Leon. 1974. "Counting the Crowd: Effects of Editorial Policy on Estimates." *Journalism Quarterly* 51, no. 2:278–85. https://doi.org/10.1177/107769907405100212.

Manning, Paul. 2013. "Financial Journalism, News Sources and the Banking Crisis." *Journalism* 14, no. 2:173–89. https://doi.org/10.1177/1464884912448915.

Martin, L. John, and Anju Grover Chaudhary. 1983. *Comparative Mass Media Systems.* New York: Longman.

Massey, Brian L., and Li-jing Arthur Chang. 2002. "Location Asian Values in Asian Journalism. A Content Analysis of Web Newspapers." *Journal of Communication* 52, no. 4:987–1003. https://doi.org/10.1111/j.1460-2466.2002.tb02585.x.

Masterton, Murray, ed. 1996. *Asian Values in Journalism.* Singapore: AMIC.

Mastrini, Guillermo-Néstor, and Martín Becerra. 2011. "Structure, Concentration and Changes of the Cedia System in the Southern Cone of Latin America." *Revista Comunicar* 18, no. 36:51–59. http://hdl.handle.net/10760/17221.

Mayer, Roger C., James H. Davis, and F. David Schoorman. 1995. "An Integrative Model of Organizational Trust." *Academy of Management Review* 20, no. 3:709–34. https://doi.org/10.5465/AMR.1995.9508080335.

McAdam, Dough. 2010. *Political Process and the Development of Black Insurgency, 1930–1970*. Chicago: University of Chicago Press.

McCargo, Duncan. 2000. *Politics and the Press in Thailand*. New York: Routledge.

McChesney, Robert W. 1999. *Rich Media, Poor Democracy: Communication Politics in Dubious Times*. Urbana: University of Illinois Press.

McChesney, Robert W., and John Nichols. 2010. *The Death and Life of American Journalism: The Media Revolution That Will Begin the World Again*. New York: Nation Books.

McChesney, Robert W., and Victor Pickard, eds. 2011. *Will the Last Reporter Please Turn out the Lights: The Collapse of Journalism and What Can be Done to Fix It*. New York: New Press.

McDevitt, Michael. 2003. "In Defense of Autonomy: A Critique of the Public Journalism Critique." *Journal of Communication* 53, no. 1:155–60. https://doi.org/10.1111/j.1460-2466.2003.tb03011.x.

McLeod, Jack M., and Searle E. Hawley Jr. 1964. "Professionalization Among Newsmen." *Journalism Quarterly* 41, no. 4:529–77. https://doi.org/10.1177/107769906404100406.

McManus, John H. 1997. "Who's Responsible for Journalism?" *Journal of Mass Media Ethics* 12, no. 1:5–17. https://doi.org/10.1207/s15327728jmme1201_1.

McManus, John H. 2009. "The Commercialization of News." In *The Handbook of Journalism Studies*, edited by Karin Wahl-Jorgensen and Thomas Hanitzsch, 218–35. New York: Routledge.

McQuail, Denis. 1992. *Media Performance: Mass Communication and the Public Interest*. London: Sage.

——. 1994. *Mass Communication Theory: An Introduction*. 3rd ed. London: Sage.

——. 2000. *McQuail's Mass Communication Theory*. London: Sage.

Mehra, Achal. 1989. *Press Systems in ASEAN States*. Singapore: AMIC.

Melki, Jad. 2009. "Journalism and Media Studies in Lebanon." *Journalism Studies* 10, no. 5:672–90. https://doi.org/10.1080/14616700902920174.

Mellado, Claudia. 2012. "The Chilean Journalist." In *The Global Journalist in the 21st Century*, edited by David H. Weaver and Lars Willnat, 382–99. New York: Routledge.

Mellado, Claudia, Folker Hanusch, Maria Luisa Humanes, Sergio Roses, Fábio Pereira, Lyuba Yez, Salvador De León, Mireya Márquez, Federico Subervi, and Vinzenz Wyss. 2013. "The Pre-Socialization of Future Journalists: An Examination of Journalism Students' Professional Views in Seven Countries." *Journalism Studies* 14, no. 6:857–74. https://doi.org/10.1080/1461670X.2012.746006.

Mellado, Claudia, Lea Hellmueller, Mireya Márquez-Ramírez, Maria Luisa Humanes, Colin Sparks, Agnieszka Stepinska, Svetlana Pasti, et al. 2017. "The Hybridization of Journalistic Cultures: A Comparative Study of Journalistic Role Performance." *Journal of Communication* 67, no. 6:944–67. https://doi.org/10.1111/jcom.12339.

Mellado, Claudia, Sonia V. Moreira, Lagos, C., and María E. Hernandez. 2012. "Comparing Journalism Cultures in Latin America: The Case of Chile, Brazil and Mexico." *International Communication Gazette* 74, no. 1:60–77. https://doi.org/10.1177/1748048511426994.

Mellado, Claudia, and Arjen van Dalen. 2014. "Between Rhetoric and Practice: Explaining the Gap Between Role Conception and Performance in Journalism." *Journalism Studies* 15, no. 6:859–78. https://doi.org/10.1080/1461670X.2013.838046.

Merrill, John C. 1974. *The Imperative of Freedom: A Philosophy of Journalistic Autonomy.* New York: Hastings House.

——. 1989. *The Dialectic in Journalism: Toward a Responsible Use of Press Freedom.* Baton Rouge: Louisiana State University Press.

Meyen, Michael, and Claudia Riesmeyer. 2012. "Service Providers, Sentinels, and Traders: Journalists' Role Perceptions in the Early Twenty-first Century." *Journalism Studies* 13, no. 3:386–401. https://doi.org/10.1080/1461670X.2011.602909.

Meyen, Michael, and Nina Springer. 2009. *Freie Journalisten in Deutschland. Ein Report* (Freelance Journalists in Germany. A Report). Konstanz, Germany: UVK.

Meyers, Christopher, ed. 2010. *Journalism Ethics: A Philosophical Approach.* Oxford: Oxford University Press.

Mishler, William, and Richard Rose. 2001. "What Are the Origins of Political Trust? Testing Institutional and Cultural Theories in Post-Communist Societies." *Comparative Political Studies* 34, no. 1:30–62. https://doi.org/10.1177/0010414001034001002.

Misztal, Barbara. 1996. *Trust in Modern Societies: The Search for the Bases of Social Order.* Cambridge, Mass.: Blackwell.

Mitchelstein, Eugenia, and Pablo J. Boczkowski. 2009. "Between Tradition and Change." *Journalism* 10, no. 5:562–86. https://doi.org/10.1177/1464884909106533.

Mitteldeutscher Rundfunk (MDR). 2013. *Anne-Rose Neumann—Die erste Nachrichtensprecherin im Deutschen Fernsehen.* Accessed February 28, 2018. https://www.mdr.de/tv/programm/sendung650352.html.

Morrone, Adolfo, Noemi Tontoranelli, and Guilia Ranuzzi. 2009. "How Good Is Trust? Measuring Trust and Its Role for the Progress of Societies." *OECD Statistics Working Papers 2009*, no. 03. https://doi.org/10.1787/18152031.

Moy, Patricia, Michael Pfau, and LeeAnn Kahlor. 1999. "Media Use and Public Confidence in Democratic Institutions." *Journal of Broadcasting and Electronic Media* 43, no. 2:137–58. https://doi.org/10.1080/08838159909364481.

Muchtar, Nurhaya, and Thomas Hanitzsch. 2013. "Clash of Cultures: International Media Training and the Difficult Adoption of Western Journalism Practices Among Indonesian Radio Journalists." *Journalism Practice* 7, no. 2:184–98. https://doi.org/10.1080/17512786.2012.753242.

Muchtar, Nurhava, Basyouni Ibrahim Hamada, Thomas Hanitzsch, Ashraf Galal, Masduki, and Mohammad Sahid Ullah. 2017. "Journalism and the Islamic Worldview." *Journalism Studies* 18, no. 5:555–75. https://doi.org/10.1080/1461670X.2017.1279029.

Musa, Bala A., and Jerry Komia Domatob. 2007. "Who Is a Development Journalist? Perspectives on Media Ethics and Professionalism in Post-Colonial Societies." *Journal of Mass Media Ethics* 22, no. 4:315–331. https://doi.org/10.1080/08900520701583602.

Mwesige, Peter G. 2004. Disseminators, Advocates and Watchdogs: A Profile of Ugandan Journalists in the New Millennium. *Journalism* 5, no. 1:69–96. https://doi.org/10.1177/1464884904039556.

Naab, Teresa K., and Annika Sehl. 2017. "Studies of User-Generated Content: A Systematic Review." *Journalism* 18, no. 10:1256–73. https://doi.org/10.1177/1464884916673557.

Nerone, John C., ed. 1995. *Last Rights: Revisiting Four Theories of the Press.* Urbana: University of Illinois Press.

Nerone, John. 2013. "The Historical Roots of the Normative Model of Journalism." *Journalism* 14, no. 4:446–58. https://doi.org/10.1177/1464884912464177.

Newman, Nic, Richard Fletcher, Antonis Kalogeropoulos, David Levy, and Rasmus Kleis Nielsen. 2017. *Reuters Institute Digital News Report 2017.* Oxford: Reuters Institute for the Study of Journalism, University of Oxford.

Nordenstreng, Kaarle. 1997. "Beyond the Four Theories of the Press." In *Media and Politics in Transition: Cultural Identity in the Age of Globalization*, edited by Jan Servaes and Rico Lee, 97–109. Leuven, Belgium: Acco.

——. 2006. " 'Four Theories of the Press' Reconsidered." In *Researching Media, Democracy and Participation: The Intellectual Work of the 2006 European Media and Communication Doctoral Summer School*, edited by Nico Carpentier, Pille Pruulmann-Vengerfeldt, Kaarle Nordenstreng, Maren Hartmann, Peeter Vihalemm, and Bart Cammaerts, 35–46. Tartu, Estonia: University of Tartu Press.

Norris, Pippa. 1999. "Introduction: The Growth of Critical Citizens?" In *Critical Citizens: Global Support for Democratic Governance*, edited by Pippa Norris, 1–27. Oxford: Oxford University Press.

——. 2006. "The Role of the Free Press in Promoting Democratization, Good Governance, and Human Development." Paper presented at Annual Meeting of the Midwest Political Science Association, World Press Freedom Day, Chicago.

——. 2009. "Comparative Political Communications: Common Frameworks or Babelian Confusion?" *Government and Opposition* 44, no. 3:321–40. https://doi.org/10.1111/j.1477-7053.2009.01290.x.

——. 2011. *Democratic Deficit: Critical Citizens Revisited.* Cambridge: Cambridge University Press.

North, Douglass C. 1991. "Institutions." *Journal of Economic Perspectives* 5, no. 1:97–112. https://doi.org/10.1257/jep.5.1.97.

North, Louise. 2009. *The Gendered Newsroom: How Journalists Experience the Changing World of Media.* Cresskill: Hampton Press.

Nossek, Hillel, and Khalil Rinnawi. 2003. "Censorship and Freedom of the Press Under Changing Political Regimes: Palestinian Media from Israel Occupation to the Palestinian Authority." *Gazette* 65, no. 2:183–202. https://doi.org/10.1177/0016549203065002005.

Nygren, Gunnar. 2012. *Journalism in Russia, Poland and Sweden: Traditions, Cultures and Research.* Stockholm: Södertörn University Press.

Nyhan, David. 1986. "Jimmy Breslin: The Bard of Queens." *Washington Journalism Review* (October): 30.

Obijiofor, Levi, and Folker Hanusch. 2011. *Journalism Across Cultures: An Introduction.* Basingstoke, U.K.: Palgrave Macmillan.

Ogan, Christine L. 1982. "Development Journalism/Communication: The Status of the Concept." *Gazette* 29, no. 1–2:3–13. https://doi.org/10.1177/001654928202900101.

——. 1987. "Coverage of Development News in Developed and Developing Countries." *Journalism Quarterly* 64, no. 1:80–87. https://doi.org/10.1177/107769908706400110.

Ogong'a, Stephen Ogongo. 2010. "The Challenges for Kenya's Journalism Education." In *Journalism Education in Countries with Limited Media Freedom*, edited by Beate Josephi, 137–54. New York: Peter Lang.

Oller Alonso, Martin, and Palmira Chavero Ramírez. 2016. *Journalism in Latin America: Journalistic Culture in Ecuador.* Beau Bassin, Mauritius: Editorial Académica Española.

Örnebring, Henrik. 2012. "Comparative Journalism Research—An Overview." *Sociology Compass* 6, no. 10:769–80. https://doi.org/10.1111/j.1751-9020.2012.00493.x.

——. 2013. "Journalism as Institution and Work in Europe, Circa 1860." *Media History* 19, no. 4:393–407. http://doi.org/10.1080/13688804.2013.844896.

——. 2016. *Newsworkers: A Comparative European Perspective.* New York: Bloomsbury Academic.

Örnebring, Henrik, Johan Lindell, Christer Clerwall, and Michael Karlsson. 2016. "Dimensions of Journalistic Workplace Autonomy: A Five-Nation Comparison." *Javnost* 23, no. 2:307–26. https://doi.org/10.1080/13183222.2016.1215833.

Parsons, Craig. 2007. *How to Map Arguments in Political Science.* New York: Oxford Press.

Pasti, Svetlana. 2005. "Two Generations of Contemporary Russian Journalists." *European Journal of Communication* 20, no. 1:89–115. https://doi.org/10.1177/0267323105049634.

Patterson, Thomas E. 1994. *Out of Order.* New York: Vintage.

Patterson, Thomas E., and Wolfgang Donsbach. 1996. "News Decisions: Journalists as Partisan Actors." *Political Communication* 13, no. 4:455–68. https://doi.org/10.1080/10584609.1996.9963131.

Paulussen, Steve. 2012. "Technology and the Transformation of News Work: Are Labor Conditions in (Online) Journalism Changing?" In *The Handbook of Global Online Journalism*, edited by Eugenia Siapera and Andreas Veglis, 192–208. Malden, Mass.: Wiley-Blackwell.

Pellegata, Alessandro, and Sergio Splendore. 2017. "Media and Corruption: The Other Way Round—Exploring Macro Determinants of Journalists' Perceptions of the Accountability Instruments and Governmental Pressures." *International Journal of Public Opinion Research* (May). https://doi.org/10.1093/ijpor/edx008.

Peters, Chris, and Marcel J. Broersma, eds. 2013. *Rethinking Journalism: Trust and Participation in a Transformed News Landscape*. Abingdon, U.K.: Routledge.

——. 2017. *Rethinking Journalism Again: Societal Role and Public Relevance in a Digital Age*. Abingdon, U.K.: Routledge.

Phillips, Angela. 2012. "Sociability, Speed and Quality in the Changing News Environment." *Journalism Practice* 6, no. 5–6:669–79. https://doi.org/10.1080/17512786.2012.689476.

Picard, Robert G. 1985. *The Press and the Decline of Democracy*. Westport, Conn.: Greenwood Press.

——. 2014. "Panel I: The Future of the Political Economy of Press Freedom." *Communication Law and Policy* 19, no. 1:97–107. https://doi.org/10.1080/10811680.2014.860832.

Pintak, Lawrence. 2010. *The New Arab Journalist: Mission and Identity in a Time of Turmoil*. London: I. B. Tauris.

——. 2014. "Islam, Identity and Professional Values: A Study of Journalists in Three Muslim-Majority Regions." *Journalism* 15, no. 4:482–503. https://doi.org/10.1177/1464884913490269.

Pintak, Lawrence, and J. Ginges. 2009. "Inside the Arab Newsroom: Arab Journalists Evaluate Themselves and the Competition." *Journalism Studies* 10, no. 2:157–77. https://doi.org/10.1080/14616700802337800.

Pintak, Lawrence, and Syed Javed Nazir. 2013. "Pakistani Journalism: At the Crossroads of Muslim Identity, National Priorities and Journalistic Culture." *Media, Culture & Society* 35, no. 5:640–65. https://doi.org/10.1177/1464884913490269.

Pjesivac, Ivanka, Katerina Spasovska, and Iveta Imre. 2016. "The Truth Between the Lines: Conceptualization of Trust in News Media in Serbia, Macedonia, and Croatia." *Mass Communication and Society* 19, no. 3:323–51. https://doi.org/10.1080/15205436.2015.1128548.

Plaisance, Patrick Lee. 2006. "An Assessment of Media Ethics Education: Course Content and the Values and Ethical Ideologies of Media Ethics Students." *Journalism & Mass Communication Educator* 61, no. 4:378–96. https://doi.org/10.1177/107769580606100404.

——. 2011. "Moral Agency in Media: Toward a Model to Explore Key Components of Ethical Practice." *Journal of Mass Media Ethics* 26, no. 2: 96–113. ttps://doi.org/10.1080/08900523.2011.559800.

Plaisance, Patrick Lee, and Skewes, Elizabeth A. 2003. "Personal and Professional Dimensions of News Work: Exploring the Link Between Journalists' Values and Roles." *Journalism & Mass Communication Quarterly* 80, no. 4:833–48. https://doi.org/10.1177/107769900308000406.

Plaisance, Patrick Lee, Elizabeth Skewes, and Thomas Hanitzsch. 2012. "Ethical Orientations of Journalists Around the Globe: Implications from a Cross-National Survey." *Communication Research* 39, no. 5:641–61. https://doi.org/10.1177/0093650 212450584.

Poell, Thomas, and Erik Borra. 2012. "Twitter, YouTube, and Flickr as Platforms of Alternative Journalism: The Social Media Account of the 2010 Toronto G20 Protests." *Journalism* 13, no. 6: 695–713. https://doi.org/10.1177/1464884911431533.

Potter, Jonathan, and Margaret Wetherell. 1987. *Discourse and Social Psychology: Beyond Attitudes and Behavior.* Thousand Oaks, Calif.: Sage.

Preston, Paschal. 2009. *Making the News: Journalism and News Cultures in Europe.* London: Routledge.

Preston, Paschal, and Monika Metykova. 2009. "From News to House Rules: Organisational Contexts." In *Making the News: Journalism and News Cultures in Europe,* edited by Paschal Preston, 72-91. London: Routledge.

Przeworski, Adam, and Henry Teune. 1970. *The Logic of Comparative Inquiry.* New York: Wiley.

Pudney, Stephen. 2011. "Perception and Retrospection: The Dynamic Consistency of Responses to Survey Questions on Wellbeing." *Journal of Public Economics* 95, no. 3:300–310. https://doi.org/10.1016/j.jpubeco.2010.08.004.

Putnam, Robert D. 1993. *Making Democracy Work: Civic Traditions in Modern Italy.* Princeton, N.J.: Princeton University Press.

——. 2001. *Bowling Alone: The Collapse and Revival of American Community.* New York: Simon and Schuster.

Quandt, Thorsten, and Jane B. Singer. 2009. "Convergence and Cross-Platform Content Production." In *The Handbook of Journalism Studies,* edited by Thomas Hanitzsch and Karin Wahl-Jorgensen, 130–44. London: Routledge.

Ramaprasad, Jyotika. 2001. "A Profile of Journalists in Post-Independence Tanzania." *Gazette* 63, no. 6:539–556. https://doi.org/ 10.1177/0016549201063006005.

Ramaprasad, Jyotika, and Naila Nabil Hamdy. 2006. "Functions of Egyptian Journalists: Perceived Importance and Actual Performance." *International Communication Gazette* 68, no. 2:167–85. https://doi.org/10.1177/1748048506062233.

Ramaprasad, Jyotika, and James D. Kelly. 2003. "Reporting the News from the World's Rooftop: A Survey of Nepalese Journalists." *Gazette* 65, no. 3:291–315. https://doi.org /10.1177/0016549203065003005.

Ramaprasad, Jyotika, Deqiang Ji, Ruiming Zhou, Fernando Oliveira Paulino, Svetlana Pasti, Dmitry Gavra, Herman Wasserman, and Musawenkosi Ndlovu. 2017. "Ethics: Ideals and Realities." In *Contemporary BRICS Journalism: Non-Western Media in Transition,* edited by Svetlana Pasti, and Jyotika Ramaprasad, 72–103. New York: Routledge.

Reese, Stephen D. 2001. "Understanding the Global Journalist: A Hierarchy-of-Influences Approach." *Journalism Studies* 2, no. 2:173–87. https://doi.org/10.1080 /14616700118394.

Reese, Stephen D., and Jeremy Cohen. 2000. "Educating for Journalism: The Professionalism of Scholarship." *Journalism Studies* 1, no. 2:213–27. https://doi.org/10.1080/14616700050028217.

Reese, Stephen D., Lou Rutigliano, Kideuk Hyun, and Jaekwan Jeong. 2007. "Mapping the Blogosphere: Professional and Citizen-Based Media in the Global News Arena." *Journalism* 8, no. 3:235–61. https://doi.org/10.1177/1464884907076459.

Reich, Zvi, and Thomas Hanitzsch. 2013. "Determinants of Journalists' Professional Autonomy: Individual and National Level Factors Matter More than Organizational Ones." *Mass Communication and Society* 16, no. 1:133–56. https://doi.org/10.1080/15205436.2012.669002.

Reinardy, Scott. 2009. "Female Journalists More Likely to Leave Newspapers." *Newspaper Research Journal* 30, no. 3:42–57. https://doi.org/10.1177/073953290903000304.

——. 2011. "Newspaper Journalism in Crisis: Burnout on the Rise, Eroding Young Journalists' Career Commitment." *Journalism* 12, no. 1:33–50. https://doi.org/10.1177/1464884910385188.

——. 2016. *Journalism's Lost Generation: The Un-doing of U.S. Newspaper Newsrooms.* New York: Routledge.

Relly, Jeannine E., Margaret Zanger, and Shahira Fahmy. 2015. "News Media Landscape in a Fragile State: Professional Ethics Perceptions in a Post-Ba'athist Iraq." *Mass Communication & Society* 18, no. 4:346–73. https://doi.org/10.1080/15205436.2014.1001032.

Rice, Tom M., and Alexander F. Sumberg. 1997. "Civic Culture and Government: Performance in the American States." *Journal of Federalism* 27, no. 1:99–114. https://doi.org/10.1093/oxfordjournals.pubjof.a029899.

Richards, Ian. 2010. "Journalism's Tangled Web: Business, Ethics, and Professional Practice." In *Journalism Ethics: A Philosophical Approach*, edited by Christopher Meyers, 171–84. Oxford: Oxford University Press.

Robinson, Gertrud J. 2005. *Gender, Journalism, and Equity: Canadian, US, and European Experiences.* Cresskill, N.J.: Hampton Press.

Robinson, Sue. 2007. "Someone's Gotta Be in Control Here. The Institutionalization of Online News and the Creation of a Shared Journalistic Authority." *Journalism Practice* 1, no. 3:305–21. https://doi.org/10.1080/17512780701504856.

Rodny-Gumede, Ylva, Viola C. Milton, and Winston Mano. 2017. "Rethinking the Link Between Media and Democracy in the Post-Colony: One Size Does Not Fit All." *Communicatio: South African Journal for Communication Theory and Research* 43, no. 2:1–9. https://doi.org/10.1080/02500167.2017.1341943.

Romano, Angela. 2003. *Politics and the Press in Indonesia: Understanding an Evolving Political Culture.* London: Routledge.

——. 2005. "Asian Journalism: News, Development and the Tides of Liberalization and Technology." In *Journalism and Democracy in Asia*, edited by Angela Romano and Michael Bromley, 1–14. London: Routledge.

Rosen, Jay. 1999. "The Action of the Idea. Public Journalism in Built Form." In *The Idea of Public Journalism*, edited by Theodore Lewis Glasser, 21–48. New York: Guilford Press.

——. 2000. "Questions and Answers About Public Journalism." *Journalism Studies* 1, no. 4:679–83. https://doi.org/10.1080/146167000441376.

Rosenstiel, Tom. 2016. "What the Post-Trump Debate Over Journalism Gets Wrong." December 20. https://www.brookings.edu/research/what-the-debate-over-journalism-post-trump-gets-wrong/.

Rotter, Julian B. 1967. "A New Scale for the Measurement of Interpersonal Trust." *Journal of Personality* 35, no. 4:651–65. https://doi.org/10.1111/j.1467-6494.1967.tb01454.x.

Rousseau, Denise M., Sim B. Sitkin, Ronald S. Burt, and Colin Camerer. 1998. "Not so Different After All: A Cross-Discipline View of Trust." *Academy of Management Review* 23, no. 3:393–404. https://doi.org/10.5465/AMR.1998.926617.

Roy, Sanjukta. 2014. "Media Development and Political Stability: An Analysis of Sub-Saharan Africa." *Journal of Developing Areas* 48, no. 2:255–73. https://doi.org/10.1353/jda.2014.0037.

Rush, Ramona R., Carol E. Oukrop, and Katharine Sarikakis. 2005. "A Global Hypothesis for Women in Journalism and Mass Communications: The Ratio of Recurrent and Reinforced Residuum." *Gazette* 67, no. 3:239–53. https://doi.org/10.1177/0016549205052226.

Russo, Tracy C. 1998. "Organizational and Professional Identification: A Case of Newspaper Journalists." *Management Communication Quarterly* 12, no. 1:72–111. https://doi.org/10.1177/0893318998121003.

Ryan, Richard, and Edward Deci. 2000. "Self-Determination Theory and the Facilitation of Intrinsic Motivation, Social Development, and Well-Being." *American Psychologist* 55, no. 1:68–78. http://dx.doi.org/10.1037/0003-066X.55.1.68.

Ryder, Norman B. 1965. "The Cohort as a Concept in the Study of Social Change." *American Sociological Review* 30, no. 6:843–861. https://doi.org/10.2307/2090964.

Ryfe, David Michael. 2006. "The Nature of News Rules." *Political Communication* 23, no. 2:203–14. https://doi.org/10.1080/10584600600629810.

——. 2009. "Broader and Deeper: A Study of Newsroom Culture in a Time of Change." *Journalism* 10, no. 2:197–216. https://doi.org/10.1177/1464884908100601.

Sacco, Vittoria, and Diana Bossio. 2014. "Using Storify: Challenges and Opportunities for Journalists Covering Conflicts." *Journal of Applied Journalism and Media Studies* 3, no. 1:27–45. https://doi.org/10.1386/ajms.3.1.27_1.

Saether, Elin. 2008. "A New Political Role? Discursive Strategies of Critical Journalists in China." *China Aktuell–Journal of Current Chinese Affairs*, no. 4:5–29. https://www.duo.uio.no/bitstream/handle/10852/15276/2/93474_saether.pdf.

Sakr, Naomi. 2013. *Transformations in Egyptian Journalism*. London: Oxford University Press.

Sanders, Jareb, Mark Hanna, Maria Rosa Berganza, and Jose Javier Sanchez Aranda. 2008. "Becoming Journalists: A Comparison of the Professional Attitudes and

Values of British and Spanish Journalism Students." *European Journal of Communication* 23, no. 2:133–52. https://doi.org/10.1177/0267323108089219.

Sanders, Karen. 2003. *Ethics and Journalism*. London: Sage.

Schlesinger, Philip. 1978. *Putting "Reality" Together*. London: Constable.

Schmidt, Vivien A. 2008. "Discursive Institutionalism: The Explanatory Power of Ideas and Discourse." *Annual Review of Political Science* 11:303–26. https://doi.org/10.1146/annurev.polisci.11.060606.135342.

——. 2010. "Taking Ideas and Discourse Seriously: Explaining Change Through Discursive Institutionalism as the Fourth 'New Institutionalism.'" *European Political Science Review* 2, no. 1:1–25. https://doi.org/10.1017/S1755773909999021X.

Schudson, Michael. 1981. *Discovering the News: A Social History of American Newspaper*. New York: Basic Books.

——. 2001. "The Objectivity Norm in American Journalism." *Journalism* 2, no. 2:149–70. https://doi.org/10.1177/146488490100200201.

Schultz, Ida. 2007. "The Journalistic Gut Feeling: Journalistic Doxa, News Habitus and Orthodox News Values." *Journalism Practice* 1, no. 2:190–207. https://doi.org/10.1080/17512780701275507.

Schwartz, Shalom H., and Anat Bard. 2001. "Value Hierarchies Across Cultures: Taking a Similarities Perspective." *Journal of Cross-Cultural Psychology* 32, no. 2:268–90. https://doi.org/10.1177/0022022101032003002.

Sen, Amartya. 1999. *Development as Freedom*. New York: Oxford University Press.

Shah, Hemant. 1989. A Preliminary Examination of Journalistic Roles and Development Reporting at Three Indian Newspapers. *Media Asia* 16, no. 3:128–31. https://doi.org/10.1080/01296612.1989.11726310.

——. 1996. "Modernization, Marginalization, and Emancipation: Toward a Normative Model for Journalism and National Development." *Communication Theory* 6, no. 2:143–66. https://doi.org/10.1111/j.1468-2885.1996.tb00124.x.

Sharkey, Heather J. 2008. "Arab Identity and Ideology in Sudan: The Politics of Language, Ethnicity, and Race." *African Affairs* 107, no. 426:21–43. https://doi.org/10.1093/afraf/adm068.

Sherwood, Merryn, and Penny O'Donnell. 2018. "Once a Journalist, Always a Journalist?" *Journalism Studies* 19, no. 7:1021–38. https://doi.org/10.1080/1461670X.2016.1249007.

Shoemaker, Pamela, Martin Eichholz, Eunyi Kim, and Brenda Wrigley. 2001. "Individual and Routine Forces in Gatekeeping." *Journalism & Mass Communication Quarterly* 78, no. 2:233–46. https://doi.org/10.1177/107769900107800202.

Shoemaker, Pamela, and Stephen Reese. 1996. *Mediating the Message: Theories of Influence on Mass Media Content*. White Plains, N.Y.: Longman.

——. 2013. *Mediating the Message in the 21st Century: A Media Sociology Perspective*. New York: Routledge.

Shoemaker, Pamela J., and Timothy P. Vos. 2009. *Gatekeeping Theory*. New York: Routledge.

Siebert, Fred S., Theodore Peterson, and Wilbur Schramm. 1956. *Four Theories of the Press: The Authoritarian, Libertarian, Social Responsibility and Soviet Communist Concepts of What the Press Should Be and Do.* Urbana: University of Illinois Press.

Sigelman, Lee. 1973. "Reporting the News: An Organizational Analysis." *American Journal of Sociology* 79, no. 1:132–51. https://www.jstor.org/stable/2776715.

Simon, Gebremedhin. 2008. "Media Ethics in Ethiopia." In *Media Ethics: Beyond Borders*, edited by Stephen J. A. Ward and Herman Wasserman, 157–71. Johannesburg, South Africa: Heinemann.

Singer, Jane B. 2004. "More than Ink-Stained Wretches: The Resocialization of Print Journalists in Converged Newsrooms." *Journalism & Mass Communication Quarterly* 81, no. 4:838–56. https://doi.org/10.1177/107769900408100408.

——. 2011. "Journalism and Digital Technologies." In *Changing the News: The Forces Shaping Journalism in Uncertain Times*, edited by Wilson Gade and Peter Lowery, 214–29. New York: Routledge.

Sjøvaag, Helle. 2013. "Journalistic Autonomy: Between Structure, Agency, and Institution." *Nordicom Review* 34 (special issue): 155–66.

Skjerdal, Terje. S. 2008. "Self-Censorship Among News Journalists in the Ethiopian State Media." *African Communication Research* 1, no. 2:185–206.

——. 2011. "Development Journalism Revived: The Case of Ethiopia." *Ecquid Novi: African Journalism Studies* 32, no. 2:58–74. https://doi.org/10.1080/02560054.2011.578879.

——. 2012. "The Three Alternative Journalism of Africa." *International Communication Gazette* 74, no. 7:636–54. https://doi.org/10.1177/1748048512458559.

Skjerdal, Terje, and Charles Muriu Ngugi. 2007. "Institutional and Governmental Challenges for Journalism Education in East Africa." *Ecquid Novi* 28, no. 1–2:176–90. https://doi.org/10.1080/02560054.2007.9653365.

Skovsgaard, Morten. 2014. "A Tabloid Mind? Professional Values and Organizational Pressures as Explanations of Tabloid Journalism." *Media, Culture & Society* 36, no. 2:200–218. https://doi.org/10.1177/0163443713515740.

Slattery, Karen L. 2014. "Ethics and Journalistic Standards: An Examination of the Relationship Between Journalism Codes of Ethics and Deontological Moral Theory." In *The Ethics of Journalism: Individual, Institutional and Cultural Influences*, edited by Wendy N. Wyatt, 147–64. Oxford: I. B. Tauris.

Slavtcheva-Petkova, Vera. 2017. "Fighting Putin and the Kremlin's Grip in Neo-Authoritarian Russia: The Experience of Liberal Journalists." *Journalism* (May). https://doi.org/10.1177/1464884917708061.

Slomczynski, Kazimierz M., and Krystyna Janicka. 2009. "Structural Determinants of Trust in Public Institutions: Cross-National Differentiation." *International Journal of Sociology* 39, no. 1:8–29.

Solheim, Margrethe H. 2017. "Journalistic Values and Challenges in Colombia, Bangladesh, Tunisia and Norway." In *Negotiating Journalism. Core Values and Cultural Diversities*, edited by Elsebeth Frey, Mofizur Rhaman, and Hamida El Bour, 77–90. Göteborg: Nordicom.

Soloski, John. 1989. "News Reporting and Professionalism: Some Constraints on the Reporting of the News." *Media, Culture & Society* 11, no. 2:207–28. https://doi.org/10.1177/016344389011002005.

Sparrow, Bartholomew H. 1999. *Uncertain Guardians: The News Media as a Political Institution.* London: Johns Hopkins University Press.

——. 2006. "A Research Agenda for an Institutional Media." *Political Communication* 23, no. 2:145–57. https://doi.org/10.1080/10584600600629695.

Specter, Michael. 2007. "Kremlin, Inc. Why Are Vladimir Putin's Opponents Dying?" *New Yorker*, January 29. http://www.newyorker.com/magazine/2007/01/29/kremlin-inc.

Statham, Paul. 2007. "Journalists as Commentators on European Politics: Educators, Partisans or Ideologues?" *European Journal of Communication* 22, no. 4:461–77. https://doi.org/10.1177/0267323107083063.

——. 2008. "Making Europe News: How Journalists View Their Role and Media Performance." *Journalism* 9, no. 4:398–422. https://doi.org/10.1177/1464884908091292.

Steiner, Linda. 2009. "Gender in the Newsroom." In *The Handbook of Journalism Studies*, edited by Karin Wahl-Jørgenson and Thomas Hanitzsch, 116–29. New York: Routledge.

Stępińska, Agnieszka, and Szymon Ossowski. 2012. "Three Generations of Polish Journalists: Professional Roles and Identities." *Journalism Studies* 13, no. 5–6: 857–67. https://doi.org/10.1080/1461670X.2012.668000.

Stevenson, Robert L. 1996. "International Communication." In *An Integrated Approach to Communication Theory and Research*, edited by Don W. Stacks and Michael B. Salwen, 181–93. New York: Routledge.

Stickland, Francis. 1998. *The Dynamics of Change: Insights Into Organizational Transition from the Natural World.* London: Routledge.

Stoop, Inek, Jaak Billiet, Achim Koch, and Rory Fitzgerald. 2010. *Improving Survey Response: Lessons Learned from the European Social Survey.* Chichester, U.K.: Wiley.

Sugiyama, Mitsunobu. 2000. "Media and Power in Japan." In *De-Westernizing Media Studies*, edited by Myung-Jin Park and James Curran, 191–201. London: Routledge.

Tandoc, Edson. 2014. "Journalism Is Twerking? How Web Analytics Is Changing the Process of Gatekeeping." *New Media & Society* 16, no. 4:559–75. https://doi.org/10.1177/1461444814530541.

Tandoc, Edson. 2017. "Watching Over the Watchdogs: The Problems That Filipino Journalists Face." *Journalism Studies* 18, no. 1:102–17. https://doi.org/10.1080/1461670X.2016.1218298.

Tandoc, Edson, and Bruno Takahashi. 2014. "Playing a Crusader Role or Just Playing by the Rules? Role Conceptions and Role Inconsistencies Among Environmental Journalists." *Journalism* 15, no. 7:889–907. https://doi.org/10.1177/1464884913501836.

Tandoc, Edson, and Tim P. Vos. 2016. "The Journalist Is Marketing the News: Social Media in the Gatekeeping Process." *Journalism Practice* 10, no. 8:950–66. https://doi.org/10.1080/17512786.2015.1087811.

Tandoc, Edson, Lea Hellmueller, and Tim P. Vos. 2013. "Mind the Gap: Between Role Conception and Role Enactment." *Journalism Practice* 7, no. 5:539–54. https://doi.org/10.1080/17512786.2012.726503.

Tang, Lijun, and Helen Sampson. 2012. "The Interaction Between Mass Media and the Internet in Non-Democratic States: The Case of China." *Media, Culture & Society* 34, no. 4:457–71. https://doi.org/10.1177/0163443711436358.

Tejkalová, Alice N., Arnold S. de Beer, Rosa Berganza, Yusuf Kalyango, Jr., Adriana Amado, Liga Ozolina, Filip Láb, Rawṣhon Akhter, Sonia Virginia Moreira, and Masduki. 2017. "In Media We Trust: Journalists and Institutional Trust Perceptions in Post-authoritarian and Post-totalitarian Countries." *Journalism Studies* 18, no. 5: 629–44. https://doi.org/10.1080/1461670X.2017.1279026.

Teune, Henry, and Adam Przeworski. 1970. *The Logic of Comparative Inquiry*. New York: Wiley.

Thompson, John B. 1995. *The Media and Modernity: A Social Theory of the Media*. Stanford, Calif.: Stanford University Press.

Thorson, Emily. 2008. "Changing Patterns of News Consumption and Participation." *Information, Communication and Society* 11, no. 4:473–89. https://doi.org/10.1080/13691180801999027.

Thurman, Neil. 2008. "Forums for Citizen Journalists? Adoption of User-Generated Content Initiatives by Online News Media." *New Media and Society* 10, no. 1:139–57. https://doi.org/10.1177/1461444807085325.

Times Mirror Center for The People & The Press. 1995. "Ordinary Americans More Cynical than Journalists: News Media Differs with Public and Leaders on Watchdog Issues." May 22. http://www.people-press.org/1995/05/22/news-media-differs-with-public-and-leaders-on-watchdog-issues/.

Tong, Jingrong. 2017. "The Taming of Critical Journalism in China: A Combination of Political, Economic and Technological Forces." *Journalism Studies*, 1–18. https://doi.org/10.1080/1461670X.2017.1375386.

Tong, Jingrong, and Shih-Hung Lo. 2017. *Digital Technology and Journalism: An International Comparative Perspective*. Basingstoke, U.K.: Palgrave Macmillan.

Torcal, Mariano, and José Ramón Montero. 2006. "Political Disaffection in Comparative Perspective." In *Political Disaffection in Contemporary Democracies: Social Capital, Institutions, and Politics*, edited by Mariano Torcal and José Ramón Montero, 3–19. Abingdon, U.K.: Routledge.

Trappel, Josef. 2017. "Market Structure and Innovation Policies in Austria." In *Innovation Policies in the European News Media Industry: A Comparative Study*, edited by Hans van Kranenburg, 9–24. Cham, Switzerland: Springer.

Tsui, Celia Y. S., and Francis L. F. Lee. 2012. "Trajectories of Women Journalists' Careers in Hong Kong." *Journalism Studies* 13, no. 3:370–85. https://doi.org/10.1080/1461670X.2011.592360.

Tuchman, Gaye. 1978. *Making News: A Study in the Construction of Reality*. New York: Free Press.

Tufekci, Zeynep, and Christopher Wilson. 2012. "Social Media and the Decision to Participate in Political Protest: Observations from Tahrir Square." *Journal of Communication* 62, no. 2:363–79. https://doi.org/10.1111/j.1460-2466.2012.01629.x.

Tunstall, Jeremy. 2008. *The Media Were American: US Mass Media in Decline.* New York: Oxford University Press.

Ullah, Mohammad Sahid. 2014. "De-Westernization of Media and Journalism in South Asia: In Search of a New Strategy." *China Media Research* 10, no. 2:15–23.

——. 2016. "Obstacles and Opportunities for Preparing Competent Journalists at Universities in Bangladesh." *Asia Pacific Media Educator* 26, no. 1:65–82. https://doi.org /10.1177/1326365X16640989.

Underwood, Doug. 2001. "Reporting and the Push for Market-Oriented Journalism: Media Organizations as Business." In *Mediated Politics: Communication in the Future of Democracy*, edited by W. Lance Bennett and Robert M. Entman, 99–116. New York: Cambridge University Press.

Underwood, Doug, Giffard Anthony, and Keith Stamm. 1994. "Computers and Editing: Pagination's Impact on the Newsroom." *Newspaper Research Journal* 15, no. 2:116–27. https://doi.org/10.1177/073953299401500212.

UNESCO. 2015. *Inside the News: Challenges and Aspirations of Women Journalists in Asia and the Pacific.* Paris: UNESCO. http://unesdoc.unesco.org/images/0023 /002334/233420E.pdf.

United Nations Development Programme (UNDP). 2014. *Human Development Report 2014—Sustaining Human Progress: Reducing Vulnerabilities and Building Resilience.* New York: UNDP.

Van Aelst, Peter, Kees Brants, Philip van Praag, Claes de Vreese, Miciel Nuytemans, and Arjen van Dalen. 2008. "The Fourth Estate as Superpower? An Empirical Study of Perceptions of Media Power in Belgium and the Netherlands." *Journalism Studies* 9, no. 4:494–511. https://doi.org/10.1080/14616700802114134.

Van Dalen, Arjen, Erik Albaek, and Claes de Vreese. 2011. "Suspicious Minds: Explaining Political Cynicism Among Political Journalists in Europe." *European Journal of Communication* 26, no. 2:147–62. https://doi.org/10.1177/0267323111404841.

Van Dalen, Arjen, Claes H. de Vreese, and Erik Albæk. 2012. "Different Roles, Different Content? A Four-Country Comparison of the Role Conceptions and Reporting Style of Political Journalists." *Journalism* 13, no. 7:903–22. https://doi.org/10.1177 /1464884911431538.

Van de Vijver, Fons, and Kwok Leung. 1997. *Methods and Data Analysis for Cross-Cultural Research.* Thousand Oaks, Calif.: Sage.

Van Zoonen, Lisbet. 1998. "One of the Girls? On the Changing Gender of Journalism." In *News, Gender and Power*, edited by Cynthia Carter, Gill Branston, and Stuart Allan, 33–56. London: Routledge.

Vanacker, Bastiaan. 2016. "'Just Doing his Job.' Journalism Defending Its Turf in a Time of Leak Investigations." *Journalism Studies* 17, no. 5:573–89. https://doi.org/10.1080 /1461670X.2014.996030.

Vanacker, Bastiaan, and Genelle Belmas. 2009. "Trust and the Economics of News." *Journal of Mass Media Ethics* 24, no. 2–3:110–26. https://doi.org/10.1080/0890052 0902885277

Vinken, Henk, and Teunis IJdens. 2013. *Freelance Journalisten, Schrijvers en Fotografen*. Tilburg, Netherlands: Pyrrhula.

Voakes, Paul S. 1997. "Social Influences on Journalists' Decision Making in Ethical Situations." *Journal of Mass Media Ethics* 12, no. 1:18–35. ttps://doi.org/10.1207/s15327728jmme1201_2.

Voltmer, Katrin. 2012. "How far can Media Systems Travel." In *Comparing Media Systems Beyond the Western World*, edited by Daniel C. Hallin, and Paolo Mancini, 224–25. Cambridge: Cambridge University Press.

——. 2013. *The Media in Transitional Democracies*. Hoboken, N.J.: Wiley.

Vos, Tim P. 2012. "'Homo Journalisticus': Journalism Education's Role in Articulating the Objectivity Norm." *Journalism* 13, no. 4:435–49. https://doi.org/10.1177/146488 4911431374.

——. 2016. "Historical Perspectives on Journalistic Roles." In *Journalistic Role Performance: Concepts, Models, and Measures*, edited by Claudia Mellado, Lea Hellmueller, and Wolfgang Donsbach, 41–59. New York: Routledge.

Vos, Tim P., and Jane B. Singer. 2016. "Media Discourse About Entrepreneurial Journalism: Implications for Journalistic Capital. *Journalism Practice* 10, no. 2:143–159. https://doi.org/10.1080/17512786.2015.1124730.

Wage Indicator Global Report. 2012. *Gender Pay Gap in Journalism*. Amsterdam: Wage Indicator Foundation & IFJ.

Waisbord, Silvio. 2000. *Watchdog Journalism in South America: News, Accountability, and Democracy*. New York: Columbia University Press.

——. 2009. "Research Directions for Global Journalism Studies: Ideas from Latin America." *Journalism* 10, no. 3:393–95. https://doi.org/10.1177/1464884909102586.

——. 2013a. "Democracy, Journalism, and Latin American Populism." *Journalism* 14, no. 4:504–21. https://doi.org/10.1177/1464884912464178.

——. 2013b. *Reinventing Professionalism: Journalism and News in Global Perspective*. Cambridge: Polity.

Waisbord, Silvio, and Claudia Mellado. 2014. "De-Westernizing Communication Studies: A Reassessment." *Communication Theory* 24, no. 4:361–72. http://dx.doi.org/10 .1111/comt.12044.

Walter-Rogg, Melanie. 2005. "Politisches Vertrauen ist gut—Misstrauen ist Besser? Ausmaß und Ausstrahlungseffekte des Politiker- und Institutionenvertrauens im Vereinigten Deutschland." In *Wächst Zusammen, was Zusammengehört? Stabilität und Wandel Politischer Einstellungen im Wiedervereinigten Deutschland*, edited by Oscar W. Gabriel, Jürgen W. Falter, and Hans Rattinger, 129–56. Baden-Baden, Germany: Nomos.

Ward, Stephen J. A. 2010. *Global Journalism Ethics*. Montreal: McGill-Queen's Press.

Wasserman, Herman. 2013. "Journalism in a New Democracy: The Ethics of Listening." *Communicatio: South African Journal for Communication Theory and Research* 39, no. 1: 67–84. https://doi.org/10.1080/02500167.2013.772217.

Wasserman, Herman, and Arnold S. de Beer. 2009. "Towards De-Westernizing Journalism Studies." In *The Handbook of Journalism Studies*, edited by Karin Wahl-Jorgensen and Thomas Hanitzsch, 428–38. New York: Routledge.

Weaver, David H., ed. 1998a. *The Global Journalist: News People Around the World.* Cresskill, N.J.: Hampton Press.

——. 1998b. "Journalists Around the World: Commonalities and Differences." In *The Global Journalist: News People Around the World*, edited by David H. Weaver, 455–80. Cresskill: Hampton.

Weaver David H., and G. Cleveland Wilhoit. 1986. *The American Journalist: A Portrait of U.S. News People and Their Work.* Bloomington: Indiana University Press.

——. 1996. *The American Journalist in the 1990s: US News People at the End of an Era.* Mahwah, N.J.: Erlbaum.

Weaver, David H., and Lars Willnat, eds. 2012. *The Global Journalist in the 21st Century.* New York: Routledge.

Weaver, David H., Randal A. Beam, Bonnie J. Brownlee, Paul S. Voakes, and G. Cleveland Wilhoit. 2007. *The American Journalist in the 21st Century: U.S News People at the Dawn of a New Millennium.* Mahwah, N.J.: Erlbaum.

Welzel, Christian. 2013. *Freedom Rising: Human Empowerment and the Quest for Emancipation.* New York: Cambridge University Press.

Welzel, Christian, and Ronald F. Inglehart. 2016. "Misconceptions of Measurement Equivalence: Time for a Paradigm Shift." *Comparative Political Studies* 49, no. 8:1068–94. https://doi.org/10.1177/0010414016628275.

Wetherell, Margaret. 1998. "Positioning and Interpretative Repertoires: Conversation Analysis and Post-structuralism in Dialogue." *Discourse & Society* 9, no. 3:387–412. https://doi.org/10.1177/0957926598009003005.

White, Aidan. 2017. "Truth-Telling and Ethics Remain the Keys to Open Democracy." In *Ethics in the News: EJN Report on Challenges for Journalism in the Post-Truth Era*, edited by Aidan White, 4–5. London: EJN. http://ethicaljournalismnetwork.org/wp-content/uploads/2017/01/ejn-ethics-in-the-news.pdf.

White, David M. 1950. "The Gatekeeper: A Case Study in the Selection of News." *Journalism Quarterly* 27, no. 3:383–90. https://doi.org/10.1177/107769905002700403.

Whitney, Charles D., Randall S. Sumpter, and Denis McQuail. 2004. "News Media Production: Individuals, Organizations, and Institutions." In *The SAGE Handbook of Media Studies*, edited by John D. H. Downing, Denis McQuail, Philip Schlesinger and Ellen A. Wartella, 393–409. Thousand Oaks, Calif.: Sage.

Wiik, Jenny. 2009. "Identities Under Construction: Professional Journalism in a Phase of Destabilization." *International Review of Sociology* 19, no. 2:351–65. https://doi.org/10.1080/03906700902833676.

Willnat, Lars, and David H. Weaver. 2014. *The American Journalist in the Digital Age: Key Findings.* Bloomington: Indiana University Press.

Willnat, Lars, David H. Weaver, and Jihyang Choi. 2013. "The Global Journalist in the Twenty-First Century." *Journalism Practice* 7, no. 2:163–83. https://doi.org/10.1080/17512786.2012.753210.

Winters, Jeffrey A. 2011. *Oligarchy.* Cambridge: Cambridge University Press.

Wirth, Werner, and Steffen Kolb. 2004. "Designs and Methods of Comparative Political Communication Research." In *Comparing Political Communication: Theories, Cases, and Challenges,* edited by Frank Esser and Barbara Pfetsch, 87–111. New York: Cambridge University Press.

Witschge, Tamara, and Gunnar Nygren. 2009. "Journalistic Work: A Profession Under Pressure?" *Journal of Media Business Studies* 6, no. 1:37–59. https://doi.org/10.1080/16522354.2009.11073478.

Wong, Kokkeong. 2004. "Asian-Based Development Journalism and Political Elections: Press Coverage of the 1999 General Elections in Malaysia." *Gazette* 66, no. 1:25–40. https://doi.org/10.1177/0016549204039940.

World Association of Newspapers and News Publishers (WAN-IFRA). 2014. *World Press Trends 2014: The Definitive Guide to the Global Newspaper Industry, in Numbers, Trends and Changes.* Paris: WAN-IFRA.

——. 2016. "Full Highlights of World Press Trends 2016 Survey." June 12. http://www.wan-ifra.org/articles/2016/06/12/full-highlights-of-world-press-trends-2016-survey.

Wu, Wei, David Weaver, and Owen V. Johnson. 1996. "Professional Roles of Russian and U.S. Journalists: A Comparative Study." *Journalism & Mass Communication Quarterly* 73, no. 3:534–48. https://doi.org/10.1177/107769909607300303.

Xu, Di. 2015. "Online Censorship and Journalists' Tactics: A Chinese Perspective." *Journalism Practice* 9, no. 5:704–20. https://doi.org/10.1080/17512786.2014.982968.

——. 2016. "Red-Envelope Cash: Journalists on the Take in Contemporary China." *Journal of Media Ethics* 31, no. 4:231–44. https://doi.org/10.1080/23736992.2016.1220253.

Xu, Xiaoge. 2005. *Demystifying Asian Values in Journalism.* Singapore: Marshall Cavendish.

Zayani, Mohamed, and Sofiane Sahraoui. 2007. *The Culture of Al Jazeera: Inside an Arab Media Giant.* Jefferson, Mo.: McFarland.

Zechmeister, Elizabeth J., ed. 2014. *The Political Culture of Democracy in the Americas, 2014: Democratic Governance Across 10 Years of the Americas Barometer.* Nashville, Tenn.: Vanderbilt University.

Zelizer, Barbie. 1993. "Journalists as Interpretive Communities." *Critical Studies in Mass Communication* 10, no. 3:219–37. https://doi.org/10.1080/15295039309366865.

——. 2004. *Taking Journalism Seriously: News and the Academy.* Thousand Oaks, Calif.: Sage.

——. 2013. "On the Shelf Life of Democracy in Journalism Scholarship." *Journalism* 14, no. 4:459–73. https://doi.org/10.1177/1464884912464179.

Zhong, Bu, and John E. Newhagen. 2009. "How Journalists Think While They Write: A Transcultural Model of News Decision Making." *Journal of Communication* 59, no. 3:587–608. https://doi.org/10.1111/j.1460-2466.2009.01439.x.

Zhou, Yuezhi. 2000. "Watchdogs on Party Leashes? Contexts and Implications of Investigative Journalism in Post-Deng China." *Journalism Studies* 1, no. 4:577–97. https://doi.org/10.1080/146167000441312.

Zion, Lawrie, Andrew Dodd, Merryn Sherwood, Penny O'Donnell, Timothy Marjoribanks, and Matthew Ricketson. 2016. "Working for Less: The Aftermath for Journalists Made Redundant in Australia Between 2012 and 2014." *Communication Research and Practice* 2, no. 2:117–36. https://doi.org/10.1080/22041451.2016.1185924.

EDITORS AND CONTRIBUTORS

EDITORS

Thomas Hanitzsch is Chair and Professor of Communication in the Department of Media and Communication at LMU Munich, Germany. A former journalist, he focuses his teaching and research on global journalism cultures, war coverage, celebrity news, and comparative methodology. He has coedited *The Handbook of Journalism Studies* (Routledge, 2009) and *The Handbook of Comparative Communication Research* (Routledge, 2012).

Folker Hanusch is Professor of Journalism in the Department of Communication at the University of Vienna, Austria, where he heads the Journalism Studies Center. He is also an adjunct professor at Queensland University of Technology, Australia, and is editor-in-chief of *Journalism Studies*. His research interests are in comparative journalism studies, transformations of journalism, journalism and everyday life, and indigenous journalism.

Jyotika Ramaprasad is Professor in the School of Communication's Department of Journalism and Media Management at the University of Miami in the United States. Her research interests are in journalism studies, international communication, and communication for social change, mostly focused in Asia and Africa. Her recent work includes the coedited book *Contemporary BRICS Journalism: Non-Western Media in Transition* (Routledge, 2017).

Arnold S. de Beer is Professor Extraordinary of Journalism, Stellenbosch University, South Africa. He is a former journalist. His teaching and research focused on South African news media, as well as journalism teaching. He was founding editor of *Ecquid Novi* (now: *African Journalism Studies*) and has coedited (among others) *Global Journalism: Topical Issues and Media Systems* (Pearson, 2004 and 2009).

CONTRIBUTORS

Laura Ahva is Senior Research Fellow in the Tampere Research Centre for Journalism, Media and Communication (COMET), University of Tampere, Finland. Her research focuses on professionalism, news audiences, and participatory journalism.

Adriana Amado is Professor at the Facultad Latinoamericana de Ciencias Sociales and the University of Buenos Aires, Argentina. Her teaching and research focus on media, journalism, and public communication. She also works as a journalist and civic activist for several Latin American nongovernmental organizations.

Kenneth Andresen is Professor of Media Studies in the Department of Nordic and Media Studies at University of Agder and NLA University College in Kristiansand, Norway. His research focuses on journalism production, transitional journalism, and media in postconflict societies.

Jesus Arroyave is Professor and Director of the Doctoral Program in the Department of Communication and Journalism at Universidad del Norte, Barranquilla, Colombia. His teaching and research focus on journalism and media studies, health communication, and communication for development and social change.

Rosa Berganza is Professor and Chair of Journalism and Political Communication at the Faculty of Communication in King Juan Carlos University, Madrid, Spain. Her teaching and research focus on global practices and perceptions of journalists, big data and journalism, research methodology, gender issues, and political communication.

Stephanie Craft is Professor in the Department of Journalism and Institute of Communications Research at the University of Illinois at Urbana-Champaign, United States. Her research addresses press practices and performance, journalism ethics, and news media literacy.

Dimitra Dimitrakopoulou is Assistant Professor at the School of Journalism and Mass Communication at Aristotle University of Thessaloniki, Greece. Her current research interests lie at the intersection of social media, journalism, and society.

Basyouni Hamada is Professor of Communication and Public Opinion at the Department of Mass Communication, Qatar University, Qatar. His teaching and publications focus on global communication, journalism ethics, Islamic communication systems, press freedom, corruption, Arab media systems, and social media.

Halliki Harro-Loit is Professor of Journalism in the Institute of Social Studies at University of Tartu, Estonia. Her research and teaching focus on media and communication law and ethics, media policy, media history, and interpersonal communication.

Liesbeth Hermans is Professor of Constructive Journalism in the Media Research Centre at the University of Applied Sciences Windesheim, Zwolle, the

Netherlands. She also works as Assistant Professor in the Behavioral Science Institute at Radboud University, Nijmegen. Her research and teaching focus on constructive journalism, journalism culture, and audience research.

Beatriz Herrero-Jiménez is a postdoctoral researcher at King Juan Carlos University in Madrid, Spain. Her primary research interests broadly fall into the areas of media discourses, journalism culture, communication and conflict, and gender studies.

James Hollings is a Senior Lecturer and Programme Leader for Journalism at Massey University, New Zealand. He is a former journalist. His teaching and research focus on journalism practice and psychology.

Jan Fredrik Hovden is Professor in Media Studies at the Department of Information Science and Media Studies at the University of Bergen, Norway. A trained sociologist, he focuses his research on the role of social class and social elites in the use and production of media and culture.

Abit Hoxha is a Doctoral Researcher at the Department of Media and Communication at LMU Munich, Germany. His research focuses on international journalism and conflict news production.

Sallie Hughes is Associate Professor in the Department of Journalism and Media Management at the University of Miami, United States. A former journalist, she is the author of *Newsrooms in Conflict: Journalism and the Democratization of Mexico* (University of Pittsburgh Press, 2006). She teaches classes on international communication, ethnic media and audiences, and Latin American studies.

Beate Josephi is an Honorary Associate in the Department of Media and Communications at the University of Sydney, Australia. Her publications and research interests center on journalism and its importance within and outside democracy, journalism education, and literary journalism.

Filip Láb is Associated Professor in the Institute of Communication Studies and Journalism, Faculty of Social Science, Charles University in Prague, Czech Republic. He specializes in visual culture, visual communication, photojournalism, theory and practice of traditional and digital photography, and the transition from analog to digital photography.

Corinna Lauerer is a research associate in the Department of Media and Communication at LMU Munich, Germany. Her teaching and research focus on the relationship between advertising and journalism, as well as on news organizations and journalistic labor.

Epp Lauk is Professor of Journalism in the Department of Language and Communication Studies at the University of Jyväskylä, Finland. Her research focuses on journalism cultures and history, media and journalism in Central and East European countries, media policy, media self-regulation, and digital and social media.

Mireya Márquez-Ramírez is Professor of Journalism Studies and Communications Theory in the Department of Communications at Universidad Iberoamericana, Mexico City. Her research interests include media systems and journalism cultures in Mexico and Latin America, role conception and role performance, sociology of news production, and mixed methods research.

Sonia Virgínia Moreira is Professor of Communication in the Graduate Program of Communication at the State University of Rio de Janeiro, Brazil. She is a former journalist. Her teaching and research focus on international journalism, journalism education, media studies, and geographies of communication.

Nurhaya Muchtar is Associate Professor of Communication in the Department of Communications Media at Indiana University of Pennsylvania, United States. A former journalist, she focuses her teaching and research on global journalism and on religion and media.

Martín Oller Alonso is Professor at the University of Havana, Cuba. Among his recent works are *La Cultura periodistica de Espana y Suiza* (2012), *Ideology and Professional Culture of Journalists in Cuba* (2016), and *Journalism in Latin America: Journalistic Culture of Ecuador* (2018).

Kevin Rafter is Full Professor of Political Communication and Head of the School of Communications, Dublin City University, Ireland. He is coauthor of *Resilient Reporting: Media Coverage of Irish Elections Since 1969* (Manchester University Press, 2019) and coeditor of *Political Advertising in the 2014 European Parliament Elections* (Palgrave Macmillan, 2017).

Verica Rupar is Associate Professor at the School of Communication Studies at Auckland University of Technology, New Zealand. Her research in journalism studies focuses on journalism as a form of knowledge production in historical and comparative context.

Vittoria Sacco works at the statistical office of the canton of Fribourg, Switzerland, as a scientific advisor. She held a postdoctoral position at the Academy of Journalism and Media at the University of Neuchâtel, Switzerland. Her research interests focused on social media, online curation, changes in journalistic practices and norms, and coverage of war and conflict.

Sonja Seizova works with the OSCE Mission to Serbia in the fields of political communications and media development and has worked as international consultant for development agencies. As a former journalist and foreign correspondent she was based in Greece. Her research interest is in comparative journalism cultures and media systems studies with a focus on new democracies.

Ivor Shapiro is Professor of Journalism at the Ryerson School of Journalism, Toronto, Canada. He is a former magazine writer and editor who teaches feature writing and media ethics and conducts research into journalists' values and identities.

Terje Skjerdal is Associate Professor in Journalism at NLA University College, Kristiansand, Norway. He has been involved in media research and development in various countries in Sub-Saharan Africa since the early 2000s.

Morten Skovsgaard is Professor WSR of Journalism at the Centre for Journalism, Department of Political Science at University of Southern Denmark. His research focuses on journalists' professional values, the conditions of journalistic production, journalists' relation with other societal actors, and the effects of journalistic content.

Sergio Splendore is Senior Assistant Professor at the Department of Social and Political Science of the Università degli Studi di Milano, Italy. He teaches media sociology and communication research.

Olivier Standaert is Assistant Professor in the Louvain School of Journalism at the Catholic University of Louvain, Belgium. He has worked as a freelance journalist for several newspapers. His research focuses on professional identities, newsroom management, and labor markets of journalists.

Nina Steindl is a research associate and doctoral student in the Department of Media and Communication at LMU Munich, Germany. Her research interests are in the fields of journalism studies and political communication.

Edson C. Tandoc, Jr., is Associate Professor at the Wee Kim Wee School of Communication and Information at Nanyang Technological University, Singapore. His research focuses on the sociology of message construction in the context of digital journalism, investigating the impact of journalistic roles, new technologies, and audience feedback on the various stages of news gatekeeping.

Alice N. Tejkalová is Dean of the Faculty of Social Sciences at Charles University in Prague, Czech Republic. She is a former TV sports journalist and host. Her teaching and research focus on sports journalism and journalism cultures.

Jari Väliverronen is a researcher and postgraduate student in the Faculty of Communication Sciences at the University of Tampere, Finland. He is a former journalist. His research focuses on political journalism, journalism change, and crisis/disaster journalism.

Arjen van Dalen is Professor WSR at the Centre for Journalism at the University of Southern Denmark. His research interests broadly fall in the area of comparative communication research, in particular focusing on the relations between journalists and politicians, as well as on economic news.

Tim P. Vos is Chair and Associate Professor of Journalism Studies and the Wallace Turner Memorial Faculty Fellow at the University of Missouri School of Journalism, Columbia, United States. He has published widely on journalistic roles, media sociology and gatekeeping, media history, and media policy.

INDEX